K

DEEP FUTURES

DOUG COCKS

DEEP FUTURES

OUR PROSPECTS FOR SURVIVAL

McGill-Queen's University Press

Montreal & Kingston • Ithaca

University of New South Wales Press

Judging from the past, we may safely infer that not one living species will transmit its unaltered likeness to a distant futurity. And of the species now living very few will transmit progeny to a very distant futurity; for the manner in which all organic beings are grouped shows that the greater number of species in each genus, and all the species in many genera, have left no descendants, but have become utterly extinct. We can so far take a prophetic glance into futurity as to foretell that it will be the c.ommon and widely spread species, belonging to the larger and dominant groups within each class, which will ultimately prevail and procreate new and dominant species. As all the living forms of life are the lineal descendants of those which lived long before the Cambrian epoch, we may feel certain that the ordinary succession by generation has never once been broken, and that no cataclysm has desolated the whole world. Hence we may look with some confidence to a secure future of great length. And as natural selection works solely by and for the good of each being, all corporeal and mental endowments will tend to progress towards perfection ... There is a grandeur in this view of life, with its several powers having been breathed by the Creator into a few forms or into one; ... from so simple a begin-ning endless forms most beautiful and most wonderful have been, and are being evolved.

CHARLES DARWIN, from the Conclusion to *The Origin of Species by Means of Natural Selection Or the Preservation of Favoured Races in the Struggle For Life*, The Modern Library, New York, 1859, pp. 373–74

Certainly we must be able to project our contemplation ahead a short time, say a hundred million years. By that time our particular species, and all other currently extant mammalian species, will exist only as fossil records. All indications of man's tenure on earth will have vanished from the surface. Man's occupation of the earth's surface leaves no permanent scars, although it certainly upsets local ecological conditions to the extreme. The conditions that will eventually prevail, after man's inevitable extinction, will be very different in detail than they would have been without him. The scars of human occupation persist for centuries, perhaps for millennia, depending upon climate conditions and the vigour of the replacing biota. But it is probable that in most areas the passage of a few millennia will eradicate the obvious scars. In time a region will resume its suitable ecological aspect again, even though the component organisms may occur in different proportions or indeed may actually be different. The effect of man's existence for a few million years, in the last analysis, will not be of any intrinsic consequence.

AC SMITH, 'Systematics and Appreciation of Reality', *Taxon*, 1969, 18: 5–19

If you don't know where you are going, it doesn't matter which bus you catch.

ANON

A UNSW Press book

Published in North America by
McGill-Queen's University Press
www.mqup.ca

and in the rest of the world by
University of New South Wales Press Ltd
University of New South Wales
Sydney NSW 2052
AUSTRALIA
www.unswpress.com.au

National Library of Canada
Cataloguing in Publication

> Cocks, Doug, 1937-
> Deep futures : our prospects for survival / Doug Cocks.
> Includes bibliographical references and index.
> ISBN 0-7735-2671-4 (bound).—ISBN 0-7735-2672-2 (pbk.)
> 1. Forecasting. I. Title.

CB161.C57 2003   303.49   C2003-902039-8

National Library of Australia
Cataloguing-in-Publication entry:
> Cocks, K. D. (Kenneth Douglas), 1937- .
> Deep futures : our prospects for survival.
> Includes index.
> ISBN 0 86840 493 4.
> 1. Social evolution. 2. Forecasting. 3. Twenty-first
> century - Forecasts. I. Title.

303.49

Cover illustration Darren Pryce
Printer Kyodo Printing, Singapore

CONTENTS

ACKNOWLEDGMENTS

Special thanks go to my friends Mike Austin and Franzi Poldy who, through numerous stimulating discussions, have shifted and sharpened my thinking on some of the major themes of this book.

Cecily Parker has similarly broadened my thinking about the human psyche, as has John Burton on the nature of conflict and its resolution.

Roger Bradbury, Michael Dunlop, Barney Foran, Graham Turner and Sarah Ryan have all read and made helpful comments on various draft chapters. Sarah clarified my view of how the book should be written when she suggested a reordering of chapters.

Inge Newman, the world's greatest librarian, has been as competently helpful with this as with my previous books.

Steve Morton and Brian Walker, present and former chiefs of the CSIRO (Commonwealth Scientific and Industrial Research Organisation) Division of Sustainable Ecosystems, have provided the fellowships which have allowed me to work inside the scientific establishment, with all the benefits that brings. Barney Foran has been a generous program leader.

Finally, it has again been a pleasure to work with John Elliot, Publishing Manager at UNSW Press.

Doug Cocks
Canberra

PREFACE AND INTRODUCTION

I am very curious about how our species will fare over coming ages. Will the human lineage survive, reasonably happily, into the distant future? Indeed, will we survive another millennium in reasonably good shape? Will the next 1000 years be particularly difficult or just ordinarily difficult? Supposing we survive the next 1000 years, will we eventually become extinct as most species do or will we evolve into a new species with which one might empathise? And, supposing we continue to evolve, will that new species or its descendants survive the death of the Sun as an energy and light source in 5 billion or so years? Beyond that, there is the ultimate question as to if, when and how the universe will end and whether, in some sense, life might best that challenge. A question which is almost as big is whether we ourselves can take steps to significantly improve our chances of being part of a long-lasting lineage. It may just be that, given such a choice, we would perhaps not take it. I will ask that question too.

I will of course die with my curiosities unsatisfied and, thereafter, I don't expect to be watching the story unfold from some heavenly vantage point. My only practicable option, in the absence of revelation, is to collect and construct some plausible well-informed stories — optimistic, pessimistic and realistic — about what might happen to the Earth and its inhabitants. In this book I am presenting some of those stories along with the ideas and facts that make them plausible in my eyes. Remember that 'plausible' does not mean 'true'. It means that if things turned out that way, one would not be too surprised.

Philosophically, I am a naturalist, meaning that I do not find stories which invoke the supernatural to be plausible. For example, when I find a gap, a lack of causal specificity, at some point in the evolutionary story — for example, what happened before the big bang, the rise of life, the rise of consciousness — I prefer to 'wait and see' rather than attribute events to a Creator, a vital principle etc. As an act of faith (and that is precisely what it is), I assume there is always a natural (causal) explanation for what has happened, even if it

cannot be accessed. For example, it is not evident that the scientific method-
ology we are using today (limited to electromagnetic and gravity signatures)
is capable of providing a full explanation of the universe.

I am also a meliorist. Meliorism is the doctrine, somewhere between
optimism and pessimism, that purposive human action can often improve
outcomes over what would otherwise be in the absence of such action. I am
certainly not a fatalist who believes there is nothing we can do to change the
future. My pessimism extends to observing that the deep future may be a shit
of a place which we can do little to avoid (I don't know) but, if we try to
make it better, it is unlikely to be worse than if we had not tried.

Put naturalism and meliorism together and you get (to use a term of
Julian Huxley's [1953–1963] which is now probably dated) a *scientific humanist*, someone who wants the best for people and thinks that science, dangerous as it often is, offers one of the better prospects for that.

Happily, we have reached an era where science and history have produced
a truckload of exciting and plausible, and sometimes contradictory, stories of
how things got to be the way they are. Anyone who takes the trouble to read
and try to understand a sample of these stories will be rewarded with a sense
of the past which is not unlike one's own memories, albeit 'false' memories
because one wasn't really there when it happened. You too can be 14 billion
years old if you wish!

And if the stories we similarly create about the deep future are plausible
enough, we can 'live' for billions more years; we can have a sense of participation in the ongoing evolutionary play. The scientific method has expanded
our understanding of life and the universe in spectacular fashion across the
entire scale of space and time (Wilson 2000). For example, 19th century geol-
ogists discovered the enormity of time and, in the 20th century, Hubble confirmed the enormity of space. By the same token, we would be foolish to
think that our present ideas about 'everything' are more than a small fraction
of what will be revealed over the almost endless years ahead. Indeed, judging
from what happened in the 20th century, many of science's paradigmatic ideas
will be overturned presently (Maddox 1998).

Therefore, within the confines of a single book I am going to set out my
shortened views on where we have come from, where we are and where we
might get to — a 'perspective on everything' if you like. And, if that is not
enough, I want to make some tentative suggestions as to what we might need
to do, and how we might need to think, in order to enlarge our lineage's
prospects of surviving reasonably happily for a very long time. When I say
'my' views, what I usually mean is the plausible ideas of others. My intended

contribution is to synthesise a large body of ideas into a graspable narrative. I have found ideas helpful to my purpose in disciplines as diverse as palaeontology, archaeology, history, sociology, psychology, geography, ecology, complexity theory, evolutionary economics and political science and, of course, cosmology.

I have written *Deep Futures* primarily for my own peace of mind (how do I know what I think until I see what I say!) but I would also like others to find my efforts helpful; I suspect that most people in modern societies lack a sense of their place in the larger scheme of things and that this makes life a little more confused than it need be. I know that the body of thought to which I have been exposed and to which I have exposed myself is miniscule but I have to describe the elephant even though I have only felt its tail. And, another thing, as Darwin wrote to a colleague, 'no belief is vivid until shared by others'. I need to share my 'creation myth' and my 'destiny myth' to fix them in my imagination.

Enough justifying. What, to cut a long story short, have I concluded about the future of the human lineage? For the moment, let me resort to allegory. Posterity, our hero, finds herself in a labyrinth of dungeons, each holding a fierce dragon. For each dragon she slays, her immediate 'reward' is entry into the next dungeon where an even bigger dragon is waiting. Her real reward is that with every dragon slain Posterity matures and grows stronger. But, and this is the question Gertrude, can she continue to outgrow the dragons she is encountering? Furthermore, for the reason that she is a flawed hero, Posterity's survival will hinge on more than just the balance of power between her growing strength and ever-bigger dragons. Sometimes she unwittingly conjures up dragons of the mind and these have to be slain just as surely as the denizens of the labyrinth if the story is to go on. To translate this allegory, the labyrinth's dragons are energetic or insidious natural hazards, the dragons of the mind are problems of the lineage's own making/makeup and Posterity's growing strength is her growing knowledge of life and the universe. What this allegory does not capture is my emergent belief that, in between anxieties, life can continue to be a great joy.

CONTENTS BY CHAPTER

Chapter 1, *21C: A difficult century*, is a selective review of what is an enormous 'futures' literature. Most excursions into describing what the future will be like (some people are willing to make firm predictions) or could be like (possibilistic futures are often called scenarios) have a 'human' time scale which means looking ahead days, months, years and, sometimes, as far out as three to four human generations. The chapter's focus is on possible developments within the global biophysical environment, the global economy, global society and global governance during the century we are standing in. Many see it as being a particularly difficult one to manage, basically because so much is changing rapidly by historical standards — Toffler's 'future shock'— and also because we have accumulated some big, demanding problems such as rapid population growth, environmental pollution, probable climate change, poverty, bubbling international aggression and a looming energy crisis. Conversely, quality of life could improve in many societies and we may well continue acquiring the knowledge of life and the universe which will be necessary if the lineage is to survive long term (happily, preferably), if that is what we want.

Chapter 2, *Deep futures,* is long on time and short on detail. While the present century can be discussed in terms of the assumption that much of what we know will persist and much of what is to come will unfold directly out of the present, this starting point for thinking about the future breaks down once you start gazing ahead for tens and thousands of millennia. Out there, a few physical landmark events and several big slow processes have some probability status but the quintessential nature of humans, post-humans and the societies they will live in are highly uncertain. One can no longer talk about particular nation states, races, demographic structures, settlement patterns, industries, continents etc. Indeed, such categories may themselves no longer exist. In this situation serious future-gazers can do little more than build plausible 'if … then' scenarios — if the world and its inhabitants turn out to be like X then they will also have to be like Y. Much of the challenge is in selecting the warp threads that will persist as the rich tapestry of the future is woven. The chapter focuses on speculations about the lineage's physical and mental evolution, possibilities for social organisation, technology developments and the macro-environment.

In **Chapter 3**, *What is the question?*, we move beyond the speculations of future-gazers towards a consideration of ends and means. We turn to asking what people might like to see happening in the future, particularly the deep future. And while there can be no common answer to such a question, the chapter moves towards a particular working answer, namely, *quality survival* or, less cryptically, *to see the lineage surviving, and surviving well*. This means a preference for a future where the human through to post-human lineage survives for an indefinitely prolonged period and that, most of the time, the majority of individuals constituting that lineage will be enjoying a high quality of life. This working answer to the question of what people would wish of the future is then re-interpreted as a collective goal, opening the way in following chapters to the question of how the lineage might need to behave if some version of such a goal is to be achieved.

Chapter 4, *Understanding how societies change over time,* is a search for theory, meaning; ideally, a plausible succinct description of some core process that, in diverse manifestations, seems to be operating when societies undergo marked change in characteristics deemed important, for example, survival and quality of life prospects. Is there a behavioural or organisational trajectory common to all societies and does that trajectory evolve in an understandable way? Armed with such a grail, it might be possible to learn how to steer a global society towards quality survival or other goals. What do long-lasting societies have in common? Ensure it. Under what conditions does life get better for a society's people? Implement them. Not surprisingly though, despite the availability of a range of very powerful and relevant ideas from a range of disciplines, the yield from this chapter is no more than some *partial theories* of societal change. That's okay.

Macro-history, systems thinking, complexity theory, evolutionary biology, ecology and the socio-behavioural sciences all contain models which can be transposed less-or-more directly to the task of foreseeing how the lineage, its organisation and its environment might change over the long future under particular conditions. For example, macro-history suggests that many failed civilisations simply became too complex to run. Systems thinking reminds us that you cannot do just one thing when managing a society. Complexity theory holds out the hope that societies can be purposively transformed if they are nudged in the right way at the right time. Evolutionary biology provides the natural selection model which not only allows us to think productively about human evolution but also about social processes ranging from economic development to fashion. Ecology explains the pervasiveness of hierarchical structures in the world and how these come about; it also explains why complex energy-degrading/converting systems, like ecosystems and societies, so commonly go through a birth–maturity–senescence–death life cycle. Sociology identifies the functions common to all societies and the tendency that all have to pass from being traditional to being modern. And so on.

Chapter 5, *A strategy for managing the deep future,* confronts both the intellectual difficulty of the task being set and the limited intellectual capacities which humans have in relation to such a task. Managing the future is a 'wicked' problem, meaning that it has no definitive formulation and no conclusively 'best' solution, and that the constraints and options confronting the problem-solver are constantly evolving. It is suggested that an approach to managing the future which is far from perfect but still worthwhile is to see it as a matter of guiding world society towards quality survival by responding collectively and selectively to a rolling (ever-changing) set of priority issues. Priority issues means those judged to have a particular bearing on whether the lineage can achieve quality survival.

Chapters 6, 7 and **8** take this suggested strategy a step further by suggesting candidate guidelines for helping society formulate responses to three families of priority issues that emerge from the discussions of social goals in Chapter 3, the nature of societal change in Chapter 4 and from the possible futures that people have foreseen for world society as described in Chapters 1 and 2.

Thus Chapter 6, *Nursing the world through endless change,* explores contemporary thinking about the way in which complex energy-degrading systems (like world society) evolve in order to find guidelines for protecting world society from its own instability and, at times, excessive stability. On one hand the reference is to any society's tendency to collapse or change direction dramatically and, on the other, its tendency to stagnate, failing to adapt to external and internal change. The true importance of the chapter is that it is arguing for a way of thinking about societal change which, I believe, will continue to generate a rich stream of insights into when and how it might be possible to move world society closer to quality survival, notwithstanding its emphasis on the unpredictability of systems like these.

The starting point for Chapter 7, *Learning forever,* is that while surviving well will require full use of what we already know, that will not be enough, at least within a framework where managing the future is interpreted as a matter of guiding world society towards quality survival via selective policy responses to a rolling set of priority issues. The chapter is a search for guidelines for making world society into more of a learning society than it is now, a learning society being one in which high priority is given to the social learning task, that is, to the building up of a sufficient body of collective knowledge (useful information) to ensure quality survival. The chapter analyses the social learning process and suggests how it can be nurtured and boosted. The importance of taking an experimental approach to social learning is emphasised. In particular, despite its many problematic consequences, scientific research must continue to have an increasing role in social learning. How it is to be channelled and what its priorities might be are addressed in some detail. For example, more knowledge of how the world and the universe work, with a degree of emphasis on human behavioural and mental processes, is particularly important.

Chapter 8, the third chapter on finding guidelines for quality survival, is *Working on perennial issues.* This is an umbrella heading which allows a little to be said on each of the four families of substantive issues (social learning and managing change are more process or 'means' issues) that collectively absorb much of world society's problem-solving capacity and will continue to do for the foreseeable future. The four families cover social, political, economic and environmental issues respectively. The social issues I have included on the basis of being most in need of guidelines are fraternal–sisterly relations, participation and the social contract, and co-operation–competition. My *Global governance* issues, chosen on the grounds of their importance for quality survival, are democracy, world government, war and oppression. Under the heading of *Production and distribution*, my global economic issues are ideology, global investment and relations between business and society. My environmental issues under *Managing the global ecosystem* are biodiversity, genes and population, and depleting non-renewable resources.

Chapter 9, *Stories to live by*, closes the book on the important idea that clear thinking about priority issues, change management, rolling strategies, social learning etc. will never be enough to ensure the lineage's quality survival if these ratiocinative activities are not supported by a critical mass of passionate people who want and believe it is possible to survive and survive well. More than that, if Posterity is to negotiate all the contingencies that no amount of forethought can anticipate, she will need role models that provide her with the style and attitudes that serve as all-purpose behavioural guides. For example, enormous insight into Posterity's challenge to achieve quality survival flows from recognising that her challenge is strongly analogous to that which every mature human faces to make the best of a finite life.

Part 1:

FUTURES WE HAVE GLIMPSED

1

21C: A DIFFICULT CENTURY

The forces that threaten global stability can probably be contained for at least one more generation, but not for much longer (McRAE 1994).

What sorts of futures have we humans foreseen for ourselves? The answer is 'all sorts'; from fleeting to eternal and, in terms of quality of life, from short and brutish to rich and fulfilling. In this first chapter we focus on the 21st century and ask what serious observers have detected in the way of possible worldly changes during this period which stand to significantly influence quality of life prospects, up or down, for large numbers of people.

Of all the centuries that comprise humanity's possible future, the 21st is particularly important for two reasons. One is that we are standing in it, most will die in it and our unborn grandchildren will grow old in it; it is the century that captures our personal interest, our self-interest, and the one which extends into what most people think of as the distant future. Second, it just may also be an especially difficult century for our species to get through without enormous suffering and, perhaps, collapse of the world system. We do not know that of course and insofar as numerous historical ages have seen themselves as uniquely challenged by the circumstances they face we need to be cautious about such a judgment. In any case, we have to pay particular attention to negotiating the 21st century simply because it's the one we have direct responsibility for and, perhaps, most control over. That was indeed my view when writing my book *Future Makers, Future Takers*, an exploration of alternative strategies for managing Australian society up to and beyond 2050.

However, while it is important to appreciate what has been envisaged for the 21st century, given that there is no escape from traversing it if we are to reach what I am calling the 'deep future', it is equally important for my present purposes (of which more later) to collate a picture (in the next chapter) of what observers have envisaged for those deep futures, the plural implying that there are multiple possibilities. This is notwithstanding the fact that what might happen in the world in coming millennia, perhaps thousands of them, rather than coming decades, has been of interest to a much smaller group of observers — scientists, fiction writers and the religious more so than the economists, political scientists, social theorists, environmentalists, entrepreneurs, gurus etc. who dominate the business of thinking about the 'immediate' future.

For much of recorded history, societies evolved in relative isolation. This began to change with the age of colonialism and today societies are intermingling to an increasing degree — a process called globalisation. The world, the globe, can be viewed as a system of interacting nations, trans-national organisations (for example, companies, non-government organisations [NGOs]) and supra-national organisations (for example, the World Trade Organisation). Systems, by definition, are networks of (many) separable components or units continuously interacting with each other according to their own behavioural rules. So, we can view the world as a system of interacting nations etc., each changing the others' social, political, economic and natural environments while collectively evolving in ways that can be described in terms of whole-of-world characteristics.

However, before looking for possibilistic future worlds under these headings, we might take a moment to scan the past century or so to see if there are some powerful trends and established patterns that might carry over into and shape this century. I am accepting Elise Boulding's (1978) view that we need to look at how the world has behaved and changed in the last 100 years if we are to have any understanding of the forces that will shape the next 100 years. This is notwithstanding Boulding's own admission that our capacity to image the future has probably been weakened by the increasing rate of change being experienced in many dimensions of the global system (cf. Snooks 1996).

GLOBAL SPRINGBOARD TO THE FUTURE

The distinguished British historian, Eric Hobsbawm (1994), has written with great insight about what happened and why in the world during the period 1914–91. This period (which he calls the short 20th century) begins with the First World War and ends with the collapse of the USSR. He divides it into:

- An 'age of catastrophe' from 1914 to the aftermath of the Second World War. Apart from the two world wars, this age includes the Great Depression of the 1930s and the rise of Fascism;

- A 'sort of golden age' of extraordinary economic growth and social transformation (for example, national independence movements) for 25 or 30 postwar years until the early 1970s (called 'the long boom' by Daly and Logan [1989]); and

- The 'crisis decades' since the 'golden age' in which capitalism, as well as Communism, has failed to deliver — as evidenced by mass unemployment, cyclical slumps, increasing divergence between wealth and poverty and between state revenues and state expenditures. An increasingly integrated world economy has undermined the institutions of all regimes. In an effort to recover, many regimes have replaced the Keynesian economic ideas which ruled in the golden age with neo-liberal and laissez-faire ideas. But followers of that path have done no better than others. This has also been the time when the potentially catastrophic ecological consequences of economic growth have begun to emerge. The growth rate of the world economy dropped from 5 per cent per annum in the 1960s to 2 per cent in the 1990s (Thurow 1996).

Overall, between 1914 and 1991 people in the advanced economies, basically the OECD (Organisation for Economic Cooperation and Development) countries, came to live longer and better (at least until the 1980s) than their parents. Technological revolutions, particularly in transport and communications, 'virtually annihilated time and distance' [sic]. But it was a murderous and barbaric century. As predicted by Marx, social relations in the first world disintegrated under the advance of asocial individualism. Capitalism (Box 1.1) has been a permanent and continuous revolutionising force.

BOX 1.1: CAPITALISM CLARIFIED

Technicalities aside, capital is the savings from past profits or wages that are available to finance new enterprises. Physical capital exists as factories, machines etc. and finance capital is wealth invested in financial instruments such as loans, shares and bonds.

Capitalism is not a dirty word. It is a term describing an economic production system characterised by wage-labour that does not own the means of production. Capitalism creates a social order characterised by constant change caused by the drive to accumulate capital by innovation and expansion of output. It is the drive for capital accumulation that energises the system — accumulate or be accumulated! Undoubtedly, the central issue in capitalist societies is the relation between business and government, the economy and the state.

HOBSBAWM'S COMING PROBLEMS

> At the end of this century it has for the first time become possible to see what a world may be like in which the past ... has lost its role, in which the old maps and charts which guided human beings, singly and collectively, through life no longer represent the landscape through which we move, the sea on which we sail. In which we do not know where our journey is taking us, or even ought to take us.
> (HOBSBAWM 1994)

Thus, beyond the 'crisis decades' Hobsbawm sees an 'unknown and problematic but not necessarily apocalyptic future' — a period of destructuring and simplification rather than destruction. Particular problems he foresees include the following:

We enter a world in which for the first time in 2 centuries there is no international system or structure — as evidenced by the emergence of dozens of new territories without any independent mechanisms for border determination. It is a world in which the first world can win battles against the third world but not wars, not in the sense of being able to control the conquered territory after 'victory'. There is a global disorder and no obvious mechanism for either ending it or keeping it under control. Hobsbawm's view matches that of Singer and Wildavsky (1993) who divide tomorrow's world into two parts. One part is zones of peace, wealth and democracy. The other is zones of war, turmoil and development in which a century of disruption can be expected.

The privatisation of the means of destruction means that it is now quite possible for small groups of political or other dissidents to disrupt and destroy anywhere. Concurrently, the cost of keeping unofficial violence under control has risen dramatically. Note though that the rapid fall of the 20th century's totalitarian and ruthlessly dictatorial regimes has effectively demonstrated the limits of sheer coercive power.

Global population will rise above 10 billion and regional differences in population change will generate great migratory pressures. There can be little doubt that friction between natives and foreigners will be a major factor in the politics, global and national, of the next decades. Eventually, the problem of how to keep world population stable will have to be faced.

The ecological consequences of ongoing economic growth will not make the world uninhabitable for humans but will change the environments in which people live and perhaps reduce the carrying capacity (numbers that can be supported) of the globe dramatically. In the long run, a balance will have to be struck between humanity, the (renewable) resources it consumes and the effect of its activities on the environment. Nobody knows, and few dare speculate, how this is to be done, and at what level of population, technology and consumption such a permanent balance would be possible. One thing however is undeniable. It would be incompatible with a world economy based on the unlimited pursuit of profit in capitalist economies of the type now existing.

While globalisation and the international redistribution of production will bring more of the world's 6 billion into the global economy, there will be a seemingly irreversible widening of the gap between rich and poor countries. The belief, following neoclassical economics, that unrestricted international trade will allow the poorer countries to come closer to the rich, runs counter to historical experience as well as common sense; protectionism regularly cuts off markets while oversupply reduces prices. A world economy beset by growing inequalities is inevitably accumulating future troubles. To judge by the tendency to inequality in the 1970s and 1980s, the major upcoming political problem of the developed world will not be how to multiply the wealth of nations but how to distribute it.

Technology will continue to squeeze human labour out of the production of goods and services, without providing either enough work of the same kind for those jettisoned, or the guarantee of a rate of economic growth sufficient to absorb them. Very few observers seriously expect a return to the full employment of the 'golden age' in the West — but a shortage of workers as populations age could change that. Demand in mass markets will continue to decline as transfer incomes (social security etc.) fall and as technology squeezes workers out of service industry jobs as well as secondary industry jobs.

Despite the difficulties of doing so, identified by Hobsbawm, many have written with great insight about what the world might be like — politically, socially, technologically, economically and environmentally — in coming decades and even generations.

Probably the three best-known future-gazers of recent times are Daniel Bell, author of *The Coming of Post-industrial Society*, Alvin Toffler, author of *Future Shock* and the prolific Herman Kahn.

According to Bell, writing in 1973, the industrial economy based on manufacturing is giving way to a service economy where the bulk of the workforce will be engaged in a wide range of non-manual occupations (and manual leisure activities). The outstanding characteristic of this society is what Bell calls 'the centrality of theoretical knowledge'. Professional and technical people, armed with a new intellectual technology, will play a dominant role. Technology assessment, forecasting models and systems analysis will replace ad hoc adaptiveness and experimentation in politics. The new scientific and technical elites will displace existing powerful groups and society will be run on the basis of rational decision-making and managerialism. Education in the new skills required will be the route to power.

A similar optimistic perspective is apparent in the work of Herman Kahn (Kahn and Weiner 1967; Kahn and Bruce-Briggs 1972; Kahn et al. 1976). He sees the connection between history and the future in terms of a 'long-term multifold trend', one important component of which is the movement towards a post-industrial society. Kahn and his collaborators foresaw continued economic expansion, linked with the growth of education, leisure and material welfare, although not in the 'non-coping' nations (after Encel 1979). Kahn's optimism contrasts vividly with the well-known but much-scorned Club of Rome study (Meadows et al. 1972) which suggested that population and industrial growth might peak and then decline drastically for the planet as a whole by 2100 at the latest.

Alvin Toffler's (1970) 'future shock' is essentially about the increasing transience of our individual experiences of things, people, ideas, organisations and places. He points out that the industrialised world is changing so rapidly that it no longer functions as a model for the non-industrialised world to emulate.

More recent writers have been less certain about what the future might hold and have talked in terms of imaginable scenarios, any of which could eventuate. Thus Schwartz (1991), starting from the position that economic forces are increasingly more important than military forces, suggests three global scenarios for coming decades:

- *New empires* — a world made up of 'blocs' of isolationist and protectionist countries.

- *Market world* — global free trade and unrestricted movement of capital and people.

- *Change without progress* — a 'blade runner' world of chaos, corruption and conflict.

Hammond (1998) also identifies three global scenarios for coming decades, two of which, *Fortress world* ('Growing inequity and environmental degradation bring conflict between rich and poor, rising social instability and violence') and *Market world* ('Free markets bring prosperity and human progress'), match Schwartz's perceptions. A third, *Sustainable world* ('Fundamental social and political reform create a more peaceful, equitable and environmentally sound world'), turns on orderly, managed development. Bossel (1998) calls his two alternative global futures *Competition* (something like Market world) and *Partnership* (something like Hammond's Sustainable world).

We turn now from such panoramic views to several thematic collations of more focused views of the world's mid-future, beginning with power politics — the ways in which nations might attempt to influence each other's actions, usually, but not always, to their own benefit.

GEOPOLITICAL FUTURES

Powershifts

Assume that the dynamic driving inter-nation relations is that each nation is seeking to survive and prosper within the community of nations (cf. Snooks 1996). For the foreseeable future, the model for inter-nation relations stands to be that of each country using threats and/or persuasion, backed up as required and feasible by tangible power, to try and make others behave as desired — what is called 'power politics'.

Power on the world stage has economic, political and military components. With the 1989 collapse of the Soviet Union, the United States became the world's only superpower; but few see America's superpower status lasting as the global competitive system expands to include Russia, China and the Middle East (Thurow 1996). For the moment, however, the ending of the Cold War does not obviously imply any immediate major shift in international relations, despite releasing previously suppressed rivalries between the United States, China, Japan and others and an outbreak of tribalism (Kennon 1995).

After the loss of US hegemony, any of a variety of scenarios would be unsurprising, including:

- A multi-state system without major alliances. This would involve coalition building between countries on an issue-by-issue basis, for example, the Australian experiences on agricultural trade, chemical weapons, Law of the Sea, Cambodia and Antarctica;

- A first world versus 'the rest' scenario (Peters 1995);

- A 'three power bloc' system built around Europe, the Americas and East Asia. The precursors of such blocs are already in place (Evans and Grant 1995) although being so diverse, ethnically and culturally, perhaps reduces East Asia's prospects for becoming a globally important entity. Defence spending was rising more rapidly in East Asia than in other parts of the world (Wilson 1996), at least until the 1997 meltdown. Conversely, the logic for eastern Europe being gradually absorbed into western Europe is overwhelming (McRae 1994). Some countries, Australia for example, are not natural members of any of these blocs.

And to even further expand the range of geopolitical possibilities, the sheer politico-economic mass of an emerging energy-hungry China could lead Japan, India and Russia to recognise their common security interests against an unpredictable giant (Goodman and Segal 1995). Although McRae (1994) observes that China and Japan are more likely to become rivals than partners, what if they find it profitable to co-operate to the disadvantage of the United States? Could Japanese militarism resurface? Friedman and Lebard (1991) concluded, and it is beginning, that Japan must at some point rearm in order to protect its access to raw materials, for example Gulf oil. Hartcher (1996) notes that, as in pre-1914 Europe, close economic integration among Asian countries does not preclude wars there, started by territorial claims, deep nationalism and competition for resources, notably oil.

Future wars and world order

What part might wars play in creating and maintaining future power standings and alignments? A world war in 2045 is used in Wagar's (1989) *Short History of the Future* as the device to trigger the end of a global capitalist economy dominated by twelve 'mega corporations'. However, most perceptions of the century's wars (but not Friedman and Lebard 1991) see the possibilities as being less total than that. For example, Huntington (1994) sees wars of the future as being between civilisations (not between nations as such), for example, between the Islamic and the Christian worlds. Against this, it is Wagar's (1989) view that while Islamic fundamentalism is likely to have some political success for a while, it will not be able to break free of the global economy because of its need for modern arms and the need to pay for these. Mid-future wars, excluding civil wars, stand to be between pairs of nations rather than coalitions of nations or 'core' nations, but always with the possibility of neighbouring states becoming involved. However, continuing advances in military technology, such as precision missiles, have decoupled territory and defence (Langford 1979; Leslie 1996). By 2020 precision strike capabilities might create the potential to achieve strategic effects over continental distances.

The so-called 'revolution in military affairs' is concerned with the military application of new technologies to the 'battlespace' including precision weapons and advanced surveillance and sensing capabilities. Audio 'lasers' allow you to whisper in the ear of someone a kilometre away and infrared binoculars allow you to see them at night. Eavesdropping devices that work through walls are already in use. Smell analysers can replace 'sniffer' dogs. High-resolution Earth observation satellites can generate geographic information of overwhelming detail and scope. When military capabilities differ markedly between warring parties, conflict is likely to take the form of skirmishes, bombings and massacres rather than battles, and practices which have been unacceptable for three centuries, such as capturing civilians and communities, stand to make a comeback (van Creveld 1991).

While trade wars to protect markets are not foreseeable at this stage, 21st century wars of redistribution would not be particularly surprising (Elkins 1995). The World Bank has suggested that some of the century's wars could be over water. Chronic water shortages already affect 40 per cent of the world's population across eighty countries. Global demand for water doubles every 21 years. In the Middle East, disputes are already erupting in the watersheds of the Nile, Tigris, Jordan and Euphrates. In South Asia, Nepal and Bangladesh are in dispute over the waters of the Ganges–Brahmaputra Basin. Nor would it be too surprising if Java were to run out of water.

But scarcities of resources other than water also stand to generate major conflicts, most notably when a scarcity of food-producing land created by population growth and land degradation leads to mass population movements, for example, sub-Saharan Africa (Homer-Dixon 1991). Fish wars are another possibility. The World Bank has warned that 'the current harvesting capacity of the world's fleet far exceeds the estimated biological sustainability of most commercial species' (Dupont 1999). In the western Pacific, where a large percentage of the marine resources are either claimed or contested, the risk of significant political–military confrontation over fish has emerged as a genuine security issue for China, Russia, North Korea, South Korea and Japan.

Oil and gas are the lifeblood of developed and developing economies. Some 80 per cent of the world's known oil resources are in areas which are politically unstable or contested, for example, the Middle East, Colombia, Indonesia and the Caspian region. Powerful nations will be prepared to take strong action, up to and including war, to ensure their continued access to what will be declining supplies.

While the end of the Cold War has led to an outbreak of tribalism and to wars within and between nations in Europe, Asia, Africa and South America, there does seem to be some possibility of a system of enforceable international law emerging in coming decades. Saunders (1994) sees the world of 2025 being more integrated with more policy being driven by international and supra-national organisations, both public and private. Certainly, no first world country is interested in using military power to establish a new empire; and, most importantly, having enforceable international law is in the interests of both business and powerful bureaucracies in the first world. Against that, many deep conflicts remain to be resolved.

Such an international administration would, at first sight, be largely built around the United Nations Organisation's establishing of minimum human rights and standards and drafting of rules for international economic and political relationships (see also Naisbitt 1994). Alternatively, the priorities might be to actively regulate the global economy or implement a 'rights of nations' charter which would protect and help nations taking actions they considered necessary for their citizens' well being. John Burton's (pers. comm.) contrary view is that the United Nations is an organisation primarily seeking to preserve the sovereignty of its nation-state members and will come to be seen to be largely irrelevant in the global economy. Thurow (1996) is also among those pessimistic about world regulation replacing national regulation of economic activities, saying 'No one can agree on who should regulate, what should be regulated, or how it should be regulated'. Whatever form the supra-national order takes, it seems likely to be a creature of the first world with others playing largely by their rules (see also Naisbitt 1994 and Boulding 1978 for discussions of prospects for world government).

Having discounted the prospect of global war, it must nonetheless be recognised that the spread of nuclear weapons remains a problem (Evans and Grant 1995; Leslie 1996) and that a 'rogue' nation indifferent to conventional notions of self-interest could trigger a major conflict across continents. Nuclear proliferation still provides a strong argument against nuclear fission as an energy source (Elkins 1995). And then there is the spectre of biological warfare. One emerging possibility is that a first world rogue nation might be willing to introduce ethnically specific 'designer plagues' into teeming third world countries seen as threatening first world security.

While the foregoing discussion envisages wars as continuing to be based on military action, other possibilities exist such as information warfare based on wholesale industrial espionage and the deliberate pollution of data transmissions underlying key systems; banking, telecommunications and power generation, for example (Elkins 1995). Alternatively, such systems are vulnerable to shutdown in an information war because they are interdependent, and the networked computers that control them have critical nodes or 'choke points' internally and at system interfaces (Cobb 1998).

Prospects for the nation state

> National sovereignty is eroded from above by the mobility of capital, goods and information across national boundaries, the integration of world financial markets, and the trans-national character of industrial production. And national sovereignty is challenged from below by the resurgent aspirations of sub-national groups for autonomy and self-rule. As their effective sovereignty fades, nations gradually lose their hold on the allegiance of their citizens ... nation-states are increasingly unable to link identity and self-rule (SANDEL 1996).

~

> Political unrest is the wild card in history's deck (HEILBRONER 1995).

Wallerstein (1995) has charted the changing legitimacy of states over the past 500 years, that is, the degree to which such are accepted/supported by their citizens. Initially weak, the cement of nationalism and the rise of the concept of the sovereignty of the people, particularly after the French Revolution, created strong nation (cf. city) states although the class struggle, for example, Disraeli's 'two nations', did threaten to de-legitimise states in the 19th century. However, support from both left wing and right wing forces, the right emphasising unity against external enemies and the left holding out the possibility of the people taking control of the state apparatus, strengthened the state and permitted the taxes which funded more services and hence more legitimacy. Legitimacy declined again in the 20th century with the failure of popular movements once in power and massive casualties in patriotic wars. Support for the state, from both the right (advocating individualism) and the left (advocating localism), has declined yet again in the last 30 years. Whatever the language, the result has been a low point in the legitimacy of states everywhere. What of the future?

Further decline in the power and role of the nation state in the 21st century is a common theme in the writing of contemporary futurists. McRae (1994), for example, identifies reasons such as:

- Power is being passed upwards to supra-national bodies via treaties and international regulations and standards. Trans-national arrangements such as the European Community and North American Free Trade Association are already overriding parts of traditional national sovereignty, for example, in social and environmental policy;

- Power is being passed downwards to regional authorities;

- World financial markets set limits on fiscal and monetary policy for most countries;

- Nations have limited scope for any actions that reduce international competitiveness;

- Trans-national companies determine investment partly on the basis of tax treatment and hence there is a limit on any country's capacity to extract tax from foreign businesses;

- The talented are becoming more mobile and can choose to live where life is good and personal tax rates are low;

- Business is increasingly participating in public policy making through lobbying aimed at influencing policy decisions.

Cerny (1995) notes the difficulties that nation states have in providing public goods such as law enforcement, regulatory structures, property and environmental protection etc. when the ideal scale for providing these services is changing, under globalisation, from national to international. But while nations are declining as political actors, the political means to control world capital have not yet emerged (Leach 1995; Fagan and Webber 1994).

Just as such international influences are intensifying, so are demands for local control, for example, Australian Aboriginal demands for self-determination. Dissociation through intra-national secession is occurring in first, second and third world countries. Giddens (1988: 129) warns that 'a world of a thousand city states as some have predicted would be unstable and dangerous'. This trend towards a world that is both shrinking and fragmenting (Camilleri and Falk 1992) is called 'glocalisation' by Courchene (1993). Hobsbawm (1994) also recognises symptoms of the loss of state power internally such as, for example, the rise of private security services and the erosion of natural monopolies such as postal services.

Nevertheless, the 'territorially rigid' nation state will continue to exist. Kennon (1995) foresees a continuation of the current division of nations into a first, second and third world, perhaps with some limited movement of nations between these categories, just as, for example, post-Franco Spain has joined the first world. Coates et al. (1996) predict that in 2025 there will be 1.3 billion people in what they comparably call the affluent world (cf. 1 billion today), 5.1 billion in the 'middle world' (3.5 billion today) and 2 billion in the 'destitute world' (1.1 billion today).

First world countries, mostly liberal democracies as in the OECD, are politically stable without having to depend on police-state methods or foreign support. They are economically advanced in terms of such indicators of a modern economy as GDP per head, price stability, inflation rate etc. They are socially developed in terms of education, life expectancy, public health and other social indicators of well-being.

Second world countries are commonly in disequilibrium because they have powerful and unrelenting internal enemies whom they control with loyal and effective police forces. The more authoritarian second world regimes put security above principle and make no claim to higher abstractions, for example, Myanmar (Burma). Others justify and legitimate themselves on ideological grounds or on the basis of economic success (for example, the newly industrialising countries of Asia). A few are totalitarian in the sense of trying to control how people think (totalitarianism and libertarianism, the idea of minimal state interference in people's lives, will remain the opposite ends of the political spectrum).

Third world countries, sometimes called the South because so many are in the southern hemisphere, are those unable to enforce their will throughout their national territories (Kennon 1995). Many are overwhelmingly burdened by foreign debt. In 1970 the fifteen most heavily indebted nations had an external public debt of 9.8 per cent of gross national product (GNP). By 1987 this had risen to 47.5 per cent of GNP. Having to make such debt repayments to first world countries ensures that schools and hospitals cannot be built and that ever-more resources will be sold off, exacerbating the problem further.

Homer-Dixon (1991) suggests that severe civil strife within the nation state is likely when:

- There are clearly defined and organised groups in society;

- Some of these groups regard their level of achievement as unacceptably low and, hence, the socioeconomic system as unfair;

- These same groups believe peaceful opportunities for change are blocked but that the authority system is capable of being overthrown.

On this analysis, the only way for a police state to cease to be a police state is to cease to be deeply divided.

The modern idea of democracy can be traced back to Locke's assertion that all people are born free and equal. The quintessence of liberal democratic government (Dahl 1999) is majority rule restrained by culture, law, custom, 'natural' rights to protect minorities and the power of a range of countervailing institutions (such as churches, unions, business, the public service, academia). It allows the individual an effective say in running the state through a process of free election of representatives under broad suffrage to make laws and carry out policy. The will of the people is the legitimate source of their own collective direction. Gorer (1966) emphasises that not only *is* majority rule restrained by a range of values ('whatever is taken to have rightful authority in the direction of conduct') in a democracy, it *must be* if democracy is to survive; that the attitude of 'winner takes all' is fatal to democracy. Government must have the consent of all the governed.

Now that is the theory, but it is not difficult to identify a rapidly growing disenchantment with government, both with the institution itself and with its ability to perform (Shuman 1978). This is despite some spreading of forms of democratic government around the world. The Freedom House organisation, which follows such matters, rated 42 countries as 'free' in 1972 and 75 as 'free' in 1994. Modelski and Perry (2002) modelled the spread of 'democracy' as an S-shaped diffusion process and predicted that the fraction of the global population living in democratic states would rise from 57 per cent in 2000 to 90 per cent in 2113. Domestic policies for managing deficits, debts and unemployment have generally been unsuccessful (Daly and Logan 1989). There is some evidence that young people are unimpressed with political processes, even in stable democracies (Eckersley 1995). And many first world countries contain a growing underclass that feels that the political process has failed it. Certainly many unemployed feel betrayed by a society that says 'If you try hard enough you will get a job'.

But how has this happened? Democracy's greatest strength, having to maintain the approval of the voters, is also its greatest weakness, namely, having to get re-elected every few years by pandering to short-sighted and greedy voters and not take account of future voters, non-voters etc. Single-issue parties can exert a disproportionate influence. Liberal democracies seem incapable of pre-empting (anticipating? forestalling?) or even seriously debating problems and, moreover, tend to overreact when they do eventually respond. The reason has been neatly diagnosed as 'pluralistic stagnation' (Lindblom 1959, 1965) wherein competing interest groups continually nullify each other: whatever is proposed by one group is commonly against the interests of some other organised group and therefore vigorously opposed. Contributing to the 'log jam' in many cases is the built-in unwillingness of contending parties to compromise, to moderate their demands. It is proposals which threaten only a diffuse and unorganised public interest which best stand to succeed. Mancur Olson (1982) talks about *distributional coalitions* or *special-interest groups* that are willing to sacrifice large national gains to obtain small gains for themselves. Olson foresees this fate for all developed countries and Kennon (1995) finds the signs already visible in Britain, the United States, Japan and Germany; but there are also signs that some groups are beginning to voluntarily restrict their capacity to gridlock the system.

Thus, failures to cope with the problems of Hobsbawm's (1994) crisis decades have undermined political consensus and participation, leaving governments vulnerable to sectional interests. However, at this stage, the liberal 'representative' democracies face little internal threat of takeover through 'direct democracy' (for example, the widespread use of citizen-initiated referenda) or through the ballot box by non-democratic groups such as Christian fundamentalists or US-style 'patriots'. Their numbers are too small.

Of more concern is the prospect of some liberal democracies becoming authoritarian police states as a response to deepening intractable divisions within the society, along with the loss of both sovereignty and legitimacy. Where such divisions are geographic (for example, Quebec in Canada, Scotland in the United Kingdom), dissociation becomes a plausible possibility, but where some 20 per cent of the community forms a diffuse underclass, it is Rio de Janeiro-style 'war' and terrorism in the cities (van Creveld 1991) that becomes plausible. Beginning signs can be seen in Liverpool, Manchester and Newcastle in the United Kingdom and in Los Angeles and New York in the United States.

But even where democracies are not deeply and intractably divided to the point of being threatened by violence and its repression, or not threatened at the ballot box by anti-democratic minorities, they are still threatened by 'creeping bureaucratisation'. Kennon (1995) sees the rise and fall of nation states as dependent on the interplay between the political sector, the bureaucratic or managerial sector and the private sector. The political sector is essentially confrontationist and that is inefficient. He notes that economically successful states of recent times are those where the bureaucracy and its specialists are able to concentrate on facilitating the activities of the private sector and solving 'technical' problems. He conjectures that first world countries intent on retaining that status, but bedevilled by pluralistic stagnation or gridlock, will gradually turn more and more decisions over to bureaucrats and specialists. The increasing role of economists is a good example of the erosion of authority by technical competence. Interest groups would not be able to play the same role as they do now in influencing government decisions. Concurrently, the core business of government stands to move from the provision of services to the administration of service provision (OSCA 1996).

The political sector would not disappear in such a 'post-democratic world', nor would it cease to have important functions: it would legitimise bureaucratic actions just as a monarchy can legitimise parliament; it would act as an ombudsman for individuals and as umpire for disputes between bureaucracies; it would channel violent tendencies into harmless theatre (as sport does); and, if things went really wrong, it could reassert itself as an authority of last resort.

GEOECONOMIC FUTURES
The globalisation process

Over the 20th century the capitalist system responded to recurring industrial over-capacity, with all that this implies for profits, in changing ways. There has been a progression from protectionism and imperialism in the first half of the century to cartelisation and then, starting in the 1970s, to *globalisation*.

Globalisation of economic activity began as a search for low-cost production by US corporations as they came under intense competition from Japanese corporations (Reich 1991). Beginning with the location of manufacturing in low-wage countries, it rapidly became a 'geographic unbundling' of business systems, that is, with research and development, design, manufacturing and service delivery being based in different locations or countries. Simultaneously, the 1970s slow-down in growth and rising unemployment fuelled a successful push for deregulation of business in industrialised countries, notably in banking (Daly and Logan 1989).

More recently, as profits again begin to falter under the influence of decreasing transport and communication costs and increasing ease of entry into many sectors of the economy, globalisation is transmuting, patchily, into a drive by trans-national corporations to provide high-value customised goods and services to the world's middle classes. That is, profits are increasingly being derived from a continual adjustment of production to customer needs (Reich 1991).

What are some of the direct consequences of these processes?

- The global economy is six times larger than in 1950, is more integrated and has significant new players. In the same period, the volume of world trade has grown consistently (at 5.9 per cent per annum between 1960 and 1988), fuelled by falling real transport costs and the progressive removal of tariff and non-tariff barriers. Trade is still growing at three times the rate of Gross World Product (GWP), while foreign investment is growing at seven times the rate of trade growth. The export of capital from trade-surplus countries has the effect of maintaining the domestic rate of profit as well as providing high profits from production in countries with low wage costs;

- National savings flow to where they earn most. National competitiveness is thus less dependent on national savings than on having the national skills which attract investment;

- Returns to a country's investors increasingly depend less on the success of their domestic companies than on the global portfolio selected;

- Globalisation appears to pit workers in different parts of the world (indeed in different regions within countries) against each other in competition for jobs, wages and working conditions (Fagan and Webber 1994). As jobs move offshore, organised labour in the industrial countries is losing its capacity to bargain with large corporations engaged in high-volume production. Concurrently, organisations have learned that it is possible to grow without growing the work force. The pain of falling real wages is moving up the organisational hierarchy;

- Productivity gains tend to show up as falling prices rather than as rising wages; there has been a shift from an inflation-prone environment to a deflation-prone environment (Thurow 1996);

- Nations can no longer substantially enhance the wealth of their citizens by subsidising, protecting or otherwise increasing the value of 'their' corporations; the connection between domestic corporate profitability and citizens' standard of living is attenuating;

- Products, corporations and economies no longer have distinct nationalities;

- Dematerialisation, decarbonisation and miniaturisation (What Buck Fuller [1969] in *Utopia or Oblivion* calls 'ephemeralisation'). Steel, chemicals, motor vehicles and oil were the world's backbone industries in the energy-intensive years of the 'long boom' (Daly and Logan 1989). Now, materials, routine labour and energy are increasingly being designed out of products as corporations respond to the two forces driving competitive markets: the hope of capturing intra-market share with a cheaper or better product; and the hope of capturing inter-market share with innovative products. Concurrently, product lifetimes and product life cycles are shortening;

- Floating exchange rates have created extreme currency instability which in turn has created an enormous mass of mobile world money susceptible to panic runs on currencies of countries with short-term debts (Drucker 1997: 162);

- The world's 200 biggest trans-national corporations are responsible for a rapidly increasing share of GWP, with sales in 1995 equal to 28 per cent of GWP, up from 24 per cent in 1982. Their combined sales exceeded the combined GDP of 182 nations, that is, all except the largest nine economies (*Canberra Times*, 17 October 1996). Yet employment worldwide in these global firms has remained virtually flat since the 1970s.

World trade

> ... if there is one rule of international econom-
> ics, it is that no country can run a large trade
> deficit forever (THUROW 1996).

It is the nature of international capitalism that as one part of the world succeeds and builds up trade surpluses, these surpluses have to be reinvested elsewhere in a process that is necessary if trade-deficit countries are to be able to
continue to trade.

It is commonly predicted that the future rate of economic growth in East
Asia, where growth is very much trade-based, will exceed that of Europe and
North America and hence contribute an increasing share of GWP. McRae
(1994), however, observes that East Asian growth is thinly based in terms of
products and export markets and is therefore fragile, for example, vulnerable
to US protectionism. Daly and Logan (1989) note that most countries of the
Asia-Pacific region are not well placed to benefit from the movement of the
world economy from labour and energy-intensive industries to services and
knowledge-intensive industries.

Thurow (1996) regards the current US–Japan trade imbalance as unsustainable and standing to have major repercussions around the Asia-Pacific
region however it is resolved, for example, by emergency tariffs. The United
States must start running substantial trade surpluses to pay interest on its
international debts or 'at some point, a falling (US) dollar is going to lead the
rest of the world to quit holding dollars'. A run on the dollar will lead to debts
in appreciating currencies (yen? marks?) becoming unserviceably high.

More generally, it is plausible to see world trade continuing to grow, partly in response to a growing world economy, partly in response to eroding
trade and capital barriers and partly in response to the as-yet-unfinished geographic dispersion of industry. Trade between subsidiaries and at 'arranged'
prices will continue to grow. Conversely, more incorporation of self-sufficiency into national goals would slow growth in world trade and a rapid esca-
lation in oil prices would stop it in its tracks.

Wealthiest of nations

Conjectures about the sorts of first world countries standing to experience
above-average rates of economic growth in coming decades include the
following:

- For the first years of the 21st century, it will remain vitally important to
  be good at making things, but gradually economic advantage will move
  to countries good at producing services;

- McRae (1994) says efficiency in the service industries will be the motor of growth. He uses a broad economy-wide concept of efficiency which includes not having to use scarce resources for ameliorating deep social problems. Crime is the most obvious of these. For example, the United States puts 1.3 per cent of GDP into overt law and order (excluding private security). The Australian state of New South Wales now has 35 000 private security guards, twice the number of police officers. The conventional family unit is an efficient way of combining child rearing with earning a living and the economic cost of family break-up is high. Health costs and transaction costs (for example, legal costs) can vary markedly between countries. Countries which want to grow richer will find it much easier if the society is well disciplined, which is not necessarily the same thing as the 'soft authoritarianism' of some 'Asian tigers';

- Because physical infrastructure (capital invested in land) and people are the relatively immobile factors of production, economically successful countries will give high priority to developing problem-solving skills and high-quality institutional and physical infrastructure. Foreign ownership and control will be of little concern in successful economies because the value of corporations lies increasingly with their mobile symbolic analysts and, as long as these do not live abroad, their home countries gain most of the benefits of their skills (Reich 1991);

- Technology is making skills and knowledge the only sources of sustainable strategic advantage (Thurow 1996). Capital in the form of land and natural resources will matter less because the industrialised world can produce its own food. Financial capital is 'always available at a price' [sic] in London, New York or Tokyo and natural resources no longer fuel economic growth (McRae 1994);

- Countries that are willing to sacrifice environmental standards, wages, working conditions, civil and political rights and ethical standards will win the economic war (a pyrrhic victory?);

- Despite current woes, the Japanese 'team approach' to manufacturing production has proved very efficient and adaptable in the face of change. More generally, a lack of sentimentality about established ways of doing things will be very important;

- An open economy will be vital to economic success (!). National security is no reason for keeping foreign firms out as, say, Albania did prior to 1990. Complete security is equivalent to autarky (full self-sufficiency). But autarky deprives a nation's citizens of all the advantages of economic interdependence with the rest of the world. In the event, trade, as a fraction of economic activity, might fall sharply of its own accord through the century if more and more products can be made more efficiently in locations close to the consumer, due to both reduced material and energy inputs and the fast pace of technology transfer (OTA 1988). It is not easy to understand how the global economy would operate under a trade decline;

• Economically successful countries will learn to initiate new 'growth industries' well before old industries begin to decline (Handy 1994). If, as seems possible, a new Kondratieff (1926) growth cycle (see page 162) is beginning, the candidate industries for driving that resurgence of global capitalism are the knowledge-intensive industries, particularly information and communications. Indeed, the US economy's 12 million new jobs in the 5 years after 1992 was a 'change dividend' attributed to this process beginning (Milne 1997);

• In a time when oil prices stand to rise markedly, the economy which steadily reduces oil use per dollar of GDP will be advantaged.

New systems for wealth creation, such as the information economy, tend to be obstructed by the traditions, codes, laws, taxes, morals, administrative arrangements etc. of the existing system and, unless it is actively countered, a wave of costly social conflict is inevitable (Arquilla and Ronfeldt 1997).

The future of global capitalism

Capitalism is an economic system energised by a drive to accumulate capital by making profits which are then invested in increased productive capacity. But continuing such investment leads to productive over-capacity, falling prices and falling profits as growth markets become replacement markets. War or 'military Keynesianism' (Knight 1987) is one way of increasing demand to solve this excess-capacity problem (the United States has, more or less, run a war economy since 1941).

Innovation is another. Schumpeter's (1934) 'waves of creative destruction' lead to the abandonment of unprofitable capital and the diversion of profits into the production of new goods and services. So, as profits from productive processes inescapably fall over time, there is a constant search for new ways of doing things, usually involving the substitution of capital for labour, or new ways of producing goods or finding new goods to produce. However, while capitalism is organised to search for and seize on profit opportunities created by technological and organisational change, there is no guarantee that these will arrive with the regularity required to maintain investment opportunities.

While we might not be too surprised to see 21st century capitalism enjoying successes and setbacks similar to 20th century capitalism, the possibility of a system-destroying setback cannot be ruled out (Heilbroner 1993). Disney's (1994) slightly less apocalyptic judgment is that during the next few decades there is a strong possibility of at least one major crisis in the international financial system, causing spectacular economic and social damage throughout the world. There is concern, for example, about the destabilising effects of massively increasing speculative international currency flows and the inhibiting effect these have on productive investment (Hutton 1996). If Thurow (1996) is right, it was fear of Communism and the dominance of the US economy that held the capitalistic world economy together for decades. The possibility of global economic collapse is increased, not decreased, by the demise of Communism and the loss of US economic hegemony.

One major reason why varieties of capitalism will provide the basis for most national economies in the 21st century is that, with the breakdown of the Soviet system in the 1980s, there are no substantive alternatives, no blueprints for a successor. This pervasiveness will be despite the obvious failures of most capitalist economies to provide full employment, high living standards, proper working conditions, rising productivity, international competitiveness, subdued cyclical behaviour, an egalitarian income distribution, inter-generational equity and a sustainable, culturally-sensitive economy.

The seventh annual United Nations Human Development Report (UNDP 1996) noted that seventy of 174 countries have lower average incomes today than in 1980. More positively, Castles (2000) points out that, in the largest of the world's poor countries, life expectancy increased by a solid 23.4 years to 63.8 years between 1952 and 1997 and that GDP per capita in the largest poor countries increased at a higher rate (3.4 per cent per annum) than in the largest rich countries (2.7 per cent per annum) over the period 1960–97. While this difference in growth rate suggests eventual convergence between poor and rich countries, the absolute gap in GDP per capita over this period (in Purchasing Power Parity or PPP dollars) grew from 1997 PPP $9024 (that is, 10 056 v 1032) to 1997 PPP $21 524 (that is, 24 761 v 3237). While such averages can be misleading, an extended data set from 80 countries over four decades (Dollar and Kraay 2000) shows that the rate of change in per capita income of the poorest quintile of a country's population is strongly correlated with and of the same magnitude as the average rate of change in per capita income. Declining prices for raw materials, the burden of international debts, the absence of an industrial base, powerlessness in key international negotiating fora as well as rising internal instability in numerous cases bodes ill for the economic future of many developing countries (OSCA 1996). Given the economic gains accruing to capital under globalisation, there is no foreseeable incentive for capitalism to reform itself as happened under the threats of Fascism and Communism.

Modern economic ideas suggest that, in unregulated markets where semi-monopolies thrive, positive feedback mechanisms are likely to allow larger companies to grow relentlessly at the expense of smaller companies. Many industries already comprise one or a few firms (Meacher 1982). In coming decades, it would not be surprising to see an ever-increasing fraction of GWP being produced by an ever-decreasing number of trans-national corporations (TNCs) and consumed in the first world and, to a lesser extent, in the second world. This would leave perhaps a hundred third-world countries with stagnant or declining domestic economies largely decoupled from the global economy or outside the trading blocs that are emerging as stepping-stones towards a more global economy. Kennon (1995) conjectures that while TNCs will have the power to topple governments, they will leave token democracies in place in all first world countries, shaping policy to suit corporate needs. If system collapse can be avoided, the 'alliance capitalism' experience of the petroleum industry provides an unsurprising scenario: as each industry is reduced to a few major players, they will cease serious competition and will instead collaboratively manage production, distribution and pricing to their mutual benefit. Similarly, one could expect financial markets to be ultimately stabilised, and a single global currency adopted. If the global economy does come to be dominated by a handful of non-competing mega-corporations, will this be the prelude to a 'post-capitalist managerialism' era in which competition gives way to 'property management'?

Meanwhile, other 'brands' of capitalism remain possibilities. The overlapping candidates include competitive capitalism, market-access capitalism, guided capitalism, crony capitalism, Fascism and social market or civic capitalism. *Competitive capitalism* means something like the free-market capitalism of economic theory. Competitive capitalism can be contrasted with *market-access capitalism* where offsets are demanded in return for allowing entry into particular markets. Asian-style *guided capitalism* sees the state playing an important role in coordinating the domestic and international operations of the nation's large corporations. Guided capitalism can degenerate into *crony capitalism* where business opportunities are gifted by the state rather than competed for. Capitalism under *Fascism* sees worker rights traded for security of employment and the protection of business from legal scrutiny. Fascism has great emotional power and many of the themes that accompanied the emergence of Fascism in the 1920s are re-emerging according to Umberto Eco (1995). In *civic capitalism,* participants accept obligations (for example, social, environmental) imposed by the (legal) framework that makes their commerce possible (Emy 1993).

At the beginning of the 21st century manufacturing output is increasing rapidly and employing fewer and fewer workers, exactly as agriculture did at the beginning of the 20th century (Drucker 2001). Assuming GWP continues to grow over coming decades, perhaps doubling by 2025 and again by 2050 (Halal 1993), the global product mix stands to continue shifting from goods to services, services being everything other than industrial and agricultural products. Travel and tourism, for example, is already the largest single industry in the world, employing 130 million people worldwide in 1993. More generally, first world economies will continue moving from extractive industries through fabricating industries to information processing and knowledge-intensive industries, but adding these sectors on rather than replacing the old 'saturated' industries. And if it survives the 'information age', globalised capitalism will exploit successive clusters of new technologies (see below).

Organisation of production

Mergers to create fewer, bigger units are not the only foreseeable change in the way production might be organised in the evolving global economy. Businesses are also beginning to learn that getting the most out of information technology requires a substantial reconceptualisation and reorganisation of the work to be done. Handy (1994) sees organisations becoming more like 'condominiums of transients', groups of project teams coming together for specific operations, rather than 'castles' where workers have a home for life. In part this is because there is less value in being able to access 'corporate memory' under conditions of rapid change. Such networks are not just between corporations but include complex coalitions with states and non-government organisations. Rooney and Mandeville (1998) locate the rise of networks and network-like organisational structures in business in the increasing need to share knowledge, particularly tacit knowledge, between firms and the role of the Internet in reducing the transaction costs of such sharing.

Emery et al. (1975) and Kennon (1995) see employment in 'new' corporations as becoming ever more specialised and bureaucratised, this being but the continuation of a long-time trend. The relationship between specialists and bureaucrats is that bureaucrats understand and coordinate the functions which different specialists can perform. Collectively, specialists and bureaucrats constitute Bell's (1973) knowledge class or professional class. Trans-national corporations are increasingly being managed and staffed by people, akin to Kennon's specialists and bureaucrats. They are called symbolic analysts by Reich (1991) — problem solvers, problem identifiers and brokers of deals. Typically, these work at terminals when not talking and otherwise communicating. They create and coordinate flows of information (intellectual capital) which evoke and blend flows of goods and services produced by smaller companies staffed by more traditional industrial and service workers. Globally, demand for their services has been boosted by declining transport and communication costs. It is because, in search of flexibility under change, big organisations are increasingly using contract inputs and contract workers for routine functions (outsourcing) that most new jobs come from small companies, not large.

Beyond capitalism

While capitalism may or may not disappear this century, we do know that it will not last forever. The very essence of capitalism is change. At some stage it will change into something else. It may be, for example, a decline in world population which makes individuals more highly valued. It may be Joseph Schumpeter's (1942) view that the mindset of economic fundamentalism might eventually destroy the minimal set of social values (private property, enforceable contracts) on which acquisitive capitalism depends. Schumpeter also foresaw that with the concentration of economies into giant corporations, capitalism would no longer have a constituency of small entrepreneurs to support it politically. Marx's 'inevitable' progression from feudalism to capitalism to Communism retains credibility for some.

Immanuel Wallerstein (1995), the father of world-systems theory, sees capitalism as doomed at some stage for several reasons: it relies on cheap labour which is slowly disappearing [sic] and it is being gradually forced to pay for environmental and other external costs it currently evades. But, most importantly, under libertarian minimalism and leftist disillusion with the state, capitalism is losing its underpinning protection and support from the state, for example, the enforceable legal environment, wage control.

Unlike all of the above, Hodgson's (1999a) scenarios for the transmutation of capitalism are driven by internal rather than external change. In an economy which is increasingly reliant on specialist skills and complex information transfers, knowledge workers cannot be tied down with precise employment contracts — their commitment must be freely given — and they are in a position to demand non-wage rewards. Ownership, control and profit-sharing are taking new and evolving forms under the emerging model of the corporation as an impermanent network of nodes of such expertise. As demonstrated by their shares of turnover, both capital and 'traditional' labour are 'subordinated' to the claims of the symbolic analysts whose skills are rewarded at rates set on world rather than domestic markets. Indeed, companies with owners wanting dividends may just become uncompetitive (Moravec 1999: 133). At some stage in this transition, capitalism, meaning 'wage' labour and the separation of ownership and management, will have become something else.

WORLD-SHAPING TECHNOLOGIES

> Technology drives social change today
> (PLATT 1966).
>
> ~
>
> The most powerful and disruptive forces of the
> twentieth century are science and technology.
> The world's most pressing political, social and
> economic problems have their origins in science
> and technology; the population explosion, eco-
> nomic growth, pollution and environmental
> deterioration, the means of war, the limits to
> growth, disparities of wealth and urbanisation
> (BIRCH 1975).

Catton (1980) calls humans the prosthetic species, dependent on detachable organs such as jumbo jets and power stations. Technologies are extensions and externalisations of people's unaided capabilities (Childe 1942; Fuller 1969). For example:

- The industrial revolution expanded our capacity to do physical work;

- The transport revolution expanded our capacity to travel long distances;

- The computer revolution expanded our capacity to acquire, store and process information;

- The communications revolution is expanding our capacity to exchange information (McLuhan's 'extended nervous system');

- The medical revolution is expanding our capacity to approach our genetic potential for longevity and to control population size;

- The dematerialisation revolution is expanding our capacity to produce given outputs from fewer inputs in primary and secondary industry.

New technologies that can be immediately applied in a number of dif-ferent sectors of the economy can be usefully called *generic technologies.* Printing is an outstanding example. Contemporary examples of ever-increas-ing importance include microelectronics, biotechnologies, telematics (also called infotronics, computer-telecommunication technologies), new-materi-als technologies and robotics (for example, Sheffield et al. 1994). Another class of important technologies are those that change the price or quality of some basic input used in most sectors of the economy; inputs such as energy, trans-port, information, telecommunications or services such as legal services. These can be called *infrastructural or enabling technologies.* In this section we have space to glance at no more than several developing families of generic technologies and several of enabling technologies.

It is the nature of capitalism that new and profitable technologies lead to production and marketing innovations in firms and, from there, to changes in the structure of economies, for example, the root cause of globalisation is technological. Economic changes, in turn, initiate social changes reflecting people's adaptations to new products and prices. The closing link in this cycle is that profits from the new products are used to fund further technological developments.

Technological change will continue to creep into our lives, changing the way services are provided, the productivity of labour, the range of goods we buy and the way we do things. But will it lead to more interesting jobs, more leisure as distinct from more unemployment, environmental protection, a greater real choice of products and opportunities, especially for the disadvantaged? As ever, technology is neutral in itself and whether technological change is used to improve people's quality of life depends on the social and economic context within which it is embedded. For example, because they have more purchasing power it is usually far more profitable to use new technologies to produce goods and services for the rich rather than the poor.

Conversely, will some technological changes prove actively harmful? While the 'revenge' or 'bite-back' potential of new technologies (Tenner 1996) is increasingly recognised, efforts to undertake technology impact assessments before rather than after adoption are minimal. Perhaps, in the post-capitalist world, technology development and distribution of the associated benefits and disbenefits will be somehow socially guided (see page 245).

Energy

> ... even the most optimistic estimates indicate commercial fusion power is unlikely to be available for fifty years or more (OLIPHANT 1992).

Even when it arrives, high capital costs and high maintenance costs may mean that fusion power (energy released when hydrogen nuclei come together) is not profitable enough to replace fossil fuels or alternative energy sources. And even when developed, fusion reactors will have severe residual radiation problems (Leslie 1996; Hardin 1993). However, Marchetti (1987) still conjectures that nuclear energy will succeed natural gas as the world's primary energy source (gas itself being the successor to oil in that role) in the second half of the 21st century, possibly being used to produce fuel-hydrogen in lightly populated areas. Uranium reserves however would be exhausted thereafter without a switch from open cycle technology to fuel reprocessing and breeder technology. Breeder technology carries proliferation and other risks but would extend the life of fissile reserves for many centuries.

Traditional calculations of future world energy needs start from information on current energy use per dollar of GDP (called energy intensity) and then make assumptions about (a) the rate of GDP growth and (b) the rate of decline in energy intensity. Grubler et al. (1995) suggest that the world will not run out of energy in coming decades even though energy needs in 2050 might be an order of magnitude higher than today. Looking further ahead again, Gilland (1995) reviews global energy demand up to 2100 and, even with a world population of perhaps 11 billion, speculates that current average annual energy consumption of 1.7 tonnes of oil equivalent per capita should be maintainable.

But what of the energy mix? With the exception of members of the Organisation of Petroleum Exporting Countries (OPEC), every major oil-producing country is already experiencing declining production (Bronner 1996). Of the world's 1023 billion barrels of proven reserves, 60 per cent or about 614 billion barrels lie beneath the sands of Iran, Iraq, Saudi Arabia, Bahrain, Oman, Qatar, Kuwait and the United Arab Emirates. Oil is also peaking in terms of market share and Marchetti (1987) sees it as having less than 10 per cent market share by 2050. He also sees most oil being convert-ed to transportation fuels, a relatively easy task technically. The World Resources Institute (1996) suggests that oil production — currently 40 per cent of the world's energy supply — could peak before 2002, in contrast to more conventional estimates that production will peak somewhere between 2010 and 2025. Thereafter, oil production could halve every 25 years or so. The energy break-even point for United States oil production (when it takes a barrel to retrieve a barrel) will probably occur in the first decade of this century. Oil will be increasingly replaced for some decades by natural gas for which only 2 per cent of known reserves have been extracted so far (Marchetti 1987). Similarly, it is efficient gas turbine generators that will drive coal from the electricity market. Absolute gas use should peak about 2060 (Ausubel 1998).

Not only will the energy mix be responding to declining oil supplies, it will be responding to a 'pervasive and persistent demand' for ever cleaner, more flexible and more convenient energy forms. There will be a continuing 'decarbonisation' as well as a 'dejouling' of the economy. Ausubel and Marchetti (1996) say the world is just past the middle point of a decarboni-sation process that will take another 150 years to complete. The precise energy mix after about 2020 will depend on both research and investment paths.

Improvements to fuel cells (these are something like rechargeable batteries) have the potential to trigger 'the big switch' from a combustion-based polluting economy to a sustainable hydrogen/electro-chemical economy (DAS 1996). Whatever the mix though, the energy sector's capital requirements will continue to be extremely large.

Energy prices are expected to rise presently, perhaps significantly enough to constitute a 'shock' or perhaps gradually enough to not constitute a major obstacle to increased energy use. A significant rise in energy prices would particularly affect transportation systems, now largely dependent on oil-based fuels. Aircraft will consume most of the fossil fuel in future transport systems (Marchetti 1991) and liquid hydrogen aircraft could be an important development for both greenhouse reasons and as a replacement for increasingly scarce kerosene (Victor 1990). Rising oil prices and limited gas supplies will stimulate, in an unpredictable way, the development of renewable energy sources (solar power, geothermal and ocean thermal power, wind power, hydro power, tidal power, biomass fuels such as ethanol and 'biodiesel' from crops) and, perhaps, new processes, beyond fusion and fission power, based on energy drawn from collapsing hydrogen atoms. New methods of sequestering (locking up) carbon dioxide away from the atmosphere or new 'clean' technologies may allow the increasing use of 'dirty' fossil fuels such as coal and tar sands. For example, carbon dioxide and heat from coal power stations could be used to grow micro-algae in vats. Active management of the demand for energy is another possibility. Overall, as natural gas runs out later this century, a scenario involving a diversity of energy sources would be unsurprising.

BOX 1.2: A DIFFERENT FORM OF RENEWABLE ENERGY

Freeman Dyson (2000) suggests the possibility of genetically engineered crop plants which convert solar energy directly to liquid fuel which is collected by 'tapping' as latex is tapped from rubber trees or collected directly into underground fuel lines. Such a technology would overcome the intermittent nature of solar energy and the costs of whole-plant processing associated with conventional biomass fuels.

Transport

Change in the world transport system stands to be a major driver of global change with benefits from an improved system coming in the form of lower production and delivery costs. Disbenefits from increased passenger and freight volumes include pollution, landscape disruption and loss of amenity values (values directly meeting human needs and wants) (GACGC 1993). Beyond the immediate costs and benefits of the transport system lurks the whole question of the net benefits of free trade and the movement towards more local production.

How might the world's transport networks change in coming decades? Conjectured increases in the value of global trade imply large increases in the physical magnitude of the transport task, despite trends to dematerialisation, to 'value-added' exports and to relatively more trade in services than goods. However, the geographic extent of the global transport network has probably already been largely set; what will change as the global economy evolves are the absolute and relative volumes and categories of people and freight, and the modal split (road versus rail etc.), on particular links. Mass tourism stands to be a major generator of people traffic.

Technologies already available, or in the research and development pipeline, suggest that reduced costs and higher speeds are possibilities for both freight and passenger transport by road, rail, air and sea. One consequence of the availability of higher speed travel might be to integrate groups of cities into 'super cities'. Marchetti (1991) argues that people spend on average about an hour a day travelling in their 'territory' and always have done; and they spend about 15 per cent of their disposable income to maximise distance travelled in that hour, that is, to maximise the size of their 'territory', given that they 'have to return to the "den" each night'. Thus, very poor people have a mean speed of 4 kilometres per hour and a 4 x 4 kilometre territory. The very rich have a mean speed of 500 kilometres per hour and a 500 x 500 kilometre territory. Average territory sizes would continue to increase if average travel speeds continue their historical increase of between 1 per cent and 4 per cent a year.

The aeroplane is the fastest means of transport and given (a) a slow decrease in real terms of the cost of air transport (helped, for example, by larger planes) and (b) increasing disposable incomes, air travel stands to be the fastest growing branch of the passenger transport business. Detracting from this prospect, deaths per air trip are currently about 10 times the automobile rate and 20 times the rail-trip rate (Weir 1999). Where passenger volumes warrant it (for example, Europe, North America), there might also be a place for the increasing use of advanced high-speed ground transport such as maglev trains or fast hovercraft in guideways. Or, more fancifully, solar-powered airships in the tourism industry? Notwithstanding, road traffic, with its relatively high emission levels, is set to rise dramatically in some regions, notably Asia (excluding Japan) (GACGC 1993). Whether total vehicle emissions rise or fall in first world countries depends on the outcome of a race between increasing traffic volumes and improved emission control technology.

Note that there is a natural limit to travel speeds, at least on Planet Earth. Given the time it takes to reach cruise speed and slow down for landing, it makes little sense to travel at speeds much above Mach 2.5 on a planet the size of Earth (Singer 1994). 'The most optimistic date for putting a man [sic] on Mars is 2020', says Dr Richard Zurek of the Jet Propulsion Laboratory, California (*The Australian*, 18 July 1996). Space travel and space colonisation will not be important to many people this century.

Computing and communications

It is the capacity to (a) manipulate and (b) transfer information ever-faster that lies at the heart of the electronics-based communications and information industries which are set to be the dominant drivers of the world economy in the next Kondratieff cycle or, if you prefer, the next long wave of economic growth. Around 20 per cent of world trade, $740 billion a year and growing rapidly, is in intellectual property. The *information industry* revolves around the creation, organisation, distribution, storage, retrieval and use of information. It has two key components: electronic publishing (for example, the World Wide Web, CD-ROMs) and information retrieval for business, entertainment and research (OSCA 1996). The key hardware that both depend on, for the moment, is silicon microchips, the heart of every computer. Fabrication of microchips is a massive global industry, currently increasing its output at the rate of 15 per cent a year. Foreseeable developments in superconductors could see them rivalling semiconductors in computer processors and boosting operating speeds, in theory, by a factor of 50. Notwithstanding, photonic computers, running on light beams instead of electron flows, will replace electronic computers sometime this century (Sceats 1992). At the low technology end of computing developments, 'throwaway' plastic microchips are coming.

The Internet provides a dramatic example of the growth occurring in electronically based communications — at the present rate of connection, everyone in the world would be on the Internet by 2003 (Negroponte 1995)!! Perhaps 300 million actually will be. What Rowland Hill did for letter writing by inventing the penny postage stamp, the Internet could do for interpersonal communication in the 21st century, provided that access is cheap enough (and, subsidised by advertising, it could be). Along with accessibility, the big issues in Internet management are likely to be accountability (in a quality control sense), privacy and security (Dyson 1998). Protecting the integrity of traded knowledge stands to become more difficult (OSCA 1996).

Arguably, the single most important thing about the Internet is that it has the potential to increase the power of the individual in relation to the state and other authority structures. For example, dissenting views can be published worldwide instantaneously; electronic discussion groups and petitions are possible; direct democracy becomes more feasible vis-à-vis representative democracy. Authorities may or may not succeed in censoring offending material. The net-based global dissent movement may, at some stage, swing from being 'against the establishment' to the promotion of a comprehensive alternative. More widely recognised though is the potential of the Internet to continue carrying an increasing fraction of global commerce and, by increasing personal productivity, to expand global commerce.

Beyond the Internet as we know it, broadband optical fibres and direct-to-home/handset digital satellite broadcasting, and then a low-power digital-radio Internet stand to allow real-time multimedia communications. This is the heart of the communications revolution — the ability to communicate one-to-one in video, audio and data modes. Multimedia technology is driving convergence of the publishing industry, the computer industry, the broadcasting industry and the recording industry (OSCA 1996). But not the travel industry. Contrary to conventional wisdom (for example, about the prospects for virtual tourism), Marchetti (1991) suggests that communication advances (ISDN, local area networks, cellular telephones, faxes etc.) may change the way travel budgets are spent but not the amount; that transport and communications are not substitutes.

Automation and artificial intelligence

Automation is the use of machines to automatically perform tasks formerly performed only by humans. When such machines have some human-like attributes they are called robots. While most widely used in manufacturing, significant achievements have been made in the automation of tasks in the communications, transport and service industries. *Artificial intelligence* is the study of how to program computers to exhibit some of the characteristics of human intelligence, for example, learning, language, reasoning, problem solving. Indeed, in some environments it is useful to program 'intelligent agents' with the equivalent of emotions as behavioural guides. At some stage, advances in bio-molecular engineering may make it possible to construct artificial brains wholly analogous to human brains and the distinction between artificial and natural intelligence will become blurred.

Commercial developments in artificial intelligence and automation have come more slowly than anticipated by many researchers in these areas. Nevertheless, more and more of the ongoing tasks required for maintaining complex first-world societies will probably continue to pass from humans to these technologies. Progress in robotics depends on using increasing quantities of computing power and memory to mimic increasingly complex nervous systems. Thus Moravec (1999) foresees robots with the capabilities of lizards by 2010, mice by 2020, monkeys by 2030 and humans by 2040. The increasing capacity of robots to undertake diverse tasks may enhance an emerging trend away from Fordist production-line manufacturing towards cottage-scale local manufacturing.

Public debate about automation recognises that while it raises the productivity of labour and has advantages for worker safety and comfort, it commonly leads to job losses and hence, perhaps, at the macro-economic scale, to insufficient consumer demand to sustain economic activity. If remaining jobs are unskilled then competition for fewer jobs drives wages down. If remaining jobs require high and therefore rare skills, they will attract high salaries. Either way, some are jobless and some are overworked and it takes time for social bargaining to level out workloads (Moravec 1999).

The key advantage of non-biological 'intelligence' is that it can be easily shared between machines and with ever-faster computers of ever-greater storage capacity the possibility of a powerful web-based 'brain' emerges. For some this raises the spectre of humans destined to become automata with our brains restricted to feeding information into computers and receiving instructions back (Harth 1999). For others, in a species which is still escaping from dependence on external authority, this would be not unwelcome (cf. Jaynes 1976).

Manufacturing nanotechnologies

> In short, replicating assemblers will copy themselves by the ton, then make other products such as computers, rocket engines, chairs, and so forth. They will make disassemblers able to break down rock to supply raw material. They will make solar collectors to supply energy. Though tiny, they will build big. Teams of nanomachines in nature build whales, and seeds replicate machinery and organize atoms into vast structures of cellulose, building redwood trees. There is nothing too startling about growing a rocket engine in a specially prepared vat. Indeed, foresters given suitable assembler 'seeds' could grow spaceships from soil, air, and sunlight.

> Assemblers will be able to make virtually any-
> thing from common materials without labor,
> replacing smoking factories with systems as
> clean as forests. They will transform technology
> and the economy at their roots, opening a new
> world of possibilities. They will indeed be
> engines of abundance. (ERIC DREXLER, *Engines of
> Creation*, 1986)

The term nanotechnology comes from nanometre, a billionth of a metre. Every living cell is an example of processes operating at this scale and a major goal of nanotechnologists is to develop bacteria-sized robots which, placed in an appropriate environment, will construct human-scale materials one mole-cule or atom at a time — just as a cell uses enzymes to construct proteins out of amino acid building blocks. The challenge is to build robots that can cap-ture the next molecule to be added to whatever is being constructed and then to hold that molecule in the right position and place while it bonds chemi-cally to the growing product. The other major challenge in nanotechnology is that if products manufactured by small assembler robots are to be cheap to produce, the robots themselves have to be self-assembling, that is, able to replicate themselves in an appropriate environment such as a solution of the right chemicals, for example, self-assembling organic solar cells.

While it is early days yet, both these challenges are being met and man-ufacturing nanotechnologies could be widely used within decades to make low-cost high-quality products ranging from computers to foodstuffs.

Biological and medical technologies

Biotechnology (biological technology) is not just genetic engineering, mean-ing the deliberate substitution of one organism's genes for another's; it encompasses a variety of techniques which allow the manipulation of microbes, plants and animals so that they produce new chemicals, grow faster, resist disease or have other useful attributes (Mannion 1995). *Somacloning* for example, allows genetically different individual cells from one plant to be grown into whole organisms, one of which might exhibit particularly desir-able characteristics. Biotechnology is of increasing importance to the econo-my in the fields, particularly, of pharmaceuticals, agriculture and environmental management.

Genetic engineering in its first and simplest form is already being wide-ly applied to the production of vaccines and other useful proteins such as hor-mones (for example, insulin) and anti-hormones. Anti-hormone vaccines for example, can increase twinning in sheep, delay sexual maturity or neuter an

animal. The transferring of 'foreign' genes into plants and animals and learning how to switch genes on and off are more difficult tasks, but potentially
more valuable. Other genetic material being transferred into crop plants can
confer resistance to salting, drought and weedicides, while offering flavour,
nutritional and textural benefits. Incorporating an improved capacity to take
up soil nutrients stands to reduce crops' needs for fertilisers. A spin-off concern here is that species with enhanced adaptive capacities may have the
potential to displace formerly unusable natural ecosystems. Most of these
applications of genetic engineering are still some way from commercial use,
one reason being that newly created genetic traits in laboratory animals and
plants still have to be spread by conventional breeding methods.

The development of biotechnologies for pest control is a particularly
promising field of research. Emerging insect-control technologies include
genetic manipulation to produce sterile males and to introduce delayed-
action lethal genes. The gene for producing, in a particular bacterium, a
chemical toxic to insects has recently been successfully transferred to crop
plants, thus enabling the plant to produce its own insecticide!

Research on vaccination against animal parasites such as cattle tick and
sheep blowfly is very active. Anti-parasite vaccines have only become possible
with the development of recombinant DNA technology (the technological
heart of biotechnology). This enables genes for protective antigens to be
'grown' in cell culture or in other organisms such as harmless viruses which
can then be released to transfer the antigen from animal to animal. That is
clever, but there is still a long way to go.

The converse idea of using carrier viruses to transfer sublethal genes (for
example, for infertility) between feral animals seems to be one of the few
prospects of ever really controlling pests such as rabbits. For example, the
myxomatosis virus, carried by fleas and mosquitoes, attacks only rabbits and
therefore is ideal for being adapted to carry the gene which produces egg-
covering proteins in rabbits. When such a transgenic myxomatosis virus enters
its victim's bloodstream, it sets off an immune reaction which makes the rabbit sterile as it destroys its own eggs in mistake for the invading virus.

Friend (1992) suggests a range of other objectives which biotechnology
is likely to achieve in the future food industry, including biological probes for
the presence of food-borne pathogens; freshness biosensors built into pack-
aging materials; natural biological preservatives; foods with extended storage
life. Other environmental applications of biotechnology are beginning to
emerge in resource recycling and pollutant degradation, for example, degradation of mustard gas, weedicides, oil slicks. *Biomining,* still in its infancy,

involves the use of organisms to extract metals from primary ores and to scavenge metals and other useful substances from waste water.

In a movement which is reminiscent of campaigns opposing nuclear power, consumer and environmental groups around the world have sought bans on the release of live genetically engineered organisms — the *biosafety* issue. While the chances of a few new genes causing an organism to become an 'environmental monster', spreading out of control (like the thousands of genes we collectively call a rabbit) are slim, legislation to control development, trialling and release of new life forms is widely viewed as desirable for both genetically engineered and conventionally-bred organisms. The public's collateral concerns, heightened by science's declining credibility, include possible problems from foods with inbuilt genetically engineered toxins and allergens and the rise of seed-vendor monopolies. Also, there is a perception that such developments are for the benefits of producers rather than consumers.

In medicine, the startling possibilities which have been foreseen for manipulating the human mind and body this century include such things as downloading memories onto disk, neurone-chip grafts, the use of drug-mediated virtual reality to extend people's vicarious experiences, limb regrowth, cryonic re-animation, artificial wombs (shades of Aldous Huxley). Nerve regeneration could allow the curing of some blindnesses, quadriplegia and paraplegia. Immunological diseases such as asthma, arthritis and some cancers could be brought under control (Regis 1990). For a long time to come though most cancers will remain manageable rather than curable.

Technologies for splitting an embryo so as to provide a reservoir of spare parts for one's old age are foreseeable and raise major ethical questions as does the use of other species to provide organ transplant material (Cravalho 1994). Growing new organs in place from injected or induced stem cells may leapfrog these particular renovation technologies. Even more fundamentally, *germ-line genetic engineering* will involve adding 'desirable' new genes to every cell in an embryo, thus making the changes heritable (unlike changes due to somatic genetic engineering). Life extension technologies based on bio-drugs such as melatonin and human growth hormone could increase first-world life expectancy at birth to 120 by 2100. This would have downstream implications for average population age, population size, inheritance taxes and a host of other issues. More controversially, if the postponement of old age becomes a growth industry in the first world it will raise questions of equity, not only between rich and poor countries but also between rich and poor groups domestically.

City-management technologies

As ever-more people move into the world's large cities this century, the result in most will be sprawl and decay. In the first world, major cities are responding to the problems of growth, particularly traffic congestion, by budding off 'edge' cities that are relatively self-contained in terms of meeting residents' needs for jobs and services locally. This relatively unplanned trend would appear set to continue, especially as finding funds to maintain, upgrade and extend urban and regional physical infrastructure looks like remaining a major problem for governments. A limited number of big cities will remain or become 'global cities', meaning that they will play pivotal, specialised and disproportionately large roles in the globalising economy, for example, London (finance), Los Angeles (media).

Apart from road and facility congestion, the maintenance of security and amenity and the control of pollution in all its forms — air, water, light, noise, electromagnetic — will remain the major challenges of city management. Seeking technological 'fixes' rather than tackling such problems at source (for example, through urban and social planning) seems destined to remain the standard response to these challenges.

In the first world, in terms of urban form at the suburb level, it will take some decades for the character of existing inner suburbs to change under prevailing densification and re-urbanisation policies (which would appear set to continue). Some new suburbs are likely to be 'experimental' in terms of neighbourhood layout, landscaping, security measures etc. but most will be of traditional design, perhaps with detached houses on smaller-sized (and therefore cheaper) blocks than today's. Houses will be increasingly 'decoupled' from traditional utilities networks through the use of composting toilets, mobile and wireless communications, geothermal and solar heating, solar power, fuel cells, water reclamation and rainwater management systems. Such decentralising and small-scale technologies have the capacity to undermine the idea of utilities being natural monopolies, and hence the regulation of such. However, complete independence from networks is not readily foreseeable. Power grids would continue to provide base energy requirements and optical fibres would provide broadband communications. While the technology to produce potable water from household wastewater is well advanced, this is an idea likely to meet consumer resistance (DAS 1996). Reinforcing the idea of the 'stand alone' house, Sheffield et al. (1994) suggest that houses in the 2040s will be burglar-proof and attack-proof. Whether housing will become more affordable for people on sub-median incomes is another question.

'Intelligent' buildings of the future will be based on modular construction and deconstruction systems and will mange their own active and passive heating and cooling systems. Sensors will warn of wearing and stress problems (DAS 1996). Perhaps geodesic-dome houses will become widely used because of their low material requirements per unit of living space (Fuller 1969). Light and strong new materials such as honeycomb concretes and laminated timbers are becoming available.

Science and technology

What role will scientific research play in producing the foregoing stream of coming technological marvels? The answer is that progress in generic and infrastructural technologies depends heavily on advances in scientific research. Companies and governments are increasingly moving to support basic and applied research in areas where advances are thought likely to translate into profitable new technologies and commodities. Conversely, research fields which do not appear to have this potential are unlikely to be well-funded, an important constraint in an era where scientific advances increasingly require access to expensive technologies. Science has always piggybacked on technology as this insightful quote from Hanbury Brown (1986) shows:

> At the time Bacon wrote — the early 17th century ... scientists were making rapid progress largely due to the new scientific instruments — the telescope, microscope, thermometer, barometer, pendulum clock and the air pump. Histories of science are often written in terms of outstanding people like Newton and Einstein so that they give the impression that the progress of science depends largely on the development of new theories. It would be nearer the truth to say that it depends on the development of new instruments and hence on new materials and new ways of making things ... our knowledge of the real world is limited by the tools which are available at the time ... each step forward in science depends on the interplay of imaginative theory and experiment.

There is no particular reason why the large companies that fund most commercial research and development would want to see any dramatic reorientation of the global research and development effort in coming decades towards 'appropriate' technologies, environmentally benign technologies and other categories of non-commercial technologies. And, if the trend to small government continues, it would not be surprising to see declining funds for public-interest research from this source, along with the privatisation of all commercially successful areas of government-funded scientific research. Indeed, since the 18th century, science has been slowly losing its autonomy and a final subordination of its spirit of free inquiry to state and business requirements has long been foreseen.

Notwithstanding, one still expects 21st century science to deliver important as-yet-unimaginable paradigm shifts as well as progress on well-recognised but difficult scientific questions such as the nature of consciousness, origins of life and the universe, genetic controls over development and the reconciliation of Einstein's relativistic theory of gravitation with quantum mechanics (Maddox 1999). (These last two, along with the structure of DNA, were the big surprises of 20th century science.)

One possibility that needs to be kept under observation is that the world may be entering a phase of diminishing returns to investment in science in the sense that while there is no drying up in the stream of new technologies, it is costing more and more (so-called 'big science') to maintain that stream.

A GROWING WORLD POPULATION

It is widely accepted that even though total fertility rates are falling in many countries, world population is likely to jump from 6 billion to more than 9 billion before beginning to fall after 2070 or so (Lutz et al. 2001).

Nearly all of this growth will occur in the developing countries in which four-fifths of the world's population already lives, that is, Asia, Africa and Latin America. This population growth can be confidently predicted for several reasons. Fertility has dropped from six to three children per woman since the 1960s but this is still well above the two children per woman required to stabilise population. Declines in mortality, historically the main cause of population growth, will almost certainly continue (Bongaarts 1998). Reason three is 'population momentum', meaning that a particularly large fraction of the female population is entering the childbearing years.

By 2030 the developing countries will contain 85–87 per cent of the world's population, even under diverse assumptions about fertility and mortality. South East Asia's population in 2100 will be 1.1 billion, up from 0.52 billion in 1990. China's population will be 2.0 billion, up from 1.2 billion in 1990. Between 1950 and 2050 Indonesia's population will rise from 80 million to 320 million.

In Europe, North America and Japan fertility has remained below replacement levels since the mid-1970s. If Japanese women continue bearing about 1.4 children, the population of Japan will fall from about 125 million today to about 55 million in 2100. Nonetheless, populations in most developed countries will continue to grow for some time because of population momentum, rising life expectancy and immigration. Population of the developed world as a whole will peak in 2025 and be back at present levels by 2050.

But a word of caution. Population projections are sensitive to small variations in fertility assumptions. If fertility were to level off at 2.6 instead of 2.1 births per woman, world population in 2100 would be 17.5 billion instead of 10.4 billion. And if fertility were to level off at 1.6 births per woman, population in 2100 would be 5.6 billion. Raising female education levels reduces fertility and delays the onset of childbearing. The increasing cost of raising and educating children is another reason for declining family size.

As well as growing and ageing, the world's population is urbanising and moving. The percentage of the world's population living in cities will rise from 45 per cent today to 61 per cent in 2025 according to UN projections. Many will be cities like Bangkok which appears to be uncontrollably decaying to the extent that the centre of the city could soon become uninhabitable because of floods, ground subsidence and pollution (ESCAP 1996).

The large-scale immigration between first world countries seen after the Second World War seems to have come to an end. The 21st century stands to be one of movement of people from poor to rich countries and, indeed, the first wave of third-worlders has already arrived in the first world (Kennon 1995). Differences in population change will generate great migratory pressures, especially between proximate rich and poor countries such as China and Japan or eastern and western Europe. Thurow (1996) foresees population movements more massive than the world has ever known. His reasons include (a) falling international travel costs and (b) the availability of western 'good life' images on third-world television screens. If tensions between Taiwan and Beijing, or between North Korea and South Korea, escalate into armed conflict, the Asia-Pacific region could see massive movements of displaced persons.

It is widely (but not universally) accepted that all countries have a responsibility to stabilise their populations as quickly as possible. At the United Nations International Conference on Population and Development in Cairo in September 1994, signatories to a 20-year Programme of Action committed themselves to formulating national strategies and programs to deal with population and development problems as an integral part of an overall development and planning process. As a further example, a declaration by the world's scientific academies, meeting in New Delhi in 1993, said that the world population goal should be zero population growth within the lifetime of our children (Graham-Smith 1994). However, short of coercion, even active and effective population stabilisation programs would not change the broad trajectory of future world population growth. Stability will come as more and more populations pass through the *demographic transition* to the lower fertility levels associated with rising incomes and better female education (Caldwell 1994).

GEOSOCIAL FUTURES

Within the framework of a growing world population, a globalising economy and a world political system marked by pressures on the legitimacy of nation-states and by US-dominated power politics (Wallerstein 1983), what has been foreseen in the way of cultural and institutional change within and between countries in the 21st century? A society's culture is the ideas, attitudes and behaviours which its individual members share and its institutions are the rules under which its members interact when contributing to the routine tasks necessary for their society's continuance.

As noted earlier, globalisation is a social process as much as an economic one, meaning that, in fits and starts, peoples/nations around the world have been moving along a path from a *traditional* to a *transitional* to a *modern society* or to a state of *modernity* (see page 169). And, in a very general way, with reversals, and certainly not in a fixed sequence, movement along this path over the last 300 years has commonly occurred in parallel with movement from a subsistence economy to an industrial economy and from authoritarian government to democratic government. We enter the 21st century with a world full of societies at different stages of political, economic and social development. Here we focus on the social rather than the political or economic aspects of what is really a single process.

The world will continue to move slowly towards being a single modern society, that is, one characterised by personal values such as (at least currently) the importance of personal success, materialism, consumerism, individualism, secularism and rationalism. Relative to traditional societies, modern societies tend to be more future-oriented, more investment-minded, more meritocratic, less corrupt, less authoritarian and more supportive of widespread education, impersonal justice and loyalties beyond the family. The dominant institutions of modern societies, leaving aside the industrial capitalism and democratic governance they are commonly associated with, include military, surveillance and security forces, incarceration and legal systems, publicly provided health and education services, other large bureaucracies (organisations capable of marshalling resources rationally and efficiently towards stated goals) and large cities. In the 20th century, Australasia, Japan and, most recently, various Asian countries exemplified the spread of modernity (Hall et al. 1992). Among its members the Organisation for Economic Cooperation and Development contains most examples of contemporary modern societies.

Traditional societies, those characterised by decision-making based on custom and tradition, particularly religious tradition, change slowly until they come under critical stress, from without or within, and then tend to change somewhat abruptly (see page 216). Starr (1996) suggests that societies take half a century to incorporate major technological changes (for example, electricity, automobiles) into basic systems such as energy and transport, perhaps a century or more to modify cultural values substantially (for example, status of women) and many centuries to reconcile historically embedded ethnic and religious differences.

Modernity itself is changing

Even as the world's societies move further along the traditional-to-modern path in the 21st century, modernity itself will continue to evolve, culturally and institutionally, primarily in the first world countries where it is entrenched. Most future-gazers take the fairly conventional view that change in modern societies is a process of social or collective learning driven by encroaching social movements which mould government responses to performance crises in ageing institutions (for example, Visser and Hemerijck 1997: 53). Sometimes, radical changes in the rules of the game are only possible after a shift in the balance of political power. At other times elites are proactive and willing to undertake planned, gradual reform.

Changing social structures

From many possible examples of what has been foreseen in the way of changing institutions in modern societies, this section discusses several which, however they evolve, will continue to strongly influence people's quality of life.

Class

Darlington (1969) defines a class in society as a group that works together and breeds together. There is no sign suggesting that class divisions in modern societies are breaking down or will break down further. Carroll's (1997) characterisation of class in Australia is probably broadly applicable to other modern societies. An upper middle class (some 15 per cent of the population) can be distinguished from a lower middle class (some 70 per cent of the population), more by its university education and cultural preferences (for example, choice of television and newspapers) than by socioeconomic differences. This upper middle class provides the political, public service, business, intellectual and media elites who guide the country. The remaining 15 per cent are recent immigrants and others who feel they do not belong in a cultural sense. This outsider group or underclass seems more likely to increase rather than decrease in relative size as tools of opportunity, such as access to health services, education and employment, become less available.

Health and education services

Welfare systems focusing on income support and the provision of health, housing and education services expanded in most first world countries after the Second World War. These systems reflected both a willingness to share the fruits of economic growth and an insurance against social conflict. Indeed, the societal goal of economic growth was 'sold' on the grounds that such growth would reduce poverty. Now the social welfare state is disappearing, slowly or rapidly, in all first world countries and poverty is increasing (Thurow 1996).

While the reasons for this decline are complex, they include:

- Widespread pressures to cut personal and business taxation (Self 1993) and balance government budgets;

- Widespread inefficiencies and failures in the operations of welfare systems;

- A resurgence of the doctrine that providing welfare benefits at any level of generosity destroys people's willingness and capacity to provide for themselves and make their maximum possible contribution to increasing the wealth of society;

- Reduced need since 1989 to maintain the welfare state as a counter-attraction to Communism (Greider 1997).

The life of the welfare state could be dragged out, perhaps, by various reforms such as competitive provision of services, but only radical changes in community values could give it a significant renaissance. The least surprising of such value shifts would be community acceptance of the 'new growth theories' which recognise that the welfare state is actually providing much of the human capital (for example, educated healthy workers) and organisational capital (for example, accessible justice) on which successful market economies already and increasingly will depend, for example, Romer (1994); EPAC (1995). Because the financing of such investments in social capital would require tax increases, it would be difficult for any country to pursue such a strategy in isolation.

The most difficult question facing health systems in first world countries in the early part of the century stands to be an ethical one, that of how healthcare is to be rationed (Singer 1992). Will it only be items with a very poor ratio of benefits to costs (for example, high-technology procedures) that have to be bought privately? It would be unsurprising to see health and education services increasingly provided by the market. This, in turn, would further disadvantage the poor and increase their resentment of what would be judged an inequitable society.

Here are some other possibilities for first world health systems:

- More attention will be given to the coming problem of pervasive obesity. For example, about 1.5 million Australians will have diabetes by 2010 at a cost of more than $1 billion a year unless people stop eating too much and doing too little exercise;

- Hospitals will become treatment centres rather than treatment and recuperation centres as they are at present. General practitioners will continue to move into group practices in order to share resources and streamline services;

- Do-it-yourself diagnosis and treatment with the help of computer-based expert systems will grow somewhat;

- After clean water, vaccines will remain the most cost-effective way to improve public health. Vaccines of the future will not just be for the prevention of infectious diseases; immunotherapeutic vaccines are being developed for cancer and autoimmune disorders such as some forms of diabetes;

- By 2010 management of neurodegenerative disorders of the elderly, such as Alzheimer's disease, will be a very major problem (ASTEC 1995);

- Mental health problems in the community, particularly the incidence of depression, could rise dramatically as people's capacity to adapt to change fractures under the influence of increasing rates of change and transience in personal contacts, ideas, organisations and possessions (Toffler's [1970] 'future shock'). A particularly important stress for many people is the loss of familiar, secure places that accompanies urban growth and development.

Law and order

Profit-seeking crime flourishes where governments are unstable and where there is wide disparity in income levels (OSCA 1996). Crime is already as powerful as government in some countries, for example, Colombia, and, perhaps, Russia (Elkins 1995). Certainly, organised crime has been quick to take advantage of weaknesses which have opened up with globalisation (OSCA 1996).

Organised crime groups are expanding internationally beyond the narcotics trade into areas such as human-organ trafficking, arms trafficking, people trafficking and information fraud. Information security will be one of the century's major growth industries. Piracy and kidnapping (for example, for child prostitution) may well become increasingly important. However, the increasing cost of law enforcement may also lead to the decriminalisation of some offences, particularly drug offences (and particularly if experiments in the privatisation of prisons do not work).

International terrorism, as distinct from profit-seeking crime, is widely regarded as a growing threat to first world countries where post-Cold War defence budgets are being increasingly spent on combating terrorism (and international crime) (Elkins 1995). It is probably only a matter of time before terrorists steal a nuclear warhead and detonate it, probably in the United States. Fear of biological terrorism centres around the ease with which anthrax, smallpox and bubonic plague can be spread. Third world countries could be subjected to food terrorism, for example, poisoning grain shipments. There are no obvious reasons why national and international law enforcement agencies stand to become more effective at combating international crime and terrorism. Certainly the Internet has so far proved more useful to criminals than law enforcers.

Within modern societies the security and justice functions are likely to be increasingly privatised. Proliferating private security firms and extra-judicial resolution of disputes through mediation etc. are examples.

The workplace

Recent changes in workforce structure in modern societies include the well-known increase in the female participation rate, more part-time employment, more underemployment, more unemployment (particularly youth and long-term unemployment), more early retirement and a shift in jobs from the manufacturing to the service sector. New jobs are disproportionately low-income part-time jobs. Conversely, an increasing percentage of full-time employees are now working (overworking?) more hours a week than a decade ago. Sweden though has introduced a six-hour working day for parents. All of these trends are still working themselves through. If workers per dependent person drop too low, elderly but longer-living retirees might be returned to the workforce.

In the setting of working conditions, individual contracts are increasingly replacing wage arbitration and trade union membership is declining in most, but not all, modern societies. Young workers are not joining unions and unions are not recruiting casuals and part-timers. In industrialising societies (for example, Korea, Brazil) unions are entering an expansionary phase.

Lifestyles

Television has now become the major source of entertainment, often more than five hours viewing a day for the average adult in modern societies. Interactive broadband multimedia channelling with a wide choice of content is presumed to be television's successor. This phenomenon, if Putnam (1993) is correct, will feed an ongoing erosion of social capital (that is, widespread amicable relations between people) in modern societies. More generally, it is from the media that most people get the lifestyle images which they then adopt as their own.

In general, modern societies are much more 'addictive' than they were in 1950; addicted to alcohol, nicotine, other soft and hard drugs, gambling and food, particularly fatty food. There is no sign of these trends abating. Car ownership is saturating in many modern societies where even the poor make heroic efforts to own a car, simply because social organisation has evolved to make this almost a necessity (and a clear example of the concept of 'relative poverty' — not being able to afford what is normal within one's society). Spending on retailed goods continues to fall as a percentage of consumption spending. Expenditure has been diverted to leisure, entertainment, health services and services that support an easier lifestyle. Specific developments which would not be surprising in the areas of entertainment and recreation activities include the following:

- For those with time and money, there is a trend is to spend more leisure time away from home, the broad choices being between commercial activities (for example, sport, theatre), nature-based activities and long-distance travel;

- For the poorer, do-it-yourself home improvements, gardening, building etc. could be increasingly important leisure activities;

- Tourism will grow and shift towards activities favoured by older people, for example, educational, cultural and history focused activities;

- Entertainment and recreation will become increasingly compartmentalised, for example, a broader selection of home entertainment; organised 'passive' mass entertainment; adventure and special interest holidays (Simpson 1992). The advent of high-capacity communications channels may or may not mean the demise of mass audiences;

- The success of open universities will prompt a growing interest in leisure-time learning;

- Experience shows that gambling (only) grows in response to new gambling opportunities so increasing numbers of casinos to boost government revenues will mean increasing participation (Simpson 1992);

- Sport will remain an important part of our lives, both as individual participants and as onlookers. Fad sports will come and go but traditional sports like golf and tennis will remain popular;

- The health culture will become increasingly ingrained in our lives with increased participation in activities like walking, cycling and swimming (Simpson 1992);

- Virtual reality will dominate the field of passive entertainment (Slaughter 1993). An important question for the tourist industry is the extent to which virtual tourism will replace real tourism;

- For many, being able to listen to one's preferred music at any time has been a great quality-of-life gain in recent decades and this privilege will spread.

Foreseeable unsurprising developments in food provision in modern societies include:

- The trend away from preparing meals from raw materials in the home stands to continue. This will take various forms such as eating out, buying meals in and using more pre-prepared foods. The range of dishes eaten will become more widely cosmopolitan;

- These trends will hold for both poor and rich, the difference being in the range and quality of food consumed, for example, fruit cordial versus fruit juice, mince versus salmon;

- More and more food for home consumption will contain natural biological preservatives and be packed in film impregnated with freshness biosensors and oxygen-scavenging polymers;

- Today's modest trends towards vegetarianism and towards a revealed preference for chemical-free foods stand to continue.

Building on Toffler's (1970) idea of 'future shock' (that is, increasing transience in all aspects of life), life for middle-class people in modern societies stands to become an increasingly frantic, ever-changing and, perhaps, fearful search for work, identity, relationships and entertainment.

Social and political movements

Behind the social and political movements which will lead in time to changes in cultures and institutions in modern societies lie changes in people's values and attitudes.

Values are the systems of preferences and norms (principles of right action binding upon members of a group and serving to produce acceptable behaviour) that characterise a society; they are general guides to behaviour (Emery et al. 1975) and are inescapably subjective. They act as rules of thumb for individuals and communities in the making of choices between re-occurring complex alternatives. Eckersley (1995) says nearly all cultures teach altruism, conformity, generosity, deference to authority, and honesty; and preach against pride, stinginess, greed, gluttony, envy, lust, theft, cowardice, non-conformity, disobedience and stubbornness. He sees these values as providing necessary balance between the interests of the individual (which don't need personal reinforcement) and the needs of the community (which do). Traditional values reflect, he believes, timeless wisdom about human interactions with one another and with the natural world.

Values in stable traditional societies evolve slowly through competitive selection — rules that work are retained, others are discarded. In modern societies the high rate of social change will increasingly challenge the capacity of the value-making process; past experience is of declining relevance to selecting present actions. Nonetheless, the search for values goes on. Applied to real-life situations, values express themselves as judgmental *attitudes*, attitudes being 'habitual ways of regarding issues'. Under the influence of the media, the education system and changing perceptions of quality of life prospects, many attitudes do appear to have been changing in modern communities in recent decades. These include attitudes towards becoming wealthy, saving, paying taxes, conformity, education, individuality and individualism, personal consumption, health, health food, work, working women, patriotism, global culture, marriage, love, the aged, the justice system, minority groups, unions, euthanasia and immigration.

Some widespread changes in attitudes and values have revealed themselves in the form of new, growing and declining social and political movements (Camilleri and Falk 1992). Significant movements seeking greater sociopolitical autonomy exist around indigenous, cultural, linguistic, local and regional/bioregional interests. Feminism and environmentalism are other powerful tides (see below). Movements with a clear potential for further growth include the anti-nuclear/peace/non-violence movement, animal rights, social and economic rights, sustainable development, land stewardship, anti-globalisation, anti-technology, fundamentalist and 'new age' religion, human potential, counterculture, vegetarianism and world government. Most such movements are seeking recognition in the form of institutional change, nationally or internationally.

Collectively, the supporters of new social movements have been seen as a 'new class' practising the 'new politics' (Galligan 1995). The *new politics* is an amalgam of causes and interests not derived from the old left–right ideological divide or ethnic–nationalist groupings. It tends to be post-materialist and universalist and based on transcendent values (Halal 1993). Will it blossom or decline? One particularly important movement, standing head to head against the new politics in a number of modern societies, is the 'radical right'. It promotes values such as monoculturalism, traditional religion, discriminatory immigration, big development projects, military conscription and tariff protection and is antipathetic to the United Nations, financial markets, big business, foreign ownership, economists and the unemployed.

Emancipation of women

Women already outnumber men in tertiary education in most modern societies. As a ratio, the range is from 1.42 in Iceland to 0.59 in Switzerland (the United States is 1.21). For transitional and traditional societies figures include 6.03 in United Arab Emirates, 2.16 in Mongolia, 1.56 in Myanmar, 1.54 in Namibia, 1.52 in Cuba, 1.33 in Philippines, 0.64 in Egypt, 0.61 in India, 0.54 in China and 0.53 in Indonesia.

While this development is likely to continue, it is less likely to translate into better jobs and higher incomes immediately. However it may do so over time, particularly in information and service economies, and as corporate cultures evolve to the point where leadership qualities such as subtlety, discernment and honesty are valued more highly than qualities such as self-assurance, bravado and brinkmanship. As women begin to dominate in education and in the professions (and possibly later in governance and the corporate sphere, where adversarial environments still prevail) something being called the *men's movement* may become more generally recognised and expand to accelerate the cultural evolution of men and help maintain (future) gender equity.

The full emancipation of first-world women in domestic life will involve a solving of the two problems of sharing unpaid home work and male violence. In many Islamic societies prospects for the emancipation of women, in either public or domestic life, seem limited.

Environmentalism

Environmentalism is the movement to more actively favour resource conservation and the maintenance of environmental quality over economic growth and development. Eminent American futurist Joseph Coates (1994) foresees a surge of environmentalism in modern societies in coming decades as affluence rises and middle-class demands for material goods and services are saturated.

Trends which support this scenario include:

- Greater ecological knowledge and awareness in the community;

- The appearance of more aggressive environmental groups;

- Increasing concern over global environmental issues such as global warming and stratospheric ozone depletion (see below).

The widespread acceptance of the concept of *sustainable development*, as popularised by the Brundtland Report (WCED 1987), can be interpreted either as a dialectical synthesis of growth and 'green' values or as a clever rearguard action by growth protagonists seeking to delay environmental regulation of their activities. The latter interpretation is more likely to be true of American, British and Australian industry where there has been stronger resistance to environmental thinking than in Germany and Japan where some industries are proactively greening themselves.

At the same time, capitalism, in its normal vigorous way, is responding to increasing demands for environmental protection; for example, in the growth of the environmental protection industry and in the rapid spread of greener technologies and products.

Religion

Religion provided a clear value system for Europe prior to the industrial revolution but this role has been giving way ever since to more secular values (Tawney 1920; Lasch 1995). However, with a loss of confidence in the 'march of progress' in recent decades (and in the secular religion of socialism [Hutton 1996]) and a clouding of people's perceptions about how the world will evolve over coming decades, there has been a resurging belief in the power of religiously prescribed behaviour to ensure a good future for the world.

More particularly, there has been a spread of Islamic fundamentalism in traditional and transitional societies and of Christian fundamentalism in modern societies (Elkins 1995). But the western fear of a fundamentalist tide advancing unchecked across the Islamic world — and then beyond — seems to be unjustified (Roy 1994; Kennon 1995). Within the mainstream versions of Christianity, Islam and Judaism, some modest ongoing reform of their existing patriarchal styles stands out as a common trend. Modern societies are also experiencing a rise in the popularity of a-rational 'new age' values such as the power of astrology. And, for many, the environmental movement provides quasi-religious values.

Rights and responsibilities

The invention of human rights is arguably humanity's greatest achievement. Civil and political rights are passably well-recognised and protected in most modern societies but social, economic and environmental rights are scarcely recognised, even by governments striving to improve social, economic and environmental quality of life for all. The reason for the latter situation, as much as anything, is that governments just do not know how to guarantee social, economic and environmental rights. There seems little prospect of formally guaranteed human rights being extended in the first world in coming decades. To the contrary, there are significant movements in a number of modern societies to have certain groups (religious, ethnic, unemployed etc.) treated as second-class citizens.

However, even without formal guarantees, people in modern societies live under a tacit social contract within which society has a responsibility to attempt to provide some sort of rising standard of living in return for the individual citizen fulfilling certain obligations and accepting certain responsibilities to the society, some legally enforceable, some not. A trend to extend and formalise responsibilities under this contract is emerging in many societies, particularly the responsibilities of the disadvantaged.

But, for much of the first world since the 1970s, society has provided a declining standard of living for an increasing proportion of the population (Thurow 1996) and it is presumably in response to this that the tacit obligations of citizenship are being eroded and replaced with political apathy, anti-social behaviour or an aggressive individualism that refuses to recognise the social basis of individual well-being.

The rich too are losing their allegiance to the social contract, but for different reasons. Their well-being is increasingly being determined in world markets rather than domestic markets. Because the fortunate thus feel less connected to and less dependent on their fellow citizens, they are less willing to invest in their futures and the social and economic gap between rich and poor is widening (Reich 1991). The dilemma is, as Reich puts it, that if the rich are taxed they will move to tax havens offshore just as, but more readily than, they have for years; but, if the rich are not taxed, public infrastructure, physical and institutional, will degrade and the rich will secede and move to private enclaves and provide their own exclusive infrastructure. In any case, as mobility increases, notions of citizenship will become more complex and may become blurred.

Localism, nationalism and planetism

The basic human need for recognition and respect for what one is (Maslow 1954, 1968) expresses itself in diverse ways, many of which involve identifying with a group, most commonly a political, linguistic, religious, ethnic or geographic group; and, as an extension of this idea, actively declaring which groups one is not in. Here we note spreading claims to a geographically based identity.

Localism (also *regionalism, bioregionalism*) is the movement to have more of people's needs, economic and social, satisfied within a local area (up to, say, half a day's travel) which, politically, enjoys significant autonomy under the nation-state. The bioregional variant of localism looks for self-sufficiency for the residents of a biophysically defined area such as a river catchment. Localism is a movement which is benefiting from the popularity of devolution as a political idea, that is, the idea that collective decisions should be made at lower rather than higher levels whenever possible.

Nationalism. Colonies, newly independent states and occupied states tend to spawn nationalist, extreme nationalist or ultra-nationalist movements, that is, movements which, to various degrees, see the independence, protection and strengthening of the state to which the movement's members belong as a primary political goal. Or a nationalist movement can arise when a putative nation-within-a-nation seeks greater autonomy. States which see themselves as being bullied by superior powers can be included here too.

While *de jure* colonialism is coming to an end, there are very few parts of the world where nationalism is not a major factor in conflictual relations between countries and, in some countries, particularly those with large ethnic minorities, in domestic politics. Unless there is a radically improved approach to conflict resolution, one based on meeting identity needs, nationalist issues will continue to soak up much political energy. While nationalism is more commonly associated with transitional and traditional societies, some modern societies will also continue to be its hosts, for example, separatist movements in Quebec, Scotland.

Planetism or *internationalism* is a movement which, in its contemporary form, recognises that a globalising world needs global governance and a high level of inter-nation co-operation if most people are to have access to a reasonable spectrum of life opportunities (Ellyard 1998). Movement towards a sense of global community is finding initial expression in the establishment of international agreements and institutions and the formation of multi-nation trading blocs and federations.

Localism, nationalism and internationalism are all, in their own ways, seeking, and will continue to seek, a redistribution of sovereign power (power to make autonomous and binding decisions on behalf of a group of people) to a geographic level which will, perhaps, yield more justice, equity or efficiency.

Mutualism

Mutualism is the doctrine that maximal individual and collective well-being is attainable only by accepting the mutual dependence between people and fostering their mutually supportive interaction, for example, Wilkin (1996). More specifically, mutualism means proactively creating a wide range of semi-autonomous non-adversarial, collaborative, voluntary, interactive, participatory, inclusive, consensual, co-operative institutional arrangements. More mutualism stands to produce an increase in inclusive citizenship, ethnic tolerance, gender equality and political democracy. Notwithstanding, there does seem to be a lack of shared perceptions about the practical institutional reforms needing to be undertaken to implement mutualism's ideas. The diffuse movement to promote mutualism can be understood as a response, mainly in modern societies, to the loosening of social controls on personal behaviour during the rise of neo-liberalism and competitive individualism in the last decades of the 20th century.

Conclusions about societal futures

So much for diverse views about where the world might be going in the 21st century in terms of the ways lives and societies will be organised. The broad picture being offered is one of societies everywhere continuing to move, slowly or quickly, from traditional to modern status, even as societies which have achieved modernity continue to change considerably, more or less in step with each other. As the products of commerce become more varied in any one location (although increasingly similar across locations), consumption-based modern lifestyles also tend to become more varied, with those variants being found across the globe. At the same time, consumerism, with its emphasis on individual wants, stands to further weaken traditional views of the significance of collectivities. In turn, this links to a growing concern over intimacy, the self and 'self development' as a project — ranging from therapy to adventure.

Change in modern societies is partly a reaction to the pace of change itself. The uncertainty of life in a rapidly changing world will continue to challenge the utility of existing values and spawn more searching for external authorities and social order, including a willingness to see the lives of others controlled. Examples have been given of how institutions will continue to change under the pressure of social movements to solve perceived problems and in response to performance failure. While it is necessary for competing values to be debated and trialled, such struggles contain two dangers. One is that adherents of opposing values settle down into paralysing or, worse, nation-shattering antagonism. The other is that frightened societies will fall prey to people peddling simplistic values as answers to complex problems.

GLOBAL ENVIRONMENTAL FUTURES

> The threat of ecological disaster is rooted in the
> inability of the market mechanism to resolve the
> global problem of pollution (HEILBRONER 1993).

An ongoing dilemma faced by modern industrial economies is that increases in the consumption of goods and services are strongly correlated with increases in energy use (Hall et al. 1992), and increases in energy use are strongly correlated with increases in environmental degradation, that is, pollution (meaning the accumulation of unprocessed residues) and ecosystem dysfunction/destruction. This three-way linkage is weakening to some extent in some economies where the product mix is changing towards services and as technologies which economise on materials and energy and low-pollution technologies emerge. However, it is not just degradation per dollar of GDP (Gross Domestic Product) that determines the overall trend in environmental degradation; it is also the total level of GDP as determined by trends in population and in GDP per head. How to identify and achieve the 'right' balance between economic growth and loss of environmental quality, so strangely called sustainable development, remains a mystery.

The earth's biosphere (plants and animals), geosphere (soils and minerals), atmosphere and hydrosphere (water in all its forms) have, throughout evolutionary time, been in the process of changing for one reason or another. But, in the last few hundred years, rates of change in these components of the natural world have been increasing in readily measurable ways. This is the phenomenon known as *global environmental change* and it is well under way. Here we note some trends in environmental quality which, driven by economic growth, are likely to continue well into the 21st century; and some possible changes which have not yet emerged:

Climatic and atmospheric changes

The most widely recognised and easily understood such change in the global environment is the modification of the atmosphere's composition by humans. Three global phenomena, widely agreed to be global problems, are involved: intensification of the greenhouse effect, and the global warming and climate change associated with that; ozone depletion in the stratosphere, resulting in higher levels of life-damaging ultraviolet radiation (Leslie 1996); and changes to the troposphere and associated phenomena, for example, photochemical smog and acid rain.

The concentration of carbon dioxide in the atmosphere has increased by

25 per cent in the last century and is currently increasing at 1.5 per cent per annum. Estimates of the 2100 level range from 540 to 970 parts per million. If human behaviour fails to change, then the anthropogenic increase in greenhouse gas production, particularly carbon dioxide and methane, will, according to best available knowledge, cause a mean global warming of perhaps 3 degrees Celsius (estimates range from 1.5 degrees Celsius to 5.8 degrees Celsius) over this century. This may not sound much, but major changes can be expected to follow, above all a shifting of precipitation zones and a rise in sea level of 65 centimetres plus or minus 35 centimetres (enough to be disastrous for many low-lying countries). Total world rainfall should increase simply because a warmer atmosphere holds more water vapour. Rainfall intensity and variability are also likely to increase, for example, droughts and cyclones. Also, cyclone intensity always increases at higher temperatures. The world's major vegetation formations (biomes) will tend to follow global temperature and rainfall shifts but, because envisaged changes represent movements in climatic boundaries of many kilometres a year, much faster than vegetation formations can spread or retreat, many formations will be increasingly poorly adapted to the climate they are experiencing.

The greenhouse effect is an indirect cause of global warming but, more directly, because all energy is eventually converted into waste heat, there is also some limit on direct energy use beyond which thermal pollution will begin to affect living organisms (Birch 1975). This is probably already occurring in big cities where high energy use creates 'heat islands', meaning zones of high air temperature.

The natural mechanisms that tend to remove anthropogenic carbon dioxide from the atmosphere have been overwhelmed in recent decades but can be expected to operate over hundreds to thousands of years. These include the storage of carbon in the oceans as carbonates and in sediments, in the soil and in additional plant material resulting from the 'fertiliser' effect of higher carbon dioxide levels.

More immediately, it has to be recognised that the chemistry of the atmosphere becomes chaotic and extremely unpredictable under pollution. The hydroxyl radicals that oxidise most atmospheric pollutants, making them soluble in raindrops, can be consumed in reactions that escalate above critical pollution concentrations. The creation of 'holes' or 'thinnings' in the stratospheric ozone layer above the poles can be traced to the escape of chemicals used primarily for refrigeration, primarily in the industrialised countries. These chemicals, which have a half-life of 75 or so years, drift up to altitudes where they are irradiated and produce chlorine which destroys ozone.

Successful international protocols already in place to limit the use of such chemicals are likely to lead to a 'mending' of these 'holes' over the next several decades.

Rain containing acid-producing industrial residues — sulphur dioxide and various nitrogen oxides — began reducing the productivity of lakes and forests in the northern hemisphere in the 1970s. The problem is slowly diminishing in the first world where technology is reducing vehicle emissions of nitrogen oxides and gas turbine power plants are replacing sulphur-emitting coal-fired plants. Sulphur emissions in Europe have been reduced 75 per cent since 1980. The problem will persist though in coal-burning regions such as China, not to mention their downwind neighbours. A 'nuclear winter' in which smoke and dust from atomic explosions in a nuclear war reduce sunlight and crop yields for some years will remain a threat as long as any country owns such devices. Nuclear war, with its residual radiation, also remains the most plausible way in which the human species could rapidly destroy itself.

During the last decade there has been a genuine shift in the scientific community's perception of global environmental processes. For example, it is now thought that the earth's climate does not respond to 'forcing' in a smooth and gradual way but in sharp jumps which involve reorganisation of the earth's climate–weather system. If so, small changes cannot be regarded with the same equanimity as previously; they may take the system across major thresholds. For example, global warming is being delayed by the enormous capacity of the oceans to absorb heat, a process which cannot continue indefinitely.

Sea ice and ocean currents

Models of global climate and ocean systems suggest that if the atmospheric carbon dioxide level reaches 2 to 3 times the pre-industrial level (that is, rise to between 550 and 800 parts per million by volume) the atmosphere and the sea will heat up to the point where much less sea ice will be formed in the Antarctic and the Arctic. One immediate effect of this is that when sea ice melts it exposes dark ocean which absorbs more heat than reflective white ice and the oceans heat up even more.

But there is a more important consequence. When seawater freezes, its salt content is left in the ocean. This makes the surface water denser and it sinks. This happens on such a grand scale that the sinking water sets up a global circulation called the *thermohaline circulation*; deep cold water moves from the polar regions to the equator and warm surface water flows back the other way. If greenhouse gas concentrations keep rising at plausible rates, the atmosphere could warm up within a century or so to the point where insufficient sea ice forms to keep these thermohaline 'pumps' operating (it has happened before, triggering a cold period). For example, the Gulf Stream which keeps north-western Europe warm might stop or reverse as the saltwater pumps in the Labrador Sea and the Greenland Sea become less effective. Also, as demon-strated in the Black Sea where there is no deep circulation to carry oxygenat-ed water downwards, the ocean depths will stagnate and all oxygen-dependent life below 1–1.5 kilometres will die (wind-driven circulation would continue to aerate the ocean down to that depth). Such stagnant oceans would also be less effective as carbon dioxide sinks.

Polar ice sheets

What does the future hold for Antarctic ice? Unless there is a change in the observed warming trend, a continuation of current retreats of fringing ice shelves along the Antarctic Peninsula is likely. This seems dramatic on the human scale but is less so on the geologic scale. The present incarnations of Antarctic Peninsula ice shelves have existed for only the last several thousand years and have, in that time, experienced cycles of advance and retreat (Clapperton 1990). The present glaciological events may be part of a normal long-term cycle. How ongoing changes to global climate affect the interior of Antarctica remains to be seen. The most sophisticated models available pre-dict an increase, not a decrease, in the volume of ice in the West and East Antarctic ice sheets in future warming scenarios. But prediction of what is a very complex process is difficult (Hulbe 1997).

Lurking methane threats

Additional methane, a very effective greenhouse gas, will be produced in sev-eral different ways as the oceans continue to warm and expand and the Earth's polar ice caps continue to melt. Large areas of densely vegetated tropical low-lands are certain to become inundated and the methane (swamp gas) that this will generate represents a feedback (a further reinforcement of the green-house effect) of ominous potential.

Another methane threat lies waiting in the tundra regions of Eurasia. A cubic metre of permafrost, on melting yields 3 cubic metres of methane. Even more worrying are enormous volumes of gas hydrates which have been formed under the low temperature, low oxygen, high-pressure conditions found in deep-sea sediments. Warming 1 cubic metre of such hydrates yields up to 160 cubic metres of methane.

Methane belched up by domestic ruminants is, surprisingly, a major contributor to the atmosphere's load of greenhouse gases. This contribution will increase as herds and flocks expand to feed a growing global population. Rice paddies are also a significant and growing contributor to atmospheric methane.

Coastal and marine ecosystems

Some 60 per cent of the world's people live near (within 100 kilometres) a coastline and human activities have been affecting coastal and marine ecosystems since the last ice age. Thus, about half the world's coastal mangroves have been transformed or destroyed; coastal wetlands which buffer the land–sea interface are disappearing. Many of the fisheries that capture the productivity of the oceans focus on predators at the top of the marine food chain and are proving to be unsustainable. As of 1995, 22 per cent of recognised marine fisheries around the world were overexploited or already depleted and another 44 per cent were at their limits of exploitation (FAO 1994). While growing, aquaculture in marine and inland waters does not appear to have the potential to maintain fish intake per global citizen in the face of population growth and a peaking of wildfish production.

Coral reefs, a major source of fish for people and a major repository of biological diversity, are under threat throughout the tropics, not only from warming oceans (corals live only within a narrow temperature range) in the longer term, but from immediate threats such as pollution and physical destruction by fishers (bottom trawling and blast fishing). Some 10 per cent of the world's reefs have already been destroyed and another 60 per cent have limited prospects of surviving the next few decades.

Land-based marine pollution is emerging as another global environmental problem. Pollution by litter and sewage are the two most publicly visible forms of human impact on the marine environment. The less visible but potentially very damaging pollutants of the marine environment include organic contaminants, such as non-biodegradable polychlorinated biphenyls (PCBs), chlorinated hydrocarbons (for example, dioxins), and heavy metal discharges (especially mercury, lead, zinc, cadmium, copper), mostly from industrial sources. Eutrophication of coastal waters is an increasing problem worldwide. It results from coastal development and land-use changes and occurs in response to addition of nutrients (nitrogen and phosphorus) to estuarine and inshore waters. Algae proliferate on the surface and deprive deeper waters of oxygen and light, killing most marine organisms. Nutrient inputs producing this effect may be from industrial sources, but are especially associated with sewage, urban run-off and agricultural practices. Nowadays, more atmospheric nitrogen is fixed by humanity than all natural terrestrial sources combined (Vitousek et al. 1997).

Land transformation and biological diversity

Most of the Earth's vegetated surface has been transformed to varying degrees by human activities such as cropping, clearing, forestry, grazing and urbanisation. One clear measure of our species' cumulative impact is that the fraction of the land's biological production that is used or dominated by people is somewhere between 39 per cent and 50 per cent (Vitousek et al. 1997). Land transformation represents the primary force driving the loss of biological diversity (biodiversity) worldwide. It seems, for example, that a great wave of species extinctions, comparable to five or six earlier such waves, is under way and is effectively unstoppable (May et al. 1995). Rainforests are extraordinarily rich in species and runaway deforestation in Amazonia, Africa and South East Asia is a particular problem. These same tropical and sub-tropical forests pump enormous amounts of water vapour into the atmosphere and are the engines which drive global atmospheric circulation.

Not only are species and locally adapted populations of species being lost at 100 to 1000 times the pre-industrial rate, there is evidence that the extinction rate is accelerating. The loss of local populations of a species reduces the genetic variation on which it relies when adapting to (coping with) environmental change. In addition to causing extinctions at a high rate, human activities are mixing flora and fauna from regions that were previously isolated from each other. Such introductions, both accidental and deliberate, can cause economic losses, human health problems and dysfunction in the invaded ecosystems. More generally, under global biological invasion ecosystems everywhere tend to become more similar and life as a whole less adaptable and resilient. A major implication for humans is that ecosystems that have been disrupted by extinctions and invasions become less efficient at providing various 'services' on which human activities rely, for example, oxygenating the atmosphere, cleaning water supplies, recycling nutrients, stabilising soil structure, providing an aesthetically and spiritually satisfying environment. Unfortunately, the cost of losing ecosystem services (life-support systems) only becomes apparent when those services start to break down.

Diseases and disasters

Based on indicators such as life expectancy, child mortality and disability, there is a consensus among experts that the world's population has never been healthier (Douglas 1996). But official predictions that modern medicine would eradicate infectious diseases have, smallpox aside, proved to be spectacularly misplaced. Diseases such as malaria, tuberculosis, measles and hepatitis are still a major cause of death in many parts of the world. 'New' diseases (for example, Lyme disease, HIV/AIDS) continue to emerge at unprecedented rates while old ones return to regions where they were on the decline. As the world fills with people, increasing interaction between humans and animals such as rodents stands to assist more diseases, like HIV/AIDS, to cross the inter-species barrier (Gibbon 1993). And, as HIV/AIDS-damaged immune systems demonstrate, old diseases can re-emerge in partnership with new diseases. In many cases, changes in the environment (for example, forest clearing, algal blooms, air-conditioned buildings, climate change) are creating new pathways for diseases to spread and take hold (Harvard Working Group 1995).

Two other major causes of disease resurgence are increasing drug resistance of causal organisms (for example, tuberculosis) and international travel. It is an open question as to whether medical science will be able to stay ahead of the evolution of drug-resistant strains of micro-organisms. The malaria parasite appears to be mutating into increasingly deadly forms, for example, cerebral malarias resistant to mefloquine. Might the HIV/AIDS virus mutate into something more transmissible? Potentially, about 45 per cent of the world's population is currently exposed to malaria and, under the climate change scenarios of the International Panel on Climate Change, this could rise to 60 per cent (Martin and Lefebvre 1995).

Given time and a reasonably stable world, diseases and populations tend to come into balance. However, increased urbanisation and increased interactions between peoples mean that the world community becomes one big disease pool. While this 'global village' means that there are no longer susceptible unexposed local populations waiting to be drastically reduced by diseases new to them (for example, the Australian Aborigines after white settlement), it also means that a virulent new disease could drastically reduce the world population (McNeill 1979). Or, less apocalyptically, pandemics of cholera, yellow fever and plague are all possible in coming decades. Loss of children and old people to disease can be tolerated in one sense but the loss of, say, 20 per cent of the adult working population stands to threaten the stability of any society.

Poverty always lowers resistance to infectious diseases, as does exposure to pollutants. And the poor tend to be more exposed to pollutants than the rich, although some pollutants, like smog, are quite democratic (Beck 1992). As measured by a greatly reduced capacity to work, there could be a drastic reduction in the 'quality' of third world populations over the next several generations due to hunger, infectious and chronic diseases.

As populations pass through the demographic transition to lower birth and death rates, causes of death change from diseases of famine and pestilence to 'lifestyle' diseases such as cancer, accidents and cardiovascular disease (Douglas 1996). Among the lifestyle diseases, smoking-related deaths (particularly in China) will rise globally to 10 million annually in a few years, eclipsing HIV/AIDS, malaria and tuberculosis deaths. The World Health Organisation predicts that road accidents will rise from ninth to third (behind clinical depression and cardio-vascular disease) as a cause of world death and disability by 2020. Finally, the possibility of germ warfare, the ultimate lifestyle disease, (a) occurring and (b) going horribly wrong, cannot be wholly discounted (McNeill 1979). Is some psychopath hoarding the supposedly extinct smallpox virus for future release into a susceptible world? Note also the possibility of biological warfare directed against crops (for example, wheat smut) and livestock (for example, foot and mouth disease).

Environmental disasters

The distribution and occurrence of natural physical hazards such as volcanic eruptions, tidal waves and cosmic events (for example, meteorites) remains unaffected by growth in human populations and their activities. What is changing however is the probability of such natural events causing major disasters, simply because there is an increasing likelihood of (bigger) communities being in the places where they occur. Cyclones and storms are a special case though. Warming the oceans, as we are doing, will extend the regions of the world where these phenomena stand to cause disasters.

And then there are the various potential disasters sitting on the boundary between the natural and the anthropogenic. Two of the potentially most disruptive are:

- The existence of many aging nuclear plants. This raises the possibility of more Chernobyls, affecting perhaps hundreds of millions of people;

- Environmental 'hormones'. These are oestrogen-mimicking compounds resulting from the breakdown of plastics, insecticides etc. It is possible that the increasingly widespread use of synthetic chemicals could precipitate a major drop in human (and animal) fertility and a major rise in developmental abnormalities (Dibb 1995).

While there will continue to be natural and man-made disasters, many proving catastrophic at regional scale, none will significantly threaten the global-scale wealth-generating process which has continued since the industrial revolution and none will threaten the human species' survival (McRae 1994).

Other pollution threats

Chlorine compounds which, in some form or other, are found in 60 per cent of consumer goods are a growing pollution threat, not just as carcinogens and as ozone destroyers but as accelerants and boosters of a variety of environmental impacts.

Apart from the global-scale atmospheric problems of warming, ozone depletion and contaminated rainfall, there are widespread local-scale air pollution problems which are likely to grow. One is indoor air pollution from the breakdown of chemicals used in clothing, furnishings etc. and from heating system residues (Beck 1992). Another is smog and fumes from traffic and industrial activity. Another is low-level radiation from various appliances and installations. Dust storms and mineral dusts from mining operations are common problems in some regions. Light pollution and noise pollution are beginning to be recognised as serious problems too.

Managing environmental quality

Despite an increasing awareness of declining environmental quality around the world, and of its origins in increasing energy and materials use, there are enormous difficulties in the way of moving towards a new balance between these two processes. One that is immediately obvious is the lack of acceptable methods of valuing the costs and benefits of moving along this trade-off curve. Another is that there is little understanding of how much time, knowledge and resources are needed to tackle established environmental problems seriously. Most programs for doing so are puny in relation to the size of the problem being addressed.

The overall difficulty though is that reducing energy and materials use inescapably reduces consumption of goods and services — notwithstanding regular technology gains in dejouling and dematerialising industrial processes. That is unpopular in a consumer society. And, for firms, reducing throughput and output reduces profits. While some firms are beginning to accept that they have responsibilities to the community and the environment as well as to shareholders, this has not progressed beyond rhetoric in most cases. In the event, both consumers and producers have a preference for environmental quality programs which address the symptoms and consequences of economic growth rather than the initial causes of those consequences, for example, low-emission cars rather than reduced car usage. Perhaps, if environmental quality problems worsen markedly, institutions will be developed for capping and taxing energy and materials usage across whole economies or even globally. To succeed, such institutions would need to be collaborations between government, business and community.

GLOBAL RESOURCE FUTURES

Assuming a 70 per cent increase in world population over this century and, perhaps, a quadrupling in the size of the global economy, the question arises as to whether the raw materials such as water, soil and minerals needed to sustain such a population and economy will be available.

Water

Being a finite resource, per capita global supplies of water are continually declining as world population increases. Already 27 countries fall into the water-scarce category — less than 1000 cubic metres of fresh water per person per year. This list includes some developed countries (for example, Belgium) and stands to be extended rather than reduced by any redistribution of precipitation associated with global warming. Part of the problem is that, while globally abundant relative to present use, fresh water supplies are unevenly distributed. The 40 per cent of the world's *accessible* water currently being used by humans will rise to 80 per cent by 2025 (Falkenmark 1998). Also to be remembered, the world's finite groundwater resources (fossil water) are being depleted at a net rate sufficient to feed 500 million people from irrigated crops.

There is considerable scope for managing water resources much more effectively. Agriculture, for example, takes about two thirds of all water used, mostly on crops and pastures, but only a third of what is applied is taken up by plants. Achieving efficiency requires an uncommonly high level of social control in areas such as water pricing, consumer education and dispute resolution. Technical and behavioural measures can reduce urban water use by 30 per cent. The structure of the economy is also important. Litres of water used per dollar of output range from very high for irrigated cotton and rice to low for services. In the mining sector, coal and bauxite production are profligate in their water use. Technologies for increasing water supplies above the natural renewable level include distillation of seawater which is an energy-intensive process and, a more promising prospect, Ocean Thermal Energy Conversion (OTEC) ships which exploit temperature differences between surface and deep waters. Industries and cities can recycle wastewater if energy for such processing is cheap.

Agricultural land

In 1995 the International Food Policy Research Institute (IFPRI) hosted a conference entitled *A 2020 Vision for Food, Agriculture and the Environment*. The central message from the meeting was that while the world should be able to provide enough food to feed 8 billion people in 2020, with the main food crops selling at even lower prices than today, more people will be hungry in the world's poorest countries — unless there are radical policy shifts. Hardest hit will be South Asia and sub-Saharan Africa where food production will barely outstrip population growth. Cereal prices were foreseen to fall by 20 per cent and meat prices by 10 per cent, a conclusion disputed by Lester Brown of the World Resources Institute (1996). Brown says that whether food prices rise depends on China's need for grain imports, already 16 million tonnes in 1995. In the IFPRI scenario, Australian cereal exports were seen to double by 2020, a matter of considerable doubt.

The conventional view is that this looming problem can best be tackled by raising incomes and therefore the buying power of the poor in developing countries. That is, given effective demand, the market will provide. Other priority actions seen as being important for reducing the number of hungry people in coming decades (Pinstrup-Andersen 1994) include:

- Strengthening government capacity to manage the economy and society in developing countries;

- Investing in the health and education of poor people;

- Managing natural resources more effectively;

- Accelerating the rate of increase in agricultural productivity. One indicator of potential here is that post-harvest storage losses amount to perhaps 20 per cent of world grain production;

- Reducing food marketing costs as a contribution to reducing retail food prices;

- Expanding and realigning development assistance.

Looking further ahead to if and when the world's population doubles, we will need to find an extra 64.5 million sq km to feed everyone, assuming that sources of food and the productivity of agricultural land remain unchanged. To get a feel for this, North America covers about 28.5 million sq km and Australia is about 7.7 million sq km. So we will need to set up a new farm equal in size to two North Americas plus one Australia. If we cannot do this, appropriately modified for productivity gains and losses, people will starve. Productivity losses from soil erosion and degradation (for example, salinisation, acidification and loss of soil structure) are central here and show no sign of declining; indeed are accelerating in many parts of the world. On the other hand, the effects of rainfall redistribution and the 'fertilisation' effect of extra carbon dioxide in the atmosphere under global warming could well offset such losses, at least until 2100. As for productivity gains, there is no new generation of land-based technologies waiting in the wings. Even if genetic engineering eventually produces nitrogen-fixing, salt-resistant, drought-resistant, pest-resistant grains, their widespread adoption will, for logistical and financial reasons, still take decades. Nonetheless, an ever-increasing fraction of the world's food will be produced from organisms genetically engineered and patented by large multinationals such as Monsanto.

It does seem fairly clear that while technologies will continue to improve in existing food-production industries, the world will only be able to feed its people by developing new supplies of cheap food from the sea (for example, whale farming, fish flour, seaweed flour), from the land (for example, meat powder) and from industrial processes. These latter include crop plants produced by hydroponic methods, cultured foods (for example, yeasts, animal and fish tissue) produced in tanks and vats and chemically synthesised foods (Prehoda 1967).

Overall, despite some not-unreasonable doubts about methods of estimating global hunger (Poleman 1996), it is problematic whether the additional billions who will inhabit the world in the late 21st century can and will be provided with the means to live in even frugal comfort. Currently 1 billion people live in quite unacceptable poverty. However, it may be that while malnutrition is rampant, starvation is relatively rare (Wagar 1989). In the Asia-Pacific region in particular, the growth of population and industry will continue to reduce the availability of arable land and countries there will increasingly rely on food imports.

Not all food-security scenarios for 2040 and beyond are as pessimistic as this. Studies for Netherlands Scientific Council for Government Policy (1995) suggest that most of the world's 15 major regions should be able to feed themselves even under the assumption of high population growth.

Minerals

Chapman and Roberts (1983) estimate that the cost in energy terms of retrieving a kilogram of minerals is likely to rise at 2–3 per cent a year in coming decades. However, there are several ways in which the major price rises this implies stand to be ameliorated:

- The trend towards recycling of metallic and other components of worn-out goods, for example, tyre recycling;

- The trend towards dematerialisation, that is, the use of smaller quantities of raw materials to achieve a product of given functional capability;

- A nascent trend towards producing 'long life' products;

- Increasing possibilities for substitution between metals (for example, aluminium for copper in power transmission) and of non-metallic for metallic materials in goods production;

- Minerals, like food, are taking, and will continue to take, an ever-smaller fraction of world trade. This is linked to the trend for western economies to produce services rather than goods;

- An increased unwillingness to accept the ecological risks of heavy metal pollution.

Overall, it is extremely difficult to see how prices for major minerals will move under the combined effect of numerous uncertain trends.

While profitable in particular situations, recycling of metals is energy intensive and will only become widespread if increasing quantities of increasingly expensive energy are needed to mine metalliferous ores of increasingly lower grades. Constructing goods with their eventual recycling in mind (for example, readily separable components) will reinforce the trend towards recycling. It may be decided of course that any emerging trend towards recycling should be actively encouraged by taxing 'virgin' construction and fabrication materials such as minerals and timber when they are used in the production process. Such taxes could extend the date at which non-renewable mineral supplies 'run out'. Depletion quotas, caps on the rate at which minerals can be extracted, could be instituted to produce the same result (see page 290).

Apart from oil and gas fields, little is known about the potential for marine minerals. On the world's continental shelves, exploration will continue for tin and gold and, perhaps, phosphatic minerals. On the abyssal plains there is likely to be exploration for manganese, nickel, cobalt, and copper nodules and polymetallic sulphides.

Global-scale resource management

Use of the world's traditional natural resources to produce traded goods is increasingly under the control of a relatively small number of large trans-national corporations, a trend which seems set to continue. One danger here is the threat to price competition as cartelisation makes the entry of new firms difficult. International regulation seems unlikely at this stage, despite the failure of US attempts to control some aspects of trans-national operations by extending its laws offshore. Rather, movement is towards multilateral agreements to free up trade and investment between countries with only minimal consideration of the environmental and labour market consequences thereof. Governments' willingness to participate in such agreements stems from the importance of contributions from trans-national corporations to government revenues and foreign exchange in many countries, even to the point where the interests of local peoples in resource-rich areas are commonly ignored.

Less traditional global resource issues, all of which may eventually experience a degree of international regulation include the use of global cyberspace, allocation of the electromagnetic spectrum, crowding of low-orbit satellites and the need for optical darkness and radio quietness (Henderson 1998a).

In the longer term, global resource management issues will only be satisfactorily resolved by partnerships between governments, business and civic organisations and there will be a movement in this direction.

SUMMARY: CHANGE IN THE 21ST CENTURY

This chapter started with some macroscopic perceptions of a 21st century world, citing Bell, Toffler, Kahn etc. and noting the triplets of global scenarios suggested by Schwartz (1991) and Hammond (1998). In a sentence which captures much of this coterie's thinking, the 21st century world will struggle, with greater or lesser success, to manage violence, pollution and capitalism. We turned then to some more detailed possibilities for the world's political, social, environmental and economic future and it is these we draw on now for a closing overview.

While there is a common view abroad that global society is in a state of flux from which clear patterns have yet to emerge, there is in fact a remarkable consensus among futurists about many aspects of the world's mid-term future, now that 1970s perceptions of a world going forward into an age of abundance and leisure (Boulding 1978) have been decisively rejected. In the 'noughties', what does seem clear, in line with the views of both Hobsbawm (1994) and Heilbroner (1995), is that global change in coming decades will take place within a cage formed by the same giant forces as those moulding recent centuries — capitalism, technology and the search for political emancipation. The difference is that these forces are no longer regarded unambiguously as carriers of progress. Rather, the outlook for the future has turned sombre because negative aspects of these agents, either unknown or unrecognised previously, are now perceived to be as important as their undisputed positive effects.

It is true that many future-gazers can be readily tagged as either global optimists or global pessimists, but closer inspection reveals not so much incompatible perceptions as different foci. The wonderful achievements painted in scenarios of technological utopias are for the rich. Most of the world will continue to be poor. Global optimists (for example, North 1995) are those concentrating on the apparent 'winners' while global pessimists are concentrating on the 'losers'. Another split is between optimists focusing on economic and technological change and pessimists focusing on environmental change.

What then are these reigning wisdoms about the great world's future? Firstly, there is recognition of some big contingencies, both catastrophes and windfalls (pleasant surprises), that would trigger an unknowable restructuring of the global system if they came to pass. The four horsemen of a 21st century Apocalypse are world war, global economic collapse, decimating disease pandemics and convulsive climate shifts:

While it is true that the Cold War is over and that democratic states, an increasing proportion of all states, have never waged war against each other, the number of nuclear states is proliferating and military capabilities are increasing, qualitatively and quantitatively, in many countries. There remain a number of plausible sequences of events (for example, Friedman and Lebard 1991) leading to all-out war between nuclear powers, including major powers.

Global economic depressions and crises (plunging GWP and threats thereof) have happened before and could happen again. Facilitating and predisposing conditions include a fragmented international money system, third-world debt, US balance of payments problems (Thurow 1996), over-investment in industrial capacity, the volume of currency sales, the speed with which financial market moods can diffuse around the world, food shortages and rising energy prices. Oil supplies could decline rapidly enough to trigger a price shock which would run through the world economy.

An outbreak of disease capable of reducing the world's human population by an order of magnitude is possible. Facilitating and predisposing conditions include increasing concentrations of people in big cities with poor public health standards, increased global travel, increased opportunities for inter-species transfer of diseases and increasingly rapid resistance of disease organisms to new medical drugs.

While it would be highly unsurprising in the 21st century to see global climates change slowly in response to greenhouse warming, there is also a possibility, albeit one with high potential surprise, that climates around the world could change massively, rapidly and in unforeseen ways. Such a spasm has the potential to fundamentally disrupt global society.

Two tantalising windfalls with the potential to bring much good into people's lives, but which would surprise most observers if they eventuated before 2050, are cheap fusion power and practical nanoscale constructor robots.

Assuming that system-restructuring contingencies do not eventuate, there are two existing overarching trends which seem reasonably set to continue running and to affect the well-being of most in doing so. One is socioeconomic and one is demographic.

Globalisation, the processes under which formerly separate societies are moving to function as a single society, economically, politically, socially and culturally, is widely expected to continue. Economically, the geographic dispersion between countries of components of the mass production system will continue. Gross World Product will continue to rise, perhaps with pauses, and most strongly driven from the Asia-Pacific region. An increasing fraction of GWP will be produced by a small number of ever-growing mega corporations.

The product mix will continue to swing away from goods towards services. Nonetheless, the global economy's material throughput (and energy use) will continue to rise despite trends to dematerialisation. This will be due to population growth and rising real incomes for many, effects that will swamp the more efficient use of materials and the saturation of some markets, for example, the rich buying services, not another car (Larson et al. 1986). Growth will be driven by the logic of capitalism, continuing trade liberalisation and expansion and by technological change, particularly in the information, communications and transport sectors. Although rationed by income, most in the first world, and a rapidly increasing number elsewhere, will presently have access to a global electronic infrastructure supporting ubiquitous personal communications and customised information and entertainment services.

The political dimension of globalisation is more problematic. The nations of the world could give the United Nations real resources and real powers to begin establishing world government. Or, the UN could become increasingly irrelevant with the rules governing behaviour between nations being set by agreements between major powers and major corporations.

Population will rise from 6 billion towards 10 billion or more late in the century, with most of that increase being in the developing countries, particularly their major cities. Urbanisation will be characterised by urban sprawl and inner-city urban decay. Despite globalisation, the world of 2050, and probably beyond, will still be divided into a first world of industrialised countries, a second world of developing countries and a third world of industrially undeveloped countries. Between and within these worlds there will be great inequalities of wealth and, in the third world particularly, widespread illiteracy, homelessness, hunger and malnutrition. Many third world countries are 'locked into' poverty and there is no foreseeable trigger that could induce the first world to behave in a way that would allow the third world to make significant progress towards meeting the basic needs of its peoples. This is not to say that such a trigger will not appear, just that none-such can be identified. So the world will be populated by 1 billion or so 'rich' people and 8 or 9 billion poor people. And they are likely to be spread over many more countries. Many sub-national groups will successfully struggle for recognition and more autonomy even as many national powers are being ceded to supra-national bodies.

While first world states will continue to be organised around a capitalist economy of some sort married to a bureaucracy of greater or lesser reach, the possibility of some struggling democracies being reduced to token or nominal status is also plausible. More generally, the proportion of the world's people living in liberal democracies stands to decline somewhat despite a doubling in the number of 'democratic' countries since 1970. The dual basis for that assertion is simply that a large proportion of the world's population growth is occurring in non-democratic countries and that democracy is losing its appeal as many democracies fail to deliver improving quality of life to their citizens.

While the catastrophe of world war might be avoided, wars over resources (from water to diamonds) and wars of liberation and emancipation for ethnic and religious groups will be widespread in the second and third worlds. In the first world, increases in crime and violence would be unsurprising, the only question being the size of the increase. Violence could extend to pervasive political terrorism and, in a worst-case scenario, to attempts by the dispossessed to physically destroy elite power. Overall, the forces of prejudice, discrimination, poverty and alienation are such that a less violent world is quite implausible.

The global environment and resource base is generally expected to continue degrading. Rates of loss and degradation of natural resources (particularly soils, water and forests) are more likely to accelerate than slow. The rate of species extinction will almost certainly accelerate. Natural disasters occur when people occupy hazardous areas and so will be increasingly common as world population grows. Numbers of disasters stand to be further exacerbated too by global climate change.

And what of other transforming social changes? Various strengthening social movements (for example, female emancipation, environmentalism) will begin to impose their values on their societies, perhaps slowly, perhaps more rapidly. In healthcare, it would be unsurprising if first-world life expectancies were to creep up while the gap between first and third world life expectancies might begin closing more slowly than at the rapid rate of recent decades. In education, it would be surprising to see an early reversal of focus from teaching vocational skills to teaching life skills.

But it could be different

A pleasing metaphor for the way in which the future evolves out of the present is that of a tree on which buds unfold, blossom and die. We expect emerged blossoms (strong trends) to run their course or wither early. And while we can identify many buds (incipient trends and immanent sharp changes), we cannot tell which are destined to develop when, if ever. Some 'buds' will inevitably escape our attention at first; the fall of Communism and the eruption of HIV/AIDS are good examples from the past. Coming from left field in the future, what about a new religion that sweeps the world? Humanity's appetency for external authority has not been killed off by the Enlightenment and could perhaps revive in an era of high change and uncertainty. What if globalisation in 30 years time is being driven by Fascism or militant environmentalism or a non-American hegemonic power?

Anyhow, this is what this chapter has been doing: identifying alternative major-change scenarios in diverse aspects of social, economic, political and environmental processes around the world and indicating whether the eventuation of one or other alternative would be seen as more or less surprising. And in a too-brief survey we have had to ignore the linkages between scenarios, that is, what eventuates in one process differentially alters the prospects for the alternatives in other processes. Asking what use can be made of such tentative 'scoping' of possible futures for the world's 21st century is the subject of a later chapter.

While it will be a very difficult century, my confidence that we will survive it in large enough numbers to ensure that we are not genetically impoverished is sufficient to make it appropriate to keep writing and sample what has been foreseen for *Homo sapiens* beyond 2100 CE and on into what I am calling the deep, deeper and deepest futures.

2

DEEP FUTURES

> I am very fully conscious that the views I have
> expressed run entirely counter to many of the
> optimistic hopes of the present age. I myself see little
> prospect of escape from the return to hard conditions
> of life, and much of my motive in setting my views
> down is the hope that they may be contradicted by
> others who have a deeper knowledge than I can claim
> of the laws of Nature. (CHARLES DARWIN, *The Next Million
> Years*, 1952, p. 27)

Having presumed a safe landing, either smooth or bumpy, in
2100 CE, what have future-gazers foreseen for the rest of time for the species
in question and its descendants? We will tackle this at three 'magnifications',
starting with some perceptions of the next thousand years (M3). Future-gaz-
ing starts to get difficult beyond that because, by then, more and more aspects
of people, societies and nature (and their interactions) as known to us will
have been displaced by new forms not obviously descended from present
forms. It made some sense for Hitler to talk about a thousand-year Reich, but
not a million-year Reich.

Then we will stand somewhat further back and look at what has been
foreseen for the next hundred thousand years, this being a best-estimate of
the duration of the coming ice age, something which we can anticipate with
some confidence and recognise as being a demanding challenge for the
species.

Finally, the chapter turns to speculations about what our descendants, if
any, might be like and what they could be doing over the millions and billions
of years between now and the several scenarios for the end of the universe.

M3: THE WORLD OF THE THIRD MILLENNIUM

CG Darwin, quoted above, the grandson of the original proponent of natural selection as the process underlying evolution, bases his pessimism on a Malthusian analysis in which much of the world's population goes hungry over the next million years, except for occasional brief 'golden ages' of plenty. As he sees the past, numbers rose after each of four 'revolutions' which reset earth's potential for feeding humans, that is, reset its 'carrying capacity'. First, mastery of fire multiplied dietary possibilities, notably by improving the digestibility of meat and tubers. Second, animal and crop-plant domestication (10–12 000 years ago) increased food production per worker and gave an advantage to larger groups in the task of running more complex societies. Third, living in cities, something which began about 6000 years ago, was the 'urban revolution' which brought division of labour, granaries and trade possibilities and again raised carrying capacity. And now we are living in the scientific–industrial revolution which, with the aid of fossil fuels, allows food for 6 billion to be produced. Unfortunately, up to a billion of these go to bed hungry each night while others eat more grain than their share in the form of bacon and eggs. And this is Darwin's point. Advances in food production do not permanently eliminate the misery of hunger. Creation of a vast new food source — a further revolution — would not solve the problem of hunger in any permanent way.

Darwin also draws attention to the exhaustion of fossil fuels as potentially triggering a population decline, a scenario which is further developed by William Catton (1980) in his book *Overshoot*. Catton sees the last four centuries of population and productivity growth as an 'age of exuberance' based on a once-only 'carrying capacity supplement' in the form of fossil energy and the use of non-renewable resources and a once-only colonisation of an under-populated New World. When non-renewable energy (including uranium) runs out in a few hundred years, and assuming no other major energy source is found, the world will enter an age of de-industrialisation and depopulation. The side-effects and pollutants (unprocessed residues) produced when using non-renewable resources hasten that day of reckoning by reducing the usefulness of, in particular, renewable resources. EO Wilson's (2000) parallel diagnosis is that the profligacy of the twentieth century has led humanity into a *bottleneck* of overpopulation and shrinking natural resources, a bottleneck through which humanity and the rest of life must now pass.

While humans have already entered a demographic transition that will see population stop growing this century, there is a small chance that this transition will turn into a population crash, a dramatic decline in numbers in the third millennium. Most plague animals, and we may well be such in biological terms, orchestrate their own decline via a hormone-induced infertility associated with high population density (rather than a lack of food), an infertility that is not necessarily reversed when numbers do decline (Morrison 1999: 134).

Worst-case and best-case scenarios

Is there more to a *worst-case global scenario* for the coming millennium than Catton's 'post-exuberance'? Certainly this century's threats of war, disease, social upheaval and environmental degradation will continue into the millennium, but are there longer-term processes in the wings, waiting to make themselves felt?

One is the next ice age. Already, at 11–12 000 years, ours is the longest inter-glacial on record and, well within a thousand years, we could be plunged into a world where, as in the last ice age, average temperatures are up to 10 degrees lower than today (although the cooling process commonly has taken much longer). Current greenhouse warming could delay this somewhat but is unlikely to permanently stall a process which, driven by recurring variations in the Earth's orbit, axial tilt and axial wobble, has operated with a basic regularity for a million years. In that cold, perhaps carbon-dioxide deficient, dry, windy world, wheat could not be produced in the breadbaskets of Ukraine, North America and Australia and, in the absence of revolutionary technology, world population would plummet.

It might well be better all round if global cooling were to occur sooner rather than later, that is, before we exhaust the stocks of fossil fuels which make mechanised, intensive agriculture possible. This would guarantee enough energy being available to build an infrastructure for coping with a cold world; such things as domed cities, linear cities, underground cities, food factories and giant greenhouses. On the other hand, if global cooling were to be delayed, naturally or perhaps by encouraging greenhouse warming, the population to be accommodated when harsh conditions arrive might have returned to something nearer 6 billion than 10 billion perhaps — assuming the continuation of contemporary sub-replacement fertility rates. In this event, the mass migrations towards the tropics which would accompany global cooling would be somewhat less disruptive of the social order than otherwise. So, apocalyptic catastrophes aside, a candidate worst-case scenario for the third millennium is one of a depopulating, de-industrialising world finding itself unprepared for a sudden ice age.

In an alternative worst-case scenario for the third millennium a 'runaway' or 'positive feedback' greenhouse effect operates. That is, every increase in atmospheric temperature triggers the release of more carbon dioxide from various sources, for example, melting permafrost. As in the very warm era of early Tertiary times this might lead to remarkably moist climates over nearly all the earth's surface (Wolfe 1985). More, this scenario envisages sea level rises of 7–13 metres as polar ice sheets melt and ocean waters expand. The resulting displacement of people, perhaps a fifth of the world's population, and the loss of coastal farmlands, could lead to the collapse of many societies and civilisations, as have earlier mass migrations.

Moving on, what *best-case scenario* for the third millennium might lie within the reach of human societies? A millennium is a blink in cosmic time and it seems unlikely that rare events like supernovae explosions, solar flares, mergers of black holes or neutron stars, large-scale volcanism or impacts by asteroids or comets etc. will kill us all in the near future (Leslie 1996). If all goes well, the human species could have stabilised its numbers and rates of materials and energy consumption by 3000 CE. Most people could be leading comfortable lives, not working too hard to meet basic physiological needs and enjoying long healthy life spans in societies able to provide significant numbers with opportunities to meet their higher needs. The threat of anthropogenic catastrophes, including wars and chronic-to-acute pollution, might have receded. The nascent great wave of species extinctions might have run its course. Greenhouse gas concentrations might have peaked and declined without causing havoc in the meantime. The struggle between counter-urbanisation and centralised technopolises as the paradigm for human settlements may have been resolved (Starr 1996). The natural world could have become a well-managed garden, replete with wild spots as well as food bowls. As early as the 22nd century, the primary challenge, the top priority, might have become the building of a global federation in which peoples can retain their identities and enjoy basic rights; and in which cycles of military and economic hegemony have been dampened (De Greene 1994).

Such a sketch still leaves numerous questions unanswered, questions to which, in many cases, there is no plausible and patently 'best case' answer. How will economic activity be organised? Will economic activity be sustained by renewable energy or by new forms of non-renewable energy? How will political life be organised, globally and locally? How will the strengths and weaknesses of competitive and collaborative behaviour be balanced? How will people's rights and responsibilities be balanced? Will religion be an important determinant of behaviour? What sort of religion? Will life be frantic or leisurely? Will people travel much? Will most people enjoy a quality of life that allows them to readily satisfy not only their basic physiological needs but also their higher needs for creative and participative activities? To what extent will robots and computers attend to the mechanics of running society? How specialised will people's roles be? Will society be strongly hierarchical? Authoritarian? Will populations be passive? Mature in the face of hard times? Will daily life be safe or dangerous? How will anti-social behaviour be defined and treated? What sorts of major projects will engage societies? Will poverty still be a problem? If so, how will poverty be distributed?

The list goes on. Alternative answers can be suggested for all these questions but few carry a sense of inevitability. What is important about the questions we feel drawn to ask about the third millennium is not that they are difficult to answer convincingly but that they are so easy to ask. What do I mean? I mean that they are questions about an updated version of the world we presently live in. As far as we can foresee, the third millennium will yield a story of people much like us coping collectively with problems much like our problems. Technologies, institutions and social forms will differ but most problems will still be recognisable as problems of managing energy supplies, the production of goods and services, environmental quality, social justice or population composition. Individuals will still be seeking quality of life based on meeting innate physiological and psychological needs. People's opportunities and constraints will present differently but they will still be opportunities and constraints. In the absence of cosmic or human-made super-disasters we will be managing a complex global society in ways which today's people could understand, at least in principle — just as we think we can empathise with what we know of those living a thousand years ago. We may of course be totally wrong, that is, it may be possible to capture a few threads of life from another age but not the fabric, not what the core concerns will be.

Biological change in M3

People much like us? While it would be highly surprising to see the extinction of humans in the third millennium, the obverse, their evolution into a new species, is just not possible in such a short time. There is serious debate as to whether human genetic evolution has effectively stopped (Jones 1993), continues as before (Richardson and Stubbs 1976) or is accelerating (Wills 1998). For example, if people can learn to behave differently as a way of coping with a new environmental stress, then those with better genomes for coping with that particular stress will not be favoured in the reproduction stakes. On the other hand, those with higher capacity for learning to cope through such behaviour change may be favoured as breeders.

But a thousand years is nothing in evolutionary time anyway and even if we are evolving biologically at an accelerating pace it will scarcely show in the third millennium. Just as we suspect a re-created Cro-Magnon baby from 25 000 years ago could grow up to don a business suit and practise merchant banking, a contemporary baby transported into the late third millennium would probably have the genetic potential to blend into that society. To be quite clear, what is being asserted here is that humans will change relatively little in genetic terms in the next thousand years. Cultural evolution, as noted below, is a different matter.

On the assumption then that human genetic evolution is proceeding at some level, coming generations of people will change genetically — and hence change in how they are predisposed to look and function and behave — in ways that accord with, primarily, Charles Darwin's principle of *natural selection*. What does this mean?

Natural selection

First, two definitions. A *niche* is those aspects of an organism's environment to which the organism (plant, animal etc.) is sensitive, meaning that the organism changes its behaviour when the niche changes. Conversely, a niche exists when there is an opportunity for an organism with particular capabilities and needs to survive. An organism's *phenotype* is the totality of its *traits* or observable characteristics, including behavioural characteristics.

In any society or, more generally, any environmental niche, people with certain traits will reproduce at a greater rate — known as having a higher *Darwinian fitness* or a *reproductive advantage* — than people without those traits. A 'favouring' of the fittest is a more accurate description here (although still somewhat circular) than 'survival' of the fittest. Conversely, 'elimination of the less fit', those leaving few descendants, is an equally accurate expression.

If that environmental niche persists over many generations and if the people with the fitter phenotype have a distinctive *genotype* (mix of genes) which (a) is necessary for the advantageous traits to appear and which (b) they pass on to their children to some extent (called inheritance of differential fitness) then that distinctive genotype will tend to become more common in the society. This is the process of *natural selection*, the process suggested by Darwin as being at the heart of the evolution of species, that is, biological evolution is what happens as a result of a long cumulative sequence of natural selections.

Note that natural selection acts directly on phenotypes and only indirectly on genotypes, even then depending on the extent to which phenotype reflects or is an expression of genotype.

Putting this another way, evolution by natural selection does not take place unless there are *relevant* genetic differences on which natural selection can work. It can take place only within a population that is genetically variable for some trait that influences the reproductive success of the bearer. If it is to produce significant changes in a species, natural selection requires that advantageous traits possessed by some people in the population should be heritable, meaning capable of being passed on to later generations to some extent, and also that the environment which makes those differences advantageous (that is, makes their possessors more likely to have offspring) should persist (or, more correctly, change only slowly) for many generations, long enough for the 'advantaged' genes to spread through the population.

It is important to understand that there are, effectively, two causal processes in evolution — natural selection of the fitter organisms by the niche and, over generations, modification of the niche by the organism. The most dramatic example of the latter is the creation of an oxygenated atmosphere following the evolution of photosynthesising organisms. A phenotype which is favoured under natural selection in any particular generation is being constructed throughout its life by an ongoing interaction between the organism's genotype and its environmental niche. Later generations are likely to be selected for success in a somewhat modified environmental niche. When its environmental niche is changing rapidly, an organism is said to be under strong selection pressure. The genotypes which survive environmental change are said to have adapted to the change.

If evolution is ever to result in one species splitting into two, it is necessary for part of the population to be isolated (no interbreeding) over many generations and subject to selection pressures different from those operating on the parent population. But, as long as a small amount of interbreeding is occurring across the entire range of a species, the mixture of genes in that population (its gene pool) will be a compromise between what is genetically best for the species in the different parts of its environment. That is, living in a variable environment makes a population genetically variable (diverse). In an M3 world where formerly separate societies are beginning to function as a single society, there is almost no prospect of humans beginning to split into several species. More than this, the human gene pool in almost every country of the world is becoming more diverse under the influence of migration and international travel. Such increased variability stands to induce a faster rate of evolution insofar as there are more phenotypes to be tested for relative fitness.

There is an argument about natural selection among evolutionary biologists which might be mentioned here but not entered into. Is natural selection best described as favouring fit organisms or fit 'life cycles' (Sterelny 2001) or fit genes or fit groups of organisms? Mayr (1994) argues that the pure Darwinian model of natural selection applies well to asexually reproducing organisms like bacteria, but for sexually reproducing species like ours, which only replicate in partnerships, it is better to regard genes as the basic replicating units, even though the fitness of genes can only be defined through their collective expression in an organism's phenotype.

The key biological argument against the existence of group selection is that there is no clear mechanism for making individuals behave in a way that is advantageous to the group, that is, there are no mechanisms that can stop 'free-riders' benefiting from group behaviour. So, unless all group members live and die together, the number of cheats will expand until the rewarding group-behaviour is no longer feasible. But, in fact, there are such constraining mechanisms, for example, tradition, acculturation, socialisation. Therefore, if there is a population of groups competing and replicating in an environment where resources are limited, then groups which constrain their members to behave in the interests of the group (for example, looking after wise elders) will expand at the expense of groups where the leverage of collective action is not exploited. While not genetic, at least initially, this process is wholly analogous to natural selection (Hodgson 1999b: 140; Plotkin 1994: 101).

Biological evolution

What are some of the human-made changes to the human environment that are likely to impose selection pressure on coming generations of M3 humans and begin to change them genetically? At a very general level, hominid evolution has been marked by an increasing use of tools (including mental and linguistic tools) and, as this behaviour continues, selection in favour of those able to use tools well should continue. Thus, the size of the human brain has more than doubled since *Australopithecus* times, but the growth has not been uniform. It has largely been in three regions: one commands the hand, another controls speech, and the third bears a large responsibility for hindsight and foresight (Bronowski 1977: 126). In general terms, an increasingly complex environment has been selecting, successfully as it happens, for an increasingly complex organism — a simple organism cannot survive in a complex environment. Whether this success can continue is not predictable.

Another probable development is that people will be selected for their ability to live successfully in crowded cities, a niche change which is likely to persist. This means people who are strongly socially oriented, accepting of highly structured lives and reduced choice and personal freedom — as in contemporary Japan, or Huxley's *Brave New World*. If observers like Lorenz (1963; 1966) and Müller (1967) are correct, co-operative, non-aggressive people will necessarily have been selected if social collapse is avoided in an over-crowded, under-resourced world. Adaptation (beneficial change in behavioural capacity) to city life is likely to have a socio-cultural component (see below) as well as the heritable genetic component we are talking of here. Even more generally, high population densities intensify the selection pressure exerted by most stresses including disease and competition for resources.

Pollution in its many forms is a major environmental stress that is probably leading to genetic change in urban populations. Atmospheric poisons particularly stress peri-natal and pre-reproductive groups (and, less importantly from an evolutionary perspective, post-reproductives). DDT and other biocides (chemicals that can kill) are ubiquitous and affect fertility, mortality and normal development of the young. Chemicalisation of the environment might lead to selection for high sperm counts. Small but continuous leaks of mutagenic radioactive isotopes from nuclear plants are of particular concern because they are cumulative, taking thousands of years to decay. Mutagens are materials which directly change the genetic makeup of those exposed to them, leading to reproductive problems such as infertility and increased birth defects.

The world will be warmer in M3, at least initially, and, as the contrasting body types of Africans and Inuits testify, the gene pools of discrete populations respond to such differences.

There is little doubt that numerous environmental stresses and selection pressures are emerging and changing in modern societies. Some forces for natural selection are getting weaker and some are getting stronger. Medical technology, for example, is increasingly making it possible for people who would have once died of disease or disability to survive and reproduce. Putting this another way, such technologies are slowing down the rate of genetic evolution. Also, given that nowadays a greater proportion of those born are reaching maturity, an increasing frequency of deleterious genes in the population can be assumed. As childbearing becomes discretionary and more onerous in modern societies, selection for maternal instinct will occur.

Infectious diseases have imposed successively more selection pressure on humans at each stage in the transition from hunter–gatherer society to agricultural villages to pre-industrial cities to modern industrial and post-industrial cities. For example, animal domestication exposed people to diseases formerly restricted to animals; measles becomes endemic only in populations above a critical size and density. Disease has undoubtedly caused the spread of many genes that were rare in hunter–gatherer times, genes that in the act of conferring disease resistance lower fitness in other ways, for example, the genes which protect against malaria while increasing susceptibility to sickle-cell anaemia. The threat of pandemic disease is conflated with the high population densities the world stands to experience for much of the third millennium.

There are a number of diseases caused by one or a few sublethal genes (for example, Huntington's disease), including deficiency diseases where particular nutrients cannot be synthesised in the body. The rate at which genes mutate, whether to a lethal/sublethal form or otherwise, is partly inherited. It follows that deliberate selection to slow the occurrence of sublethals (by genetic testing of prospective parents for example) will slow evolution in general and select for genes which counter the effects of the sublethal mutations. On the other hand, helping people with genetic defects to survive increases a population's genetic variability, even though it is allowing deleterious genes to accumulate (Huxley 1953, chapter 6). It needs to be appreciated, especially given current enthusiasm for gene therapies, that only a few diseases are tightly linked to one or a few genes. Most inherited diseases occur as a result of complex interactions between a set of genes and their environment. Their associated risk level is likely to decline with age and with the operation of physiological compensation mechanisms.

Degenerative diseases of old age, meaning those that strike after the reproductive years, may be an advantage in a society where reproductive life is limited — raising the reproductive capacity of the society (possible births per capita) without lowering the fitness of the individual If the post-reproductives in a society are a burden then societies with a high incidence of such diseases will expand more rapidly than societies without such diseases, for example, a community where every woman dies of cancer at 55 might be more prosperous and fertile than otherwise. Even if post-reproductives are not a burden, there will be no selection against genes which confer both fitness in youth and degenerative disease in old age. Rather, there will be active selection for such genes. If post-reproductives are actually beneficial to a society, they cannot be selected as individuals but the society or group they belong to may well expand at the expense of other groups.

Socio-cultural change in M3

As a general rule, rapid change in the physical environment (for example, changing food supplies) leads to strong selection pressures and causes accelerated evolution of the gene pools of the species that are caught up in it — or their extinction. However, in the case of human societies, it also leads to *socio-cultural evolution,* that is, gradual change in social organisation (institutions) and in cultural norms and values — a strategy which has the effect, when successful, of coping with or taking advantage of environmental changes that are occurring too rapidly to allow adaptation by natural selection. Under socio-cultural evolution both individuals and groups learn new behaviours which are not based on genetic changes even though these may eventually lead to genetic changes (Boyd and Richerson 1985). Instead of, like natural selection, waiting a generation before even beginning to move a population towards adapting to a new environment (remembering that this can only happen when some relevant phenotypic variability is present), candidate cultural changes can be devised and trialled in, sometimes, weeks, for example, fashion, slang. And if such prove successful, communication, particularly through language, can spread the new behaviour rules rapidly through the benefiting parts of the population. Some cultural changes such as new ideologies, religions and racial attitudes may take generations to spread but the process is still much faster than natural selection.

At the heart of any society's *culture* are the ideas that a significant proportion of its members share, ideas about how the world works (for example, religious beliefs), and, also, the shared *behavioural rules* (so-called production rules) its members make use of. These rules (or precepts) take a general 'if ... then' form — *If* you find yourself in such-and-such a situation (environment), *then* behave in such-and–such fashion. More specifically, rule-based behaviours take forms such as rituals, routines, customs, conventions, institutions. Cultural change takes place when most people drop existing behavioural rules or new behavioural rules are developed for use in newly recognised categories of environments or reformulated to be more discriminating in recognising variants of existing environments. New behavioural rules are developed and improved by an *individual learning process* which is well described as innovative trial-and-error. Cultural change turns into cultural evolution when a sequence of past cultural changes is recognised as having had an overall direction.

The search for new behavioural rules is triggered when an innovator perceives that his or her ('hir') inherent needs/goals are not being as well met as they might be. Once developed and apparently successful, new behavioural rules spread through the society as people imitate each other. New ideas about relationships between entities (how the world works) are similarly assimilated into a society's culture by teaching or imitative acceptance if they help people towards a more comprehensive or cohesive and useful world view.

Not dissimilarly, *social evolution* — accumulated social learning — is the changes in behaviour and behavioural rules that accumulate as a *group* of people learn to behave in a coordinated way to meet some collective need, for example, to maintain institutions such as government, the legal system, the economy etc. Social reorganisation involves the specification of a new or redefined behavioural role for each group member. Most such refinements start from a pervasive behavioural rule or principle (which is at least partly genetic and hence unlearned [Wilson 1975]), namely, that an individual's needs can often be more effectively satisfied by co-operation (mutually beneficial exchange) with others than by the individual acting alone.

While group learning can make institutions more effective over time, reciprocal exchanges can also become unbalanced with some members acquiring more of the things that all want. When reciprocity does give way to unequal structures of differentiation and power, new rules for guiding coordinated action have to be devised if groups, organisations and institutions are to remain legitimate in the eyes of their members. As Boulding (1978) says, institutions collapse when the lower members of the social hierarchy withdraw their legitimacy. The resulting shift in political power opens the way for radical overhaul of the failed institution's rules. *Social learning*, meaning the ways in which groups acquire new rules for exploiting the 'leverage of collective action', is discussed further in Chapter 7.

Adaptation feeds on itself

Just as behavioural changes can feed back via differential reproduction rates to produce population-wide genetic changes, they can, and indeed generally do, also lead to further socio-cultural changes. Adaptation, meaning beneficial change in an entity, feeds on itself. Organisations and the socio-cultural environments in which they find themselves co-evolve, that is, each evolves in response to changes in the other. For example, businesses adapting to market change stimulate further market change.

As noted above, some cultural forms such as fashions change frequently (perhaps every month) while others such as religions change infrequently. Such differences parallel the speed at which the environments of the different forms are changing. For example, fashion is tracking or responding to cohort change (people moving between age groups), while religion is responding to major increments in human knowledge of the world (Wilson

1975: 560). In our time, institutions are notoriously slow to change whereas technological change is perceived to be breathtakingly rapid.

This raises the more general issues of *cultural lag* and *cultural overload*. Just as individual lives in the 21st century are likely to require adaptation to more frequent changes in relationships of all sorts, the rate at which whole societies experience challenges and opportunities is also likely to increase, at least in the first part of the third millennium. When challenges come at some supra-critical rate, resources for developing new social technologies for dealing with them may not be available, that is, the society's capacity for cultural adaptation gets overloaded and the end result might be poorly functioning institutions or, in the extreme, social collapse. Even accepting that the rate of socio-cultural change is increasing, we still cannot foresee the point at which the capacity to adapt will be exceeded. What we can do is wonder whether the 'fatal flaw' of cultural evolution is that it has initiated change at a rate to which we cannot adapt culturally. When the rate of external change exceeds the rate of internal change the end is in sight perhaps.

Paradigm shifts in M3 social organisation

Given the foregoing basic appreciation of the socio-cultural evolutionary process, what major socio-cultural transformation has been foreseen for the third millennium? Here are several.

Historically, the invention of agriculture, role specialisation and systematic technological progress are the three socio-cultural transformations which, supported by the invention of writing as a communication tool, have rough-hewn human society over the past 12 000 years. And, while further evolution of all of these may well continue over coming centuries, such trends are in no way inevitable. Similarly, there is nothing inevitable about the continuation of more recent trends such as urbanisation and globalisation.

What we can say is that societies will continue to experiment with innovative ways of solving problems — such as those in the best- and worst-case scenarios — which are blocking the achievement of social goals and bringing the legitimacy of the reigning social order into question. In systems where problem-solving fails badly despite attempts at innovation, the overall system stands to fail too, to become disorganised. Or, alternatively, there might be a reorganisation, a paradigm shift in social organisation towards new goals and new problem-solving recipes.

One plausible scenario for a major paradigm shift in M3 societies emerges from the observation that humanity is currently confronting a morass of technology-induced problems, from global warming to the nuclear threat and overpopulation. Material technologies which have frequently solved major immediate problems have, all too often, 'bitten back' with unforeseen consequences, creating multiple 'new' problems at a later date. Public awareness of this process has led to a degree of technophobia which, if it persists and strengthens, could eventually induce a massive switch in society's social learning efforts from devising material technologies to devising *social technologies*. These are the building blocks of social organisation, 'recipes' developed to solve social problems, meet social needs or achieve a social objectives, for example, the alphabet, standard time, coinage, credit cards, human rights, representative government etc. The solution of social problems lags behind material technology because we have not looked seriously for ideas to deal with them (Platt 1966).

Another quite fundamental shift in M3 social organisation which would not be totally surprising would be a switch from an adversarial approach to conflict resolution to a consensual, dialogic problem-solving approach. Modern societies seem to favour an adversarial approach to resolving conflicts at all levels from international relations (the doctrine of deterrence) to domestic relations (family courts). Given the modern world's poor record on resolving pervasive, debilitating conflicts, the possibility of trying a fundamentally different approach might well become an 'idea in good currency' (see page 271).

A less palatable answer to the problem of conflict, suggested as a real possibility by Toynbee (1971: 81), perhaps even a necessity if we are going to survive, is an authoritarian world government. Most probably, this would be in the form of a dictatorial world state in the style of the Roman or Chinese empires, one with real power to stop wars. Accepting such a dictatorship for a time could be the right choice if it allowed humans to avoid liquidating themselves.

A dictatorial world state or authoritarian world government might also be the most effective way of responding to the systemic intractable problem of social injustice. How can the world economy and political system be remodelled to deliver reasonable access to life opportunities to all? The initiative for narrowing the rich–poor gap lies with the rich countries. They may act voluntarily, but if they refuse they will eventually be confronted with a choice between being deposed or holding the majority down by establishing a worldwide fascist regime (Toynbee 1971: 135).

A democratic federation of the world's nation states is not an impossibility but it would have to be strong enough to tax rich countries and allow 'unionisation' of the poor countries, meaning that they would be able to bargain collectively to sell labour and raw materials to rich countries (see page

273). If this new world order were to grow out of the United Nations, all experience with federal systems suggests that a direct link between people and government would be needed, that is, people as well as states would be represented (Toynbee 1971: 150). Any movement to a true world federation would probably need to be accompanied by a widespread attitudinal shift from nationalism to planetism (Ellyard 1998), that is, people seeing themselves as, first and foremost, citizens of Planet Earth, rather than of a nation or region.

Summary: Prospects for M3

At this stage in the human story, nuclear war and genetically engineered viruses are the two anthropogenic hazards which could destroy the human species. As far as extinction is concerned, everything else, including cosmic events, is a second-order threat.

If we can get through the third millennium's first century with its already-existing plethora of human-made problems, challenges and hazards without collapsing our highly interconnected global society, we should be better equipped to face the rest of the millennium. Not just because the present suite of problems will, by definition, have been dealt with somehow, but also because the very fact of our survival will indicate that we have learnt something of how to cope with and contain war, disease, environmental degradation, hunger, social disorganisation etc. Perhaps even how to forestall such blights. The presumption here is that, no matter how slowly, societies learn from non-fatal experience.

As for the rest of the millennium, there are three contingencies which have the capacity to collapse societies around the world and destroy civilisations. Runaway global warming with its implications for weather, climate and sea level is one. Global cooling is the second, especially if the primary energy resources which would allow its effects to be ameliorated are exhausted. The third is a lack of global governance. While the world is increasingly functioning as a single society, it is not being governed as a single society. Problems such as poverty, conflict, international capital flows, myopic technologies, pollution and exploitation manifest at a global scale and must be managed at a global scale. Whether this can be done democratically is as big a challenge as whether it can be done at all.

Perhaps the possibility of disease epidemics in a world of highly connected mega-cities should be included on this list. While people will change little in genetic terms, socio-cultural change will be enormous and, if our energies are not depleted in battling the big challenges, life in the third millennium could be rich for an increasing proportion of people. That is the best I can offer.

THE NEXT GLACIAL AGE

In the last ice age, ending 12 000 years ago, huge ice sheets advanced and retreated over most of Canada, northern Europe and Russia. Sea levels rose and fell by as much as 200 metres in concert with this locking up and releasing of much of the world's water from glaciers. The advancing glaciers, covering up to 27 per cent of the earth's surface, obliterated most plant and animal life in their paths and pushed the inhabited temperate zones of the northern hemisphere south. Much of the tropics became cool deserts. More generally, cold-climate vegetation types tended to replace warm-climate types.

Within the next few thousand years another glacial age that will last 100 000 to perhaps 120 000 years will probably begin on Earth, reducing mean temperatures from current levels by as much as 10 degrees Celsius at times. Indeed temperatures were already dropping steadily prior to the industrial revolution with its accompanying acceleration in the emission of greenhouse gases. If it is like previous ice ages of the last million years this one too will have warmer and cooler periods reflecting periodicities in various cosmic and solar processes. It will be dry and windy. And as temperatures rise and fall over millennia the world's *biomes* or major vegetation types — boreal, temperate and tropical forests, shrub lands, woodlands, grasslands and deserts — will respond by advancing and retreating across the landscape for hundreds, perhaps thousands, of kilometres on every continent. As in the last glacial age remnant islands of retreating biomes will persist in particularly favoured locations, exploiting all of their genetic plasticity to hang on for millennia even, ready to seed new waves of expansion as conditions become suitable once again for their spread.

While conditions were harsh for much of the last ice age, it was a period in which our hunter–gatherer ancestors, equipped only with stone-age technologies and fire, spread out (or were forced by climatic change to spread out) across much of the globe. It was also a period in which our capacities to solve problems by inductive reasoning and to function as complex co-operating social animals evolved rapidly. So, if *Homo sapiens* apparently handled the last glacial age so well, would not the same be true for our descendants? They will have technologies which amplify raw human capabilities by orders of magnitude and organisational skills which already allow the maintenance and development of societies with hundreds of millions of members. Compared with our hunter–gatherer ancestors they will have the tremendous advantage of knowing what is happening, how bad it might get and how long it might last.

Perhaps so, but how well the species survives in terms of measures such as mortality rates and quality of daily life will still depend on factors such as:

- How climatically severe this glacial turns out to be;

- How much primary energy is readily available for human use;

- How many people have to be fed, clothed, sheltered; where they are located;

- How effective our food production technologies are in a dry, cold world;

- How resilient our techniques of social organisation prove to be under hardship;

- How much time and energy are available for social and cultural development after meeting people's basic physiological needs;

- How many additional shocks, natural and human-made, co-occur with periods of low temperatures, low rainfall, windiness and fluctuating sea levels.

In fact the last ice age was a close call for humanity. About 65 000 years ago a volcanic winter occurred and, combined with the cold conditions, reduced human numbers to about 10 000 (!) (Pinker 1997: 205).

Provided that we do not enter the coming glacial age with a much higher human population than now, dwindling energy resources and fragile or collapsing cultures; and provided that we do not become victims of major cosmic or planetary accidents, it would seem that our prospects for surviving well, that is, with our knowledge base and genetic base reasonably intact, are quite high.

Best-case and worst-case glacial scenarios

Under a best-case scenario, humanity's collective knowledge continues to accumulate throughout the glacial and, come the next inter-glacial, the population remains large enough to have preserved most of the genetic diversity the species currently enjoys. There is a wide spread of cultures. Cities, the environment in which social evolution appears to occur most readily, continue to be important components in the pattern of settlement. Peoples remain co-operative beings. A global communications network links people everywhere and a global transport system facilitates the movement of people and goods around the world. If life is hard, it is not so hard as to stifle creativity. Given such a scenario, one might anticipate a wave of cultural development once the next inter-glacial lifts the yoke of coping with an adverse climate. Just like last time.

Under a worst-case non-terminal scenario, humanity emerges from the coming ice age organised into small competitive tribes or bands of hunter–gatherers, confined to a limited number of low-latitude refugia, with only a fraction of our technical skills and little knowledge of the past or of the rest of the world. Great wars do not have to be scripted in to achieve this. All that is required is a slow decline in the primary energy available to maintain complex societies after giving first priority to the production of food and shelter under difficult conditions (Cottrell 1955). Population too would adjust to the inherent 'carrying capacity' of a glacial world, corrected somewhat for any ongoing fossil fuel subsidy. Any loss of capacity to maintain medical and pharmaceutical services would send mortality rates soaring and, as HIV/AIDS has shown in Africa, a loss of 10 per cent of the adult working population is calamitous for an economy. As with a best-case scenario, one could anticipate a cultural blossoming with the arrival of the inter-glacial, although from a low base. But not as low as last time for the reason that, since the last ice age, we have developed a higher level of individual consciousness and an enhanced capacity to reason 'scientifically'. These features which, conventionally, are extraordinarily useful on a day-to-day basis, are unlikely to be lost during the next glacial.

Biological evolution during the next glacial

During the last ice age conditions were ideal for populations to start differentiating from each other genetically, namely many small isolated populations subject to repeated climatic change. Genetic 'inertia' makes it difficult for adaptive changes to become fixed (present in all individuals) in large populations. Still, to the extent that humans prove unable to ameliorate the stresses of the coming ice age by cultural means, genetic evolution could be expected, boosted by the high genetic variability being built into breeding populations by migration and outbreeding today. Humanity is moving towards sharing a single large gene pool and a single human type and away from having a number of smaller 'racial' and 'tribal' gene pools.

Evolutionary physical changes which have been foreseen as possible within, perhaps, a few hundred thousand years, include a rounded skull, smoothing of the area above the brows, a reduction in size and number of teeth and a shrinking of the face, loss of body and head hair, loss of the appendix, a reduced sense of smell and increased height. Such changes reflect the loss of attributes once needed for a hunter–gatherer lifestyle. Could human brains start getting smaller as we make more and more use of 'external' memories such as libraries and have less need to store information internally? There is some evidence that modern humans have smaller brains than Neanderthals of 30 000 years ago.

Will evolution be managed?

It is widely assumed that, at some stage, perhaps by the time of the next glacial, humans will attempt to consciously control and direct their own evolution, both biological and socio-cultural. *Eugenics* is the study of how to improve the capabilities of a human population by changing its gene pool, basically by controlling breeding behaviour but also by inserting and deleting genes in the gametes (eggs and sperms) of breeding individuals. The sorts of measures discussed are both positive — pursuing the good — and negative — avoiding the bad.

Positive eugenics attempts to raise the reproduction rate of individuals with 'desirable' heritable characteristics, thus spreading their genes. For example, as evidence accumulates that behavioural traits are heritable, we might ask which behavioural qualities best enhance humanity's survival prospects. Human culture began through interpersonal and group co-operation and, it can be argued, co-operation is now as important as intelligence for survival. It should be possible to select for individuals with congenial non-aggressive behaviour, as well as mental and physical 'superiority'. Selecting for submissive behaviour, on the other hand, would open the door for demagogues (Richardson and Stubbs 1976: 205).

Negative eugenic measures include the use of abortion and birth control and social controls such as incest taboos to reduce the incidence and spread of supposedly deleterious genes, for example, sterilising intellectually disabled people. Many such deleterious genes arise by mutation and negative eugenics, in attempting to reduce the rate of deleterious mutations, is likely to be reducing the rate of all mutations, including potentially useful ones. This is because a species' mutation rate, while moderately heritable, is a rate common to most genes, not just those being targeted in eugenics programs. Against this, geneticist Hermann Müller (1967) has argued that anything lifting the mutation rate in humans would push the species close to extinction, an unsettling observation in light of radiation and chemical levels in modern environments. Macfarlane Burnet (1970: 137) notes that in a stable population where most children born survive to reproductive age, there will eventually be a random accumulation of minor genetic inefficiencies such as eye defects, migraines and allergies. Those populations which are last to leave the era of high birth and death rates will retain their genetic quality best.

This then is the first of three major difficulties with eugenics. That is, it is only useful in a stable environment where loss of genetic diversity is unimportant. And how can a stable environment be guaranteed? Similarly, ongoing agreement on long-term stable social goals has to be assumed because, for eugenics to significantly change a population's gene pool, persistent action over many generations will be required. For example, does one keep selecting for mathematical intelligence, emotional intelligence or linguistic intelligence? Preferences may well change. A superior or 'fitter' person is only superior until the environment changes. Third, it is socially divisive, arousing the resentment of those judged genetically undesirable or lacking in physical or behavioural attributes judged worthy of enhancing Despite many well-meaning advocates, eugenics is not an idea in good currency in today's world, having been associated in practice with gross abuse of human rights. In any case, there are less drastic ways of raising 'cleverness' levels — better education for example.

Nevertheless, at some time in the deep future it may become obvious that the species' well-being and survival requires people with certain attributes and there will need to be debate as to what mix of eugenics, socialisation, education, social engineering, prostheses and euphenics will best achieve what is required. *Euphenics* is a term for biological ways of improving on the genetic capacities of people as they are, for example, through healthcare, exercise. The use of folic acid to prevent the expression of genes predisposing to spina bifida is a good example. Care will be needed to avoid producing a species incapable of surviving without massive systemic support and without the genetic variability to resist new diseases.

Glacial age technologies

Could the planet be warmed? That is one fundamental question on which glacial age technology will undoubtedly be focused. Should it be?

Unless glacial age science has progressed enormously compared with today, there would be concern about adverse unintended consequences of artificially changing global climate. This would be particularly so in the case of approaches based on modifying the Earth's wobble and tilt (see page 75). Modifying the Earth's orbit around the Sun, even if it could be done, would seem, *prima facie*, to be a quite unacceptable option. Approaches based on modifying the courses of major ocean currents, for example, the circumpolar currents, would also be likely to raise great trepidation.

One less interventionist possibility would be to enrich the atmosphere with various greenhouse gases (as is happening inadvertently today) and so trap outgoing radiation. Carbon dioxide would be an obvious candidate given that its atmospheric concentration is commonly low during ice ages. Another approach would be to decrease the reflectance of the Earth's surface so that more of the Sun's incoming radiant energy is absorbed rather than reflected back into space. For example, black coal dust spread on ice sheets would have this effect. Positioning giant mirrors in space to reflect more solar energy earthwards is another seemingly benign possibility. Perhaps there will be ways of storing energy during periodic warm times for release at colder times. Any 'earth-warming' strategy carries some risk of 'overshooting' and producing a super-hot Earth when the next interglacial arrives.

All the foregoing scenarios involve large investments of energy and scientific capabilities well beyond, but not unimaginably beyond, what we have today. They clearly could not be pursued under the 'worst-case' scenario sketched out earlier.

The complement to the above earth-warming approaches to global cooling would be an 'adaptive' approach based on accepting and then attempting to live comfortably in a cold world. In general, presuming high costs for generating and transferring energy, one might expect a glacial world where regional communities were largely self-sufficient in terms of food and energy. Migration of large populations to low latitude regions with their lower heating requirements and better crop production possibilities would be a first option provided that this did not involve displacement of existing populations. Regions with winds suitable for generating wind power might attract population, as would regions able to readily tap geothermal power and heat sources. Technologies for making geothermal power (heat from the earth's core) more widely available would be sought.

Keeping the populations of large cities warm and well fed would be difficult. Cities would have to be rebuilt to incorporate ideas such as giant, transparent, heat-trapping 'bubble' domes covering buildings constructed wholly or partly underground. Even in an ice age a constant base temperature of 15 degrees Celsius could be maintained without artificial heating just a few metres below ground level. Linear cities built along a single transport axis would be energy efficient in other ways.

Given the difficulty of growing agricultural crops outdoors in most regions, factory-style 'vat farming' of micro-algae, yeasts etc. and hydroponic vegetable growing would be important perhaps. High transport costs would encourage the development of recycling technologies for human and other organic waste. There could be a place for controlled hunting of wildlife for food but not for raising livestock which is energetically inefficient. To the extent that trade across oceans continued, efficient wind ships and ways of keeping ports ice-free have been foreseen.

Summary: Prospects for the next glacial age

With some important provisos, it does seem that our prospects for surviving the next glacial age well, that is, with our knowledge base and genetic base reasonably intact, are quite good. In particular though, we would not want to enter the coming glacial age with a much higher human population than now, or with dwindling energy resources or with a fragile or collapsing world society. And it would be better not to become victims of major cosmic or planetary accidents.

If energy is readily available we could do much better, increasing our knowledge of humanity and the human situation and using it to build needs-meeting, resilient societies, well-equipped to adapt and evolve through the next billion years of life on earth. It is only with energy to spare over and above requirements for meeting physiological needs that communities will be able to divert people into creating and maintaining knowledge. Conversely, if a glacial age forces humans back to living in much simpler societies, we will have lost 100 000 years of opportunity to improve society's long-term survival prospects and billions of people will have been added to the roll-call of those for whom life was basically miserable.

BEYOND THE NEXT GLACIAL AGE

Here come the slow variables

Thinking about the next 100 000 years of human existence centres on if and how a complex energy-intensive global civilisation is going to survive a great winter without fossil fuels. But how does thinking about the future have to change once we make the assumption that humanity does get through the next ice age reasonably well and sees the rest of time before it? The big difference is that we now have to start taking account of vast processes of which we know relatively little and which, in human terms, are proceeding so slowly that we accept them as 'fixed' background when thinking about a mere 100 000 years or so.

What are these uncertain but all-important processes? In broad terms there are four. Humans could evolve or change themselves into some form of post-humans within as little as half a million years. The Earth could become uninhabitable within as little as a billion years. The Sun could die within as little as 5 billion years. The universe could become uninhabitable for any form of life within as little as 10 billion years. None of these might happen or, alternatively, all might happen but more slowly or more rapidly than suggested.

There are two main ways of speculating about such deep futures. One is to write science fiction stories in which, typically, humanity's descendants have personal attributes, social organisation and technologies which differ from the historical experience; and the story may or may not involve inter-action with other purposive life forms. The other is to write science-based non-fiction scenarios which construct possible futures compatible with what scientists and other scholars have hypothesised about how diverse physical, biological and social processes work. Speculation about what science's long-term agenda might be is an important part of such scenarios.

The list of famous writers who have told stories about believable and unbelievable, frightening and comforting, near and distant future societies is long and distinguished, for example, Bacon, Rabelais, Rousseau, Defoe, Swift in earlier ages and Wells, Huxley, Bradbury, Asimov, Orwell and Stapledon in our own time. Olaf Stapledon's (1930; 1966) *Last Men, First Men* is perhaps the grandest of all such stories, serving as a template for numerous succes-sors. It carries humanity's story forward through an evolutionary chain of nineteen successive species of diverse form and consciousness, ending with a problematic attempt to reach other galaxies as the death of our solar system approaches.

Stapledon saw that if you are going to think about future events on a planetary and cosmic scale, you have to think about the future of life on a comparable scale. Given that few species exist for more than a few million years, particularly mammals, this means thinking in terms of the *post-human lineage*, the succession of 'species' which might evolve from *Homo sapiens*. What might the post-human lineage be like? Will it be able to or even seek to sustain itself in the face of planetary and cosmic change? The term 'species' here is arbitrary but useful. All forms of life are continuously changing at rates modified by chance and environmental circumstances. One species may undergo rapid change while another exhibits few 'design changes' in tens of millions of years. Rapid environmental change has usually meant either extinction or rapid speciation. The point is that our descendants will change markedly and, if it is convenient, we can break the sequence of changes into species. In practice we only have enough causal understanding to talk gener-ally about the post-human lineage.

The particular power of fiction as a device for generating descriptions of future societies is that, through elaborate detail, it can convey a 'virtual' expe-rience of living in some future society and hence strong views on whether to seek or avoid such a future for one's own society. However, to the extent that it depicts societies fundamentally different from our own, it has little power to guide us in the here and now. It is for this reason that much sci-ence fiction is not highly regarded by many professional futurists. Coates

(1994) suggests that such stories have a certain cautionary value to be acknowledged when asking 'what should we be doing' but that they are usually of little direct value.

Fiction writing grades into qualitative forecasting where individuals, often inspired, have believed that they can see the future into which the forces of the present are propelling us. Notable examples are Adam Smith and Karl Marx. Smith envisaged a future of economic growth accompanied by the intellectual and moral decay of the labouring class while Marx projected a 'drama of self-destructive capitalism laying the basis for the constructive tasks of socialism' (Heilbroner 1995). Prophets like Nostradamus are somewhat different. They too believe they can see the future, but through revelation rather than an appreciation of how the future unrolls out of the present, step by causal step.

But in this chapter we are talking about futures so distant that it is hard to think of anything which could happen today, apart from a cosmic or planetary accident such as a severe volcanic winter perhaps, which would affect what happens after the next glacial in any *predictable* way. The effect will be there but not accessible. Even if the chain of cause–effect consequences of contemporary actions could be identified, such consequences would only be known probabilistically at best. At each link in the chain of consequences possible outcomes would ramify, cumulating into an effectively innumerable suite of possible post-glacial outcomes. On the scale we are talking about, a major war might equate to the butterfly wing beat which, in the right circumstances, causes a cyclone — but an unpredictable cyclone.

The other approach, this book's approach, to speculating about deep futures, namely writing science-based non-fiction scenarios, cannot produce fiction's detailed absorbing 'future histories'. But it can suggest some plausible limits or boundaries within which, with our present understanding, it would not be too surprising to see the future evolve. Equally, it can identify futures which are currently impossible in the sense that we can imagine them but not the causal steps which would generate them. Anyone who is clear about what they want the future to bring may also be able to extract an optimistic scenario and a pessimistic scenario from the sketchy realm of the 'not impossible'.

What we turn to then is:

- A short uncritical review of some major transitions which planetary and cosmic science has hypothesised for the deep future;

- A spotty collation of speculations as to how the post-human lineage might evolve and collectively organise itself over such extended timescales and in the face of major planetary and cosmic transitions.

Planetary and cosmic futures

Within the limits of our understanding of the physical processes that will shape the world and the cosmos for the rest of the effective life of the universe, a number of possibilities which are important from humanity's point of view can be foreseen, most of them unpleasant. It may be of course that our present understanding is badly astray or that our post-human descendants will find ways around the very high hurdles that it currently looks like they will have to jump.

A respite from glacials?

The Pleistocene epoch of ice ages or glacials began about 2.5 million years ago after 250 million years without an ice age. Because 250 million years is the time it takes the solar system to revolve around the centre of the galaxy, we can speculate that there is a cloudy, Sun-dimming region which the solar system encounters for several million years once every revolution. If that is so, there is a possibility that the present epoch of ice ages might be the last for another 250 million years.

Reshaping the continents

With the acceptance of the theory of *plate tectonics*, the continents are recognised to be 'crustal plates' some hundred or so kilometres thick, floating, rising and falling on slowly swirling plumes of molten rock, the Earth's mantle. For example, the tectonic plate carrying Australia is moving northwards at about the rate that fingernails grow. In about 25 million years the Australian plate will grind into Indonesia and, as a separate continent, Australia will again cease to exist. In perhaps 80 million years 'Australia' will have reached Japan. And in perhaps 100 million years all the continents will again come together in a single super-continent like Pangaea, the last super-continent. It was about 200 million years ago that Pangaea split in two and the half sailing under the name 'Gondwana' began a further splitting into Antarctica, Australia, Africa and South America. *Plus ça change …*

Science cannot model these future plate movements in any detail. We can assume though that they will be accompanied by fundamental changes in global climate patterns and, through diastrophic processes, by the formation of plateaux and mountains on a grand scale. In other words, the world in 100 million years will be unrecognisably different from our world in terms of its land–ocean configuration and its climate regimes.

No plants, no water

Under a 'permanent total drought' scenario from James Kasting (2000) of the University of Pennsylvania, the energy of the Sun (which at times has been up to 30 per cent less than it is today) will increase by about 1 per cent every 100 million years. As the oceans warm an increasing concentration of phytoplankton will absorb carbon dioxide from the atmosphere, eventually precipitating it as carbonate rocks. As the continents warm they will weather faster, increasing the rate at which silicate rocks react with and 'lock up' carbon dioxide. Consequently, in about 900 million years the level of carbon dioxide in the atmosphere will fall below the critical level for photosynthesis and the biosphere will be extinguished.

And that is not all. In about a billion years the Earth's angle of inclination to the plane of its revolution around the Sun will increase from 23 to 60 degrees causing very major climatic changes. Not only will evaporation from the oceans continue, there will also be a loss of ocean waters beneath the globe's tectonic plates. The Earth is only about 500 parts per million of water by weight and, as a result of these processes, the Earth will be a planet without surface water in about 1.2 billion years. Heavy cloud formations associated with increased evaporation from the oceans might slow, but not stop, this process.

Long days, long nights

When the proto-Moon struck Earth a glancing blow about 4 500 million years ago (Taylor 1998) and skidded back into space, it set the Earth spinning once every 3–5 hours. Day and night were created but it took another 3.5 billion years for rotation time to slow to 18 hours. Currently the Earth's day length is increasing by a second every 62 500 years. As the Earth rotates more and more slowly the Moon is spiralling away from the Earth at a rate of about 2.5 millimetres per lunar month. The Moon of our delight will be but a pinpoint of light one day.

Eventually, under the influence of the Moon's gravity and the loss of rotational energy in the form of heat generated by the friction of tidal movements, the Earth's rate of rotation will slow to one revolution per 1100 hours. Thereafter, in theory, due to some complicated effects associated with the Sun's gravitational pull, the Earth's rotation rate would increase and the Moon would start to come closer to Earth again. Ultimately, still in theory, the moon would be so racked by strong 'tides' that it would break up into a ring of small fragments orbiting the Earth. While the Earth would be too big to break up, it would, at this time be rotating once per 10 hours and inundated by massive tides sloshing back and forth every 5 hours (if there were still any oceans left to slosh about).

In practice, long before this 'Moondeath' scenario, the Sun will begin to die (see below) in, say, 7 billion years when a day would be about 55 hours long and the moon would still be retreating. The implication of all this, from a survival perspective, is that with lengthening days the extremes of both day and night temperature will increase to levels requiring a lot of adaptation.

And, at any time ...

Once we begin thinking about futures measured in millions rather than thousands of years, scenarios such as volcanic winters, asteroid strikes, geomagnetic reversal and the loss of the geomagnetic field become plausible possibilities as distinct from possibilities which would be highly surprising if they occurred in the next millennium.

The axis on which the Earth rotates shifts when there is a weight redistribution due to erosion, glaciation etc. and this in turn realigns ocean depths around the world (the equator moves and the oceans 'bulge' near the equator). In geologic time a number of such moves have changed sea levels by more than a thousand metres and it will happen again. The similar realignment of slowly flowing 'oceans' of magma beneath the Earth's crust stand to initiate major periods of volcanic activity (Strain 1997).

Volcanic winters, which have occurred many times in Earth's history, are events where particulates are ejected from active volcanoes in such quantities that the amount of sunlight reaching the Earth is much reduced for periods of years and, in principle, possibly for centuries. The main effects for humans would be reduced ambient temperatures and reduced crop production. In a worst-case version of this scenario, humans would be wiped out through starvation.

Of the near-Earth asteroids (bodies orbiting the Sun), those called the Apollos have the capacity to do us deadly damage as they are in earth-crossing orbits. There are estimated to be more than 1000 of them although only a couple approach the Everest-sized body that extinguished the dinosaurs 65 million years ago (Taylor 1998: 112). We can expect a strike from an asteroid of 8–10 kilometre diameter every 100 million years and one of 4–5 metres diameter every few months.

The asteroid which exploded above Siberia in 1908 had the energy of a thousand Hiroshima bombs. The real danger however would come from an asteroid landing in the Atlantic or Pacific oceans. Simulation models suggest that an asteroid 5 kilometres in diameter would produce a tsunami ('tidal wave') high enough to inundate coastal areas currently containing half the world's population.

The Earth is protected against most cosmic radiation by a magnetic shield formed by its iron core functioning as a large magnet. Occasionally in Earth's history, the polarity of this molten, swirling magnet has reversed rapidly and, during reversal, the shield has weakened, exposing all life to dangerous levels of radiation. Given that Earth is unlikely to cool to the point where its molten core solidifies, thereby precluding magnetic reversal, there is no reason to assume that this will never happen again.

Besides breaking up meteoric particles, the atmosphere also reduces cosmic ray effects by several orders of magnitude and solar particle effects even more. The risks from high-energy solar disturbances are perhaps less serious than previously thought. Also on the plus side, we are at a safe distance from places where rare but powerful supernovae explosions are likely to occur.

Sun death

For most of its life a star like our Sun sustains itself by burning hydrogen nuclei to produce helium and starts to die as its hydrogen fuel runs out and the fusion of helium into heavier elements becomes more important. In our Sun, which is already 4600 million years old, this conversion, at the rate of 150 000 tonnes of hydrogen a second, could continue for perhaps another 5–7 billion years before the Sun swells up fifty-fold to become a 'red giant' star, incinerating the inner planets before collapsing into a 'white dwarf' star and, ultimately, into a burnt out 'black dwarf'. Depending on the rate at which the Sun loses mass and hence gravitational pull, the inner planets could survive, but as 'dead' planets, because they will retreat into larger orbits. For a preview of the 'red giant' phase, take a look at Betelgeuse in the Orion constellation.

An uninhabitable universe

It is not easy to understand and condense sophisticated debates about the ultimate future of the universe to a few paragraphs. All scenarios for the end of the universe are highly speculative. I have found Taylor (1998), Hawking (1988), Davies (1983) and Heidmann (1989) all helpful. The continuation of any form of life which requires a more or less regular passing of energy through matter would, however, appear to be inconsistent with either of two contending theories: that the universe might continue expanding and cooling till the same deadly cold temperature (the 'big chill') prevails everywhere; or that the universe might eventually stop expanding and collapse in on itself in a 'big crunch' (an all-engulfing black hole) to form a 'cosmic egg' in which even sub-atomic particles get melted down. Similarly, under the 'forever expanding' theory, matter (nucleons) would disintegrate eventually into energy (photons) (Heidmann 1989). The idea of a universe which oscillates back and forth for eternity (Wheeler 1977: 3–33) in a sequence of big bangs and big crunches is out of favour.

Current thinking is leaning towards the suggestion that the universe was expanding (meaning well-separated galaxies moving further apart) at a decelerating rate till 5 billion years ago (implying an eventual long-term collapse), but is now expanding at an accelerating rate and will continue to do so. Just when the universe becomes uninhabitable will depend on the form in which life exists as well as on the physical conditions at the time, but it could well be more than 15 billion years. Figures of the order of 100 trillion years have even been suggested (Dyson 1979). Along the way, our galaxy will become a graveyard of dead stars and black holes — and even the black holes will eventually decay. Atoms themselves may have a finite lifespan, in which case 'life' could only survive as magnetic fields and electric currents! All will be dark except for rare flashes of light from the populous galactic centre as dwarfs collide.

This then is the speculative physical background against which further speculation about the future of our descendants needs to be tested for compatibility. In light of this planetary and cosmic scenario, how long and how well will they survive?

Late-human and post-human history

Extinction is the norm

The fate of most biological species that have ever lived has been extinction. When a species' environment changes it either adapts and slowly evolves into something different or it dies out. A few environments — like that of the saltwater crocodile, cousin to the dinosaurs — have remained relatively constant over millions of years and allowed the inhabitants thereof to survive unchanged. The probable duration of an 'average' species may be between a half and five million years; and we have no reason to believe from the fossil records that recent mammals, including humans, have a life expectancy of more than a few million years. Humanity may now be in its second million years and, with very good luck, may survive another one or two million. One phlegmatic view of that brevity is captured in the frontispiece quotation from taxonomist Albert Smith (1969).

Indeed, more than 17 distinct human species have walked the earth at different times but only ours remains. In Africa *Homo habilis* coexisted with and eventually replaced gracile *Australopithecus*. Later *Homo erectus* coexisted with and eventually replaced *Homo habilis* In Java modern humans coexisted with and eventually replaced *Homo erectus* (Wills 1998).

Okay, but what could happen?

What is of interest for present purposes is not how long *Homo sapiens sapiens* (modern thinking man) lasts but whether and for how long the line of descent from humans through various species of post-humans (called anagenesis) continues. What form of post-humans could we evolve into, or evolve ourselves into, species after species, before the line dies out?

For example, there is plenty of time before, say, the possible onset of permanent total drought in about a billion years for our lineage to evolve, if environmental conditions were right, into a flying, burrowing, arboreal or marine animal. Or indeed speciate into all of these, as the original Australian marsupials did. But why would we? What plausible environmental shifts might induce any such quantum adaptations? Our past evolutionary success has rested on being functionally unspecialised, relying on intelligence and its products to exploit diverse niches. If necessary, we can use our prostheses to 'fly', 'burrow' and 'swim' without being locked in genetically to such behaviours. Prostheses are 'exosomatic instruments' produced by humans but not belonging to the human body.

We are far more likely to evolve by losing adaptations which were useful in hunter–gatherer societies (for example, strong jaws) but not in complex big-city societies where individual roles are highly specialised. Conversely, if future human environments continue to be highly urbanised, the genes of people who are successful at living in such environments (dextrous, placid and quick learners?) will be favoured and increase as a proportion of the human gene pool; as will be the genes of people with the ability to avoid unhealthy lifestyles.

But there is nothing inevitable about a permanently urbanised future. For example, after the next glacial age humanity might equally well comprise 800 million people living in a dispersed network of high-technology villages, each collecting solar power locally and living more-or-less self-sufficiently. Such a method of social organisation might even facilitate a balancing of humanity's inbreeding and outbreeding tendencies, just as clans did in tribal times and social stratification did in cities until the 19th century. While it is widely accepted that some degree of outbreeding is beneficial, the underlying mechanism, robustness of the immune system perhaps, is not fully understood (Alexander 1979: 195). It is the balance between inbreeding and outbreeding which determines the balance between conforming and creative/dysfunctional individuals in a society according to Darlington (1969). Even under a village-based social organisation, speciation would seem unlikely, given the small levels of gene flow between sub-populations required to ensure the maintenance of a single breeding population.

A cautionary note needs to be introduced here. There are two sorts of genes — *structural genes* which contain instructions for synthesising various proteins and *regulatory genes* which control *epigenesis*, the timing and type of cellular differentiation that occurs in an embryo or immature animal (Schwartz 1999). There is evidence that major changes of the sort accompanying speciation can rapidly follow the mutation and subsequent spread of one or several regulatory genes. Whether such *punctuated speciation* as distinct from *gradual speciation* based on mutation and selection of structural genes could only be successful if there is a vacant ecological niche to be filled is another open question. In the pre-human genus *Australopithecus*, a mutation in the genes regulating the time at which the brain stops growing may have opened the way for the emergence of the big-brained genus *Homo*. Rapid, unpredictable speciation of humans into a lineage of post-humans, largely through epigenetic evolution, has to be accepted as a plausible possibility.

Looking well ahead then, what are the possibilities for truly fundamental change in the post-human lineage relative to modern humans? Could there ever again be something as transforming as the evolution of language? Or walking upright? Or the invention of agriculture? Or the emergence of consciousness? Three candidate areas where one might look for the possibility of major change are in the reproduction process, in socio-cultural organisation and in the nature of the (post)human mind.

Post-human reproduction

Staying with DNA

As long as our descendants continue to die, some form of reproduction in which each generation's members produces approximate replicas of themselves will be necessary if the lineage itself is not to die out. But could the individual genome become structurally different, with or without the help of our descendants, from what it is today — twenty-three pairs of chromosomes collectively bearing 30 000 or so genes, each in the form of two alleles (versions), one from each parent?

For example, could humans evolve into a parthenogenetic species where there are no males and females produce offspring genetically identical to themselves, that is, *clones* of themselves? There would seem to be no evolutionary advantage to such a development and some disadvantages. In particular, sexual reproduction is an effective way of generating genetic variability in a population and, with it, a capacity to adapt to environmental change. This capacity would be lost in a parthenogenetic species. Another point is that reproducing sexually is effective in inhibiting the spread of certain parasitic diseases. In any case, parthenogenesis is not possible in mammals where, unlike insects, normal development of the embryo requires the presence of both a maternal and a paternal set of chromosomes.

Perhaps the Y chromosome, which only males have, will continue, as it has, to get simpler and simpler over time, carrying less and less genetic information. Ultimately, as in reptiles, the maleness of a developing embryo might be determined by the environment in which it is developing (for example, ambient temperature) rather than the presence or absence of particular genes. More probably, in perhaps 10 million years, when the Y chromosome has disappeared, the sex-determining gene(s) will be found on other chromosomes. If this happens in different sub-populations it could lead to different species of hominids.

Rather than getting simpler, could the human genome become more complex in time? The human lineage has probably acquired additional genes over evolutionary time, perhaps through the incorporation of viral and bacterial genetic material. Deliberately, or through natural processes, further such additions are not inconceivable, leading perhaps to the enhancement of traits such as (for example) the capacity to tolerate environmental extremes or to resist certain diseases. Beyond the incorporation of genes from other species lies the possibility of constructing totally new genes and chromosomes; or of inducing mutations specifically designed to achieve particular effects. Doing this sort of thing successfully would require an understanding of molecular biology orders of magnitude beyond current knowledge.

However, there may be intrinsic limits to genetic complexity. Copying more than 5000 million nucleotides (the 'letters' of the 'alphabet' in which the protein-making instructions of the genetic code are written) during each cell division, a number which is only about twice the number found in the human genome — even using 'proofreading' techniques based on the enzyme exonuclease — transmits an unacceptable number of errors (mutations) (Jantsch 1980: 194).

In fact, in these, the early days of molecular biology, there do not seem to be any obviously useful ways in which, at the level of cellular processes, our DNA-based method of reproduction and evolution might be improved, either by natural or artificial means. Not while we remain animals anyway. DNA is a remarkably efficient way of transmitting basic information between generations; changing a single nucleotide changes the information transmitted. Epigenetic evolution and Darwinian natural selection together suggest that humans have an enormous capacity to evolve biologically without having to change the way the human genome functions and is constructed.

Assuming 30 000 genes each with two variant alleles means that, in principle, three raised to the power of 30 000 genetic combinations are possible.
Most of these will never be used.

Our descendants might well decide that guiding the lineage's genetic
evolution is a less effective and flexible way of adapting to and modifying an
evolving environment than guiding the lineage's socio-cultural evolution. Or,
more probably, they will see the challenge as one of seeking an explicit balance between slower genetic responses to long-term change and faster cultural guidance of short-term change.

Could we evolve into robots?

Life on Earth owes its existence to the properties of water and carbon, and to
the fact that both of these are abundant. Carbon forms a staggering variety of
compounds of great stability. It also lends itself to forming compounds that
are more weakly bonded (less stable), and it enters into multiple bonds. These
double- and triple-bonded molecules, among other useful properties, absorb
photons of ultraviolet light which have just enough (and not too much) energy to break many types of carbon bonds and allow complex reactions among
the resulting molecular fragments. This process leads on to the synthesis of a
diverse variety of more complex molecules. Water, at terrestrial temperatures,
is one of few available liquid mediums within which such reactions can take
place at reasonable speed.

Could life evolve to be other than carbon- and water-based? At lower
temperatures ammonia or hydrogen cyanide could serve as a liquid medium.
Silicon-silicon bonds look more promising than carbon bonds, in terms of
reaction times for making structures at lower temperatures. Nevertheless, sili-
con compounds seem to have limited potential for life-like processes in both
high- and low-temperature worlds; they do not form double bonds. Silicon-
oxygen bonds are slightly more stable than carbon-carbon bonds, but they
tend to produce molecules like the silicates, which are crystals of the same unit
repeated over and over again, rather than the molecules with the aperiodic side
chains which signify a potential to carry high quantities of information.

Notwithstanding, will we remain carbon-water animals with a DNA-
based method of reproduction? Could we evolve into *robots*, machines made
of inorganic materials which simulate (post)human behaviour? Or into
androids, robots made of flesh and bone? Or into *cyborgs*, dahlek-like creatures
that are part-robot and part-biological life form? Moravec (1999) describes
how rapidly robots with human and supra-human capacities, physical and
'mental', are being developed. Progress is a function of computing speed and
memory and, as these increase, the evolution of nervous systems from insects

to humans is being recapitulated. In principle, future robots would be able to run complex societies unaided (and as 'zombies' without consciousness). They will presently be designed to be self-replicating, and to evolve in physical capacities and artificial intelligence by a form of natural selection — sometimes called exosomatic (out of body) evolution. As such they would qualify as 'synthetic life', at least in environments compatible with their replicating capabilities. Given the efficiency of DNA at encoding and manipulating information, computers may be DNA-based for a period in the future. This not only suggests a possible technology for robotic 'natural selection', it raises the idea of some form of DNA interchange between post-humans and 'biocomputers' or androidal robots.

But the answer is no. Carbon-based life will not evolve into non-biological synthetic life. That is, no one has been able to think of a plausible set of steps whereby mutation and selection might convert, over many generations, a nerve synapse into a transistor, or an eye into a video camera etc. More subtly, could human germ plasm be modified to carry *nanobots*, very small constructor robots, capable of being turned on and off by regulator genes and making synthetic organs, molecule by molecule, from non-biological materials such as composites and plastics? This is conceivable and is a description of a true cyborg, as distinct from a scenario where non-biological prostheses (for example, strong limbs, artificial brains) and the organs they are supplementing evolve together (co-evolve) but do not reproduce together. For example, there is some evidence that human brains have shrunk a little since the advent of 'off-line' memory. Conversely, evolution of human intelligence could possibly speed up when computers overtake humans in information processing capabilities. Such co-evolution would be no different in principle from the discovery of cooking leading to the evolution of smaller human jaws.

Moravec (1999), and others before him, dismiss the possibility of advanced robots competing with and wiping out humans. Precluding that scenario requires only that robots be programmed to always obey humans. Perhaps it is not that simple. Especially if humans cannot understand how future generations of robots are processing information to make decisions. So, what might be the role of humans in a society where most work and decision-making is being done by robots? Would humans be something like pampered pets? Or, at the other extreme, would humans work collaboratively and symbiotically with synthetic life forms on the ultimate challenge of acquiring the knowledge to take the lineage through such tests as total permanent drought on planet Earth?

Immortality and all that

The role of death, evolutionarily speaking, is to allow a lineage to adapt to its environmental niche, or, more broadly, to allow a lineage and its niche to co-evolve. That is, each new generation has a non-zero probability of being a little fitter, a little more likely to reproduce itself than the last. If a species' generation time is long it can, at best, only adapt slowly. The more rapidly the niche is changing, the more important it is to turn generations over quickly if the species is not to become maladapted to the point of extinction. Alternatively, at least in the case of humans and post-humans, social and cultural adaptation can replace genetic adaptation to a greater or lesser extent, for example, dietary rules can supplement genetic selection for resistance to food-borne pathogens.

It may become accepted in time then that genetic evolution has a much smaller role to play in a society's adapting to changing circumstance than social and cultural evolution. If so, the lineage will be freed to actively pursue individual immortality or, more accurately, longevity. For example, sperm and eggs could be stored till their donors 'proved' their capacity to live beyond their reproductive years, and then used (although it might be simpler to just encourage breeding among people with long-lived parents).

Other more interventionist possibilities include various sorts of genomic manipulation (for example, of mitochondrial 'longevity' genes), hormone 'rejuvenation' treatments, replacing failing organs with animal organs, with organs cloned from stem cells or with prostheses. Nanoscale constructor robots might be placed in the body with the task of rebuilding failing organs *in situ*. Retaining quality of life would presumably be as important a goal of such technologies as increasing life span. Question: if a failing brain can be replaced with an electronic equivalent, should it with the brain of the person as they were at 20? 30? 40?

Just as longevity is an impediment to genetic evolution, it stands to be an impediment to socio-cultural evolution. Sociologists recognise that an accustomed way of behaving persists as long as circumstances allow. Humans acquire habits, attitudes and behavioural patterns in early adulthood which tend to remain with them for life. A paradigm shift in a society's thinking even now requires a generational change. A society where many people are some hundreds of years old could be a very conservative, maladapted society in the absence of social technologies for reprogramming and re-educating the aged. Assuming a stable population, it would also be a society with a small proportion of children. There may be other unexpected problems with longevity such as a failure in the 'will to live' after a certain age.

Perhaps 'cybernetic immortality' involving the survival of the individual's mental organisation in a computer will be the way out (Joslyn et al. 1997). The physically dead could still be consulted and, indeed, allowed to develop mentally by being appropriately briefed.

Clearly longevity is not an unalloyed good. In the deep future its pursuit is likely to be traded off against other evolving individual and social needs in ways we can only dimly apprehend.

The post-human mind

What we start with

The mind is what the brain does (Pinker 1997: 21) and what the brain does is process information. It is, as Stafford Beer says, 'a slightly alkaline three pound electro-chemical computer running on glucose at 25 watts'. Humans have a triune or 'three-in-one' brain, each doing its own job with some degree of independence, even competitiveness, and each taking control of behaviour as circumstances dictate. The brain stem or primitive 'reptilian' brain (hindbrain) acts reflexively, without thought, controls bodily functions and, when threats appear, the 'fight or flight' response. The limbic or early mammalian midbrain is the source of emotional responses; it has a capacity for visual memory and a very limited language capacity (yells, screams, expletives). The neocortex or late-mammalian forebrain is a greatly enlarged version of the olfactory analysis centre which was so important to our shrew-like ancestors. Over time its function has changed from smelling to thinking.

The neocortex is further divided, physically and functionally, into a cerebral left-brain and a cerebral right brain. The left brain is in control when we are thinking in an analytical, mathematical, technological or problem-solving mode. It swings into action when a considered response to an emotional trigger is called for. The right brain is in control when we are thinking in an imaginative, synthesising, artistic, conceptual or holistic mode (holism is the recognition and study of emergent properties). The limbic brain is similarly divided into left and right halves. The limbic left-brain is in control when we are organising, planning, or controlling events. The limbic right brain is in control when we are immersed in interpersonal, emotional, musical or spiritual experience.

Behaviour (directed action) that occurs without thought and which follows tacit, innate (inherited) behaviour rules is *instinctual behaviour*. A behavioural rule is one or more instructions of the form 'If the environment is like X, then behave like Y'. What we call instincts are the particular things animals tend to do in particular settings. Instinctual behaviour can be contrasted with *learned behaviour.* Learned behaviour follows rules *acquired* as a result of individual experience. New behaviour rules can be acquired in basically two ways. One, called *programmed learning* or *inculcated behaviour* or *socialisation*, is a process of imitating other people or of being conditioned by (emotional) rewards and punishments to respond to particular stimuli. It provides cultural behaviour rules such as traditions and customs for recurrent situations. The other, variously called *creative learning* or *reasoning* or *problem-solving*, produces new behaviour rules specifically for responding to novel situations, often through a trial and error process or the mental simulation of such. It is sometimes useful to divide creative learning into *generative learning* — changing the mental model being used — and *adaptive learning* — changing behaviour to cope with changes in the external world.

Problem-solving behaviour, managed from the cerebral left-brain, commonly involves conscious thought and relies on information from memory to build and (so consciousness thinks) choose among mental models (scenarios) of alternative behaviour possibilities. More correctly, the act of choice is not conscious, only the setting up of the choice problem and the response to a choice once made. The important point is that making decisions within an analogue of the real world has many advantages over real-world trial and error.

The left brain's reasoning capabilities started to evolve away from what we recognise today as the right brain's instincts and culturally 'fixed' behaviour rules as recently as, perhaps, 3–4000 years ago (Jaynes 1976: chapters 4–5; Wilson 1980: 117). Since then, self-conscious choice, apparent or real, rather than 'authoritative voices in the head', has increasingly functioned as the rationalisation of behaviour. What has evolved includes the capacity to build mental models of the external world which include the model-maker, seeing oneself as if from the outside. Along with being able to remember one's previous thoughts, this is a large part of what is meant by consciousness of self.

Until that advance, discoveries (for example, the wheel, the plough, fire) were deductions from general principles observed in nature. But development of the cerebral left-brain initiated our powerful capacity to use inductive reasoning, that is, generalising from particular events, to create knowledge. Storing information externally (for example, following the invention of language and writing) further increased the species' problem-solving capabilities.

Strange as it may seem, the adaptive value of consciousness is not at all obvious. It is not inconceivable that consciousness is an epiphenomenon with no functional value, like the roar of a jet engine (Harnad 1982)! Csikszentmihalyi (1993: 34) uses the fact that the mind experiences an unpleasant chaotic disorder when not engaged in some goal-directed activity to conclude that consciousness is an important safety feature that keeps us doing the things needed to survive, including, most importantly, prioritisation of those activities. Or, since we only remember things we have been conscious of, is consciousness a way of tagging things worth remembering?

Looking forward

The physical brain and what the brain does in terms of generating and processing information appear to have co-evolved and might be assumed to continue doing so. Our opening question then is whether the natural brain, through genetic evolution, individual learning, acculturation or self-organising behaviour in collaboration with other brains is going to think in a markedly different way as we move through hundreds and thousands of millennia to come? Certainly a number of changes have been foreseen in terms of what the different parts of the brain will do, in how well they will do it and in how well different brain parts will coordinate. As Jaynes (1976: 36) says, 'the function of brain tissue is not inevitable, and ... perhaps different organisations, given different developmental programs, may be possible'.

For example, might reasoned behaviour based on knowledge from past learning and a capacity for problem solving increasingly replace instinctual behaviour? Or, putting this another way, will we learn or evolve to better suppress instinctual behaviours which are readily accessible to modern people but which we judge to be maladaptive in a post-Neolithic world? Eating salt for example. Will we evolve or learn the discipline that allows us to stop short of damaging indulgences, given that religion and tradition no longer provide that discipline? Will we learn to use reasoning to turn over cultural behaviour rules at a rate which balances the virtues of stability (social cohesion, ease of communication) with the virtues of innovation? Will we learn to routinely detect the ego's protective distortions of reality? Some certainly think we are at a transition point on a path between behaviour being controlled by reason and being controlled by instinct and culturally fixed behaviour (Darlington 1969: 62; Csikszentmihalyi 1993).

Reason, culture's rules and instinct are all 'mind tools'. Through much trial and error, instinctual behaviour evolved as if to guide behaviour in routine situations relevant to primate survival — mating, hunting, territoriality etc. Cultural behavioural rules evolved as if to guide decisions in more complex but still slow-changing societies. Reason evolved as if to conceptualise, evaluate and choose between alternative behaviours in non-routine situations, for example, undertaking forced migration. Reason requires dedicated neural networks, is metabolically expensive and is prone to various operating weaknesses such as a poor capacity to estimate and combine probabilities or to factor in longer-term consequences. Freud and Marx both debunked reason in their different ways. Freud saw it as rationalising the satisfying of suppressed desires while Marx saw it as rationalising class interest. Postmodernism revives the perennial view that only experience, not reason, can produce knowledge.

It is early days yet for the 'big brain' experiment and reasoning will probably continue to improve over millennia as a decision-making tool, through both learning and genetic evolution. While a place for 'low-cost' instinctual behaviour is likely to remain, one can imagine people having a much clearer awareness of how 'head' and 'heart' appetencies can both be present and indeed in conflict; and how they can best be reconciled.

Consciousness, so new in evolutionary terms, was only made possible, perhaps, by the prior development of words for describing psychological states as distinct from external happenings (Jaynes 1976). Even now it is little more than a thin inaccurate story of what we did and why, overlain on a vast amount of unconscious processing. The question is, what might it evolve into in the deep future? For example, might we learn how to experience, at will, a state of heightened awareness of ourselves and our surroundings, what Wilson (1984) calls 'perceiving reality directly'? I am thinking of something like Maslow's (1954) 'occasional peak experiences' in which people have moments of intense happiness as they apprehend their life-situation and pay attention to the world around them.

Or, looking inwards rather than outwards, could we become more mystical? Mystical experiences, what Huxley (Wilson 1984: 24) called 'mind-at-large', are most readily understood as recapitulations of the stage in human evolution which preceded rational thought (giving reasons for choices) and individual consciousness, of times before there were egos. In other words, the world as experienced through the mind of an early hominid. More prosaically, control by the neocortex is being suppressed in favour of the limbic brain. Achieving widespread access to the mystical state has been foreseen as a basis for universal empathy with others, to foster a sense of oneness with the world and as a foundation for the religious dimension of a universal culture (Parker 1973).

More generally, might we learn how to consciously and routinely access the right brain's activities (the subconscious mind) or even the brain stem's autonomic activities (for example, as it regulates blood pressure)? There is evidence that yogic and meditative techniques can show the way here, not to mention psychoanalysis and psychotropic drugs such as mescalin. Carl Jung mastered the ability to dream while awake (not quite like daydreams), what he called *active imagination*, as a means of accessing the unconscious activities of his right brain (Wilson 1984: 76) and of working towards optimal collaboration and understanding between his left brain and right brain 'selves'. While consciousness is a mystery we do not yet know how to think about, it may help here to remember that it is always consciousness *of something*, from a pinprick to what is occurring in the right brain.

At a practical level, a capacity to manipulate as well as access right-brain activity would be useful for such tasks as damping down the body's stress responses when neither flight nor fight is possible (Selye's 1978 general adaptation syndrome); and for inducing the anti-stress *relaxation response* (Goleman and Gurin 1995). Psychosomatic diseases which we might eventually learn to manage by psychological methods include arthritis, asthma, some gastrointestinal problems and, perhaps, some cancers. Psychological control of the immune system is a possibility. For example, particular sorts of brain activity affect the white blood cell count. A related evolutionary inheritance which is also potentially manageable is that, under stress, mature adults regress to an instinctual infantile selfishness (Stove 1995: 114). Just being able to track the transfer of behavioural control from one part of the brain to another would be of value and a step towards Hegel's (1807; 1971) 'culmination of history', namely, mind having full knowledge of itself.

There are various other presumed improvements that have been foreseen. Alan Snyder (1999) has suggested that, in time, everyone might learn to release powers such as *idiot savants* display, for example, drawing like da Vinci, composing like Bach and performing amazing mental calculations. Others foresee that we will learn how to massively improve both short-term and long-term memory, without producing information overload (Broad 1925, chapter 5). In fact, it is commonly believed that humans use only a small fraction of the brain's information-processing capacity and that harnessing such more fully might accelerate both biological and socio-cultural evolution, although not necessarily in expected directions (Wills 1998: 229).

Consonant with the idea of the 'underused brain', William Calvin (1997), a neurophysiologist, has foreseen the possibility of retraining alternative cortical areas to replace lost functions and to break up obsessions and hallucinations. Nonetheless, competition for cortical 'territory' is a well-established principle. Thus if nerves serving a certain function develop early in a particular part of the cortex, then nerves which serve other functions may be inhibited from developing in that same area. This leads to the idea of *cognitive trade-offs* in which training up certain skills can lead to a loss of other skills (Donald 1991). Could one implication of this for the future be that people are trained to be specialist thinkers in certain areas, knowing that this may reduce their capacities in other areas?

At the heart of problem-solving capabilities lies *intelligence* which, in general terms, is the capacity to perceive relationships between things. We may learn how to train this capacity more fully or we may develop psycho-pharmacological drugs which enhance general or specific intelligences. Under either approach there will be some selection pressure favouring those who learn well or who respond well to 'smart pills'.

Learning to perceive relationships between things which are widely separated in space or time has not come easily to the human lineage. Hunter–gatherers relied on instinct to cope with seasonal change and variation. The peasant and the herder learned to look ahead a whole year and, eventually understood the 18-year lunar cycle. But looking ahead for several human generations has generally proved too much for our newly developed rational faculties; the part of the brain which controls impulsivity is still developing. Or, perhaps we do have some such capacity but choose not to exercise it? Or, perhaps in an uncertain world it is entirely rational to heavily discount the foreseeable future? If there do not appear to be any net survival or welfare benefits from further extending human planning horizons, long-term planning will not be pursued by our descendants any more actively than we do.

Learning to think in terms of networks of causation (you can't do just one thing) rather than chains of cause and effect has proved similarly difficult. Early humans learned to deal with problems on an ad hoc basis and the need to see a problem embedded in the context of other problems rarely arose. We still find it difficult to believe that solving a problem generates other problems, not to mention new selection pressures.

Even from this short survey, it is clear that the scope of what has been foreseen in terms of possible new and augmented ways in which individual human minds might function in the distant future is enormous. And that is without including speculations about humans having paranormal powers which they may further develop in time, for example, telepathy, precognition, psychokinesis. The emphasis above has been on individual minds. The next section brings together some speculations on how minds in the distant future might interact and function collectively.

Global brain

Information exchanges between members of primate social groups are carried out in many ways, including audio-visual and chemical (for example, pheromone) signals, genetic material and, for humans only, language and writing. Most recently, the communications revolution of the 20th century, based on the transmission and reception of electromagnetic impulses, massively expanded the capacity of individuals everywhere to exchange information directly with each other. Also, computer-based communication networks, like books before them, have allowed individuals to access voluminous stored information. It would be unsurprising if the efficiency of what is now a global-scale communication–information network were to continue improving in terms of numbers connected, speed, ease of access etc. For example, within a matter of decades, we will probably be able to tie our brains directly into vast computer databases without using voice-recognition or keyboards (Wills 1998). Already, simple nerve impulses can be transmitted from person to person and person to computer via the Internet. Reality is truly overtaking Marshall McLuhan's metaphor of the 'extended nervous system'!

But is there something other than better communications and better-informed behaviour implied by the prospect of this widely accessible *Globalnet* of bigger, faster computers? For instance, might Globalnet become the infrastructure for a *Noosphere,* the name given by French Jesuit and palaeontologist Pierre Teilhard de Chardin (1959; 1964), to 'an envelope of thinking' which he saw as eventually spreading across the globe, just like the biosphere from which it would emerge? Both Teilhard and Peter Russell (1982), with his concept of a *global brain,* are talking about more than improvements in information storage and transfer around the world. They are foreseeing the possibility of a group or collective mind emerging in which individual minds act as 'neurones' in processes analogous to individual consciousness, reasoning and learning.

For example, somewhat similar conscious thoughts might pass in a wave from individual to individual in some region of the collective mind. Or individual brains might work in parallel on the one decision-making problem. Or relationships and patterns newly perceived by one individual might then be perceived more readily by other individuals. In the extreme, a single global consciousness might replace all individual consciousness processes.

It is a small step from here to imagining a role for artificial intelligences in the global brain. A partnership perhaps between networks of super-intelligent and capacious information-processing computers and a network of inter-human communications? At present we rely on subconscious processing to reveal behavioural options and choose between them. Perhaps it will seem little different to be instantaneously connected to and prompted by 'intelligent agent' software when faced with a decision problem.

While the global-brain scenario is highly speculative and offered here without plausible process-level mechanisms, it gains a touch of support from what is understood about the evolution of complexity. Jacob Bronowski (1973) explains:

> Nature works by steps. The atoms form mole-
> cules, the molecules form bases, the bases direct
> the formation of amino acids, the amino acids
> form proteins, and proteins work in cells. The
> cells make up first of all the simple animals, and
> then the sophisticated ones, climbing step by
> step. *The stable units that compose one level or
> stratum are the raw material for random
> encounters which produce higher configura-
> tions, some of which will chance to be stable* ...
> Evolution is the climbing of a ladder from sim-
> ple to complex by steps, each of which is stable
> in itself. The tumult of random combinations
> occasionally produces a new form of organiza-
> tion. [my emphasis]

This tendency towards complexity could be disrupted at any time but, if it is not, and provided that a large number of stable (persistent) units — human and artificial intelligences in this case — are interacting, not too much and not too little, the preconditions for the emergence of new stable units — a collective mind in this case — have been met. However, complexity theory offers no way of predicting whether something new and stable will actually emerge. Nor can theory predict any properties of such an emergent collective mind. All that complexity theory can say is that whenever independent *holons* (see page 174) do come to together to form 'super holons' with novel behaviours, the component holons will lose some of their former behavioural flexibility. So, if some form of global brain were to emerge from Globalnet, it would imply that participating individuals were judging that their gains in terms of access to information and information-processing capacity outweighed any loss of mental independence. As a tantalising suggestion, a global brain might tend to have thoughts comparing the choices confronting large groups, even global society, rather than thoughts about individual choices.

Such a collective mind would not be exactly new. As Gustave Le Bon (1947: 18) points out, crowds can behave like 'evolutionarily prior organisms'. A collective mind can be temporarily formed with all taking the same direction, often under the influence of a leader. The worrying thing with crowds is that the more intolerant and dictatorial the leader, the more people are willing to stop thinking and taking responsibility (Jaynes 1976, Chapter 3). A collective mind emerging from Globalnet could be maladaptive just as well as it could be beneficial to the lineage.

Post-human society

What we start with

Our history as social animals began 130 million years ago when insect-eating shrew-like mammals took up an arboreal lifestyle and began living in groups for mutual assistance, protection and food finding, activities which all strengthened band cohesion and led to forms of social organisation that eventually gave rise to human culture. These early developments importantly included some notion of hierarchy or dominance ranking among group members, a fight-flight repertoire and pairing between males and females. I like Pattee's (1969) definition of a hierarchy as a descending arrangement of constraints.

In general, all species of social animals divide into separated groups where individuals in a group are friendly to a degree among themselves and hostile to other groups and individuals. Aggression (behaviour intended to threaten or inflict physical injury on another) between groups of the same species appears to have evolved as a means of protecting each group's social stability and its territory, or, more generally, of maintaining a system of territories among multiple groups. The organisation of groups into more-or-less stable territories is an efficient way, for much of the time, of distributing and exploiting a region's food resources. A group defending its core territory almost always succeeds in repelling an attacking group. In primitive human societies aggression is channelled and limited by customs rules, taboos etc. It is further limited by the weapons available.

Within tribal groups or bands of humans (the simplest group structures), behaviour is further regulated by rules of co-operative conduct (for example, gift exchange) which are partly instinctual and partly learned. Co-operation is best thought of as a strategy for amplifying the benefits of what can be achieved by individuals acting alone. Pooling of muscle-power, food, memory and artifacts are examples relevant to a tribal society. If it is to survive, co-operation has to be monitored to ensure that its dividends are fairly distributed. Co-operation based on direct reciprocity (immediate mutual aid) presumably evolved at some stage into a memory-dependent system of indirect reciprocity where co-operative behaviour could be legitimately rewarded at a later time and by people who had not benefited directly from the initial altruism. Indirect reciprocity is clearly an efficient rationale for co-operation but how it could have evolved through natural selection is a matter of some debate.

The role of aggression and hostility *within* the group lies mainly in the establishment of hierarchical standings and in the protection of the male–female pairing relationship, behaviours which can both be argued to have adaptive value. Having a leader is the extent of hierarchical organisation in tribal groups. A group with a courageous, skilled and aggressive leader stands to multiply and gain the security of greater numbers and a larger territory at the expense of other groups. Conversely, the efficiency of hunting and gathering for producing food declines beyond a certain group size. Tribal groups therefore tend to have upper and lower limits on their size and much of our species' social behaviour is adapted to living in groups of, say, less than a hundred where all are known to each other.

The important conclusion emerging here is that a code of co-operative behaviour and a code of competitive behaviour are the twin foundations of tribal and inter-tribal social organisation. The further genetic role of these codes has been in maintaining the system of small isolated groups which has been an ideal setting for rapid biological evolution. Both of these codes are elaborately adapted to the hunting and gathering mode of food production which hominids have followed for 99 per cent of their history. But in the Holocene era, that is, the last 12 000 years, starting with a switch in the mode of food production to herding and cropping, these deeply ingrained, largely unconscious, behaviour codes — probably what most people mean by 'human nature' — were increasingly required to guide behaviour in circumstances under which they had not evolved.

But despite being faced with this need to adapt, the social instincts — the instinctual components of humanity's social-behaviour code (including both competitive and co-operative instincts) — have changed little in 12 000 years. Conversely, the learned or cultural parts of that code have changed massively, co-evolving with changing consciousness, changing modes of production and the invention of diverse social and material technologies — cities, feudalism, nation states, social classes, war, religions, mechanisation, industrialism and science, to name a few. Consider these four enormous changes in postglacial social behaviour/organisation:

1   *The decline of traditional and customary behaviour and the rise of*
    individualism
        It was the success in the Aegean civilisation of problem-solving based on individual rational choice which began the loosening of religion's constraints on individual behaviour, a trend which continues to this day in modernising societies (see page 153). Recent expressions of individualism in modern societies include the rise of political libertarianism and religious 'new ageism'.

2   *The rise of coercive leadership*
        Eisler (1998: 205) suggests there was a big switch in the early Holocene (post ice-age) from a collaborative or partnership model of social organisation to a coercive or dominator model of social

organisation. Among other factors here, agricultural surpluses allowed standing armies to be maintained. In hunter–gatherer societies, leaders tended to be people of influence rather than authority. Like Australian Aborigines today, people decided collectively what to do rather than being told what to do. But for most of pre-history and history, most societies have been led by self-interested callous bullies capable of destroying whatever delicate social organisation is in place, for example, feudal societies, absolute monarchies. It is only recently with the rise of democratic states that the pendulum has begun to swing back towards collectivism, notwithstanding the modern democratic state's near-monopoly of coercive power to control instinctive 'anti-social' behaviour when conditioning fails.

Somewhat surprisingly, even thousands of years after the spread of higher consciousness, groups of all sizes have been very willing to accept aggressive leadership. This tractability or indoctrinability, this apparent need for authority figures, does not appear to be declining in modern societies, but it may be that elites are simply improving their capacity to manufacture an orthodoxy (dominant discourse) which does not allow threatening new ideas through.

3   *The decline of tribalism and the rise of nationalism and planetism*

Hunter–gatherers had both an instinctive and a culturally reinforced appetency to participate in tribal activities, including social rituals and confronting other tribes. As the economically optimal size of a social unit increased with improvements in communications, transport and agricultural technology, people learned to adapt their need to belong socially to larger and larger social units. While loyal membership of the nation state, that is, nationalism, is readily inculcated into most people, especially as tribes lose their distinctive identities within nations, there remains an instinctive need to also belong to smaller, more tribe-sized groups of people one recognises — communities, classes, interest groups etc. Nationalism began replacing religion as people's primary loyalty from the close of the Middle Ages.

Conversely, as the world's separate societies have moved at an increasing rate towards functioning as a single society (globalisation), a small but increasing number of people have found their primary loyalty to be towards the whole human family rather than the tribe or nation. This is planetism (see page 52) and is potentially of enormous importance for the persistence of the lineage.

4   *Changing roles of the sexes*

The privileged elites in most (arguably, all) Holocene societies have been men, and the women they have owned have shared in that privilege. Most women have been restricted to caring roles, menial roles and, in recent times, to sub-professional roles. As societies have moved from traditional to modern, and as childbearing and rearing have become volitional and costly functions, women are inexorably moving to access the full range of roles which modern, but still patriarchal, societies can offer. While ever fewer such roles rely on physical strength, that is only a part of the story. In the short term this trend might be expected to continue to the extent that societies where women are emancipated are economically advantaged.

Looking forward

In Chapter 1 the world of the 21st century was depicted as one where societies would continue to move from being traditional to being modern, and that modernity itself would continue to evolve. Here we are asking what has been foreseen of the spectrum of possibilities for social organisation in the distant future.

If science fiction is any guide, the dimensions of the possible, although not the particular mixture they come in, has already been revealed in history. That is, late-humans and post-humans will still be organised into societies which, once the technological props are stripped away, will be analogues of social systems the world has already seen, such as democracies, dictatorships and oligarchies. When not confronting environmental or psychological challenges, distant societies will still be engaging in war, trade and material production to ensure survival while diverting economic surpluses into population growth, education, science, art, sport, entertainment and religion.

With the expansion of the forebrain, the role of the social instincts in determining social behaviour has declined relative to the roles of socialisation and reasoning. And while it would be unsurprising if this relative decline continued, our lineage's instincts for competition and co-operation will disappear only slowly, perhaps over hundreds of thousands of years, even if being strongly selected against (which they are probably not). The implication, should this be the case, is that 'human nature' will increasingly be a product of socialisation and reason, not the social instincts. Eventually, if late-human society wants its members to be co-operative, competitive etc. they will have to be 'programmed' that way. The difference will only be one of degree from today where, as Eric Fromm (1942) puts it, all societies socialise people so they want to do what must be done to keep society functioning.

What is also implied here is that far-distant societies will inescapably have to match their choice of a 'human nature', a value system to be inculcated, with their choice of a 'world view', a philosophy of or, perhaps, model of social organisation which is judged best for advancing the society's goals. Can the range of options for such a model be identified?

Three sorts of societies

All persisting societies rely on a mixture of three sorts of relationships between people (constraints on individual behaviour) to ensure completion of the ongoing tasks that keep the society operating smoothly. These are *coercive, contractual* and *consensual (or voluntary)* relationships. They correspond to Lindblom's (1977) recognition of command (or authority) systems, market systems, and persuasive systems as the tools of social organisation. Boulding (1978) suggests that institutions and organisations come into being through the activities of three analogous organisers — threats, exchange and love (altruism). Following the same line of thought, social theory commonly locates human relations within the realms of either the state, the economy or 'civil society' (Frankel 1987). It is not difficult to map these perceptions into the idea that competition and co-operation are the foundations of social behaviour.

Societies that are largely organised by coercion, command, threats and enforceable rules and seek to minimise the use of contractual and voluntary arrangements can be said to have *hierarchical* or *structured* forms of organisation (van Asselt et al. 1996), for example, autocracy, dictatorship, representative democracy, pluralism, corporatism. General arguments in favour of hierarchical social organisation include the putative benefits of specialisation and efficient coordination. The basic social technology for the organisation of a hierarchical society is some sort of mechanism (for example, the class system) for assigning people to functional roles (for example, military, religious, political, economic) and resolving conflicts between functional groups (for example, the judicial-legislative-bureaucratic system).

Societies that are largely organised by consensus, persuasion and love and seek to minimise the use of contractual and coercive arrangements can be said to have a *voluntarist* or *mutualistic* form of organisation, for example, true anarchy, Quaker society. General arguments in favour of mutualistic social organisation include the putative benefits of improved co-operation and sociality. The basic social technology for the organisation of a mutualist society is some form of participatory process delivering agreement between people to work towards agreed goals.

Societies that are largely organised by contracts, markets and exchanges and seek to minimise the use of coercive and voluntary arrangements have *individualistic* forms of organisation, for example, libertarianism, neo-liberalism. General arguments in favour of individualistic social organisation include the putative benefits of competition-driven efficiency and personal autonomy — freedom from state interference in one's life. The basic social technology for the organisation of an individualistic society is the legally enforceable contract between 'legally defined individuals', for example, people, companies, groups.

Take your pick

The foreseeable plasticity of human, late-human and post-human behaviour is such that there is no possibility of predicting the particular form of social organisation that will reign at any time in the distant future. Certainly it is meaningless to extrapolate existing trends. In any era, any of a diversity of mixtures of contractual, coercive and mutualistic social forms would be possible and individuals would presumably be socialised to facilitate the smooth workings of the chosen social form. And to the extent that particular forms of social organisation persist through future evolutionary time, social instincts will evolve to mimic learned behaviours. Perhaps there are potential forms of social organisation outside my triangle of ideotypes but they do not suggest themselves.

Conversely, there are instinctual social behaviours which have been identified as being in particular need of urgent reform if the lineage is to survive in a civilised manner. Deceitfulness is one but aggression, particularly aggressive leadership, is seen as the main culprit. Bion (1961) believed aggression to be 'an original, self-subsisting, instinctual disposition in man, and ...the greatest impediment to civilization ... [as a consequence] ... civilized society is perpetually threatened with disintegration'. For Freud, the question was whether culture could succeed in mastering this so-human instinct of aggression and destruction. For Koestler (1967: 73), our basic deficiency is too strong a need to belong, with this leading to levels of inter-group hostility which are no longer appropriate. On the surface, the eventual challenge for socialisation is to extend the individual's feelings of amity to much larger groups, ideally to all humanity.

The obverse to the suggestion of overly aggressive leadership is to ask if people are too willing to be lead and will, at some future time, be socialised to be more individualistic. A passive society is unlikely to be a creative society and there are times ahead when the ability to innovate will be critical. A passive society is also more likely to be inequitable and dominated by power elites. On the other hand, no society can persist without a base of widely obeyed behavioural rules and a society driven by competitive individualism stands to be fragmented and alienating. Alexander (1987: 78) says it is how we will deal with conflicts of interest that will determine the fate of the world and the future of humanity.

It is clear that even if the future rate of social evolution does lie within society's control, the challenge of where to set that rate in different eras will be enormous. The function of inculcated values is to provide more or less automatic guidance to people and societies when choosing between alternatives. As society's perceptions of the consequences of past choices change, values must change or become impediments to adaptation rather than useful decision aids. Adaptability requires facing the long-term future without attachment to any aspect of the existing society, even fundamental values like democracy.

Ultimate technologies

Here we turn to speculations about the sorts of material technologies that, from where we stand today, would seem to be needed if the post-human lineage is to survive for billions more years. It would be foolish to rule out any conceivable technological effect as forever impossible but there are many effects which, in light of our current understanding of how the world works, would be impossible to bring about. Time travel, perpetual motion, teleporting and paranormal feats (such as precognition and psychokinesis) are good examples. Even here, the door marked with the impossibility of time travel has been opened a crack: Einstein's special relativity unites space and time into a single continuum in which it is theoretically possible for tachyons (hypothesised particles) to move faster than the speed of light. Under that theory, a tachyon 'message' from a rapidly receding source could arrive before it left. And 'quantum entanglement' ideas suggest the possibility of a form of teleportation. Just as today's world exceeds the wildest imaginings of Verne, Wells, da Vinci, Bacon and Archimedes, so might the deep future seem to contemporary humans. Mind you, it will be hard to beat the suggestion that one day we may be able to set off a big bang in the laboratory and create a new habitable universe (*Nature News Service*, 27 May 2002).

Moving even closer to the edge of science fiction, Moravec (1999) suggests that our descendants may develop means to venture beyond our 'reality' into worlds where the major physical constants (for example, the speed of light, the attraction of electric charges, and the strength of gravity) differ somewhat from those in this world. Quantum mechanics does predict such worlds. It is a source of amazement to many that small changes in any of the six or so major physical constants would make life as we know it quite impossible. My more Irish view is that if we were not adapted to the constants we have, we would not be here; and that the 'constants' we live under must have been more or less stable for a very long time.

Here, we will stick to candidate technologies which science has already glimpsed as approachable possibilities — not that this is the place to discuss mechanisms. Many of these, as a background requirement, assume the availability of huge quantities of energy. Others carry an overhanging dread of enormous unintended consequences.

Free energy?

In a finite space there can only be finite quantity of usable energy and the second law of thermodynamics assures us that this usable energy will irrevocably dwindle away. Nevertheless, new technologies may be able to increase the amount that is usable in practice to something that is nearer the amount that is usable in theory. Thus 'breeder' nuclear reactors can transform fertile but non-fissionable material into fissionable fuel but, in no way, as popularly believed, can they 'produce more fuel than they consume'.

And of course, if humankind's energy dowry is finite, the faster we use energy, the quicker we bring on the extinction of the lineage. Even a so-called stationary or steady state economy will run down the stock of usable terrestrial energy. If the post-human lineage is still in existence in the last days of an expanding cooling universe, it will be scrabbling around to extract usable energy from randomly distributed 'warm' spots.

So far, the nearest thing suggesting an ultimate energy bonanza has been the discovery of antimatter. Antimatter particles are mirror images of particles of normal matter, but oppositely charged, for example, normal electrons and antimatter positrons. A gram of antimatter will annihilate a gram of ordinary matter to produce two grams of energy. Perfecting a technology to control this process would yield a thousand times the energy obtainable from hydrogen fusion.

Perhaps at some far-off time post-humans may develop an 'ultimate' technology for regulating and aligning the Sun's output of radiant energy, for example, damping solar flares, stoking the Sun's furnaces with 'spare' planets? In the meantime, taking the Sun's flow of radiant energy as given, we have the opportunity to learn how to harness more of that flow. Enormous quantities of solar energy (some 5300 Q) are intercepted by the earth's atmosphere each year and, of the half which is not reflected back into space, life uses less than 0.1 per cent. The total usable energy stored on earth as fossil and other fuels and in other energy sources is similarly minuscule in relation to this annual solar flow. Several proposed technologies for capturing a significant part of this flow were mentioned earlier and others are likely to appear as the basic difficulty associated with capturing solar energy is further addressed, that is, compared with terrestrial energy sources, solar energy is highly diffuse. It comes like a fine rain but, unlike rain, does not collect into creeks, rivers and oceans. The alternative to seeking technologies which do concentrate solar energy is to seek technologies for adapting to its diffuseness, just as photo-synthesising plant life has done.

Managing the spheroid

In light of possibilities sketched earlier for planetary and cosmic futures (see page 97), a need may be eventually perceived for technologies which allow basic planetary behaviour to be adjusted. For example:

- Tilting the planet's axis relative to its plane of revolution around the Sun;

- Changing the planet's speed of rotation (day length), for example, increasing it by moving some form of mass towards the poles;

- Changing the planet's distance from the Sun, for example, to slow the rate of warming.

Technologies for diverting or destroying threatening asteroids and comets will almost certainly be needed in the long term, for example, putting pul-verising robots on asteroids to disperse them into space, exploding or deflect-ing asteroids with nuclear charges, attaching solar sails or rocket motors to change an asteroid's course. It is likely that technologies for protecting the planet from radiation bursts in outer space will also be needed in time, for example, extended electromagnetic fields.

Threats from within the planet are also likely to spawn big technologies. 'Magma seas' of molten materials flow through the earth's mantle on a timescale measured in millennia in a kind of giant 'weather system'. The effects are numerous, ranging from continental drift and lift and Earth-axis shifts to volcanoes, tsunamis and earthquakes; maybe even ice ages and coal ages. Efforts to manage this system (magma management) are likely to be made in time.

Atmosphere and ocean replenishment

James Lovelock (1989) believes that Mars is now dry because there was no photosynthesis, therefore no oxygen build-up and therefore no ozone (a form of oxygen) to combine with hydrogen in the outer atmosphere to prevent lightweight hydrogen molecules from drifting into outer space. Over billions of years this process would lead to a loss of the planet's oceans. It may well be that as Earth shifts to a hydrogen economy, a similar process could begin here, and be accelerated over the next billion years as the Sun's radiant energy slowly increases and as photosynthesising plant life declines. Technologies for slowing hydrogen loss or reversing it by capturing hydrogen from space may be developed. Perhaps the key to retaining Earth's atmosphere and oceans as long as possible will be the systematic capture of comets, the icy bodies which probably provided most of Earth's water in the first place?

Managing big 'weather' systems

In addition to persistent surface currents, the deep oceans experience 'weather' and 'storms', turbulent water flows which can last for years and strongly influence atmospheric rainfall, temperatures and winds (Moravec 1999: 156). It is conceivable that these oceanic systems will be directly managed in time, along with the management of atmospheric climate and weather.

Managing the biosphere

For present purposes, the biosphere is the mosaic of ecosystems that cover the Earth's surface. An ecosystem can be broadly defined as a biotic community (community of living organisms) and its abiotic (non-living) environment. As emphasised in popular texts such as Fritjof Capra's (1996) *Web of Life*, the reigning paradigm of ecological science is to see ecosystems in terms of 'food chains' or 'nutrient cycling'. Carnivores, at the top of the food chain, eat nutrients in the form of herbivores which eat nutrients in the form of plants. Plant and animal by-products and plants and animals which die uneaten are broken down by micro-organisms (the decomposers) from complex to simple nutrients which are taken up by plants to be cycled up the food chain once more. Ecosystems differ primarily in the groups of species which play these generic roles. These same generic roles have existed for much of the time of life on Earth and, to the best of our knowledge, will continue, but played by different species, into the deep future.

Throughout most of geological time individual species and their immediate descendants have lived about a million years. They have disappeared naturally at the rate of about one per million per year and newly evolved species have replaced them at the same rate, maintaining a rough equilibrium. Occasionally, the species extinction rate has soared and the birthrate of new species has declined as the natural environment has been destroyed for one reason or another. Palaeontologists recognise six such mass extinctions during the past half billion years. Typically, after a large part of Earth's biodiversity has been destroyed, there is a bloom of 'disaster' species such as fungi and ferns that fill the environment's empty niches, then a few 'Lazarus' species expand in numbers and types and, within 2–5 million years, life is back to its previous variety.

Just as the world's ecosystems cycle nutrients such as nitrogen and phosphorus up and down the food chain they also play a major part in cycling (that is, appropriating but also replenishing) oxygen, carbon and water vapour on a world scale. Virtually all atmospheric oxygen is the product of past plant photosynthesis, a process that, with the aid of photons of sunlight, starts with the splitting of water into oxygen, protons and electrons. Atmospheric water vapour is replenished by both plant transpiration and evaporation from free water surfaces. Atmospheric carbon dioxide is replenished by volcanic activity and reduced by sequestration in organic materials and during rock weathering.

The key point about the biosphere's recycling systems, is that for some 1500 million years, with short exceptions, the temperatures and compositions of the atmosphere, the oceans and the Earth's crust have been remarkably stable, fluctuating within the limits that permit the survival of DNA-based life forms. The non-living environment has been kept within these limits by a range of feedback processes which swing into action, quite unconsciously of course, but as if to counter any movements towards life's environmental limits. For example, oxygen build-up towards lethal limits is eventually balanced by the burial of organic matter, a process which takes oxidised materials out of the atmospheric cycle (Salthe 1993: 281). Perhaps the same will happen with the voluminous wastes high-energy societies produce; they could become a substrate for quite new recycling processes.

This perception that (feedback processes within) the biosphere creates and maintains environmental conditions favourable to its own existence is James Lovelock's (1989: 144) famous Gaia hypothesis. A stronger version of the same hypothesis, one which adds nothing for me, is that the Earth is a sort of super-organism regulating its own 'metabolism' via a range of homeostatic mechanisms.

Now we can talk about the future. For a long time to come the human lineage will be relying on the biosphere to provide, at very least, most of its food and water and a breathable atmosphere. It would be wrong to assume that because life has for so long created and maintained environmental conditions favourable to its own existence that this will continue irrespective of human and post-human activities such as land clearing, carbon dioxide production, polluting, species extinction etc. While life in general has survived past massive losses in biodiversity such as are occurring now, particular species, families and genera have obviously not. It is at least possible that *Homo sapiens* will be part of the present mass extinction.

Still, supposing otherwise, and supposing further that the lineage continues to consume large quantities of exosomatic energy, what if this so disrupts one or more of the major geochemical cycles that life rapidly becomes very difficult? One option would be to reduce energy use and hope that the biosphere's feedback processes would, unaided, restore environmental conditions to tolerable levels. The other option would be to attempt to actively manage the biosphere and the cycles it participates in. Remembering the complexity of the interactions between different components of the biosphere and the various geochemical cycles, including some puzzling lag effects, this latter would be enormously difficult. Things could go disastrously wrong. Certainly, contemporary humans have neither the understanding nor the technologies to do this. Nonetheless, looking ahead millions of years, such active management of the co-evolution of the biosphere and the physical environment may well become feasible

Indeed, it will have to become feasible if, as suggested earlier, the unmanaged biosphere could begin dying in about a billion years as temperatures rise, oceans evaporate and carbon dioxide is locked up in oceans and weathered rocks. Ultimately, it may be necessary to construct an artificial biosphere which performs most of the functions of the natural biosphere.

Space travel and settlement

The sunlight-filled vacuum of deep space is a benign environment for mechanical, electronic and optical processes, just as it is lethal for the wet chemistry of organic life (Moravec 1999: 144). Space may well become home for a range of extra-terrestrial industries relying on such things as large structures, intensive energy use, massive computation and the labours of advanced robots.

In his *Foundation* trilogy, Isaac Asimov (1995, 1996) describes humanity at some distant future date as comprising 40 billion people spread across the galaxy. But, at this stage, it is difficult to envisage a plausible future for post-humans which includes escaping from Sun death by trekking to nearby stars. Completing a trip to the stars within a human lifetime would require a spacecraft that could accelerate to a cruising speed of 16 000 kilometre per second within 10 years. Perhaps such a craft could be propelled by radio waves but we really have no idea. While it may just be possible to reach stars in the local group of galaxies (those bound by gravitation to our galaxy) it would be impossible to 'catch up' with other galaxies on the retreat into an expanding universe.

When the time to leave does come, the technology for extending the lineage might involve constructing a self-sufficient 'free planet', one able to wander through space indefinitely; or we could take the Earth with us.

Superintelligences

The tasks that might be allocated to and within the capabilities of machine-based artificial intelligences in the distant future can be perceived only dimly.

There is however a generic capability which will be persistently sought because it lies at the heart of what we mean by intelligence. To repeat, intelligence is the capacity to perceive relationships between things. Identifying relevant new examples of relationships between things is what we think of as creativity. Post-humans will be looking to develop *superintelligences* — entities which can create intelligence greater than their own — which can make creative discoveries in nominated areas of existing knowledge in a totally routine way and at great speed. A closely linked technological objective will be to develop a capacity to routinely identify gaps in existing knowledge which are bottlenecks to suites of further discoveries. Whether it will be the role of post-humans or robots to then fill those gaps is an open question.

Little can be foreseen of the processing software, databases and encodings that such capabilities might rely on. They might not necessarily be understandable by even post-human minds. As for the hardware supporting these superintelligences, enormous speed and memory will obviously be required. Moravec (1999: 162) notes that any neutron star contains very dense, closely-packed matter that could perhaps be shaped into a 'mind' which, having very close-spaced components, could work a million times faster than any processor based on regular matter. Heady stuff!

OVERVIEW: DUNGEONS AND DRAGONS

In Chapter 1, the big uncertainty identified as lurking in the 21st century is whether humans have already or are in the process of initiating massive irreversible climate change which has so far been delayed by the export of heat to the deep oceans. And it is also uncertain whether we will be able to cope with several other massive challenges of our own making, namely the consequences of rapid population and economic growth — both made possible by the growth of scientific knowledge. Still, leaving aside thermonuclear war and engineered viruses, the species will probably survive the 21st century — miserably or not so miserably, with or without civilisation.

In this chapter, moving beyond a 21st century perspective, we have reviewed various speculations touching on the future of the human lineage at three timescales: the next thousand years, the next hundred thousand years and the next ten-plus billion years.

The big uncertainty of the third millennium CE is whether the next great winter, already overdue, will start and, if so, whether we will have a sufficient residuum of fossil fuels to construct refugia, keep ourselves warm and well-fed or whether population will drop dramatically. Conversely, will the greenhouse effect 'run away' and produce a warm, moist world, a 'coal age', in which most coastal civilisations are inundated? People themselves will not change much in a thousand years and it is possible that the co-operative instinct plus an evolving rationality will win out over self-interest and instinctual aggression to produce a reasonably peaceful global federation in which peoples can retain their identities and, as individuals, enjoy basic rights and opportunities for self-realisation.

The big uncertainty of the next 100 000 years, given that most of that time will be an ice age and that fossil fuels (including nuclear fuels) will no longer be available, is whether the human lineage will survive. While it is true that the human population may have fallen as low as 10 000 in the middle of the last ice age, this was due to the superimposition of a 'volcanic winter' on the rigours of an ice-age climate. Not only did the species survive last time, socio-cultural evolution, in parallel with language developments, actually accelerated. On balance, the odds on surviving the next ice age, even without fossil fuels, look good; not so good on surviving comfortably.

If we do survive the next glacial comfortably, it will probably mean that we have learned to live within the constraints of a renewable and even re-expanding energy supply. This would allow us to evolve freely, culturally and mentally. Indeed, organic evolution of the brain stands to be much more significant than evolution of more readily observable physical characteristics. But in the timeframe of a single ice age we will not be evolving into a new species.

Once the lineage has made it through a millennium of self-inflicted problems and the next glacial it might have a respite of a billion or so years in which to learn more and more about surviving well, even while building a capacity to tackle a damoclean round of massive challenges to the integrity of the biosphere, the oceans and the atmosphere. Our descendants will need to acquire technologies for ameliorating terrestrial and extra-terrestrial shocks such as volcanic winters and asteroids.

From then on the track gets steeper, with post-humans having to live in an ultimately doomed burnt-out solar system with, on current knowledge, not much prospect of escaping to more habitable parts of the galaxy, much less the universe. And beyond that lies the prospect of a universe which either implodes or contains no usable energy.

In terms of social organisation in the deep future, we may or may not find an alternative to living as populations of role specialists in big cities. As individuals, a billion years from now we could still be complex mixtures of the rational, the emotional and the instinctual (because that is more interesting?) or behaviour could be ruled by just one part of the triune brain. Governance may or may not come to be centrally concerned with individual quality of life. It would be surprising though if it were to find an organising principle outside some mixture of contracts, coercion and co-operation. If the power of reasoning continues to evolve, developments in governance, social organisation and 'post-human nature' in the deep future will be conscious choices, not chance happenings.

As reported in this and the previous chapter, the future of the human to post-human lineage is, in the first instance, a story of dungeons and dragons, an escalating struggle between knowledge and catastrophe. Each threat surmounted bestows time to improve our understanding of life and the universe in preparation for the next threat. New knowledge will not necessarily improve our long-term prospects though; it might make our long-term prospects either better or worse depending on how it reconceptualises threats and capabilities. We know that the world, ultimately, is physically constrained and some futures are just not possible. On the other hand, we have only just started discovering the rules of matter and space.

But not all threats to the lineage are external. The period which began with the post-glacial expansion of agriculture has been fraught with perils flowing from the difficulties inherent in supplementing imitative learning and instinctual behaviour controls with ratiocination, the power of reasoning. This process, we may suppose, has been going on for 2.5 million years but it has accelerated twice in the last few thousand years, once with the rise of reasoning as we know it in Greece in the second millennium BCE and once with the rise of experiment-based modern science after about 1500 CE.

Here is the potentially tragic dilemma. Science and the cumulative technological knowledge it spawns offer the lineage one slim hope of surviving into the deep future. But, for the very reason that it offers hope — that it has the potential to massively change people, societies and the planet itself — science is a two-edged sword. This is because it is being wielded by a species which, to date, has not been able to control its instinctual aggression, its hostility to outsiders and competitive self-interest in a world where these are increasingly inappropriate.

This mattered less before Galileo but is enormously important now that we can destroy ourselves or, less dramatically, destroy civilisation's capacity to efficiently generate new knowledge. Knowledge has produced knowledge capable of halting the production of knowledge! The danger will persist until, at least, we have learned much more about how the mind works. The 'big brain' experiment could go badly wrong (speaking from a contemporary perspective) in other ways too. Replacing instinct with reason as the dominant control over behaviour could lead to the loss of the curiosity that drives science and the will to survive which we take for granted.

This then is the spectrum of our lineage's possible futures as collated from science-based and other serious speculations. The dungeons and dragons allegory needs to be extended to include an ever-stronger but flawed hero, to recognise that the dragon-slayer's sword of knowledge is becoming mightier over time, but also increasingly dangerous to the wielder until she can overcome an appetency for self-mutilation. And sometimes she unwittingly conjures up her very own dragons which then have to be slain. In this sense, the future is written both in the stars and in ourselves.

Outside religious circles, few have embraced alternatives to this 'quest and looming tragedy' vision of the lineage's future. While prophets from Rousseau to Freud have thought civilisation a failure and recommended returning to an earlier primitive existence, it can't and won't be done, at least not deliberately. Nor, without collective purposive intervention, will society self-organise and evolve into something capable of planning its own long-term survival.

It is now time to move on from what could happen to what 'should' happen. What, reasonably, do we want to happen? How should we plan to manage individual and societal evolution and the accumulation of knowledge so that what we want becomes more likely? And, to guide our planning, what have we already learned about how societies change over time?

Part 2:

UNDERSTANDING THE TASK

3

WHAT IS THE QUESTION?

Chapter 1 asked where informed and thoughtful people think humanity is going in the 21st century and Chapter 2 asked the same question for the rest of time. We were interested in what those people thought would or could happen, not what 'should' happen. In this chapter, we turn to asking what people might like to see happening in the future and the conditions under which such preferences might become goals that they set out to actively achieve.

While there can be no common answer to what people might like to see happening in the future, especially the deep future, the chapter moves towards a particular, flexible working answer, namely, *quality survival* or, less cryptically, *to see the lineage surviving, and surviving well*. This means a preference for a future where the human through to post-human lineage survives for an indefinitely prolonged period (certainly many billions of years) and that, for most of this time, most individuals comprising that lineage will be enjoying high quality of life. This working answer to the question of what people may collectively wish of the future opens the way in following chapters into the question of how the lineage might need to behave if some version of such a goal is to be achieved. The hardheaded question of whether such a collective goal is ever likely to be adopted is left until the final chapter.

WHY DO PEOPLE THINK ABOUT THE FUTURE?

In the end we cannot but think about the future. It is an existential burden all of us carry, some more constructively than others. The great psychologist Abraham Maslow (1968) said that thinking about the future and planning for the future are central attributes of a healthy human personality.

At a practical everyday level, people think about the future because they want the future to be kind to them (or to others, such as their grandchildren); and planning for the future — thoughtfully choosing today's actions with regard to their future consequences (consequentialism) — may help that to happen. Even when it appears that one's future situation cannot be influenced by today's actions, it may still be judged useful to plan responses to the occurrence of any of various scenarios of possible futures.

People can also think about aspects of the future in a disinterested way, that is, without interpreting what might unfold in terms of their own self-interest. This sort of thinking may just be curiosity driven or it may stem from a concern for others, for society if you prefer. Or perhaps from a concern for life in general? Who cares whether our lineage survives for a thousand years, a million years or 5 billion years? Who cares whether our descendants are going to lead rich self-fulfilling lives? The answer is that some do, some feel actively malevolent towards posterity and most are too busy surviving from day to day to think about such things or, indeed, have never been prompted to think of such things. And, for many, their religion provides them with an image of the future which they accept as revealed truth not needing to be further thought about.

WHAT DO PEOPLE WANT OF THEIR OWN FUTURES?

What more can be said about what people want from the future, either for themselves or for others or for society?

In principle at least, people do not want what they regard as impossible to have. What we want is conditioned by what we think might be possible. Most would agree that, ultimately, there is much in individual life one can do little about. Buddhism is built on the premise that suffering is ubiquitous. Death is a fact for you and those you love. However, while people might sometimes think it would be wonderful to be immortal, they aspire, not to immortality, but to something which, in the right circumstances, they think might be achievable, say a long healthy life. And, as a natural corollary to having such an aspiration, they might plan and take action to achieve a long, healthy life, that is, set longevity as a personal goal. A goal is something which you want and are prepared to take action to achieve.

Maslow (1954, 1968) provides a comprehensive and widely accepted theory of 'human nature' that clarifies and elaborates what individuals are seeking from the future and hence, by implication, what their goals are. People, he says, strive to satisfy received physiological and psychological needs for life, safety and security, for belongingness and affection, for esteem, for respect and self-respect and for self-actualisation (personal development, realisation of latent potentialities). As more basic needs (for example, food) are met, attention switches, in a hierarchical fashion, to satisfying higher needs (for example, for creative activity). Doyal and Gough (1991) define *needs* as that which 'persons must achieve if they are to avoid sustained and serious harm'. Another definition, one with implications for how society 'should' be organised is that a need is a want which society agrees is also a right.

Maslow's theory follows plausibly from the observations that humans are purposive and that human needs have long been proxies for evolutionary success. Directedness or 'drive' is an attribute of all life, to be found in organic as well as mental activity (Sinnott 1950; 1962: 83). Life and its actions are not random; they are regulatory and either maintain a reference state already achieved or move towards one which is yet to be realised. Purposive activity, as seen in its highly developed, conscious form in humans, is a specialised and elaborated kind of directed activity concerned mainly with mastery of the social and material environment. Natural selection has preserved individuals with 'purposes' or intentions that are conducive to survival and reproductive success — which 'want' the 'right' things. While Maslow's needs are not easy to measure directly, they can be readily interpreted as being conducive to such evolutionary success.

Raising the idea of a needs hierarchy allows us to introduce a further idea that recurs throughout this book, namely, *quality of life*. Following Maslow, a person enjoying high quality of life is one able to largely satisfy his or her higher needs. Birch (1975) similarly suggests that quality of life is measured by a person's feelings that their potentialities for creative activities and relationships with others are being satisfied. After conceding that it is more easily experienced than measured, Wilkin (1996) says high quality of life consists of perceptions of satisfaction relative to one's personal set of values. As a general and uncontroversial assertion then, most individuals, tacitly or overtly, have the enjoyment of high quality of life over a long period, a 'better' life, as an umbrella goal.

WHAT SORT OF SOCIETY DO PEOPLE WANT?

People have been imagining and describing 'ideal' societies for at least 3000 years (Schaer et al. 2000; Carey 1999). Some of these utopias have been seen as desirable because of the benign natural environment in which they are placed but more have been built around ideas of how individual improvement (for example, developing the 'non-attachment' to worldly things which all the major religions preach) and particular social structures (for example, just societies governed by rule of law) can contribute to creating societies in which people would want to live (Huxley 1938, chapter 3). Despite their often-good intentions, offering people a picture of what to strive for, many imagined utopias seem bleak and constraining to those not sharing the author's world view.

Beyond imagining and describing, many 'reformers' — from the Pilgrim Fathers and the Russian Bolsheviks to sects, cults and ideologues — have tried to physically create their ideal society. Many are the rocks on which such efforts have foundered, one being attempts to impose a permanent static structure on the reformed society, a strategy which ignores the juggernaut of change. Indeed, the evolutionary success of humans has commonly been attributed to avoiding fixation of both group structure and productive infrastructure (not to mention the ways in which individual needs are satisfied). Experimental utopias have often turned into dystopias (places where one would not want to live) which have to be rescued by a vision of a further new utopia.

Theory and practice suggest then that the lesson for anyone seeking a generalisation about what sort of society people want is 'be cautious', certainly not dogmatic or tightly prescriptive. Nevertheless, for this book to move forward, some working suppositions about preferred future societies are needed. So, from asserting that people in general have a goal of high-quality extended life based on satisfying a hierarchy of needs, I will take the small step to presuming that most people would therefore want to live in a society which is conducive to their achieving that goal. I will call such a society a *nurturing society*, meaning one fostering opportunities to satisfy inherent human needs.

And if individuals want high quality of life for others, such as grandchildren, as well as for themselves, it follows in another small step that individuals will want a society that nurtures all its members, present and future, in this sense. After all, one's grandchildren could be located anywhere on the social scale in future society and, drawing on Rawls' (1971) 'veil of ignorance' argument, the best guarantee of their well-being is that future society should nurture all its members.

The question of how society might be best organised to achieve comprehensive long-term nurturing is at the heart of this book but can be put aside for the moment to ask if societies, as distinct from individuals, can have goals.

CAN SOCIETIES HAVE GOALS?

Edgar Dunn (1971) makes the useful observation that collective goals are simply the personal goals that prompt a group of individuals to exploit the leverage of collective action. He is recognising that in many situations co-operation between individuals is synergistic (synergic, synergetic), that is, able to achieve more than the sum of what can be achieved by individuals acting alone. So, if a hunter–gatherer wants meat, he will obtain more by co-operating with others and sharing the kill than by hunting alone. All have the same (collective) goal.

But it gets more difficult from here on. In structured societies it is task specialisation which generates the synergistic benefits of co-operation. People therefore do not have identical immediate objectives and social technologies such as contracts and coercion and governments are needed to coordinate individual activities and distribute the dividends of voluntary and involuntary co-operation. Custom and tradition can also coordinate a society's diverse activities. In the Middle Ages European societies saw their paramount pur-pose as serving God (Tawney 1920). Having a clear social purpose disap-peared with the arrival of the industrial revolution and the rise of individualism (Wallerstein 1995: 1–7) and has never really been regained — with the exception of seeking victory in wartime, perhaps; or in the early days of some communist societies.

Perhaps societies do not need to express goals? Perhaps they do not carry the 'existential burden' identified by writers like Sartre (1948; 1975) and Camus (1946) which mandates that individuals have no option but to con-sciously choose the goals they want their behaviour to achieve? Certainly those of a libertarian bent reject the idea of a society with explicit goals por-tending collective action. Their claim is that any collective action based on goals that are not specifically agreed by all participating parties is illegitimate. This, they would assert, has the implication of limiting the role of the state — the vehicle by which modern societies articulate and implement Commons' *collective will* (Hodgson 1999b: 151) or Hirst's (1997: 88) *general will* — to that of a 'night watchman', ensuring little more than legal protection for those entering into contractual arrangements.

Others opposed to or indifferent to the overt expression of social goals include various sorts of teleologists and determinists. For example, some tech-nological determinists see societal development as being driven by irrepress-ible market-mediated technological change, and hence unable to purposively approach declared social goals. In similar vein, those who have a teleological view of history as a process working itself out along a purposeful trajectory will see the expression of social goals as a pointless diversion. More of this in Chapter 4 where the process of social change is explored from several per-spectives. Privileged elites are another group who may oppose the search for social goals on the unacknowledged grounds that such are likely to have an egalitarian thrust which could threaten privilege.

It is doubtful then if any complex contemporary society can develop collective goals that are both explicit and able to command the informed assent of all the society's members. Notwithstanding, modern states commonly invoke the language of social goals and visions, in part as 'carrots' to encourage people to participate in coordinated behaviour and in part to guide the search for further collective action. Calls to adopt a national goal, 'a genuinely shared sense of national purpose' (to quote an Australian prime minister), describing where the community wants to be in several generations' time can be seen as analogous to an individual affirming her life goals.

'Vision' has emerged in recent years as a word in good currency, replacing 'goals' to some extent but having a similar meaning. Perhaps it has a slightly 'richer' ring to it than goals. Thus:

> The motivation underlying the specification of any vision is to articulate a set of goals and aspirations for the future in order to generate debate about alternative strategies for the present (SAUNDERS 1994).

> ~

> ... a national vision should not be viewed as a 'wish list'. The goals it contains must certainly be ambitious and challenging, but they must also be realistic, achievable and compatible with each other. In short, the vision must not only be desirable but feasible (ARGY 1992).

On balance, provided that the process is not abused or mismanaged, it is probably more rather than less useful for a society to articulate its higher-level goals. Let me expand.

For many, having a vision of their society's future increases their sense of purpose and the confidence and energy with which they tackle the present. It draws them forward. Thinking about what the future holds stands to reduce 'fear of the unknown'. Even to know what we do not know offers a measure of reassurance.

And for those who, like myself, find it helpful to view the relationship between the individual and society as a rational *social contract*, knowing where society is heading allows the individual to assent to (or question) that contract in a more informed way. More strongly, every society has a responsibility to its members to explain its collective purpose; every citizen has a right to be informed of that purpose. I am drawing here on Rousseau's (1762; 1968) *The Social Contract* which was undoubtedly the most important political essay to come out of the eighteenth century Enlightenment. Its basic idea is one of a fair system of co-operation between and within generations (Rawls 1993). On one side of this contract, society has a responsibility to protect and promote a negotiated set of individual rights. On the other side, each individual has a duty to contribute to the smooth functioning of society, fulfilling specified obligations and accepting certain responsibilities to the society, some enforceable, some not (see page 264).

THE PROCESS OF SETTING SOCIAL GOALS

Accepting then that every society has a responsibility to articulate the collective goals which are the ultimate rationale for its existence, what procedural guidelines can be suggested for those seeking to formulate such goals? We have space for some brief indications.

First, as far as possible, the process should be participatory, that is one which includes the views of all affected people. This is just not possible when choice of goals will affect people not yet born. Nor is it possible in a large society, where logistical problems make full participation impracticable. The process should also be dialogic rather than adversarial (an exchange is dialogic when parties are able to state the others' position to the others' satisfaction). Participation, apart from helping to legitimise goal setting, is the main way, outside formal education, that people learn to be good citizens as Rousseau (1762; 1968) argues.

Next, there will be more chance of reaching consensus if the goals to be sought are modest. This is because 'human beings of all cultures, as a result of their genetic and cultural evolution, are basically animals with a small-group, parochial, geographically local, short-term outlook' (Ornstein and Ehrlich 1989). On the other hand, bold goals which it would be surprising to see achieved, may help lift what is actually achieved, even if this falls short of what is sought. A balance between ambition and modesty, between what is ideally wanted and what is possible, needs to be struck.

Social goals must always be open to revision by due process. This allows recasting in the light of new knowledge and changing attitudes and priorities among present and future group members. Bertrand de Jouvenel (1964) suggested the need for a 'surmising forum' engaged in continuing dialogue.

In order to subsume the goals of as many individuals as possible, and hence command wide support, social goals need to be expressed at the highest level of generality compatible with not being vacuous. For example a goal to create 'heaven on earth' is not operational. It contains no hint of what needs to be done if it is to be achieved, or of what would constitute success.

QUALITY SURVIVAL AS A GOAL FOR WORLD SOCIETY

It was argued above that people, as individuals, tend to have high quality of life over many years as a broad-brush personal goal. And that they will therefore want to live in nurturing societies where they and others can have high quality of life. Those 'others', in many cases, will include members of future generations.

It is a further small step from recognising the importance of quality of life for the individual to suggesting *high quality of life for all*, including people of future generations, as an appropriate goal for any society of people intent on choosing and pursuing a common goal. Clearly, this is a social goal which is entirely consonant with the pursuit of high quality of life as a personal goal. And, like any social goal, it presumes that, in some sense, acting collectively can boost quality of life for every individual.

My argument is now at the point of being able to suggest that the goal of high quality of life for all — the goal of becoming a nurturing society — is appropriate for what can be called *world society* (Burton 1972). By this I mean a society which is seen to include all humans and their descendants over whatever period of time the human to post-human lineage persists; and, furthermore, I mean a society which is able to take collective action on behalf of its membership in some reasonably legitimate way, for example, via a world government. Despite globalisation and the existence of institutions such as the United Nations, there is no world society now and there may never be. Nevertheless, for the purposes of this book, a world society is a convenient, not altogether improbable, scenario which will allow me to discuss strategies for managing the deep future on the global scale at which I think it will have to be managed.

It further suits my expository purposes to postulate that a world society might well have a second collective goal in addition to 'high quality of life for all for as long as society survives'. I refer to the goal of survival itself, indefinite survival for as long as the universe lasts. Survival per se is a more problematic goal though than quality of life for all. Why would individuals, singularly or collectively, have a preference for a long-lasting society over a short-lived one? If high quality of life for all at all times could be guaranteed then it would seem reasonable to prefer society to persist indefinitely. If people are enjoying the trip, why cut it short? But if high quality of life cannot be guaranteed, and it cannot, surviving when life is not worth living would seem to be a doubtful achievement. For example, Kavka (1982: 105) suggests that it is morally wrong to create 'restricted lives', meaning lives that are significantly deficient in one or more of the major respects that generally make lives valuable and worth living.

Some may see a religious imperative or duty to seek the indefinite survival of the lineage. Some may see the Kantian ethic, the golden rule, as dictating that no generation should be deprived of quality of life through being extinguished and hence that the lineage should not come to an end. I prefer to look elsewhere to justify indefinite survival as an appropriate goal for world society.

A preference for a society lasting at least a few generations is understandable in terms of concern for kin, but, just as most of us have no personal feeling for the *Homo erectus* individuals who were our direct ancestors, few can empathise with their equally unknowable descendants 100 generations from now. Evolution is a game in which the only prize is to stay in the game, that is, avoid extinction. While the possibility of human extinction is commonly bemoaned, implying some preference for indefinite survival, reasons why extinction would be so bad are rarely given. After all, there are no tangible benefits for today's humans if their lineage lasts, say, 2 billion instead of 1 billion years. Notwithstanding, various writers, including Wilhelm Reich (1946) and BF Skinner (1971), have proposed survival as a primary value for society. For me, the primary reason for world society adopting indefinite survival as a goal is that this is the ultimate problem to be solved and we are a species which takes pleasure in problem-solving. Just watch a baby learning how to walk. Perhaps there are some psychological reasons too. Indefinite survival is a quixotic goal; the prospects for success are not good but there is something energising about taking on grand challenges.

Clearly, a scenario of world society adopting a goal of indefinite survival is less plausible than one of world society adopting a goal of being a nurturing society for as long as such a society exists. Nevertheless, I want this book to explore how a world society which adopts both these goals might best reach out for them. And to simplify frequent references to this pair of global social goals, I will introduce the term *quality survival*. Thus, much of this book is written under a scenario of a world society emerging and adopting a collective goal of quality survival, namely, to create a nurturing society with good survival prospects.

But, there will be a caveat. If the unavoidable price of survival turns out to be major suffering, quality survival may well be judged an unacceptable goal (replaced by one of exiting gracefully perhaps?). For example, the welfare of the individual and of society are clearly in conflict if the welfare of the individual is seen to be wholly a function of his/her freedom from socially imposed constraint. Conversely, the two sub-goals may reinforce each other. It would be helpful to know the trade-off, if any, between quality of life and survival.

More generally, social goals will always be evolving. We can be sure that people in 100 000 years will see things very differently from us. We have little idea what post-humans will want from their future. Within just the modern period, the dominant social goal in many societies has shifted from serving God to serving Mammon (or, more politely, to accumulating material wealth) and may be shifting again to sustainable development (balancing wealth accumulation with environmental protection). Proposing a goal of quality survival is appropriate for the moment.

FROM GOALS TO OBJECTIVES

Upcoming chapters address the question of how the lineage might need to behave if some version of the quality survival goal is to be achieved. It will usually be helpful for such a purpose if, as a first step, the quality survival goal can be broken down into operational *objectives*. These are a set of intermediate 'goals' which assert in explicit terms what needs to be first achieved if a top-level goal such as quality survival is to be eventually achieved. Such objectives are most readily expressed as target values for various *partial measures* or *indicators* of, say, the 'average' quality of life enjoyed by members of a society; or of the society's survival prospects.

Under such thinking, average quality of life is judged to have improved (deteriorated) when a relevant indicator moves up (down) over time, for example, life expectancy. But there is no such thing as a necessary and sufficient set of quality of life indicators, covering all aspects of human needs at all times and places. Nor can changes in different indicators be confidently combined together to get a measure of overall change in quality of life. All that can be said is that if an indicator changes in the 'right direction', while other things remain the same, people are 'better off'. Using an indicators approach to quality-of-life measurement is an acknowledgement that it is difficult (impossible?) to measure universal quality of life directly.

Having earlier accepted Maslow's theory of human needs as the starting point for operationalising the quality-of-life idea, it would seem to follow that quantitative indicators should be developed around components of the hierarchy of qualitative needs identified in his writings. Doing this would provide very direct indicators of individual quality of life but these would still need to be aggregated somehow to deliver society-wide indicators.

As an example of the difficulties of aggregation, some will think 'average' quality of life quite inadequate as a measure of a society's overall quality of life. Thus Rawls (1971) argues that it is the quality of life of the most disadvantaged members of the society that best measures the quality of life of the whole society. For example, for a society's quality of life to be judged high, the poor must have reasonable choice in relation to all aspects of consumption — food, transport, accommodation, healthcare, clothing, education, communications and recreation activities. These are the 'tools of opportunity'.

Indicators of long-term survival prospects are equally likely to be contentious. What does it mean for a society to 'survive'? Does the survival of a few individuals qualify? Somehow it means avoiding 'total social breakdown', the loss of those social processes that allow daily life to continue meeting people's basic needs. Thinking of world society as a living organism, total social breakdown would equate to death. We are talking here about changes in world society that would render it unrecognisable, for example, a totalitarian order or a disorder of feuding warlords in an environment bereft of a collective social and physical infrastructure. In our era, social breakdown means low life expectancy, high maternal mortality, little access to primary healthcare, clean water and sanitation, illiteracy, malnutrition, injustice, oppression of women etc.

The above is all that needs to be said here about quality survival indicators. That is because this book is not so much about producing concrete plans for managing the deep future as it is about mulling over *how* to produce such plans.

CAN WE SHAPE THE FUTURE?

The reason for asking this question (and it comes up again in Chapter 6) is that unless we believe we can shape the future (HG Wells' evocative phrase) to some extent, that is, bring various indicators of quality survival towards nominated target values, there is little point in developing social goals — images of the consequences we hope will follow our collective actions.

Deliberate attempts to reform society were rare before the modern era. Heilbroner (1995) detects three basically different attitudes towards shaping the future in humankind's long history. For most of that time, until about 1750, most people accepted, with resignation, that the future would be much the same as the present, with the social and economic order changing little from generation to generation; and that, basically, the future was beyond human control. From about 1700 onwards, under the influence of three great forces, namely the capitalist mode of production, technology and political emancipation, people began to believe in 'progress' and expected the future to be better than the past. But, from about the middle of 20th century, the prevailing attitude towards the future has become more one of 'post-modern' apprehension. Matching these attitudes to current perceptions of what directed behaviour (that is, actions) can achieve, they identify firstly the view that actions cannot influence the future (resignation); secondly that actions can influence the future for the better (progress); and thirdly that actions influences the future but, for better or worse, we know not (apprehension). More concretely, people believe it is getting harder to shape the future, an attitude which may be self-reinforcing if reformers get disheartened.

The human species has undoubtedly set forces in train which are shaping the course of history. But those forces are not manageable by individuals or even, perhaps, great nations. Each individual has no choice but to live in a socio-politico-economic environment that has been largely moulded by others. However, within the parameters set by that environment, the individual can make things happen, can be more or less successful in achieving quality of life.

Similarly, it is an idea central to this book that, like individuals, societies, to some limited extent, can purposively determine (ameliorate) their own future with respect to targets such as quality of life and prospects for long-term survival. Ultimately though, it cannot be demonstrated that a society such as ours can deliberately improve its quality survival prospects, to a degree that is worth the effort, over and above what prospects would have been in the absence of collective intervention in the societal process. All that can be said is that optimists believe it can and pessimists do not. This is not to deny the various arguments that can be made in favour of one or the other position, nor that people do change camps under the influence of such arguments.

Thus, pessimists see quality survival prospects:

As being overwhelmingly determined by forces outside any control by governments or other collective bodies; or

As being strongly affected by the actions of collective bodies, but in quite unpredictable ways.

And some who are pessimistic with respect to society's ability to control its own future may be Panglossian optimists (she'll be right) when it comes to believing that the world will be kind to us (even if we do not recognise that kindness), irrespective of whether we actively seek such an outcome. Ranged against the Panglossians are the fatalists and deep pessimists believing that the world will be unkind to us, regardless of what we do.

RECAPITULATION

This chapter's task has been to give purpose to the rest of the book. It argues the case for accepting a sequence of propositions which lead to a central question I want to answer as well as possible in later chapters.

The starting proposition is that most humans have a general goal of high quality of life for themselves and others of concern and that high quality of life flows from being able to satisfy a hierarchy of inherent needs ranging from the biological to the need to be creative.

Next it is argued that all societies have a responsibility to their members to declare the collective or social goals which are the ultimate reason for any society's existence and, further, that high quality of life for all of its present and future members is a social goal which flows naturally from the quality-of-life goals of a society's individual members, including future members. Wanting to live in a nurturing society where quality of life can be pursued leads to wanting to live in a society where the nurturing of quality of life is a collective goal. And, while there is yet no such entity as a world society able to set social goals and make collective decisions on behalf of the global population, it is suggested that, supposing there were, high quality of life for all would be appropriate for that society too.

Finally it is argued, somewhat tentatively, that survival for an indefinitely long period might serve as a second goal, alongside quality of life for all as a high-level goal for an emerging world society. That is, there is a widespread drive to avoid extinction of the species and its descendants. The term *quality survival* is coined to encapsulate world society's two high-level hypothesised goals, namely indefinite survival and quality of life all round.

While humans clearly can and do shape the future strongly, it is not clear that a world society could purposively shape its future so as to approach a major social goal such as quality survival. Nevertheless, the question is important enough and open enough to make it worth asking over coming chapters. Can humanity and its descendants create a (very) long-lasting and nurturing world society? If so, how? What should we do to bring it about?

4

UNDERSTANDING HOW SOCIETIES CHANGE OVER TIME

My primary reason for wanting to understand how and why societies change over time is that such understanding may suggest how to move world society towards my proposed goal of quality survival. Obversely, it may help the lineage to avoid a painful Hobbesian extinction. Not that one's expectations as to what can be immediately learned should be too high. This chapter identifies just a handful of useful broad-brush models of social change. Beyond that, it draws out some issues that recur when deciding how to collectively manage such change. I will use the term *societal change* or, equivalently, socio-cultural change, in the wide sense of including social, cultural, political and economic forms of change within societies.

Looking back to the advent of structured societies in Neolithic times, societies and systems of interacting societies have changed in ways we infer from the historical (written) and archaeological record. Some of what can be created from this record are social histories of everyday life and group experiences, but more are political histories — narratives of empires, kings and wars. Our particular interest here is in how and why societies appear, thrive, decline and disappear and in how and why collective quality of life has changed over humanity's post-glacial (last 12 000 years) history, that is, I am accepting that such change has been a reality and look to understand the processes involved.

I am also accepting that the process by which societies change over time, at least when they are not busy collapsing or being dramatically reorganised, can usually be described as *evolution*, in the general (supra-biological) sense of that word. An *evolutionary process* within a system of interest is one where, over a period which is long relative to the lifetimes of the components of the system, certain fundamental features of the system are preserved while others change apparently irreversibly, often in a way which, with hindsight, appears cumulative (see Box 4.1 for a note on 'system'). For example, sociologists who are cultural materialists, such as Harris (1979), perceive all societies to have an infrastructure (arrangements for the production of people, food, energy etc.), a group structure (groups linked emotionally and groups linked functionally) and a mental and cultural superstructure. These components may change in detail over time but will be retained in some form in all socio-cultural systems.

Our starting point for understanding societal change will be macro-history, that branch of the discipline which looks for patterns, generalisations, similarities and 'law-like statements' within and across the narratives (life stories) of the multitude of cultures, societies, nations, civilisations, empires etc. which have existed since hunter–gatherer tribes began settling in farming villages. Narrative history, the history of events, provides the raw material from which recurrent basic processes can be inferred. Macro-historians ask questions such as: Do societies have life cycles? Developmental stages? What triggers transitions between life-cycle stages? How important are initial conditions in shaping a society's subsequent development? Why has history taken very different courses on different continents? How do societies solve problems? What, if any, is the role of the individual in societal change? Are there processes which drive change in many societies simultaneously? What sorts of societies succeed in meeting people's needs and which fail?

Because historians, with a few exceptions, have been more interested in differences between civilisations than similarities, the body of macro-historical generalisations is thin. Some of the most important contributors of macro-historical insights have come from other disciplines such as sociology, anthropology, ecology, geography, social psychology and economics. In particular, sociology's perspective on historical change is explored here.

A second approach to the challenge of understanding how societies change over time is to recognise that societies are *dynamic systems* (Box 4.1) and hence open to the insights of a growing body of theory describing how and why entities which qualify for such description change over time. In particular, societies, including world society, are *dissipative* or *energy-degrading systems* whose behavioural characteristics flow from the diverse ways in which they process incoming energy into building and maintaining internal structures, depending on how incoming energy levels are varying over time (see Appendix). Among the implications for societal change are the conclusions that such change can be slow and directional or fast and disorganising but rarely predictable over any length of time.

Beyond history and systems theory, the chapter's third approach to understanding societal change is to ask if societies can be plausibly regarded as examples of or analogues of classes of dynamic systems that have been studied in other disciplines, notably the empirical biological sciences. If so, insights already obtained into how such comparable systems behave over time might be applicable to societies. Specifically, I will be asking whether aspects of societal change are analogous (similar in a process sense) to (a) changes in the lineages of biological species (evolutionary biology or phylogenesis) and (b) changes in the organisation of ecosystems (plant–animal communities) over time (ecosystem dynamics).

The conclusion I will be coming to is that, like macro-history and systems thinking, these biological sciences have much to contribute to an understanding of societal evolution. In the case of ecosystems, the main reason is that these, like societies, are dissipative systems. More particularly, unlike societies, they are well-studied as dissipative systems. Many of their dynamic behavioural characteristics appear to have direct analogues in societal behaviour, particularly the way in which they slowly get more complex and more vulnerable to disturbance over time. Indeed there are other biological sciences (for example, molecular genetics, biochemistry, immunology, embryology) which study dissipative systems and which could be searched for behavioural rules which might be transposable to societal change but time, space and a lack of knowledge on my part preclude this.

The situation is somewhat different with evolutionary biology. The processes by which species differentiate over evolutionary time scales to give lineages of species could be studied as dissipative systems but normally are not (Wicken 1987). They are studied as a process of competitive selection in populations of self-replicating entities. While populations of societies cannot be studied in this way, there are some important populations *within* societies which can be, for example, populations of firms. Understanding what strategies make certain members of a population successful under one form of competitive selection, namely phylogenesis, turns out to be helpful for understanding a range of competitive processes leading to change in human societies.

There is a risk of confusion here which needs to be pre-empted. Looking for whole-of-society analogues in the behaviour of other classes of biological systems might obscure the fact that ecological and other biological processes also play a *direct* role in much societal change, certainly to the point where these processes need to be kept in mind when contemplating scenarios for the future of world society. Disease (for example, McNeill 1979; McMichael 2001) and resource degradation (for example, Diamond

1992) are the obvious examples. Christopher Lloyd (pers. comm.) goes as far as to say that macro-history is merging to some extent with the historical sciences of geology, biology and ecology, that human societal history is intricately linked to natural history rather than in opposition to it.

IDEAS FROM HISTORY

> The past, like a cricket in the corner,
> Whines in its low persistent voice. (SHU TING)

> ~

> … as one particular pattern of human exploitation of the environment began to encounter difficulties, thanks to exhaustion of one or another key resource, human ingenuity found new ways to live, tapping new resources, and thereby expanded our dominion over animate and inanimate nature, time and again (McNEILL 1979).

Stages, trends and defining events in world history

As a frame on which to hang some queries and generalisations about the macro-historical process, let me recapitulate some basic trends and turning points in the development of world society. Remember though that historical facts are not so much 'facts' as accepted judgments. I draw heavily on McNeill (1979) for the pre-modern part of this story.

Throughout the last ice age, which lasted, with warmer and colder periods, from 115 000 years BP (Before Present) to 15 000 years BP, society was organised into small (less than 100) unstratified bands of hunter–gatherers. Mastery of fire was the technological key to their survival.

About 65 000 years BP a volcanic winter reduced the human population to perhaps 10 000 people. It has taken most of the ensuing interval for that genetically homogeneous group of *Homo sapiens* to populate the world, reaching, for example, Australia circa 50 000 years ago and North America c.12 000 years ago. Language then was a primitive instrument (for example, possibly without nouns [Jaynes 1976]), generating some information (commands, warnings, opportunities) additional to the senses as well as allowing, for the first time, useful information to be stored outside the individual's genes and memory. Despite being a primitive tool, language allowed humans to move to the top of the food chain.

While the human genome has changed little since, the speed of cultural development began to accelerate from about this time. For example, stone tools improved dramatically with the length of cutting edge obtainable from a source rock improving perhaps 10–12 fold between 65 000 years BP and 40 000 years BP.

12 000 BP–6000 BP

Coming out of the ice age, some 12 000 years ago, perhaps as the well-watered grasslands of the African–Asian steppe were drying out and as large food animals were becoming less abundant, humans started growing their food (for example, cereals) rather than obtaining it all from hunting and gathering. This was the Neolithic revolution in which, across the Eurasian continent, people began to live settled and relatively peaceful lives (although not necessarily longer and more leisurely lives) in agricultural villages. Life was mostly peaceful because food was produced only in subsistence quantities and this left no opportunity for non-producers such as priests and soldiers to be supported by farmers and little temptation to attack other villages in search of food. Population grew by the spatial spread, rather than the intensification, of settlement. Religion, art and magic became important tools for managing society.

6000 BP–3000 BP

Then came large-scale irrigated agriculture, beginning about 6000 years ago and, with the invention of writing, the beginning of history proper. Sumeria, the first real civilisation (meaning a society supporting cities and specialist occupations), appeared about 5500 years ago in southern Mesopotamia in the flat lands around the lower reaches of the Tigris and Euphrates rivers. Soon after, circa 5000 years ago, a Nilotic civilisation appeared. The complexities of managing irrigation systems devolved to a specialised priestly class which was fed from large grain surpluses (partly explainable by the invention of the plough as well as by high yields under irrigation), as was the warrior class which emerged to protect those same surpluses from marauders. As marauding increased, command (military) management replaced priestly management in the Mesopotamian and other irrigation civilisations. As urban populations grew in the irrigation civilisations additional specialist occupations (for example, metal working, transporting goods) emerged and the technologies associated with these new occupations advanced in step with the numbers who practised them.

Food surpluses induced a second surge in human numbers, this time in urban rather than rural areas. But waterborne diseases (boosted by close human contact) and the need to sustain armies acted as major checks on population growth. Only rich urban civilisations could sustain viruses and armies which ate but did not produce. While urban populations acquired some

immunity to the new diseases of crowded civilisation, rural peasant populations did not — an important determinant of the success of urban elites in
controlling outlying areas.

By about 3500 BP the Middle Eastern civilisations had been joined by
an Indian civilisation in the upper Punjab area and a Chinese civilisation on
the middle Hwang-Ho. The Mesoamerican and Andean civilisations began
around 3500 BP. The classical Greek civilisation on the Aegean Sea came
about 3100 BP. Across Eurasia societies were now coming to be organised
into spatially extensive politically independent imperial command structures.
Government-at-a-distance was achieved through the bureaucratic principle
of delegation. Taxes, collected on commission for the centre by feudal warlords, were the price of military protection. Difficulties with transport and
communications were persistent challenges to the management of empires, as
were fluctuations in crop yields. For instance in 3628 BP the Santorini vol-
cano exploded, destroying, by tidal waves [sic], the Minoan civilisation and
initiating a period of volcanic winter, and political instability, worldwide. In
the words of McNeill (1979), most of Eurasian political history can be viewed
as unending fluctuation between imperial consolidation and peripheral feudal unrest, punctuated at times by epidemics of invasion by mobile horse-riding nomads from the animal-producing steppes which lay beyond areas
suitable for cropping.

3000 BP–2000 BP

The millennium beginning around 3000 BP saw not only the continuing
expansions and contractions of Eurasia's empires but the decline of the
magic-based religions that had controlled social behaviour since the early
Neolithic. In what Jaspers (1953) calls the 'axial age' of new religions, the
period circa 2800 BP to 2200 BP saw the emergence of Taoism and
Confucianism in China, Buddhism and Hinduism in India, monotheism in
Iran and the Middle East and Greek rationalism in Europe. Beneath their
obvious differences all shared a concern for how to cope with the misery of
life (oppression and disease), how to transcend personal weaknesses and how
to live in peace in a flawed world. (Armstrong 2001). Morality had become
central to religion.

Even more importantly, both Jaspers (1953) and Jaynes (1976) identify the
axial period as a time of marked expansion in human consciousness, most
spectacularly in the Aegean civilisation (from where it spread through Eurasia
with the growth of the Alexandrian empire). What is involved here, and the
process is probably still in progress, is a transition from rationalising decisions

already made subconsciously to a rationalisation of decisions as choices between alternatives formulated by a conscious self; the species was beginning to escape its dependence on both external and internal authority. Primitive thinking in which (for example) names and images were perceived to be real properties of the things they signified began to give way to critical thinking, that is, thinking about the thinking process (Turchin 1977). Searching for a trigger for this transition, such adaptation and learning might begin when existing mental models of the consequences of actions fail, as may well have happened in the struggles to manage turbulent empires. Decisions based on custom, tradition and divine authority fail when conditions change.

2000 BP–1000 CE

And indeed, by about 2000 BP, the beginning of the Common Era (CE), a sort of stability had been reached in humanity's response to the advent of urbanisation. Circa 200 CE most of the world's people were to be found in four major civilisations stretching from the Atlantic to the Pacific ocean, north and south of the Mediterranean and across southern and eastern Asia. To the east of the Roman empire was the neo-Persian or Parthian empire (covering Iraq, Afghanistan, Iran). To the west of the Chinese empire was the Kushan empire covering parts of northern India, Afghanistan and central Asia. But not for long.

Trade within the protective boundaries of individual enlarging empires had grown slowly from the time of the irrigation civilisations, but some 2000 years ago long-distance trade and transport between civilisations by ship and caravan began to expand rapidly. Wind energy, captured by bigger sailing ships and utilised through trade, began to change power balances (Cottrell 1955). It was a development which, while bringing material benefits, new ideas and new technologies, inaugurated a thousand years of instability across Eurasia. The initial impact of this first move towards a globalisation of commerce was epidemiological disaster as the separate disease pools of each empire (plague, smallpox, measles, syphilis) mingled together. For example, drastic depopulation in parts of the Roman empire contributed to its disintegration. Conflict between the main religions raged. Weakened empires were beset by rebellion from within and raids from the steppes without. In 535 CE, atmospheric dust and debris from a major natural event, perhaps a comet or asteroid, but most probably the eruption of Mount Krakatau in the Sunda Strait, initiated several years of low temperatures and reduced sunlight. This led to crop failures around the world, followed by some decades of climatic instability (Keys 1999); plagues, droughts and floods placed further pressures on social organisation and this period saw the collapse of numerous societies including the major civilisations of South East Asia and South America. The 6th century, after 535 CE, was a period of major political reorganisation right across Europe and Asia, for example, the collapse of the southern Chinese empire during this time led to the consolidation of northern and southern China into a single empire.

From the 8th century, Islamic civilisation arose to unify the core of the western civilised world from Spain to India, while Sinic civilisation spread through Korea and Japan, and Indic civilisation throughout southern Asia. By 1000 CE complex global trading routes linked the centres of manufacturing production in the Middle East, China, India and Southeast Asia to underdeveloped suppliers of raw materials in Russia and Europe (Goldstone 1998).

1000 CE–Present

The first thousand years of the Common Era can be usefully interpreted as a seesawing struggle between authoritarian systems and market systems for control of the Eurasian civilisations. Which of these systems would determine how resources were to be mobilised into projects large and small? But after circa 1000 CE the balance between command and market systems began tipping inexorably towards the market as the major determinant of economic activity, first in China, then in the West. The undermining of western feudalism began after the 1300s with the slow emergence of rich and powerful non-aristocrats including merchants and landed gentry. It was in 1430 when, by peremptory imperial command, China withdrew from all trade, land and sea, opening the way for a European dominance of sea trade for centuries to come.

Gengis Khan and his sons and grandsons were the last great horse-riding marauders from the steppes. By the late 13th century their Mongol empire spread from the Pacific to the Black Sea and from Siberia to near-India. As much as anything it was bubonic plague which was responsible for its subsequent rapid break-up and the permanent closure of the great overland trade routes. Also, the spread of hand firearms allowed the formerly invincible mounted nomads to be repulsed.

Notwithstanding, an Islamic revival began in 1301 with the founding in Anatolia of the state which was to become the core of the future Ottoman empire, eventual master of much of Europe until the siege of Vienna in 1689. The Ottomans, together with two other Islamic empires, the Persian and the Mughal, controlled Eurasia from the frontiers of Austria and Morocco to the borders of China, plus much of northern India by 1639. Thereafter, these land-based empires began to give way to the seafaring Dutch, French and

English. But for 300 years the rise and spread of Islamic civilisation, with its great art, architecture, science and conquests, was the most important feature of Eurasian history.

While the biggest civilisations continued to break up, the advantages of large centrally organised armies for defence meant that the states which succeeded the large empires were still territorially extensive. Gunpowder was decisive in achieving political consolidation of these emerging states, for example, control of cannon, including the metals used for their construction, allowed castles of resisting warlords to be invaded.

Europe, however, remained unconsolidated. War there, commonly religious war, was endemic because no state had clear superiority. One consequence of this was an 'arms race' improvement in weaponry which was to later ensure the military dominance of Europe over the rest of the world. Also, there was greater scope for market-driven behaviour in Europe than elsewhere because capital could move between countries when the command system became too demanding. Because mercantile wealth could not be readily appropriated by bureaucratic authority, private and, subsequently, state wealth began to accumulate rapidly, feeding on itself. The new wealth accumulated preferentially in metropolitan areas at the expense of the rural peripheral peasantry who remained subject, not to market forces, but to feudal control over their lives.

The trend towards European dominance of trade and capital accumulation was only reinforced by the industrial revolution. After the 18th century European states were able to use both cheap manufactured goods and military superiority to dominate and extract surpluses from peripheral states around the world in a frenzy of colonisation. And in this they were helped by the decaying of the gunpowder empires that had arisen in the 15th and 16th centuries.

Of equal importance, the European Enlightenment of the 18th century brought three revolutionary changes of perspective, all of which spawned powerful secular trends which are still being worked through worldwide. Heilbroner (1995: 112) calls these the promise of science, capitalism's capacity to utilise resources and the legitimacy of the will of the people as the source of their own collective direction. To quote Harris (1977: 264) on the third of these:

> In anthropological perspective, the emergence of bourgeois democracies in seventeenth- and eighteenth-century Europe was a rare reversal of that descent from freedom to slavery which had been the main characteristic of the evolution of the state for 6000 years.

Throughout the 19th century, science and technology continued to provide capitalism with the inventions and innovations that, among other things, underpinned successive waves of economic growth and facilitated medicine's success in sharply reducing infant mortality. The former, economic growth, was strongly correlated with increasing fossil-energy use, first deep coal and then oil/gas, a relationship which led in the 20th century to pervasive, as distinct from what was a previously spotty degradation of the world's terrestrial and marine ecosystems and natural resources. The latter, reduced infant mortality, led to the 20th century population explosion which only now is being tempered by a worldwide demographic transition to fewer children per woman.

The 20th century, as noted in Chapter 1, was one of 'murderous and barbaric' wars over ideology and access to resources. Societies everywhere continued to move erratically along the path from traditional to modern and modern societies moved further towards marketism and individualism. Energy-hungry technologies allowed the capabilities of the food, transport and communications systems to grow enormously, thereby accelerating globalisation, this being the process whereby formerly separate societies come to function as a single society, economically, socially and culturally.

Two cautions

Short as it is, my potted history of world society mentions many of the factors that have featured in diverse attempts to interpret history — great men [sic], great ideas, great social movements, natural disasters, environmental change, resource availability, resource degradation, human nature, religion, culture, trade, war, disease, social stratification and technology (particularly new energy sources and their applications). It also throws up two cautions for those who would seek the quality survival of world society, that is, high quality of life for most people into the indefinite future.

One is that societies, particularly large societies, come and go with depressing regularity, at least on the scale of historical time. Against that of course, while individual societies tend not to survive, society as a whole has persisted. Perhaps the ultimate danger in globalisation is that it leaves only one society to disappear!

The second caution is that quality of life, at least as measured by the basic indicators of food availability, health and freedom from coercion, has been poor for most people for most of recorded history.

Encouraged perhaps by improvements in quality of life for ordinary people in limited parts of the world in recent centuries we might ask the historians if history has been directional in senses that matter for the present inquiry. And, taking up the other caution raised, what do they have to say about why societies come and go?

Is history directional?

The ancient Greeks certainly thought so, believing that societies pass through successively harsher ages they named as gold, silver, brass, iron etc. Nearer our own time, there has more commonly been an optimistic willingness to see history as progressive in some sense or other, that is, that things have tended to get better. Thus Benedetto Croce (1941) saw history as a story of increasing liberty, Arnold Toynbee (1934; 1961) saw it as a saga of successively higher religions. Von Ranke and Hegel (1837) in the 19th century, saw history as an unfolding of the human essence of reason. The Israelites and their successors saw history as the progressive working out of God's purpose.

Some have been willing to extrapolate trends they see in the past into the future. Most famously, Karl Marx, was willing to predict an eventual fundamental change in social organisation, namely from capitalism to socialism. With the fall of Soviet Communism, Francis Fukuyama (1992) thought he could administer the coup de grace to Marx and triumphantly proclaimed the 'end of history', meaning that capitalist liberal democracy was here to stay and spread. History in the Marxist sense of movement from one form of social order to another was over!

I myself have no difficulty in identifying trends in world history, notably increasing human knowledge, declining importance of instinct in determining human behaviour, increasing complexity in social organisation, increasing energy use and increasing size of political units. But I stop short of seeing any necessity for such past trends to continue into the future — a process which obviously requires the persistence of the conditions which initially nurtured the trend. Any trend can be disrupted or run out of the resources which feed it. Also, whether such trends are progressive in the sense of unequivocally promoting the lineage's quality survival is not at all clear. As Haldane (1932: 62) asked, is the history of the last 6000 years in the process of being replaced by a new historical process which will not obey any 'laws' we can detect in the old history?

The importance of initial conditions

While projecting historical trends is problematic, a simpler question may be more answerable. Are there directions which world history will not take? Are there constraints within which history is free to wander but beyond which it cannot go? It is a question which has been addressed by historical geographer Robert Dodgshon (1998). His list of the constraints (historical bindings) which reduce society's spectrum of possible future paths include natural laws, physical limits and logical, technological, economic, ethical, psychological, cultural and political constraints. But predicting in concrete terms when and how such constraints will operate is more difficult.

Dodgshon is particularly concerned with society's inertia or tendency to resist change. Intuitively, there are many large changes which are not possible over short periods, but what if the period being considered is a billion years? Society's inertial tendencies slow rather than stop change. For example, the physical use of space in the past (for example, structures erected, forests cleared) raises barriers against and reshapes opportunities for future change. A second example is institutional inertia. The standard analysis of institutional change sees ageing institutions becoming trapped in a performance crisis until a political crisis shifts the balance of power, allowing a radical overhaul of the 'rules of the game' (Visser and Hemerijck 1997: 53). Dodgshon's third example is 'knowledge inertia'. Societies transmit information in the form of cultural norms (how to behave) from generation to generation and while there is a degree of selection and novelty in what is passed on, most is handed down unchanged.

Inertia is not necessarily irrational. For example, 'lock in' is the name given to the situation where an institution or organisation recognises that a new goal-seeking strategy would be more cost-effective than current strategy (equals initial conditions) but for the investment cost involved in switching to the alternative.

Change depends on opportunity

Accepting then that societies are always constrained in how they can change, that they resist change, and that past trends may not continue, does macro-history have anything to say about how societies do change? Yes it does, a little. Just as a society's initial conditions — everything it has inherited from its past, including a culture and a biophysical environment — mark out what it cannot readily achieve, they also suggest, tentatively, what that society might attempt to achieve, and perhaps succeed in achieving.

The most powerful exposition I know of the importance of initial conditions is Jared Diamond's (1997) analysis of what is perhaps history's broadest pattern, the very different courses of history on different continents. Why did Aboriginal Australians remain stone-age hunter–gatherers while agriculture and empires were arising among Native Americans, and while widespread literacy and metal tools were arising in Eurasia? Why were Europeans the ones to conquer Africans, Aboriginal Australians and Native Americans, and not vice versa? Without going into detail here, Diamond shows that early Eurasians had access to plants and animals that were intrinsically susceptible to domestication, that this was less so in the Americas and even less so again in Australia. And indigenous peoples succumbed readily to European invasion partly because their 'initial condition' did not include resistance to European diseases or firearms.

Toynbee (see Somervell 1946: 569) too attempts to identify initial conditions which spawn major civilisations. After excluding 'benign environments' and 'racial superiority', he suggests that vigorous societies might arise where the environmental conditions faced are difficult rather than easy, but not too difficult, for example, the Viking emigrants from Norway responded well to the severe challenge of Iceland but collapsed before the severer challenge of Greenland. More generally, it is not just biophysical stresses which can prompt the flowering of a society. Toynbee's list of stressors includes the stimuli of military defeat, constant pressure from invaders and the strictures imposed by a larger society on one of its groups, for example, the outcast Jews or the enslaved groups that became powerful Christian societies.

For this study, the relevant question is whether there has been any identification of initial conditions which are positive indicators that a society has good survival prospects and quality of life prospects. While later chapters will be attempting to show that there may be, this is not something which emerges as such from the writings of macro-historians. More has been written on the converse question of why societies fail or, rather, flourish and then fail.

Is history cyclical?

As reviewed by Galtung and Inayatullah (1997) most macro-historians see societies developing in organisational complexity and then declining, one replacing the other. But only for some is such cycling superimposed on a progressive trend towards greater enlightenment and civilisation.

At their simplest, cyclical theories of history are perceptions of, a belief in, a repeating pattern in which cultures necessarily traverse a metaphorical sequence of birth, youth, old age and death, in a manner akin to the life cycle of biological organisms. The biological metaphor may or may not be extended to incorporate 'evolutionary' trends which persist through generations of cultures. Spengler's (1932) famous book, *The Decline of the West*, is archetypical; for him, the western European civilisation which arose circa 1000 CE reached the peak of its cultural achievements during the 18th century Enlightenment and is now in its old age.

Arnold Toynbee's view in *The Study of History* (see Somervell 1946) is more sophisticated. Civilisations grow out of earlier civilisations or a fusion of earlier civilisations or, occasionally, spring directly from 'primitive life'. For him, civilisations develop under the stimulus of creative individuals or small minorities whose innovations spread through and energise the society. But most civilisations eventually 'break down' when their creative minority becomes a merely 'dominant minority' and loses the allegiance of the majority. Social cohesion and unity is lost. Note though that breakdown does not necessarily proceed to disintegration or collapse, that is, to the demise of the state. Upheaval might be a better word.

States have risen and collapsed with bewildering rapidity in all parts of the world in the past 5000 years. When a complex society collapses it suddenly becomes smaller, simpler and much more egalitarian. Population falls, and energy use, information flows, trade and economic activity all dry up (Fagan 1996: 193). Joseph Tainter (2000), one of the few archaeologists to have made a comparative study of collapsed societies, points out that an initial investment by society in developing complexity in its organisation is a rational way of trying to solve the problems of the moment. At first the strategy works. For example, agricultural production increases through more intensive farming methods, an emerging bureaucracy manages production and distribution well, expanding trade brings wealth to a new elite who use their authority and wealth to undertake great public works. Then as the less costly solutions to society's problems are exhausted, it becomes imperative that new organisational and economic answers be found, even though these may well be decreasingly cost-effective. As stresses develop, a complex society such as that of the Maya becomes increasingly vulnerable to collapse: there are few reserves to carry it through natural disasters; groups within society see that centralisation and complexification are not working and withdraw their support; the trend towards decentralisation and collapse becomes unstoppable.

Collapse is thus a rational, albeit traumatic, response when increasing stress and malfunction demand organisational change. Tainter does point out though that all-out collapse will not occur unless there is a power vacuum in the sense that there is no strong neighbouring state waiting to absorb the vulnerable state (cf. Toynbee's 'fusion' of civilisations). Tainter's insight is that complexification is a strategy for solving a society's problems which is often successful in the short term but which, in the long term, may well increase that society's vulnerability to collapse. Western civilisation has avoided this fate so far, he says, through a combination of luck and ingenuity which has allowed complexification to continue. He is referring to the discovery of the New World and finding and learning how to use fossil fuels. Catton (1980: 3) points out that the fossil fuel 'solution' has generated a whole new raft of problems to be solved — more complexification.

Models of long economic cycles

Economic historians have long noted *stages* in the development of market economies. Marx's long-term perspective focused on the feudalism-capitalism-communism sequence. Rostow (1953), working in a post-1750 timeframe, and with little support from available data, postulates five stages of economic development, that is, five stages of increasing human productivity, starting with traditional agriculture and ending with a mature industrial economy.

Economic historians have also long recognised that mature market economies go through superimposed *cycles* (of different length) of increasing and decreasing economic activity (for example, Berry 2000). Most cycles so recognised are measured in months or years, but there has been one bold attempt, largely ignored by today's mainstream economists, to understand how and why economic activity rises and falls over decades. *Kondratieff cycles* are named for the Russian whose massive study of social and economic time series data first identified them (Kondratieff 1926). His empirical observation was that many innovations and processes diffuse through society over time in a way which can be described by an S-shaped (sigmoid) curve, that is, slow growth at the beginning, followed by accelerating and then decelerating growth culminating in market saturation, for example, mainframe computers 'saturated' around 1995.

Periods of global growth and expansion in economic activities last about 55 years under this model and are punctuated with phases of fundamental change in the structure of the economy, the technological base and many social institutions and relations. Towards the end of a growth phase in the economy, many markets saturate and growth slows. The search for revitalised profits induces a cluster of new technologies which slowly at first, and then more rapidly, penetrate markets (Grubler and Nakicenovic 1991). Why 55 years? Berry (2000) finds economic activity strongly correlated with a lunisolar cycle of that length, one which affects crop production regularly and just sufficiently to nudge (entrain) various aspects of economic activity into step with each other and with the lunisolar cycle!

Is history recurrent?

Historians, as well as detecting directions and cycles in history, have also perceived categories of society-shaping processes which, while not strictly cyclical, have re-occurred frequently enough to warrant their recognition by future generations as ever-present contingencies.

The work of the Australian economic historian Graeme Snooks (1996) is a good example. After concluding that 'we have no consistent explanation of the rise and fall of civilizations', Snooks presents his own innovative interpretation of the dynamics of human society over the past 2 million years. He suggests that individuals in a competitive environment generate community growth by investing in the four dynamic strategies of family multiplication, conquest, commerce and technological change. He argues that the rise and fall of societies is an outcome of the opportunistic (not cyclical) development and exhaustion of these strategies. He uses his dynamic-strategy model to discuss future outcomes for human society, arguing that far from leading to ecological destruction, growth-inducing technological change is both necessary and liberating.

Less sanguinely, CD Darlington (1969) says that the big lesson from history is that humans destroy the resource base on which they depend. Diamond (1992) notes three situations in which human populations tend to wreak great damage on their environments:

1   When people suddenly colonise an unfamiliar environment, for example, Maori destruction of megafauna in New Zealand (Flannery 1994), European settlers in Australia;.

2   When people advance along a new frontier (like the first peoples to reach America) and can move on when they have damaged the region behind;

3   When people acquire a new technology whose destructive power they have not had time to appreciate, for example, New Guinea pigeon hunters with shotguns.

Diamond (1992) says it has always been hard for people to know the rate at which they can safely harvest biological resources indefinitely, without depleting them. Decline may be difficult to distinguish from normal year-to-year fluctuations and by the time the signs are clear enough it may be too late. We of course have no such excuse; we know what has happened before and we know how to model sustainable harvesting and the importance of precautionary behaviour.

While well-recognised as important in isolated cases (for example, Easter Island), resource degradation has also been the recurring process behind the steady westward movement of the centre of western civilisation over several millennia (Diamond 1992). Particularly in arid and variable climates, deforestation, time and again, has led to soil erosion and the destruction of dams and terraces for example, in the classical Aegean civilisation. As a rule of thumb, irrigation-based civilisations such as first arose in Egypt, Mesopotamia and the Indus Valley several thousand years BCE, seldom last more than a few centuries before degrading the soil resource through salting and waterlogging. In general, it is intensification in resource use which leads to environmental depletion and, from there, to either sudden collapse of the cultural system or a shift to a new mode of production. Even when resource degradation has not been fatal, adjustment to it has usually been painful in quality of life terms for ordinary people.

Extreme events and *trigger events* are other recurrent determinants of historical change. Events which are small in themselves can sometimes trigger large changes — the 'butterfly effect'. As the Papua New Guineans found, 'one steel axe can ruin your stone age culture' and their country moved from a stone age to a greeting-card culture (literally) in forty years. Perhaps the triggering of the First World War by the assassination of Archduke Ferdinand is another. The conditions under which small triggers induce major change will be discussed presently. At other times it is the encountering and survival of extreme events which determine a society's subsequent evolution — the Irish potato famine, wars of independence, great droughts and so on.

One of history's most common recurrent processes is *conflict* and *competition* in all its forms — between individuals, between social classes, between regions within a society and between nations. Throughout history, social structures at all scales have normally been organised into a powerful ruling minority and a ruled majority, playing out a struggle between authority and freedom (Haldane 1932; 1937: 63).

For example, Wallerstein's (1974) notion of dominant core regions always developing at the expense of dependent peripheral regions can be applied to all societal change from early times, for example, colonialism, imperialism, lagging regions within a country. Incorporation and peripheralisation and the conflict it engenders is a recurrent historical process in nations, empires and world society. Conventional balance-of-power thinking about international relations (Alexander 1987: 108) is another example (see page 274). Such sees nation states as striving to ensure that others behave in ways acceptable to them by the use of deterrence or, if that fails, violence.

History tends to record only breaches of the peace, but obverse processes of *co-operation* and *coordination,* sometimes voluntary, sometimes coercive, are just as ubiquitous as conflict. Indeed, conflictual and co-operative behaviours may well have co-evolved to the extent that in early history the main function of human groups was protection from the predatory effects of other human groups (Alexander 1979: 222). Beyond predation, the tribe, the neolithic village, the medieval city and the modern nation-state all benefit their members through processes which amplify what can be achieved by individuals acting alone, for example, specialisation, concerted action. People co-operate particularly well when engaged in inter-group competition, but, conversely, find it particularly difficult to co-operate with an adversary to resolve conflict (Burton 1997). Since Spencer's popularisation of social Darwinism, historians have had some difficulty in recognising that co-operation and competition have played comparably important roles in history.

Summary: Things that keep happening

While it could be much extended, the list of processes that keep recurring in the historical record and which I have singled out because I think they will continue to be important in managing the future include population growth, trade, war, and technological change (Snooks' four), resource degradation, catastrophes and competition–co-operation within and between societies.

Role of the individual and the small group in history

In traditional, unchanging societies, individuals play their scripted roles and return from whence they came. In describing societies which are changing — expanding, contracting, replacing social forms, technologies etc. — historians and social scientists routinely view individuals and small groups as lead agents of change. Individuals and social movements may be depicted as autonomous agents of social transformation or simply as the tools of larger historical forces (who's going to lead the revolution?). More complexly, it may be recognised that people's capacities and propensities to act as change-agents are moulded by the environment they seek to change, for example, a society where people are hungry is more likely to spawn revolutionaries than fabians (see page 172).

Arnold Toynbee (see Somervell 1946: 588) is an historian who argues that a vital culture is always the product of a small creative minority whose ideas and innovations diffuse widely. In a society's growth stage, creative individuals lead successful responses to successive challenges. In the disintegration stage they appear as saviours *of* or *from* the disintegrating society. Haldane (1932; 1937: 62) too accepts the importance of individuals in history but suggests it is inventors rather than artists, philosophers and generals who have shaped history, this being 'the story of man's attempts to solve the practical problems of everyday life': Pasteur and Darwin were the two greatest biologists of the 19th century but whereas Pasteur changed the world, Darwin only affected the way we think about it!

In principle, every human life changes the subsequent course of history forever. In practice, the effects of most lives are not detectable in the historical record. Those who make a major innovative or disruptive or incompetent contribution can be detected over centuries and a very few religious, intellectual and military leaders appear to be still affecting social and individual behaviour worldwide after millennia, for example, Jesus, Buddha, Plato, Confucius, Genghis Khan, Alexander the Great. It has to be assumed that it is the coming together of a particular fluid historical environment, one where great social forces are colliding, and a particular personality (which is itself a product of the historical environment) that produces historically significant individuals, that is, both are necessary. Even then, to quote Geoffrey Barraclough (1991: 92), 'the interplay between the individual — let us say a Bismarck — and the society in which he works remains as mysterious as ever'.

Small groups can also be important for genetic reasons. One of Darlington's (1969) main themes is the great contribution made to all societies by the progeny of hybridisation between immigrant and local populations, for example, the contribution of the Huguenots to English society. This eminent and controversial geneticist, argues that inbred societies produce genetically uniform populations suited to historically stable conditions and that outbreeding societies produce a proportion of specially talented individuals (and a matching proportion of misfits) who, over many generations contribute to every field of activity and culture. Conversely, migrants who breed only among themselves will be more likely to produce useful but unremarkable members of society. A similar argument applies to breeding across class lines within a society (his definition of a class is a group that works together and breeds together), for example, Leonardo, Erasmus. Just to complicate matters, the effects of a resident population outbreeding with a migrant group are likely to be different in terms of talented and deviant progeny depending on whether the resident population is itself outbreeding or inbreeding.

In general, outbreeding produces the genetic variability which allows a population to adapt to environmental change by natural selection. But too much variability is disruptive of social control and an environment-specific balance between endogamy and exogamy (inbreeding and outbreeding) needs to be struck. What that means in practice is not self-evident although, as a rule of thumb, societies change most rapidly where interaction between people, and hence interbreeding, is not constrained by barriers of religion, poverty or language (Darlington 1969: 677).

SOME SOCIAL PSYCHOLOGY

Psycho-history — leaders and followers

We have been pack animals for a very long time. It can be postulated that the adaptive values of a dominance (leadership) hierarchy in primate groups are that it allows rapid decision-making under pressure, facilitates control of behaviour within the group and facilitates interactions between groups. Both willingness to be led and the will to lead are at least partly instinctual, but since late Neolithic times the history of humans can be characterised as a process of growing individuation, particularly with respect to the declining importance of instinct in determining behaviour — including leader–follower behaviour. It is here that social (cf. individual) psychology offers more insight than history into the way in which leaders and followers interact in shaping historical events.

Particularly since the renaissance, since the 16th century say, humans have been increasingly freed from the religious and social bonds which formerly inhibited their capacity to develop their intellectual and emotional potential as individuals, that is, to individuate. But, as argued by Fromm (1942: chapter 1), these bonds satisfied people's instinctual need to belong to a group and to have authority in their lives, telling them what to do. This loss of social and religious roles makes contemporary people responsive to confident leadership and hence susceptible to fundamentalism — political, philosophical, religious — and authoritarianism. This appetency for submission to internal (for example, conscience) and external (for example, public opinion) authority, an innate desire for freedom to individuate and a will to power are the three psychological components of a society's *social character,* jostling to determine how strongly and to where a society will be led.

More generally, a society's social character is those motivators/drivers of actions and feelings which are common to most of its members. According to Fromm (1942: 14), it is shaped primarily by (but is not the mere shadow of) the economic system of production and the sort of work available simply because this is what the individual has to accept and adapt to in order to live. This is also why certain definite changes in social character take place at certain historical epochs. For example, Protestant doctrines prepared people to accept the roles they were required to play under industrialism. Or, another example, after the renaissance, economic activity became respectable whereas in medieval times salvation was the primary concern. Putting it this way, the modern individual emerged from the destruction of the medieval social structure. And the process continues. The success of industrial capitalism requires consumption and, presto, a social character with accumulation as its central concern has emerged (with, as Postman, Chomsky and others contend, a little help from the advertising industry).

A view of human nature

What is being proposed here is a view of *human nature(s)* as being neither biologically nor culturally fixed. Social character can be thought of as the expression of human nature in a particular historical setting. It evolves with circumstances, adapting to but perhaps lagging behind the cultural pattern (just as shifts in the genetic component of leadership and followership tendencies will lag behind cultural shifts). Strivings to satisfy basic physiological and higher needs are not malleable in themselves, but the psychological drives mediating the ways in which these satisfactions are sought will vary. That is, they will vary between societies while showing a degree of uniformity among the members of particular societies at particular times.

The extreme plasticity of social character under socialisation and social conditioning is both a force for and a danger to societal survival. It allows societies to adapt reasonably rapidly to necessity (for example, wartime mobilisation) but can be badly misdirected, for example, Nazi Germany. While despots and heroes can reorient social behaviour in the short term, societies which continue to ignore or deny basic needs will be forever unstable (Henderson 1998b: 216). John Burton, pioneer of modern conflict resolution, nominates identity, recognition, security and personal development as the human needs most relevant to conflict avoidance and resolution (Rubenstein 2001).

The above is a view of human nature which is out of step with Freud's view of history as being the result of psychological forces which are innate and not conditioned by changing circumstances. And it is a view which is out of step with a behaviourist psychology which assumes that human nature has no dynamism of its own but is totally determined by the prevailing culture, that most behaviour is learned involuntarily through a mechanistic feedback process (Skinner 1971).

These differences are matters of degree, perhaps, and the position I will be taking forward is that social character does change and therefore probably can be purposively changed, within limits. In principle at least, societies should be able to somewhat reshape the ways in which both leaders and followers are motivated and hence behave.

Although leadership of hierarchical structures by individuals — usually competitive males — is established in all aspects of all complex societies, it has not been regarded kindly by psychologists. Freud's rival, Alfred Adler (Wilson 1972: 160) puts the drive to seek dominance, a sense of superiority, at the centre of his thinking about personality — not as an irrational impulse but as a rational strategy for protecting against one's insecurity and inferiority. Erich Fromm sees a drive for power as an expression of an individual's inability to stand alone and live, a desperate attempt to gain secondary strength where inner strength is lacking.

SOCIOLOGY AND SOCIETAL CHANGE

Sociologists study societies as they are functioning at a point in time. History can thus be thought of as sociology projected backwards in time. Sociology grew from attempts to counter social disorder by creating a theory of social order, locating order and disorder in the quantity and quality of social relations. This led to the idea that social order is maximised where social relations are densely knit and suffused with value consensus; and a disorderly society exists where social relations are atomised and deranged by dissensus over values. From there it is a short step to seeing the heart of the social process as movement from one sort of society to another (Wolf 1982: 9). In particular, sociology has been concerned with how 'modernisation' has occurred in different societies in the last few hundred years. We have space to mention three strands of thought in mainstream sociology — structural–functionalism (what a mouthful), cultural materialism and power-and-conflict thinking. All have a perspective to contribute to understanding societal change (Etzioni-Halevy 1981).

Received perspectives

Structural–functionalism starts from the idea that any social structure (set of 'fixed' relationships between a set of social entities) which evolves must have a useful function. As developed by Merton (1957) and Parsons (1949), it sees social evolution proceeding through successive differentiation of subsystems within society. First, the political, cultural and judicial subsystems become distinct and autonomous; then, when the economy and the technology on which it is based become fully autonomous, modernisation occurs. In time, these differentiated subsystems become (magically?) reintegrated. Societies, under this view, are relatively stable, but strains (for example, unrest) can emerge when traditional goals are not being met and this can precipitate major change. There is more emphasis though on how structural subsystems fit together and function as an integrated whole rather than on how they change.

Adherents to a *cultural materialist* view of society (Elwell 1991; Harris 1979) are 'infrastructure determinists' who suggest that the entire structure (organisation) of any socio-cultural system rests on the way the society exploits its environment to meet the biological and psychological needs of the population. That is, the mode of production determines the forms of families, collectives and other group structures which in turn determine the behavioural and cognitive superstructure of society (cf. Fromm above). Infrastructure is given this leading role because it reflects the way a society adapts to its environment to meet basic needs — society's primary task. Group structure and mental and cultural superstructure must necessarily adapt to be compatible with the 'given' infrastructure (our values depend on the age in which we live).

There is a clear debt here to Marx's basic idea that social life is shaped by the way people engage nature through production and that the mode of production can be referenced to identify forces guiding social alignments such as class. Cultural materialists nonetheless view societies as very stable systems with most changes in structure, infrastructure or superstructure being resisted and dampened elsewhere in the system. Most successful social changes start with a mutual change in both the production system and its environment. Elwell (1991: 11) claims that many of these reconfigurations have been changes that extract more energy from the environment, particularly where this favours the well-being of elite groups. Intensification of the production system in this way leads eventually to some form of environmental depletion and then to either a sudden collapse of the cultural system or a shift to a new mode of production. If the culture shifts successfully, intensification starts all over again.

The post-1950s *power and conflict* school of sociology rejects the structural–functionalism emphasis on value consensus and integration. Like cultural materialism it starts with Marx but broadens the idea of social conflict to power in general (Dahrendorf 1959). Thus Mills (1959) partitions society into power elites (political, military, economic) and masses. The elites manipulate the masses into accepting their rule, apparently believing that the masses do not have the organising ability to challenge their power. Gramsci (Etzioni-Halevy 1981: 58), developing what he calls 'hegemony theory', suggests that the ruling classes gain a large degree of consent from the masses (for example, through mass culture, advertising, mass production) and therefore do not need heavy-handed coercion to keep control of society. An important principle emerging from power-and-conflict thinking is that when class conflict is institutionalised it becomes containable.

Weber and Durkheim

Two other giants of early sociology, Max Weber (1864–1920) and Emile Durkheim (1858–1917), must be mentioned in the present context of understanding how societies change. Like Marx, Weber worked out an elaborate theory of the rise of capitalism. Where Marx saw economic factors and class conflict as prime movers of history, Weber's explanation added the individual's values and ideas to Marx's economic explanation. For example, he identified a 'spirit of capitalism' which encouraged entrepreneurs to re-invest rather than consume (Weber 1905; 1958). For Weber, the distinctiveness of modern western society lies in its rationality as evidenced in ends-means thinking, organised schemes of thought, the decline of myth and magic etc. *Rationalisation* is a habit of thought involving ongoing evaluation of the best means for achieving given ends. Bureaucratic thinking about human organisations and technocratic thinking about industrial processes are two examples. It is rationalisation which produces ongoing change. Weber's contribution, apart from rationalisation, was his distinction between the stability of traditional society and the flexibility of modern society (see comments on Anthony Giddens below).

Bureaucracy (not in the 'red tape' sense) is a most effective form of social organisation, capable of marshalling resources rationally and efficiently for undertaking large or small projects. Its method and effectiveness lies in its coordinating of the contributions which different specialists can make. It has several weaknesses, the first being that its concentration on means-efficiency can lead to a failure to question organisational ends and overall goals. Second, bureaucracies are notorious for alienating their members, producing in them a sense of powerlessness, isolation and meaninglessness in the face of conditions they cannot control and consider oppressive.

Durkheim (1893–1964) recognised that the interdependence of individuals in a modern society is created by the division of labour and expressed in contractual relations. But, he argued, contracts alone are insufficient to explain the integration and cohesiveness of modern societies. Behaviour in human societies is also strongly affected by norms — principles of right action binding upon members of a group and serving to produce acceptable behaviour. For example, contracts are useless without an expectation that they will be honoured. People acquire norms by being taught and by observing and imitating the behaviour of others. Culture is information stored in human brains that, together with individuals' genes and environments, determines their behaviour. Since culture is communicated from one person to another, individuals sample from and contribute to an evolving cultural pool, much as they do an evolving gene pool.

Without such *collective representations* (shared ideas), individuals aspire beyond what is possible in their society and anomie (normlessness, lack of direction) and strains on the fabric of society (cf. structural–functionalism) result. Recall an earlier reference to Fromm's observation that all societies socialise people so they want to do what must be done to keep society functioning. In order to provide society with effective problem-solving institutions, people's behaviour must be patterned and controlled. Roles and behavioural norms are set up and the effectiveness of the resulting organisation is reinforced by assigning hierarchical status to roles. Quality of life for participants in such arrangements depends in part on how well they have been socialised into their roles.

Giddens the synthesiser

Anthony Giddens is a much-lauded contemporary social theorist who, in developing an understanding of the dynamism of modern societies, has synthesised ideas from many sources, including Weber's thinking about the role of the individual and Durkheim's thinking about the role of collective ideas in the process of social change. Also, drawing on power-and-conflict thinking, he sees four subsystems ('institutional clusters') in modern societies — capitalism, industrialism, bureaucratic control of the population, military power — which are the foci of organised conflict and struggle in society (cf. Marx's class struggles). While change within each of these four subsystems is fast and wide-ranging compared with traditional societies, the subsystems themselves remain in place — 'shells' with unchanging names and functions but changing methods.

His 1979 theory of *structuration* (cf. Eisler's [1998] theory of *cultural transformation*) addresses the problem of whether it is individual acts or major social forces that shape society. He asserts that it is human agency in the form of purposive behaviour by individuals which continuously reproduces (maintains) social structures such as belief systems, institutions, organisations, interpersonal relations etc. Putting this more simply, unless people keep acting in particular ways, playing their roles, social structures will break down. If this is so, it means that one or more individuals can change structures in sociopolitical systems over time by making slightly different decisions, acting differently but not too differently. So social structures form a context which neither determines human actions fully nor leaves them entirely unconstrained. Ultimately, structure and agency are capable of transforming each other. As an example, Schon's (1971) description of the emergence of ideas-in-good-currency when existing ideas are failing would seem also to be a description of structuration at work.

Understanding institutional change

What is an institution? It is useful to view each of society's various institutions as groups of people playing interacting roles according to recognised rules, usually with the purpose of solving problems of a particular type. Institutions are the subsystems of society. All institutions are mechanisms which reflect ideas about how to best deal with practical problems and, being abstractive, they all follow a common strategy of attempting to lower the transaction costs (for example, 'the costs of doing business') and the uncertainties (for example, how will X behave?) associated with interactions between people in a particular problem setting (North 1993). It is important to note that all institutions are a form of co-operation (see page 269).

The standard model of institutional change (new rules, new roles etc.), as noted earlier, is that institutions change only when a political crisis allows their declining performance to be addressed (Krasner 1988). It is a view that does not acknowledge the possibility of institutions attempting to proactively improve their real or perceived performance and adjusting to ever-changing circumstances.

Institutional performance can degrade in various ways. For example, an institution which originally offered its participants a mutually beneficial exchange becomes unbalanced, rewarding some participants unduly (Blau 1955). Once a pattern of system failure appears and target problems are not being solved, demands for change begin and the institution loses legitimacy. Not that a failing institution dies easily. Vested interests and habitual behaviour ensure that time and a sustained effort are needed to deliver renewal. When the need for institutional change first becomes demanding, the institution's initial response is to change superficially by finding new ways of doing and thinking which do not upset existing power and status arrangements. But, as the need for change continues to press, theory suggests there must eventually be a choice between progressive and regressive change (Borgeryd 1998: 235). Regressive change involves stricter conformity to tradition and, commonly, a loss of effective aspects of the institution as well as dysfunctional aspects. Progressive change brings the institution more in line with its professed ideals.

What we have here is a view of institutional change which sits easily with Giddens' concept of structuration. Institutions exist because people keep acting in ways that reproduce them but, while they cannot be changed at will, institutions can be slowly changed by purposive individual actions. And, episodically, there will be crises which allow/force institutions to change dramatically.

SYSTEMS THEORY AND SOCIETAL CHANGE

The starting point for applying systems theory (Box 4.1) to societal change is to recognise that societies (including world society) are dissipative (energy-degrading) systems. The fundamental property of dissipative systems (Glansdorff and Prigogine 1971) is that they continuously take in energy, physical materials and information (a form of energy with special properties) from their environment and continuously excrete (dissipate) materials, information and degraded energy — energy of a lowered quality in terms of its capacity to do work — back into the environment, for example, waste heat. Within its boundaries, a dissipative system's intake of energy, materials and information is used to build and maintain persistent processes called structures. The appendix on page 327 describes, very succinctly, the basic properties of such systems. It will be difficult reading for those unfamiliar with such ideas but, given the richness of this way of thinking, worth an effort. If societies are dissipative systems, sometimes at least, they should change over time in ways which can be interpreted as examples of processes which are characteristic of such systems. In following sections we note various efforts, mainly successful in my view, to read such processes into observed societal change. Discussion is organised under the three headings of self-organisation, feedback and complexification.

Many of the societal-change processes to be identified as examples of the behaviour of dissipative systems have of course been previously described, here and elsewhere, in the languages of other disciplines. The question then is whether thinking in systems terms identifies important processes previously unrecognised, or highlights the importance of previously recognised processes.

BOX 4.1 WHAT IS A SYSTEM?

The concept of system has arisen as part of humanity's efforts to make sense of the world it finds itself in. By definition, systems are networks of semi-independent components or entities or subsystems or holons (a useful word invented by Arthur Koestler) continuously interacting with each other according to their own behavioural rules or decision rules. For example, a component's rules for transforming inputs into outputs or for transferring outputs of materials, energy or information (a 'packet' form of energy with special properties) to other system components (most processes amount to some form of transformation or transfer). Once the concept is discovered of course, the world turns out to be full of 'systems'!

While components of any properly identified system interact with 'the rest of the world' (which means other systems), this inter-action will be muted compared with the intensity of interactions between components within that system. While the act of putting a (permeable) boundary around some part of the world and calling its contents a system and everything else 'environment' is ultimately arbitrary, there are those who argue that the living world at least is full of 'natural' systems formed by chunky sets of transformational processes that are comparably 'fast' or 'slow' — that is, which take similar times to experience significant change — or that take place at comparable spatial scales. In practice, a system's environment is not 'everything else' but those temporal fluctuations external to the sys-tem (called drivers) to which its behaviour is responsive.

When a system (for example, a community of organisms) contains components that function on distinctly different space-time scales (for example, organisms are constrained to live in a smaller space and for a shorter time than the community to which they belong), the system is said to be hierarchical or hierarchically organised.

System dynamics is the study of how systems change over time although the term is also applied to an approach to system modelling developed by Jay Forrester (1961).

Self-organisation

A self-organising system is one with the capacity to markedly change its behav-iour rules, and hence its structure, in response to appropriate change (fluctua-tion) in its external environment or in the environment of one of its internal subsystems. If the flow rates of energy and materials through the system's envi-ronment change by more than some critical amount the system collapses into disconnected subsystems, and if they change by less than some critical amount the disturbed system homeostatically resumes its prior behaviour.

Historically, the truly spectacular examples of societal self-organisation (think of it as reorganisation) have been triggered by new energy sources becoming available — fire, animal power, water power, wind power, coal power, oil power. Cottrell (1955) argues convincingly that the amounts and types of energy employed not only condition society's way of life materially, but set somewhat predictable limits on how society can and will be organ-ised. More generally, it has been the endogenous development of social technologies (task specialisation, human rights, democracy etc) and material technologies (metal working, printing, remote communications etc) which have ushered in 'threshold' reorganisation. External triggers for reorganisation include natural disasters, war, famine and disease, all these being triggers which first lead to a loss of current organisation.

Not that systems theory has much to say on how societies will specifically reorganise in response to major innovations and disturbances. Responses will be shaped by the determinants of change but just how and to what extent society's structure, superstructure and infrastructure will change is problematic (see page 169). Putting this differently, steering a self-organising process is very difficult.

Perhaps the best that can be done is to create a *context* of constraints which will exclude various sorts of unacceptable change-trajectories from eventuating, for example, prohibit profiteering and reduce trade barriers during food shortages. Context takes the form of physical structures in the case of a natural environment, formal and informal institutions in the case of a social environment and norms and values in the case of a cultural environment. More generally, societies which are in a process of reorganisation are constrained in terms of what changes will be possible. As noted earlier, the sorts of constraints which reduce the spectrum of possible future paths to reorganisation include natural laws, physical limits, logical constraints, technological and economic constraints and psycho-socio-cultural constraints. If over-constrained though, the society will not be able to find any feasible way of reorganising itself.

Self-organisation and resilient behaviour

Self-organising systems which are *resilient* do not reorganise themselves unless strongly perturbed; nor are they easily disorganised. Empirically, societies which have survived large disturbances historically are perhaps more likely to be resilient in the face of future disturbances but not necessarily. Surviving small disturbances is no test for resilience. Systems that suddenly break down in the face of disturbances that they could previously absorb have clearly lost resilience. But that is knowledge after the event. Does systems theory help to identify societies which are resilient *a priori* and hence less likely to change markedly tomorrow? For example, a society with 'buffered' components that learn new behaviours or reorganise rather than collapse in the face of disturbance — a system with resilient subsystems — is more likely to be resilient overall.

Like immature ecosystems compared to mature ecosystems, simple societies are more likely to be resilient than complex societies. From a proactive perspective, simple societies stand to be more resistant to change. A complex society with many highly interdependent institutions, organisations and individuals will be susceptible to small disturbances to any of its many feedback links, but just how much disorganisation this precipitates is again unpredictable. Indeed, small disturbances may lead to reorganisation rather than disorganisation.

Dynamic behaviour

Theory recognises that a dissipative system can show a variety of intrinsic dynamic behaviours, that is, patterns of change over time, depending on the mix of feedback processes operating inside the system rather than on the way in which the system has been disturbed from outside. As noted above, these include cycling, oscillating, sigmoid growth, explosive growth, rapid decline and chaotic behaviour. Examples recognised in societal systems include:

- Myrdal (1944) argued for the idea (winning a Nobel prize along the way) that group disadvantage is a form of cumulative causation or positive feedback that makes economic development in third world countries very difficult to achieve. Conversely, advantage tends to breed advantage unless countered by government;

- Long waves of economic activity (see page 162) involve sigmoid growth and depend on both positive and negative feedbacks triggered by product innovation and market saturation;

- Kenneth Watt (1992) argues that depressions and wars are consequences of ineffective feedback controls, notably on the rate of repatriation of war debt;

- Technological change is commonly seen as a self-accelerating process dominated by positive feedback, that is, new technologies make further technologies possible;

- Mode-locking is the tendency in dissipative systems for oscillations in different parts of the system to synchronise with each other. Examples can be found of social phenomena (for example, birthrates) moving in step with economic activity. More generally, mode-locking leads to a synchronising of economic activities which are cycling with periods of different lengths (see page 162). It is generally recognised that systems showing mode-locking and increasing oscillatory behaviour are often near a level of (hyper)complexity from which they can be reorganised by a small disturbance into one of several markedly different dynamic behaviours (see page 219).

If a societal system is not behaving as desired, it may be possible to deliberately introduce new feedback loops, positive or negative, to improve behaviour, for example, reward desired behaviour or punish unwanted behaviour. Such *feedback control* can be contrasted with *feed-forward* or *pre-emptive control* in which action is taken now to modify some anticipated future state of the system, for example, change the way children are educated.

Critical states and chaotic behaviour

Dissipative systems which have self-organised themselves into a condition of extreme complexity, sometimes called hypercomplexity, where they are liable to change dramatically under the impact of small disturbances, are said to be in a *critical state* (Bak 1996) or at the *edge of chaos* (Kauffman 1995). Buchanan (2000) suggests that a large proportion of natural and social systems are in such an unstable critical state most of the time and that recognising the 'ubiquity' of the critical state is a valuable starting point for understanding what has happened in history and will happen in the future. When change is triggered in a hypercomplex sociopolitical system it can be of several broad types which can be characterised as disorganisation, chaotic reorganisation or orderly reorganisation.

Disorganisation for an animal or plant means death and the loss of all levels of organisation from the conscious to the biomolecular. For a society, disorganisation may just involve the loss of some higher levels of organisation (for example, the legal system in Colombia or the financial system in Argentina) while lower levels (for example, village life) continue to function. Catastrophe theory does suggest that when a system is collapsing from the top down, the upper levels will fail quickly and the lower levels more slowly.

When an orderly (non-chaotic) system reorganises it behaves as though programmed to leave one phase of a developmental or life cycle and enter a new phase (see Appendix). There is continuous directional change in most aspects of the system, with some parts growing or declining and some disappearing or newly emerging. For example, a society retains its essential character even as some quality of life measures continue to improve and others to deteriorate. Multi-stage theories of economic development are identifying such a process (see page 162).

When a system in a critical state reorganises chaotically, its behaviour fluctuates, within limits, in an apparently random fashion, but the particular way it behaves depends sensitively on the state it is in when it begins to reorganise. That is to say, a slight difference in the state it is in prior to reorganisation makes a major difference to the chaotic path it subsequently follows. Another way of putting this is that in dealing with a chaotic system one can never confidently associate a given outcome with a given set of initial conditions because those initial conditions can never be known precisely enough.

Notwithstanding, even though the behaviour of such bifurcating (fork-ing) chaotic systems may not be predictable far enough ahead to be useful (for example, weather forecasting) they might eventually prove to be manageable (steerable like a car) simply because they will respond to a series of small nudges (Moravec 1999: 155). A bottleneck in the availability of some resource is an example of such a leverage point. More generally there may be phases of intrinsic dynamic behaviour that are more favourable to system change than others. The challenge is to learn how to reliably identify which is which.

While it is of no help for predicting the immediate behaviour of a chaot-ic system, many such systems fluctuate or produce recurrent outcomes which, over time, follow a power law. That is, small fluctuations/events are common and large fluctuations/events are rare and the frequencies with which differ-ent sized events occur are systematically related (see Appendix). The sizes of wars as measured by body counts are a good example. The implication is that in a power law system there is no event of typical size and big events will eventually occur. One thing that can be said is that power laws tend to show up in systems that are being driven slowly away from equilibrium (by cap-turing more and more energy) and in which the actions of any individual component are dominated by its interaction with other components (Buchanan 2000: 96).

Seeing societies as complex adaptive systems

The term *complex adaptive system* is becoming widely used to describe, among others, a particular sort of biosocial (dissipative) system, namely, one where the system's components are a medium-sized number of intelligent adaptive agents (meaning organisms, people or organisations capable of changing their 'if … then' behaviour rules), each exchanging decision-making information locally with a small number of other agents in the system and each attempt-ing, self-interestedly, to reduce the implementation costs and uncertainty about the outcomes of their decisions, for example, How can I ensure that I will not be cheated, robbed by others? Holland's (1995: 10) briefer definition is 'a system of interacting agents described in terms of rules … which change as experience accumulates'. An *adaptation* is a small putatively beneficial change in behavioural capacity.

The principle underlying all complex adaptive systems is that collective order (patterns of ongoing behaviour) can emerge, without upper-level guid-ance, from the dispersed interactions of individual agents. The groping by buyers and sellers in a competitive market towards an equilibrium price is a simple example.

Students of complex adaptive systems search for individuals' behaviour rules which collectively generate *social organisation*, that is, mutually agreed collective rules which constrain each individual member of the system in such a way as to reduce uncertainty for all decision makers. For example, if you and I trust each other to be honest — a tacit, unenforceable 'rule' — our interactions will be that much more productive. *Agent-based modelling* is one strategy for discovering the behaviour rules of individuals in a complex adaptive system. This involves matching, in a computer simulation, the dynamics generated by candidate behavioural rules and the observed dynamics of a real world system.

Participants in a complex adaptive system constantly experiment with novel inter-agent behaviour rules (as well as rules for coping with other aspects of a variable environment) and those rules that are successful in reducing uncertainty or, more generally, increasing the well-being of the decision maker, tend to be retained and, in time, spread to other decision makers (a form of social learning; see page 192). The extraordinary difficulty of understanding complex adaptive systems comes from the fact that every one of the system's individual participants is simultaneously 'trying' to implement the same rule-enhancing strategy! Complex adaptive systems never come to a steady state in which participants' behaviour rules are no longer changing, although these may be relatively stable in a slowly changing external environment.

Society then is a complex adaptive system in which many participants are interacting and modifying their own behaviour in response to others, that is, co-evolving. People are continually coming together for common purposes such as forming specialist groups to address special needs. The 'rules' they devise for group members include tacit values and ethics as well as explicit injunctions. The society can be as small as two people or as large as the United Nations.

Co-operation is the basic form of social interaction. Competition, a popular alternative candidate for that title, is but a useful sorting–selecting process within a prior framework of co-operation, for example, competitive markets can only work within a legal system for enforcing contracts. By the same token, any new co-operative action is always constrained by the need to largely conform to a context of existing social norms, values and institutions. Co-operation starts with a hypothesis about the beneficial effects of some possible co-operative behaviour and, depending on how effective that behaviour is when put into practice, the hypothesis is confirmed and the behaviour reproduced (an example of circular causation). The possibilities for new co-operative behaviour rules are thus twice constrained. Once to conform to the existing social context and once in terms of the balance between the benefits of leverage from co-operation versus the disbenefits of constraints (meaning loss of behaviour options) on individual behaviour. The process (a form of self-organisation?) is one of converging on joint goals by sequential trial-and-error, but not the 'blind' trial-and-error of random mutation and natural selection. Trial-and-adjustment might be a better term.

Note though that the uncertainties caused by conflict of interests are never wholly eliminated by co-operation. This is because rules of co-operative behaviour reduce uncertainty only for the specific problem for which they were developed. Rules that regulate co-operation on the roads are useless for regulating intimate relationships. Rules can only reduce uncertainty to a socially acceptable level for particular circumstances.

Emergence and hierarchy

Complex adaptive systems in the form of human societies can range from highly centralised command systems to highly decentralised consensual or voluntary systems. A highly decentralised system is one in which there are few constraints imposed on participants so as to limit their behavioural autonomy. Observation suggests that systems which rely almost exclusively on decentralised control (for example, anarchic or libertarian societies) adapt to change and converge on their goals relatively poorly as do those with highly centralised control (like totalitarian societies). Overly decentralised systems are too uncoordinated to react coherently to environmental change and overly centralised systems are rigid and unresponsive. While one can imagine there being an optimal level and distribution of social control for any environment, identifying that optimum is another matter. Does democracy and majoritarian consensus rule offer a good level of control? Is a society seeking quality of life for all less adaptable? When is tradition better than law as the source of society-wide behavioural rules?

From a systems perspective, much of the hierarchical organisation of a society (multiple levels of behaviour control/constraint) arises 'bottom up' when individuals co-operate to act with a common purpose. Further hierarchical levels arise when such collectives themselves combine to act collectively. The self-organising or reorganising process by which centres of higher-level control arise through the co-operation of lower level centres of control is called *emergence* or *co-evolution*. Obviously emergence cannot happen until stable (persistent) lower-level units have been created, just as an emergent higher-level control centre must be stable if the hierarchical system is to persist. Whatever comes into being has to be self-consistent, meaning consistent with its former self and everything else.

The hierarchical method of organising complex adaptive systems is efficient in that it economises communication and negotiation (Boulding 1978) and in that it allows specialist subsystems to evolve. Specialist subsystems are those which can carry out tasks important to the system's survival in a particularly effective manner but at the price of losing some of their own capacity to cope with a variable environment. For example, a specialist employee may be unemployable outside his/her company.

As Simon (1973) points out, the emergence of stable hierarchies is a process which explains why the evolution of living systems, from species to societies, tends to have a consistent direction over time, namely, towards systems displaying more levels of control. When stable components come together to form a new level of control, it is a process which will not be reversed spontaneously. By definition, individuals participating in the emergence process are better adapted than non-participants and will be favoured by natural selection. Or, putting it another way, participants would be disadvantaged by becoming independent again in what is now a new environment. While higher levels of control may or may not emerge in a system, there is no process which, in a stable environment, could lead to fewer levels of control (Allen and Starr 1982). Indeed, the story of all evolution, not just biological evolution, is one of survival of the stable. An example from the early history of the universe is the occasional coming together at high temperature of hydrogen atoms to form stable helium molecules. The emergence of consciousness and purposive behaviour from the human nervous system is a recent example. One reason that hierarchies tend to survive is that if their upper levels are destroyed, they can rebuild from their lower level components when supplies of usable energy improve.

Evolution by natural selection has been a sequential process of hierarchical elaboration (cells, multi-cells, organs, hormones, mind, instincts, emotions, reason etc) although not usually recognised explicitly as such. It is a process in which increasing the number of levels of control leads to increasing stringency of control by upper-level on lower-level components. That is, a new level of control constrains behavioural possibilities at all lower levels. Allen and Starr (1982: 226) similarly suggest that the evolution of society towards more levels of organisation (for example, a globalised society) may involve more detailed and explicit control over individuals.

Complexification

The next characteristic of complex adaptive systems which we will look to see expressed in human societies is complexification.

Societies, through the process of emergence, have tended to become more complex over time, that is, more feedback links get built into the social system and more subsystems are incorporated into or formed within the system. Complexification in one subsystem leads to 'complexity races' with all subsystems having to become more complex simply to cope with an increasingly complex environment. Factors allowing ongoing complexification include society's increasing capacity for information storage and communication and increasing possibilities for building on and processing acquired knowledge. And no rigid energy constraint has yet been encountered.

Most basically, it is increasing knowledge which leads to increasing complexity and, perhaps surprisingly, to increased uncertainty about the results of one's decisions. Uncertainty increases because it is more difficult to calculate outcomes of decisions in a more complex world, rich with circular causation (Dörner 1997: 5). Further, society's context-setting institutions have difficulty in coping with growing complexity (solving a problem generates other problems) and this adds further to uncertainty (Tainter 2000). For example, there is usually more law in societies that are larger, more dense, more differentiated, more complex, more stratified (Alexander 1987: 248).

Does increasing complexification mean that societies become more vulnerable to collapse? Systems theory suggests that this may be so. Subsystems which have to manage an increasing number of interactions will have to use more energy (incur higher costs) to get the same result, for example, to cope with red tape. Alternatively, if the society's energy throughput does not increase as it complexifies, less energy will be available to maintain each part of the society.

Life cycles

More generally, the theory of dissipative systems suggests that complex adaptive systems which are becoming more complex, more highly connected, are simultaneously losing even the resilience to cope with low levels of environmental fluctuations and avoid disorganisation. How does this happen?

Under the control of a sequence of autocatalytic (positive feedback) processes, each triggering the next in a self-organising succession, all dissipative systems have a potential *life cycle* or *developmental trajectory* broadly comprising five stages — birth, immaturity, maturity, senescence, death (disorganisation). Progress through a life cycle, up to the point of senescence–death, is characterised by increasing exergy (usable energy) flow through the system as a whole but decreasing exergy flow per unit of information (meaningful patterns) stored in the system (structures to be maintained, biomass etc.). Stored information is still increasing but at a decreasing rate as the system approaches maturity. Positive feedback processes are stable (have an innate propensity to survive), simply because they are creating something faster than it is being destroyed. Note that the reference is to a dynamic stability with growth and senescence occurring when there is an imbalance either way in the rates of generation and degeneration of the components of the cycle.

Obviously not all dissipative systems complete a life cycle. There has to be a sufficient flow of usable energy available to support the complexification of the system up to the point where it becomes fragile due to being over-connected. Alternatively, at any stage, a large decline in available usable energy will disorganise the system or reduce it to a less complex state. But basically, a dissipative system's potential to move through a life cycle is always there.

This tendency to follow a life cycle holds for all 'living' dissipative systems, whether they are self-replicating and self-maintaining as organisms largely are, or whether they are fortuitously self-assembling as ecosystems and societies are. Recall the earlier discussion (page 160) of studies by Toynbee and Tainter of collapsed societies.

What might also be noted at this point is that if a dissipative system happens to contain a population of short-lived (relative to system life) self-replicating entities of any sort, the way is open for a process of natural selection to kick in and better adapt that population to its niche, or expand its niche, in the overall system. This is the link between Darwinian and dissipative-systems thinking. Because the 'population' comprising the world's societies does not meet this requirement (for example, societies do not replicate), it is more rewarding to view the international relations system as a complex adaptive system than as a population of societies evolving through natural selection (Dark 1998).

Collapse is not inevitable

Despite the emergence of many smaller states in recent times, the long-term historical trend in human society is towards larger political and urban groups. Larger sociopolitical units have obvious competitive advantages over smaller units, including informational and industrial economies of scale. But, as a state grows larger and more complex, more and more decisions are required to maintain it (reproduce it through time) and, because the potential for change is latent in every decision, change becomes increasingly likely. The more complex a system the more likely it is to change.

If the number and quality of a society's decision-makers does not increase with the complexity of the system, more frequent decisions will be required of each decision-maker leading to more mistakes and poorer policy. Also, effective decisions get harder to find as parts of a system become more inter-dependent — each part is so dependent on the other parts behaving in par-ticular ways that change in any one is likely to produce instability in the whole. This is the problem of hyper-coherence or 'long-chain dependency', well-illustrated by the consequences of a strike at one small motor compo-nent factory.

Quality decision-making requires information to be acquired and processed at a sufficient rate. If information is under-supplied the system can-not reproduce its own structures and is liable to collapse. Collapse may also occur if sufficient information is delivered but cannot be processed rapidly enough (called 'turbulence' [Dark 1998: 133] or information-overload).

So complexity, rate of decision-making required, propensity for change (because present in every decision) and tendency towards system collapse all increase together.

Coping with complexification

Rising complexity can be coped with in at least five ways. One is to actively simplify by shedding parts (for example, abandon colonies) or reducing total energy use. Another is to stabilise the external environment so that it is not as threatening (for example, a security pact). Another is to acquire further resources (for example, new colonies) which yield a surplus that can be applied to decision making. Another is more efficient information processing (for example, computerisation). The fifth is to (re)organise decision-making hier-archically (Simon 1973; Boulding 1978) for example, by devolving power to smaller units or, conversely, by grouping units into a new form of organisation.

Hierarchically organised decision-making systems, such as representative democracies and federations reduce the overall demand for decision-making information. If collapse is to be avoided, both decision-making and informa-tion-processing must keep pace with complexification. As the system first com-plexifies, opportunities for innovative decision-making increase simply because ever-more decisions have to be made. But, at some stage, possibilities for further non-disruptive change decline, the system becomes increasingly 'path-depen-dent' and adaptive flexibility is lost. Dark (1998) draws on catastrophe theory to suggest that when collapse comes (and it may not) it will be sudden, rapid at first and then slowing as complexity declines. He further suggests that a 'replace-ment system' is likely to form shortly before a sociopolitical system collapses, at a time when the rate of innovative decision-making is still high. Because both collapsing and replacement systems coexist for a while under this model, Dark prefers to talk of 'waves' rather than 'cycles' of recurring sociopolitical systems.

Collapse can be forestalled, even for centuries perhaps, and, when it comes, the transition to a new form of societal organisation does not necessarily imply plunging quality of life. The trajectory of change might involve many small changes rather than one large change.

ECOLOGICAL THEORY AND SOCIETAL CHANGE

Now we turn to the biological sciences, starting with ecology, for insights into how societies change over time.

An ecosystem, broadly defined, is a biotic community (community of living organisms) and its abiotic (non-living) environment. In principle that includes communities containing humans and there is a science of human ecology. In practice, most ecological theory excludes humans who complicate things enormously with their diverse and plastic behaviour. Our interest here is in whether an understanding of change in ecosystems which do not include humans can be applied to societies, these being ecosystems dominated by humans. For example, one lesson from ecology is that species which are too successful are likely to precipitate structural environmental changes to which they are maladapted. Indeed, all species modify the environment on which they depend — a law we cannot repeal!

Ecological communities and human communities exhibit the same basic principles of organisation (Odum 1983). Further similarities flow from our capacity for behavioural differentiation which leads to different groups in society being analogous to different species in ecosystems, interacting in analogous ways (Catton 1980: 102). Both forms are networks that are organisationally closed but open to flows of materials, energy and information. There are many differences of course, such as language, consciousness and culture. However, ecosystems have great capacity to renew themselves over time and the principles of successful (persistent) ecological organisation therefore may offer guidance to human communities seeking to survive in acceptable form for hundreds of years.

Capra's principles of ecosystem persistence

Capra (1996) identifies five such principles:

1   *Recycling*
    Processes in ecosystems are cyclical. Successful ecosystems retain (hold within their boundaries) the materials (for example, nutrients, substrate) on which their member organisms depend; or, at least, materials 'leak' from the ecosystem no faster than they are acquired from outside. Ecosystem members are linked mutualistically (interdependently) through an intricate set of feedback relationships in which the

well-being of any member depends on the well-being of many other members. These feedback loops are the processes by which materials are cycled. Most coastal cities lose most of their food-nutrient inputs offshore as sewage, that is, fail to recycle.

2   *Solar power*
The cycles of nearly all successful ecosystems are powered by solar energy that is transformed into chemical energy by photosynthesis or into the physical energy of winds, tides etc. Human communities seeking to organise themselves on the same principles as ecosystems would similarly rely on solar energy in its many forms — wind, tides, biomass, hydro power — rather than the 'detritus' of coal and oil.

3   *Co-operation and competition*
The properties of successful ecosystems emerge from both competition (for example, shading out competitors) and co-operation. The basic relationship between parts of ecosystems is one of mutual interdependence or symbiosis — a process of unwitting co-operation. Competition for resources is good insofar as it weeds out entities that use resources inefficiently and frees those resources for other uses. Co-operation, the pursuit of common goals, is good insofar as it allows resources to be saved through the benefits of specialisation. Since the creation of the first nucleated cells over 2 billion years ago, evolution has proceeded through ever more intricate arrangements of co-operation and co-evolution. Successful ecosystems continually upgrade their capacity to survive by creating and selecting for both new synergistic and new competitive relations between community members. Provided they are in dynamic balance, co-operation and competition release resources that can be used to improve adaptability, meaning an increase in the system's resilience and diversity (see 4 and 5).

4   *Resilience*
Successful ecosystems are resilient or flexible. That is, they have developed processes that allow them to cope with extreme events and rapid changes from one state to another, for example, weather changes. While resilient systems can cope with such stresses on a temporary basis, prolonged stress will breach any system's tolerance limits and destroy it. Survival is a matter of avoiding threshold stress. Maintaining reserves of energy and materials, analogous to holding uncommitted capital in human societies, is fundamental to the capacity of ecosystems to survive hard times (Odum 1983).

   Another result which can be hypothesised to apply to societies is that a modular or compartmentalised structure facilitates resilience and resistance to stress. Perturbations to one module of the system cannot be transmitted easily to other modules, simply because there are few connecting paths between modules. But fragmented communities, those with recently broken links between parts, are unlikely to survive further environmental change. Aboriginal Australia was a good example of a modularised society. The converse of the modularity argument is that destroying a 'keystone' node in a system, one with connections to many other nodes, stands to disrupt the whole system.

5   *Diversity*
Successful ecosystems are diverse, meaning that they have a wide variety of member-classes (for example, species) interacting in a wide variety of ways. When its environment undergoes permanent change (for example, climate change), a diverse ecosystem is more likely to find, within itself, relationships that fit it to survive in the new environment; allow it to successfully reorganise. This is the importance of having different species (cultural groups?) with different responses to environmental change each playing the same role in the food chain (economy?) (Chapin et al. 1997). As a rule of thumb, frequently disturbed systems tend to have low species (occupational?) diversity and vice versa. A simple system in a fluctuating environment is likely to be as persistent as a complex system in a stable environment.

While recycling and the use of solar power can be given ready meaning as survival principles for human communities, it is more difficult to interpret the competition–co-operation balance, resilience and diversity in human–society terms. A continuously changing strategy is probably required. Chapter 5 offers some guidance.

Concept of the adaptive cycle

The portion of contemporary ecological theory which offers most insight into how societies change over time is CS Holling's (1973, 1987) *adaptive cycle theory*.

At one level, adaptive cycle theory is what results from applying the abstractions of dissipative systems theory, as explored above, to the particular reality of ecosystem dynamics. However, in making that application, Holling and his followers have extended, enriched and concretised those source ideas. More than this, the Holling school has actively sought to interpret societal change in adaptive-cycle terms, their purpose being to understand how regional communities might better manage the natural resources on which they depend (Gunderson et al. 1995).

At the centre of adaptive cycle theory is the idea that a region's ecosystems normally pass through a succession of cycles, each lasting somewhere between years and centuries, and each characterised by four phases. A rapid *growth* phase (renewal) leads into a prolonged phase of biomass accumulation, increasing complexity and increasing 'brittleness'. This *accumulation* phase is inevitably followed by a sudden, externally triggered *collapse*. Next comes a short *reorganisation* phase during which now-empty niches are reoccupied, either as before or by new species or by 'fitter' versions of the previous occupants.

While the process of assembling an ecological community following disturbance — called succession — can take many paths, it is nevertheless constrained in where it can eventually go by its first few steps. This reorganisation phase is the time at which it becomes possible for the ecosystem to begin developing in a way that differs from previous cycles. What actually happens will depend on such things as the colonising species available in neighbouring communities and differences between the ecosystem's pre- and post-disturbance environments. Once the basic structures and processes of the reorganised ecosystem are established, rapid growth begins again. Over evolutionary time, the suite of available species changes and species acquire attributes that specialise them for particular stages in the local successional process. For example, early successional species develop adaptations such as high reproductive rates or dormancy that allow them to fill new habitats quickly. Late successional species acquire traits such as the ability to grow in shady places and overtop early species.

For the Holling school, the idea of an adaptive cycle that alternates between long periods of aggregation and transformation of resources and shorter periods that create opportunities for innovation is fundamental to understanding complex systems from cells to ecosystems to societies (although there are many exceptions). By analogy, a successful society is setting the stage for its own downfall as stresses and rigidities accumulate (see Chapter 6). Institutions fail to cope with slow changes that are invisible or too complex for people to agree on a response. Societies which survive do so by finding ways of managing (rather than avoiding) such cycles so that they are minimally destructive (Westley 1995). For example, the reorganisation phase of a society's adaptive cycle might focus on social learning, the renewal phase on visionary goal-setting and the consolidation phase on strategic planning. More generally, it is foresight, plus a hierarchical social organisation and having an understanding of the adaptive cycle which may allow it to be managed.

The dynamics of hierarchies

Adaptive cycles are normally embedded within larger adaptive cycles, for example, ecosystems within eco-regions. More generally, the whole biosocial world can be viewed as an ever-changing hierarchically linked system of adaptive cycles. *Hierarchy dynamics*, meaning the interactions between larger and smaller adaptive cycles, have been studied by Holling and other ecologists and, like the concept of the adaptive cycle, have been used to reflect on several aspects of how societies and communities change over time.

Each level in a dynamic hierarchy serves two functions. One is to conserve and stabilise conditions for the faster and smaller levels; the other is to generate and test novel possibilities for its own behaviour each time there is a reorganisation. Behaviour and structure change so slowly at the upper levels relative to the lower levels that the lower levels can normally operate as if the environment provided by higher levels is more or less stable. Or, putting this another way, lower levels are constrained to behave in ways which are compatible with the context provided by higher levels in the hierarchy, for example, the way a patch of burnt forest regenerates depends on the species available in the surrounding forest. Notwithstanding, there will often be 'windows of opportunity' when the upper-level cycle is ripe for reorganisation and such shifts can be triggered by appropriate lower-level behaviour, for example, the triggering by hormonal accumulation of stages in a young animal's development, or canopy development in a regrowth forest.

Translating this perception to human societies, larger, slower (low-frequency) adaptive cycles are the more inclusive collectives, such as tiers of government, and lower levels are individuals and groups. Governments enforce laws which constrain individual behaviour, but individuals and groups can, under the right conditions, secure changes in laws which enhance their behavioural possibilities. Revolution is a pervasive example of strong change in human systems, one which Goldstone (1998) suggests as being more likely when reorganisation is occurring simultaneously at several hierarchical levels. A modest hypothesis might be that, inherently, societies tend to change slowly most of the time but sometimes more rapidly. External shocks can impose further change at any time.

EVOLUTIONARY THEORY AND SOCIETAL CHANGE

Whereas ecologists study the structure and behaviour of biological communities over, perhaps, hundreds of years, evolutionary biologists study the structure and behaviour of all life (the biosphere) over billions of years. That is, the ecological and evolutionary perspectives differ in degree rather than kind. Both focus on the phenomenon of interacting life forms but at massively different spatial and temporal resolutions.

At its broadest, the story of life on earth is one of co-evolution (meaning 'evolving together in a way which involves circular causation') between life forms and their physical environment. This means that while change in life's physical (land-sea-air) environment have been driven by external forces such as vulcanism, the luminosity of the Sun and plate tectonics, they have also been driven by biological processes. For example, over a billion years, micro-organisms produced sufficient oxygen to first oxidise the earth's surface (for example, haematite deposits) and then create an atmosphere which allowed air-breathing life forms to evolve.

Co-evolution between life forms is similarly important for explaining the changing mix of life forms over evolutionary time. For example, land animals could not evolve until the land had been colonised from the sea by plant life. Even more generally, all food chains and all niches are the products of co-evolution.

While the idea of co-evolution is central to understanding the history (and future) of the biosphere, the primary focus of evolutionary biology has long been more narrowly on *phylogenesis*, meaning the slow change and split-ting of species, basically through *natural selection* (see page 78) and related processes such as genetic drift and sexual selection. In this framework, a species' evolution is seen as being driven by the selection pressure imposed on it by its biophysical environment but the reverse influence of the species on the environment, the co-evolutionary dimension, is poorly recognised (Griffiths and Gray 2001). Most effort goes into understanding the way in which a population of short-lived, approximately self-replicating, similar but still variable individual members of a species interact with each other such that, over time, the gene pool and the range of physical forms and behaviours in the population change markedly.

The power of the idea of natural selection is not restricted to phylogen-esis. It is a 'foolproof algorithm' (Dennett 1995: 50) such that any population of 'replicators' which make a surplus of near-faithful copies of themselves over their limited lifetimes will evolve and adapt over time. Many sorts of popula-tions have been asserted to have the 'replicator' characteristics which initiate *competitive selection* (a broader term than natural selection). Many more have been described using natural selection as a metaphor for their evolution. However, the 'population' made up of the world's societies does not meet 'replicator' requirements and, while societies might rise and fall, the process cannot be usefully viewed as competitive selection in action.

More modestly therefore, this section considers attempts to view the process of phylogenesis as a metaphor or analogue for one particular aspect of societal change (socio-cultural evolution). Specifically, we consider efforts to explore the value of biological evolution as a model for social or group learn-ing — a process so central to humanity's survival prospects that it will get a chapter to itself presently.

Space does not permit discussion of the equally illuminating attempts to interpret the process of structural change in capitalist economies as one of competitive selection in the manner of phylogenesis. Hodgson (1999b) reviews the problems with orthodox economics which led to the development of *evolutionary economics*, so named because, at least initially, it progressed by finding analogues for many aspects of modern economic systems in the neo-Darwinian synthesis of Mendelian and Darwinian ideas.

Social learning

In the broadest sense, *social learning* is nothing more than purposive cultural change. As used here, it denotes the process by which whole societies become more knowledgeable in terms of widely accepted behavioural rules and beliefs about how to coordinate the activities of individuals and organisations to better achieve common goals. The emphasis is on learning *with* others rather than processes of learning *from* others as in imitation, socialisation and meme transfer (Pardon and Clark 1995; Bandura 1971) (memes, to use Daniel Dennett's [1995: 344] phrase, are distinct memorable ideas which spread from person to person in the community). Nor am I considering, for the moment, the experimentation-based processes by which technical knowledge is accumulated in a modern society, although these too have been likened to Darwinian evolution (Popper 1972). Toulmin (1972) too had an evolutionary view of society's changing concepts, emphasising that overwhelmed concepts could resurface, just like unsuccessful species.

As a further clarification, our interest here is in learning at the level of the political collective rather than at the level of voluntary associations. Writing specifically about modern societies, Peter Hall (1993) defines social learning as the 'deliberate attempt to adjust the goals or techniques of policy in response to past experiences and new information. Learning is indicated when policy changes as a result of such a process.' Edgar Dunn (1971), in a still-relevant pioneer study, defines social learning or *sociogenesis* (his term, devised to emphasise the parallel with phylogenesis) as activities which guide society towards collective goals by redesigning the way society is organised.

Comparing social and genetic learning

While there are also major differences, socio-cultural evolution through social learning is a process strongly analogous to natural selection (Hodgson 2002). In what way? Trial and error (change and evaluate; test and regenerate) variants of a culture's existing rules, or new 'mutant' rules, are tested for effectiveness in meeting group or individual needs and wants and those that are relatively more effective are 'reproduced' in others by imitation and teaching, that is, others 'inherit' the new behavioural rules (Dunn 1971). Doubts over what to call the units of inheritance in social learning (production rules, social innovations [Henderson 1998b], social technologies, policies, even memes perhaps?) do not obscure the parallel between social and biological evolution. Indeed, just as biological mutations cannot change an organism very much if it is to remain viable, social mutations which are not constrained by the realities of available knowledge, continuity requirements etc. will fail or damage society. And, like most mutations, most ideas for improving social organisation (generative learning) or for reorganising to cope with external change (adaptive learning) will fail.

Dunn attempts to liken the redesigning of social goals and the reorganisation of society — what he calls extraordinary problem solving — to *adaptive generalisation* in biological evolution, this being the process in which evolution takes a markedly different direction such as happens when a genetically variable species encounters a new type of life zone, for example, a marine species encounters a shoreline habitat. And what he calls normal problem solving — improving the way the existing system works — is likened to *adaptive specialisation*, the process in which a species comes to use its existing resource base more efficiently. Typically, extraordinary problem-solving is called for when social learning experiments fail to achieve any goal convergence. It could involve recasting the system's organisation and boundaries to capture externalities by implementing a new layer of control or spinning off a new quasi-independent system.

Just as adaptive specialisation leads to new species when part of an interbreeding population is isolated and reliant on a somewhat different resource base, new cultures and new societies have arisen historically where social groups were isolated and learning to exploit a unique environment. Today, of course, cultures are converging rather than diverging, particularly with regard to knowledge that is useful across many environments, for example, new artifacts, cognitive processes and social forms.

Note that both biological evolution and socio-cultural evolution involve the creation and transmission of knowledge, that is, useful information. In purely biological evolution, information specifying the organism's behavioural possibilities is transmitted via genes (recipes for making proteins). In social evolution the replication and transfer of acquired knowledge is also via a material embodiment (exosomatic or exogenetic heredity), namely language in the form of gestures, words and then writing. The true brilliance of language is that it can convey knowledge of the past, possible futures and the imaginary as well as the present. Also, in a loose way, a specific beneficial arrangement of neural connections is being passed on when knowledge is passed on. The accumulated language-based knowledge of a population is intriguingly comparable to its gene pool.

One major difference between the two processes is that the spectrum of candidates for selection as new behaviours is generated consciously and purposively by people seeking more effective goal achievement. Darwinian natural selection operates 'blindly' on whatever collection of differing phenotypes is available at the time an environmental stress is imposing selection pressure on the population. Because what is passed on is something that the learner was not born with, inheritance of the products of social learning is more Lamarckian than Darwinian. The reference is to Lamarck's doctrine of the inheritance of acquired characteristics as the mainspring of biological evolution.

The efficiency of social learning

Looking deeper into this particular difference, socio-cultural evolution does not inescapably suffer from what has been called biological evolution's 'fatal flaw', namely its short-sightedness (Potter 1990). Biological evolution has a predilection for short-term gain. Selection promotes what is immediately useful, even if the change is to prove fatal in the long run, for example, leading a bird species to feed on a single species of plant which eventually goes extinct. Socio-cultural change, however, can embody foresight in the sense that people and groups can develop behavioural rules for environments and situations which are anticipated but have not as yet eventuated. It can also 'pre-test' a range of candidate behavioural rules by mentally rehearsing how each might perform in possible future environments and choosing the one which is pre-judged to perform best, that is, appears to offer maximum goal convergence. While natural selection works only to maintain or raise a species' population (the implicit goal being to maximise Darwinian fitness), socio-cultural learning can be consciously directed to better satisfying any socially mandated 'symphony' of a population's diverse needs. More than this, as discussed in Chapter 3, societies can revise their working goals as circumstances and mental models of reality change. Compared with socio-cultural evolution, natural selection has 'tunnel vision' as well as being short-sighted.

So, are there other ways in which social learning is also more efficient than genetic learning?

- Unlike useful new genetic information, useful new information acquired under social learning can spread within as well as between generations, and hence more rapidly;

- At least in principle, the knowledge pool built up under social learning tends to be widely available. The pool of genetic information, for a number of reasons, tends to become fragmented among sub-populations;

- Because social learning commonly leads to new and more specialised social roles, it increases the diversity of people's behaviour. Competitive genetic selection, however, tends to reduce genetic diversity, making people's behaviour more uniform and hence less likely to yield further useful novel behaviours;

- Feedback from the physical or social environment as to the success of an evolutionary experiment is much more direct in sociogenesis than in phylogenesis, especially if success in terms of goal convergence is being actively monitored;

- Social learning can test novel ideas without killing the carriers of failed ideas;

- Social learning can consider changing the environment as well as adapting to it;

- The very articulation of social goals can stimulate further search for novel behaviours.

Pointed questions about social learning

Having lauded the efficiency and flexibility of social learning relative to genetic learning, there are several pointed questions which need to be asked:

1   *Is knowledge acquired through social learning more secure (less likely to be lost) than the knowledge embedded in genetic change?*

    Provided that the numbers involved are not too small, any sample of the human population will carry most of the genetic information that has accumulated over the species' history. Conversely, much knowledge acquired through social learning is stored exosomatically (outside the body) and can be lost or destroyed, for example, the great library of Alexandria. Also, much cultural knowledge is held by small specialist groups whose loss would disrupt society, for example, only electrical engineers know how to run power stations. The inference to be drawn is that such contingencies should be guarded against.

2   *Can it be claimed that social learning has generated significant achievements?*

    The outstanding achievement of humanity's social learning is that it has allowed groups to adapt to, to survive in, a range of environments worldwide. This has required the development of mobility in the first instance and then of the ability to tolerate new environments. The latter, in turn, involves learning an appropriate response as each expression of the new environment is encountered. As well as mastering specific environments, humans have learned how to learn; have learned how to be adaptable as well as to adapt.

One clear failure of social learning to date is that while it is routinely applied to the scientific control of the physical environment, we have yet to learn how to purposively transform social environments, for example, to eliminate poverty. The irony here is that it is success in manipulating physical systems that has generated organisational inadequacies and a corresponding need for social technologies, for example, control of nuclear weapons. More generally, all social learning transforms the physical and social environment and so triggers the need for further learning — a co-evolutionary treadmill from which there may be no escape. Indeed, social learning may have its own 'fatal flaw' in that it is currently initiating a rate of change in some subsystems of society to which related subsystems are unable to adapt rapidly enough. The result is an overall lack of coordination; and uncoordinated systems fragment.

Another failure is that we have little idea of how to design promising social experiments under conditions of high uncertainty and high risk, for example, decriminalising recreational drugs (see page 241). Somehow, conditions of great uncertainty require imaginative and flexible probing, not seesawing between vacillation and commitment.

3   *Is social learning getting more efficient?*

Stated so broadly, this question is unanswerable. Inter alia, it depends on the scale at which the question is being asked. The knowledge base on which the social learning process can draw is ever-expanding and there is no doubt that in some areas, and the 'new' technologies may be an example, constant or increasing returns to efforts at social learning can be seen. The areas where progress, even inefficient progress, is not being made are intrinsically uncertain or starved of resources. In other cases, progress is being made in individual subsystems but lack of coordination with related subsystems is stifling progress in the overall system.

Then there is the question of how much harder it is to achieve social learning in a social system which is getting increasingly complex. Are problems proliferating faster than they can be solved? When do diminishing returns set in? Rescher (1980) argues that exponential growth in the size and costliness of science is already necessary to simply maintain a constant rate of progress (see page 247). Finally, at the broadest scale, there is the puzzling question of whether social learning is taking complex societies into evolutionary blind alleys.
Now that would be inefficient.

Three conclusions about social learning

First, the idea of social learning is useful in itself, just recognising that societies, either by design or by an unmanaged process of emergence from below, acquire institutions, organisations, social technologies etc. which persist because they help achieve some goal.

Second, recognising that the process by which such arrangements are generated involves 'artificial' selection from a range of competing candidates in a process which is comparable to the natural selection of fit phenotypes provides ideas for improving social learning. For example, and this is an important part of Dunn's contribution, identifying the ways in which social learning is more efficient than genetic learning immediately suggests avenues for further improving the social learning process. Unfortunately, post-Dunn, there is little follow-up literature seeking analogues in socio-cultural evolution of the expanding range of ideas in post-synthesis evolutionary theory.

Third, in terms of steering world society towards a collective goal such as quality survival, managing social learning would seem to be considerably more important than managing genetic learning, that is, humanity's physical evolution. While that is true now and for a long time to come it may not always be thus. Dunn is so convinced of the importance of social learning that he names it as the fourth great threshold of human development (The other three are (i) communication by use of symbols as generalisations, (ii) discovery of the amplifying power of co-operative behaviour, (iii) discovery of the knowledge-generating power of experimental investigation [science]).

It is my perception also that intelligent social learning has to be at the heart of any strategy for achieving quality survival. That is why Chapter 7, among other tasks, will assemble a variety of guidelines for nudging world society in that direction.

Coda on biological evolution and societal change

Many have warned against using biological analogies in social science. Some of this is a reaction against simple-minded social Darwinists proclaiming that what 'is' in evolution, for example, 'survival of the fittest', equates with what 'ought' to be in human affairs; those who are poorly equipped to make their way in life should not be helped. The real question of course is: What works best? Where danger lies is in thinking that evolutionary metaphors are the whole truth.

I have briefly described the contribution of evolutionary thinking to understanding one aspect of 'public' learning, namely social learning, and mentioned one aspect of 'private' or bottom-up learning, namely long-term economic change in a capitalist economy. Other examples abound. The term *universal Darwinism* (Dawkins 1982) summarises the view that competitive selection is an important driver of evolutionary change in variable populations of self-replicating entities and that there are many such populations including organisms, memes, prions, immune systems, routines in firms and, as we have just explained, cultural rules in societies. I repeat though that populations of societies per se are not normally regarded as exemplifying competitive selection; just populations of certain processes within society.

The conclusion I find useful for present purposes is that the evolution of most social structures within a society is likely to contain an element of competitive selection from among alternative courses of action or, more briefly, an element of *evolutionary* or *historical learning*. Further, the challenge for managing the deep and not-so-deep future is not to reject competitive selection but to make it as effective as possible. Equally it would be wrong to totally reject models of societal change which involve equilibrating or homeostatic mechanisms. For example, equilibrium-seeking models have a role in studying short-run change in an economy, but not long-run change. Since much social learning is about doing what is necessary to maintain rather than develop society, homeostatic and historical views of societal change are complements rather than alternatives.

OVERVIEW: A PLURALITY OF FRAMEWORKS

What have we learned?

Consider where this chapter has taken us, starting with wanting to understand how and why societies change over time. Such understanding was proposed as a basis for managing quality of life in world society into the deep future. The first half of the chapter is a distillation of ideas about societal change from history, sociology and social psychology, these being disciplines with an explicit interest in societal change, albeit from quite different perspectives. We return here presently.

The second half turns to a selection of ideas from the sciences of dissipative complex systems, ecosystem dynamics and biological evolution. Here the first question is whether societies (or world society) are examples of these processes. If they are, then what has been learned about them can be applied directly to societal change. If they are not, the question drops back to asking if these processes are useful metaphors for societal change.

As currently conceived, the focus of research in biological evolution is the adaptation and differentiation of species through the process of natural selection. This is neither an analogue nor a metaphor for changes in world society nor the population of societies in the world (no self-replication at above-replacement levels). But it is an illuminating reference point for viewing change in many *populations within societies*, including populations of ideas, knowledge of various types and economic units.

Self-evidently, both societies and ecosystems are examples of dissipative complex systems and we can learn much by looking for societal analogues in the behaviour of dissipative systems in general and ecosystems in particular. Some of the behavioural tendencies of societies that can be asserted as a result of this mapping are:

- Societies are always changing, sometimes slowly over long periods and sometimes rapidly. All societies are historical, that is, are born, develop and will one day cease to exist either through disintegration or fundamental transformation;

- Like all dissipative complex systems, societies are hierarchical, meaning, inter alia, that different parts of any society (its different subsystems), change at different rates. A society's different subsystems tend to have their own characteristic dynamics, meaning that, depending on a subsystem's dominant feedback links, characteristic variables in the subsystem trend upwards or downwards or oscillate, converge on a fixed value etc. Subsystems which change slowly and produce strongly trending variables (for example, population growth) create an environment to which faster subsystems (for example, food production) have to either eventually adapt via reorganisation (equals co-evolution) or eventually they will collapse;

- Societies change slowly because most agents (purposeful actors) keep following, repetitively, the routine behaviour rules which keep the society's structures functioning — an approximately homeostatic process. Some change inevitably occurs because a few agents inadvertently modify the rules they are responsible for implementing and a few agents proactively modify society's behaviour rules within the limits of what is feasible and deemed necessary (it is a learning process) to correct imbalances between the operations of different subsystems;

- However, the longer a society continues to change slowly, the harder it becomes to find corrective changes in any subsystem which do not trigger cascades of rapid change in other subsystems. Conversely, depending on purpose, the easier it is to find changes (leverage points) which do just that (bring on the revolution!). How commonly societies reach and maintain such a critical state, and what the symptoms are is an open question (see page 219);

- Societies in which collapse or widespread reorganisation has been long delayed are those which have kept simplifying their organisation in a controlled way (for example, into largely independent modules) or improved their information processing capacity or raised their energy throughput to service an accumulating complexity;

- Rapid change, usually in the form of collapse to a much simpler structure or widespread reorganisation can be triggered by external shocks as well as internal agents. When it comes, the severity of a collapse (for example, number of control layers lost) and the system's subsequent dynamic behaviour (turbulence, oscillations etc.) is not predictable (see page 221);

- Because all societies are unique non-repeating systems, their behaviour cannot be captured in laws — these being assertions as to what will happen under repetition of some situation. What we have here are 'law-like' statements of tendency, of ensembles of possibilities, which are better than guesses (Dunn 1971: 129). While science has made little progress in learning how to predict the behaviour of dissipative complex systems, it has winnowed out various properties of such systems which provide a first understanding from which we might begin to purposively manage them (Waldrop 1992; De Greene 1994). This challenge is taken up in the next chapter.

Returning to historians and sociologists, while they rarely use the somewhat abstract language of dissipative complex systems, they are constantly drawing attention to 'template' events and processes comparable to those which this chapter is presenting as characteristic of such systems. They are putting flesh on the systems skeleton. Conversely, systems thinking provides a reductive skeleton for the body of history. That is, while history cannot be reduced to systems theory and ecosystem theory, it is compatible with these frameworks when the interpretive effort is made.

A reasonable conclusion then is that the historical disciplines and systems thinking provide complementary ways of looking at societal change. Each may be best for particular purposes. Both recognise that change in a society over time can be broken up into episodes from various categories, with the category-names for the same episode under the two perspectives being interchangeable. A revolution is an example of self-organisation. Population growth is a positive feedback process. And so on.

But the historical disciplines go deeper. Their perspective is emergent. They premise that something can only be understood by knowing how it was constructed. By identifying and modelling the productive, institutional and mental processes that underlie broad-scale societal change, such changes can be plausibly, although subjectively, explained as well as described. The process is scientific in the sense that history's generalisations are assertions (hypotheses) that may or may not be contradicted by future knowledge.

Given the goal of managing world society into the deep future, the task here is to extract from the psycho-socio-historical literature a working set of rules-of-thumb, conceptualisations, causal tendencies, templates etc. which can be incorporated into tentative guidelines for managing the future. There is no space here to fully extract such a typology from the present chapter and elsewhere, but when particular guidelines are presented in Chapters 6–8, they will be briefly justified in terms of the processes that history finds in society's structures, superstructures and infrastructures.

Working assumptions about people

Notwithstanding, I do want to collate here a few working assumptions about human behavioural tendencies which I believe have emerged up to this point and need to be kept in mind when planning how to manage the future, particularly in terms of achieving high quality of life for most people. Paramount here is the reference point that aspects of human behaviour reflect genetically based instinct and aspects reflect socially acquired character.

Our hunter–gatherer ancestors lived in small inbreeding isolated groups held together by pair bonds, dominance hierarchies, territoriality, ritualisation of hostility etc., just as many animal groups still do (see page 116). People in such societies do not question the social order; they behave as their ancestors did for thousands of years, as integral parts of a closely knit, highly organised social organism, feeling amity for those within and enmity for those outside the group. The amity–enmity dichotomy is the source of the dual standard of morality which most people still unconsciously hold, that is, judging 'strangers' differently from members of one's own 'tribe', be it a gang, class, ethnic group, nation or football club. It is also the source of humans' still-strong need to 'belong' (Koestler 1967).

Human societies have been hierarchically organised since neolithic times in the sense that strategic decisions are taken by an elite subset of the population, be it a priestly class, a warrior class, a political class, a business class or a bureaucracy (see page 116). The patent advantages of hierarchical organisation, such as decisiveness, flexibility, specialisation and improved prospects for short-term group survival are (more than?) offset by the almost total failure of hierarchical societies to have provided reasonable quality of life (by the standards of the day) to non-elite majorities or to have improved long-term survival prospects.

Here is the dilemma. Societies initially form and cohere around co-operative practices which permit all members to get more than they could alone or in smaller groups. Specialisation is frequently the basis for such co-operation but specialists' activities need to be coordinated by leaders. Over time an originally reciprocal exchange becomes unbalanced with some members accumulating more benefits than others, including economic and political power. Invariably, once a group has obtained such power it is unwilling to return to a more equitable co-operative organisation of society. Worse than that, the near-universal tendency is for ruling elites to become corrupt, exploitative, coercive and self-seeking. Quality of life for the majority is sought only to the extent that this consolidates the position of the ruling minority. Turning this around, defence of privileged self-interest is the fundamental impediment to raising quality of life for most. Even when societies have changed markedly and their current elites displaced, their structures have always reverted into a powerful ruling minority and a ruled majority. Part of the explanation for this 'musical chairs' view of society is that while most people have a strong need for authority in their lives they also have a limit to their tolerance of inequality.

It is only in the last few thousand years, starting with limited democracy in the Greek city states, that humans have moved a small way from seeing societies as naturally divided into all-powerful rulers and masses with minimal rights. In international relations, there has been an equally small move away from the idea that the only way to conduct foreign policy is to make yourself as powerful as possible.

The human mind also began changing in two important ways from about the same time. Capacity for applying rational thought to formulating and solving problems has increased, as has the degree to which people are conscious of themselves as individuals with needs, motives, drives, emotions, values, beliefs and knowledge. Politically, this self-awareness has led to the invention of human rights and to individualism as an ideology. While the genetic origins of various 'fixed' instinctual behaviours are well accepted (for example, mating behaviour, concern for kin, living with others), it is still not widely recognised, even in modern societies, that humans are largely products of their cultures, that what is uniquely individual is a small part of anyone's nature. Individuals are moulded by their society towards a social character which fits them to play appropriate roles in its infrastructure, structure and superstructure. Indeed, a degree of superficial individuality fits people to play the role of consumers in a marketised society. While there is justifiable anxiety about the plasticity of human behaviour being deliberately exploited to serve elite interests, this should not obscure the fact that a choice always has to be made between managing acculturation and letting it happen. When does education become social engineering?

It is no disgrace to recognise that as a species we are still young and still 'childish'. For example, we still have little ability to look ahead and little capacity for incorporating the long-term into decision-making. It may take millennia to learn how to best capitalise on the emergence of reason and consciousness.

CONCLUSION

This chapter is intended to convince others, as I am convinced, that the ways in which societies have changed in the past can be reasonably well explained using the tools and ideas and templates developed by historians, social scientists, biologists and systems theorists. I am equally convinced that our capacity to explain the past in these ways will continue to improve and indeed that there is an increasing consilience among the disciplines that have been used to illuminate societal change in the present chapter (Depew and Weber 1995). Two of the paradigmatic ideas behind this coming together of disciplines that study change in diverse spheres are those of temporal development, life cycles for example, in dissipative complex systems and of evolution through competitive selection in self-replicating populations.

But what of the future? Will the same tools and templates allow societal change in the next century, millennium etc. to be plausibly explained in retrospect? Whether the future is one of convulsive technological or political change or 'end-of-history' somnolence it should be possible to explain what happened within something like the framework of ideas developed here. Is there some way in which the world might fundamentally alter (short of the lineage going extinct) such that history, systems theory, sociology, social psychology, ecology etc. will give us no understanding of the dynamics of world society? I do not believe so. Certainly the futures foreseen in Chapters 1 and 2 are quite compatible with the change processes being described here.

Our real interest here is not retro-diction of course. Nor is it in predicting change in world society, much as we would like answers to some big questions: Is world society getting more vulnerable to collapse? More prone to inequity? Predicting societal change is much too difficult. Our purpose is to use an imperfect understanding of societal change to help fashion a tentative strategy for managing world society so that it survives into the deep future and delivers good quality of life to its members along the way. We turn then to just that.

Part 3:

TAKING CHARGE

5

A STRATEGY FOR MANAGING
THE DEEP FUTURE

PICKING A METAPHOR FOR THE DEEP FUTURES PROBLEM

In this book's Introduction, our lineage's journey into the future was likened to a Dungeons and Dragons adventure with Posterity, our hero, being confronted with a yet bigger dragon after each successful battle. While happy with that as a first metaphor for the lineage's life story — a series of escalating challenges to be surmounted — I am now in need of a metaphor which evokes the enormous intellectual complexity of the problem of managing the near-to-distant future to achieve quality survival. For brevity, I will refer to this as the *deep futures problem*.

My choice is the metaphor of Posterity the gardener. Managing the deep future is like being temporarily in charge of a large garden — Earthgarden to give it a name — which is intended to provide sustenance and delight for generations to come. Regardless of what Posterity does, Earthgarden will keep evolving, developing, changing, reorganising. But Posterity wants to do what she can to ensure that the garden continues to provide sustenance and delight. While she has to dig and sow, plant and prune every day, she also has to plan, conditionally, what to dig, plant, sow and prune tomorrow, next year, next century. She has to think both tactically and strategically. What are the big issues that need to be tackled now? Which can be deferred? Where to put, flowers, vegetables and wild areas? Can she improve her digging, sowing etc. routines? What preparations should be made for uncertain changes in future tastes, aesthetic and culinary? How can the different needs of different visitors be satisfied? Can the garden be storm-proofed? Locust-proofed? What should be assumed about the future availability of various seed stocks? What beds to dig up and what to save for the moment? Is there room for experimental plantings? All of these and other questions facing Posterity parallel issues that need to be addressed as part of drawing up a substantive strategy for guiding world society towards quality survival for the human and post-human lineage. Each generation is momentarily a steward of the lineage.

But the above sorts of questions about Posterity's garden cannot be answered immediately in any specific way. This is because the issues are intertwined. How Posterity responds to one issue depends on her responses to other issues. If she storm-proofs the garden by planting windbreaks, they will make the adjacent soil too dry for vegetables. And so on.

What can Posterity do? Perhaps she should draw up various scenarios — meaning 'possible futures' or 'could be' stories or 'ensembles of possibilities' — imagining the evolution of her garden and, of those which appear feasible, attempt to steer her garden through the scenario yielding most in terms of sustenance and delight. That is a very positive strategy but maybe she should be more conservative, more 'risk averse', and concentrate on protecting her garden against contingencies which stand to wreck it. Or just concentrate on improving the bits of Earthgarden that are not contributing to the goals set for it? Perhaps Earthgarden's very charter needs revising?

WICKED PROBLEMS

One reason for my choice of metaphor is that both the deep futures problem and the Earthgarden problem are 'wicked' or ill-structured problems (Rittel and Webber 1973). A wicked problem has several defining properties: There is no definitive formulation of the problem and no conclusively 'best' solution. The problem exhibits itself as an evolving set of interlocking issues, constraints, objectives and options for action. Ends and means overlap. You do not solve wicked problems, you manage them until you decide to stop managing them (or run out of resources). Your understanding of the problem, and hence your 'working' formulation of it, evolves as the problem unfolds and as you take various actions, each of which is intended to be a partial solution, that is, to improve some aspect of the total problem.

In terms of being wicked, the deep futures problem is comparable to many other problems facing societies. The political scientist CE Lindblom (1959) has argued that very few situations can be changed other than marginally in democratic societies and that a philosophy of 'muddling through' by making frequent small changes in the 'right' direction without particular reference to ultimate destinations is in fact an optimal strategy for managing society — not terribly effective but optimal. It is worth recalling that 'myopic' evolution works the same way, through a series of small adaptations. The point must be made however that muddling is a slow process, not suited to tackling urgent problems nor to achieving paradigm shifts in societal organisation.

ACCEPTING THAT RATIONALITY IS BOUNDED

The very concept of a wicked problem is an admission that human rationality, our ability to think clearly, step by explicit step, and devise solutions to problems, is imperfect. The phrase 'bounded rationality' is Herbert Simon's (1982), introduced to make the point that, whatever the problem, humans never have the time or the knowledge to solve it as they can see it should be solved. But there are many more reasons why we do not think as well as we might. One fairly general reason is that, for many problems, we think too slowly relative to the speed at which the problem is unfolding (Dörner 1997: 133) and we resort to taking *shortcuts* such as:

- Acting before getting goals sorted out;

- Solving problems sequentially rather than in parallel;

- Simplifying relationships between variables;

- Extrapolating trends linearly;

- Ignoring side-effects and long-term repercussions;

- Using simplistic models of parts of the problem because of a limited capacity to absorb new concepts.

While there is no standard method of teaching people to cope with complexity and uncertainty in their thinking, they can be taught to reflect on their own thinking and learn such basics as:

- State goals clearly;

- Recognise that it may be necessary to compromise between goals;

- Recognise the possibility of 'good enough' solutions;

- Recognise that it may be necessary to establish priorities and ignore some relevant considerations;

- Anticipate side-effects and long-term repercussions of decisions made;

- Collect just the right amount of new information and know why you need it;

- Avoid excessive abstraction;

- Avoid assuming that multifaceted events have one central cause;

- Learn to analyse errors before trying again;

- Learn to identify one's assumptions and attitudes as a basis for upgrading them (the thrust of Argyris' [1976] 'double loop learning' theory).

Nowadays there are also numerous computerised decision-support systems for helping people organise and visualise their thinking about such things as influence paths (multiple intertwined causal paths), 'trees' of sequential and conditional decisions and the flow and structure of a complicated argument (called argument mapping) (see, for example, www.philosophy.unimelb.edu.au/reason/critical/argument_mapping.html, accessed 23 July 2002). Computer simulations of wicked problems can be instructive but must be treated cautiously.

It is equally important for people to realise that others will often be better able to see the flaws in one's thinking than oneself. There is a role for collaborative inquiry based on a diversity of opinion, a tolerant attention to the opinions of others and a willingness to abandon the indefensible.

Perceptual and emotional barriers

As well as falling down on procedural requirements we need to be equally wary of a variety of common emotional obstacles to rationality. For example:

Beware of optimism and pessimism: In the absence of theory many decision-makers are guided by optimism (for example, many technocrats) or pessimism (for example, most deep ecologists). Once taken as a general stance, either of these attitudes becomes a procrustean bed which leads to biased perceptions.

Beware of exponential growth: People find it difficult to appreciate the rapidity of exponential processes, and hence to manage them.

Beware of groupthink: It is uncomfortable to stand alone in your thinking. We all need to be part of the group and to largely conform.

Beware of authority figures: We all have a tendency to readily accept the views of an acknowledged expert. But discipline-based expert advice can frequently lack context and may also be partial. Increasingly, the inaccessibility of parts of the social stock of knowledge brings its legitimacy into question.

Beware of mind reading: Because it is difficult to deliberately forget what you now know, you may not appreciate the ignorance of others.

Beware of the unthinkable: It is difficult to think clearly about events which, while being possible, would be highly surprising if they occurred.

Beware of space and time discounting: Discounting the significance of events which are remote in space and time is a way to reduce the complexity of a decision problem, making for an easier but not a better solution (Linstone 1994), for example, it supposedly takes a nation a generation to discount the horror of war and become prepared to engage in another. It does seem we are biologically programmed to ignore slow change but pick up fast change in the world about us. Our preference for immediate over delayed gratification makes matters worse. The problem of temporal myopia in human affairs is well illustrated by the story of the sirens on a Mediterranean island who lured sailors to their death with song. Ulysses' self-knowledge of his own limitations allowed him to foil the deadly lure of the present and live on.

Beware of linear causation: We have difficulty in thinking about problems which cannot be visualised. This may explain why we tend to think in terms of chains of causation rather than the reality of cycles and networks of causation.

Failing to learn from the past: Toynbee (1971: 74) suggests that while it is possible for societies to learn from past experience, they seldom make the effort until goaded into it by suffering. His examples include France and Germany learning not to try and conquer Europe and the English learning to give up their colonies. Without deceiving ourselves, we must be willing to interpret past experiences in terms of success and failure.

Beware of stress: Under even slight pressure, people revert to simplistic conceptualisations of complex problems.

Dangerous myths and beliefs

Myths are stories that people live by, stories they draw on to guide their lives, largely by showing how contradictory ideas can be reconciled (Salthe 1993: 245; Lévi-Strauss 1958; 1963). My Earthgarden and Dragons metaphors (allegories) have the potential to be myths. Myths, especially religious and tribal myths, have given many people the strength and courage to endure miserable lives. They have provided, and still provide for many, an explanation of human existence. They have inspired the good and the evil. My immediate concern is that there are myths — and other belief systems — with the potential to seriously divert the pursuit of quality survival because they consume people and impose arbitrary constraints and tendencies on their behavioural choices.

Foremost here are identity myths where a group grounds its identity in some historical mix of religion, ethnicity, culture and territory and is willing to engage in violent conflict to protect that identity, usually with other groups equally protecting their own identity myths. The world is awash with examples.

Heavenism is the idea that what happens on Earth does not matter because our immortal souls are going to spend eternity in heaven and getting there is what we need to focus on, not making the best of being mortal. This idea is only dangerous to those of us who do care what happens on Earth and regard heavenists as lead in the saddlebags. Other religious beliefs that are less than helpful are that the Devil is real and that God created the world about 6000 years ago.

Not all dangerous myths are religious in origin. *Scientism* is the belief that all of humanity's problems can be solved by the application of modern Cartesian–Newtonian science. The basic assumption is that there exist objective universal laws governing all natural phenomena, that these laws can be ascertained by scientific inquiry, and that once such laws are known, we can, starting from any set of initial conditions, predict perfectly the future and the past. More recent thinking about uncertainty and circular causation has challenged this paradigm but, partly because it works well in a limited range of situations, it remains strong and, in public discourse, leads to deceit and self-deception.

Economism is the philosophical stance that, because people are primarily strivers after material gain [sic], decisive importance should be given to economic considerations when making policy decisions. Neo-liberals make the further assumption that material gain will be higher in a fully marketised economy than under any other form of economic organisation.

Isaiah Berlin (1999: 159) once described the history of thought and culture as 'a changing pattern of great liberating ideas which inevitably turn into suffocating straitjackets'. Communism, liberalism and the other political 'isms' which emerged from the French Revolution come to mind.

More generally, *utopianism* is the idea that it should be possible to build an ideal society which would then not need to be further changed — a quite unrealistic belief in a changing world. The regressive form of this belief, held by both Rousseau and Freud (in *Civilization and its Discontents*) is that civilisation is a failure and we can and should return to an earlier primitive existence.

Enough. I have space to list only a few of the many myths and ideas with the power to inhibit the creation of alternative possible behaviours. The message for those seeking to address the deep futures problem is beware the (wo)man who has found the truth!

A STRATEGY OF RESPONDING TO PRIORITY ISSUES

Still, bounded rationality or not, the question remains, how do we conceptualise and manage the deep futures problem? How will we have to think to have any prospect of quality survival? My tentative and pragmatic working suggestion — see it as a bolder, less incremental version of muddling through — is to conceptualise the deep futures problem as one of *constantly searching for improvement by responding collectively to an unrolling set of priority issues.* There are several steps involved:

- Identify issues (potential problems, ungrasped opportunities) which are currently seen as most needing attention if quality survival is to be more nearly achieved;

- Design a series of alternative candidate responses (policy systems, programs etc.) to one or more of these priority issues;

- Implement the alternative promising to most improve quality survival prospects;

- Continue, that is, update priority issues.

As a recipe for responding to this or any other wicked problem, these steps beg many questions and are but a starting point. For example, the recipe as presented does not draw out the importance of tackling wicked problems on multiple fronts simultaneously, of breaking a complex of vicious circles collectively, as far as resources allow (Varis 2002). What I will do in this chapter, drawing on earlier chapters for ideas, is nominate several broad priority issues relevant to achieving quality survival. In following chapters I move on to suggesting a range of guidelines to be kept in mind when formulating alternative responses to those issues, or bits of them. I will not be creating any specific responses to the suggested priority issues (that is, I am not producing a 'grand plan'), simply collecting some injunctions which, in principle, might help to shape such specific responses. I particularly want to demonstrate how a basic understanding of societal change and of natural science lead to a rich (but far from exhaustive) suite of guidelines for addressing aspects of the deep futures problem. Some will disagree with some of my suggested guidelines but this simply means that in the eyes of these readers the offending guidelines should have zero influence on choice of actions. That is the beauty of *indicative guidelines* — they do not have to be followed. Having said that, I will also be suggesting some *imperative guidelines*, meaning that I strongly believe such should be followed.

What I am saying is that while we do not know with any real confidence how to manage world society to achieve quality survival, what we already know about the world and about humans and their societies suggests some priority issues and numerous qualitative guidelines or principles or hints that are probably worth following, to a greater or lesser extent, if that is the task. If followed, guidelines create areas of possibility within which evolutionary processes can unfold. As Jacob Bronowski (1973: 436) says, we shape our conduct by finding principles to guide it.

FOUR PRIORITY ISSUES

In Chapters 1 and 2 I presented ideas from a multitude of sources on people's perceptions of the human lineage's possible future experiences. In Chapter 3

I argued that people and societies need to establish goals if they are to think productively about what they want from the future and how to achieve what they want. A case was made that quality survival is a rich and appropriate societal goal, quality survival being shorthand for high quality of life for all members, present and future, of a society lasting over innumerable generations. In Chapter 4 I reviewed ideas from various disciplines on how and why societies change over time. My conclusion was that the processes underlying broad-scale societal change can be understood and explained to a useful degree and that the flow-on task is to produce guidelines for managing these processes.

What, I am now asking in light of all this, are the priority issues, the handful of really major concerns at this point in the history of the lineage, that have to be addressed if the lineage is to have some prospect of achieving quality survival? There is no right answer but, restricting myself to four, my choices are:

1   Nursing the world through endless change;

2   Raising the quality of social learning;

3   Confronting near-future threats and opportunities;

4   Anticipating deep-future challenges.

Chapter 6 will draw out some guidelines for responding to the first of these priority issues. Chapter 7 will find some guidelines relevant to priority issue 2, raising the quality of social learning. Chapter 8 will do likewise for priority issue 3 under the heading 'Working on perennial issues'. Some guidance on addressing issue 4, deep-future challenges, is worked into Chapters 6 and 7.

6

GUIDELINES I: NURSING THE WORLD THROUGH ENDLESS CHANGE

Let the great world spin forever down the ringing grooves of change. (ALFRED TENNYSON, from 'Locksley Hall')

Behind my nomination of 'guiding endless change' as a priority issue is a conviction that it is a legitimate and productive world view to see the deep futures problem as involving unceasing intervention in the irrepressible development of a dissipative complex system called world society. It is a view I would like to see more widely accepted but many are sceptical. It might be said, for example, that seeing the quality-survival challenge in this way is interesting but offers little of substance to those asking what needs to be done when by whom; that applying developmental systems theory to world society is just a re-labelling of the phenomena of history. There is of course equal scepticism for the utopian polar alternative of identifying an agenda for change with a beginning and an end and rigidly pursuing its implementation.

At the heart of the 'guiding endless change' perspective is the idea that it would be unsurprising if, left to its own devices, world society, and, equally, its component societies, exhibited the full range of dynamic behaviours associated with dissipative complex systems. These include convulsive changes as in natural disasters and revolutions; stagnation and stubborn resistance to change as in many traditional societies; modest reforms to the lives of ordinary people as favoured in liberal democracies; and the rolling back of reforms by reactionary forces. While the context and political interpretation will differ, the themes of slow and rapid, continuous and discontinuous changes impacting for better or worse on the quality of people's lives will persist as long as world society persists. This, I am saying, is the core process which has to be guided and which, to some extent, can be guided (see page 145).

We turn then to a sample of general-purpose guiding principles, suggested by our limited understanding of dissipative complex systems under four headings:

- Managing the change rate;

- Managing trends;

- Managing fragility and senescence;

- Managing unpredictability.

MANAGING THE CHANGE RATE

Karl Polanyi (1944; 2001) argued that the pace of societal change is often as important as the direction, but whereas we often have little control over direction we do have some control over rate. Indeed, the great ideological debates since 1789 between conservatives, liberals and socialists have been largely about the rate of reformist change (Wallerstein 1995). Rate of change is an important part of quality of life for the reason that rapid transformation destroys old coping mechanisms and old safety nets while creating new demands before new coping mechanisms are developed.

The modern world is extremely dynamic. The pace of social change is much faster and the scope much broader than in any prior historical system. Nonetheless, as in any hierarchical system, different things change at intrinsically different speeds and, if society is not to be disrupted, these relativities must be maintained. A society's infrastructure, structure and superstructure need to co-evolve. More specifically, institutions, technologies and people's values need to change in concert (Linstone 1994). The function of values is to provide semi-automatic guidance to people and societies when choosing between alternatives. As society's perceptions of the consequences of past choices change, values must change or become impediments to adaptation rather than useful decision aids. Being adaptable includes facing the long-term future without attachment to any aspect of the existing society, even fundamental values like democracy.

Thurow (1999) says societies must be organised so old vested interests can be swept aside by the new. Social systems have to be built in which entrepreneurs are free to destroy the old — but not too easily. He cites medieval China and 19th century Russia as examples of too little and too much order. Successful societies manufacture a tension between order and chaos without letting either get out of hand (see below). New ideas are easily frustrated if society is not receptive to the turbulence that comes with change.

But achieving such adaptability may not be easy. It must be recognised that societal systems resist change (see page 158). A well-adapted society does not willingly seek change. Sociologists say an accustomed way of behaving persists as long as circumstances allow. Because systems tend to counter imposed changes, you end up making little progress — Ridley's (1995) 'red queen' hypothesis. Or, more pessimistically, the harder you push, the harder the system pushes back — Tenner's (1996) 'revenge effects' hypothesis. System maintenance processes are powerfully mobilised in turbulent times. As dissipative systems theory suggests, a generalised force acting on a system far from equilibrium will cause the system to reorganise itself in the direction of the force in such a way as to minimise its effects (Nicolis and Prigogine 1977). The possibility that major change will not be achieved without major conflict and major pain needs to be born in mind, for example, the enclosure movement and the industrial revolution in Britain. Or, to quote AN Whitehead (in Hirschman 1991: 88), 'the major advances in civilization are processes which all but wreck the societies in which they occur'.

At some times, particularly when adaptive responses are not emerging rapidly enough, it may be desirable to slow the speed of change, for example, the slowing by the Crown of the English enclosure movement because of the social dislocation it was causing. At other times, the aim will be to remove barriers to change. For example, an economy can get locked into certain development strategies because of inertia and the 'changeover' costs of moving from one strategy to another. In such a situation, where the changeover is an all-or-nothing one, it takes great courage to calculate that the benefits of change exceed the costs and then act.

MANAGING TRENDS

Much of the observable change in societies is in the form of trends, that is, some indicator of change keeps moving in one direction, growing or declining, for a period that is long relative to the interval between decisions that take account of that indicator's value. Most trends are consequences of positive feedback processes and can range from slow and linear to fast and (hyper)exponential; or a mixture thereof. The accumulation of economic resources by those who are already rich, what Myrdal (1944) calls the 'Matthew effect' (Unto those that hath …), is a powerful example. Again, having power over coercive resources generates further power — armies conquer territories and that allows more military power to accumulate. Marchetti (1987) notes the homeostatic behaviour of large societal systems, able to hold their growth trajectory even when subjected to significant external shocks, for example, world population growth under plague.

However, systems dominated by positive feedback also reach limits, for example, the limiting of population growth by carrying capacity. At the heart of directional changes in society lie processes of diffusion, spread and accumulation of largely imitative or repetitive entities, ranging from ideas to artifacts. And, as previously noted, the temporal patterns of accumulation or growth of many of these entities are sigmoid (S-shaped) rather than linear. At the turnover point on a sigmoid growth curve, the rate of spread stops increasing and starts declining as niches for the diffusing entities become scarcer or more attractive to competing diffusion processes, for example, the saturation of new road links. Handy (1994) uses the idea of 'linked sigmoid curves' as a normative model for national, business and personal development, making much of the need to embark on new paths before growth or development rates decline. His message is to start on a new path *before* the old begins to peter out.

The problem of *overshoot* appears when trends in society which start out being productive/adaptive become counterproductive/counter-adaptive. Economic growth may be an example. What management guidelines can be suggested? Given that there are limits to the amount of short-term change that can be effected, ameliorative action has to start early if major tensions are be avoided. While society is regularly caught napping by the totally unforeseen (for example, HIV/AIDS), the fact is that almost all major problems (and opportunities) are identified well before they become threatening (are lost). The greenhouse effect has been foreseen for decades by scientists. Rachel Carson wrote *Silent Spring* in 1969. And so on. However, history constrains the possible rate of response to such early warnings because it bequeaths us a complement of societal capital that we are loath to abandon and that is not optimal for effecting change. A further difficulty is what is known as 'assumption drag', that is, 'We must accept … that we have to live for some time with the future before we recognise it as such' (Emery et al. 1975). Or, 'We see the past superimposed on the present, even when the present is a revolution' (Debray 1967: 2). Newly emerging trends are most difficult to detect when they are being quietly nurtured by existing parts of the system which are still playing their traditional roles, for example, cancerous cells, social movements.

These brakes on the rate of proactive change can be a force for stability but, if we want to deal with problems that current trends suggest will begin to bite in the medium- to long-term future, it may be that we need to start redirecting those trends now. Conversely, there is a danger of 'oversteering' when managing trends. Many cause–effect links in societal systems are not closely related in time and space and failure to understand this can lead to an overreaction when the system does not appear to be responding, for example, raising interest rates to slow economic growth. Built-in lags can also lead to premature assumptions that a trend is over.

MANAGING FRAGILITY AND SENESCENCE

Being dissipative systems, world society and its component societies have a tendency to pass through a sequence of developmental stages metaphorically equivalent to birth, immaturity, maturity, senescence and death, the last implying disorganisation or collapse (see page 183). For example, Modis (2002) fits a sigmoid curve describing the world's increasing complexification and concludes that the maximum rate of complexification has already passed. The idea that the world *in toto*, including human society, is on the way to a point where further viable changes will have great difficulty in emerging is a startling one.

An important management dilemma facing a mature society is that actions taken to successfully solve current problems — which usually means extended roles for individuals or collectives — carry a hidden cost, namely an increased susceptibility to future disruption triggered by external or internal fluctuations. In shorthand terms, complexification increases fragility. The more complex a system, the more likely it is to change of its own accord. A more fragile society carries an increased risk of both large and small losses of functionality, that is, of the capacity to meet needs. As theory suggests, increased complexity does not mean increased stability; it is more likely to indicate a low-change environment.

Can such increased fragility be diagnosed? A hypercomplex society (see page 178) may indicate its status through an increased frequency of fluctuations in various performance indicators. If the sizes of such fluctuations follows power laws (see Appendix) this may be an additional indication that the society is in that critical state where even a small breakdown in internal processes or in inputs from the environment could trigger reorganisation, disorganisation, upheaval or collapse. Mode-locking, the process in which various cyclical phenomena become synchronised, may be another indicator of fragility, for example, crises at several hierarchical levels simultaneously. The implied guideline is that such things need to be monitored even though they are in no way firm predictors of the size and timing of future breakdowns or reorganisations. Indeed, there are no practical ways of measuring a society's complexity or hypercomplexity.

In addition to fragility, there is a second, more obvious, cost of complexification. While it may solve target problems, it stands to (a) create further problems and (b) to make solutions to related problems harder to find. And there always are related problems; all problems exist in the context of other problems. As complexity increases, solutions to problems in one node of the system require a chain of adjustments to behaviour in other nodes of the system, 'waves of co-evolution' as it has been described. Complexification spreads and options narrow (path dependency). Eventually a point of *stagnation* or *senescence* is reached, a 'critical state' where there seem to be no ways of improving behaviour in one node of the system without causing other nodes in the system to malfunction. So, problems become apparently insoluble — another indication that hypercomplexity has been reached.

In summary then, complexification, primarily showing up as modifications and extensions to individuals' roles as decision-makers and problem-solvers, leads to the solution of society's immediate problems but, in time, it also leads to fragility and senescence, that is, to a susceptibility to disorganisation or reorganisation under stress and to an incapacity to solve further problems. Still, there is no reason, in principle, why a society should not last millennia without collapsing. While such survival might be quite unplanned, it stands to be assisted by a strategy based on ideas such as:

• Improving society's capacity to handle complexification;

• Periodic rejuvenation through controlled simplifications; (reductions in complexity)

• Avoiding and anticipating unplanned simplifications, large and small;

• Balancing further complexification with simplifications.

Confronting complexification

There are several ways of helping functionaries cope with the extended roles that come with complexification. All involve a loosening of constraints on individual and group capacity to solve problems and make decisions. One way is to increase the energy flows and prosthetic capital that decision-makers can command. Increasing one node's energy 'subsidy' can solve an immediate problem but at the price of increasing complexity overall. Putting a cap on total energy used, without constraining how it is used, will slow both complexification and environmental degradation but needs to be allied with an efficient system for transferring energy between uses.

The ecologist's perspective on energy use may be instructive here. Organisms that are successful in finding ways to extract more energy from the environment for their own use will live longer and leave relatively more copies of themselves. But, when organisms become too successful in extracting energy from the environment, they may destroy it and themselves in the process, for example, hungry elephants, koalas. The systems perspective is that if a dissipative system does not capture increasing amounts of exergy (usable energy), it will not proceed through a life cycle, that is, it will not reach a level of complexity at which it is vulnerable to collapse. There is no scientific law that systems must use ever-more energy, but, if they do not, they will not complete a life cycle.

Other hints for enhancing a society's capacity to solve ever-more problems under increasing complexity include:

- The level of trust and co-operation between people. Transaction costs and interaction costs fall when co-operation and trust between people rise. Trust allows contracts to be implicit rather than explicit. Other approaches to reducing transaction costs include well-regulated markets and creating organisations which internalise transactions (Coase 1937);

- Improved information flows, as facilitated by modern communications and information technologies, are particularly effective although, as Linstone (1994) warns, it can also be dangerous to speed up information flow in complex systems; increasing the flow rate simply allows the system to move more rapidly towards a fragile senescent state. For example, it may be advisable to slow information flow in an oscillating system;

- Making maximum use of self-managing systems. One reason the world has become more complex is that humans have taken over more and more naturally self-managing systems and undertaken to change and manage these themselves. This in itself is difficult enough, but when all these 'new' systems begin to interact in ways which could not have been predicted, human managerial capabilities may be exceeded.

Controlled simplification

An alternative to improving problem-solving capability as a way of deferring the collapse of a complexifying society is to deliberately initiate frequent small reorganisations (mini-collapses?) and occasional major reorganisations. A society following this 'complexity aversion' strategy will be both complexifying and simplifying at any time, sometimes moving further, on balance, towards fragility–senescence and sometimes towards maturity–immaturity. Too far in one direction and the system becomes excessively rigid. Too far in the other direction and the system loses the structure to behave coherently. The premise here is that ongoing simplification creates a 'space' within which priority problems can be tackled without pushing the society to the clogged-up point where problems have no solutions and the smallest of internal perturbations or external shocks might trigger a major collapse. The hope is that each time the society re-complexifies after simplification there is an opportunity to ask if priorities have changed, that is, complexification–simplification is a strategy which allows refocusing on changing priorities; simplification stands to free up resources to tackle priority issues.

Any strategy of controlled simplification will be complicated by the numerous uncontrolled, unplanned simplifications which all societies recurrently experience — war, epidemics, famine, natural disasters etc. While any simplification makes room for re-complexification, the complexification that occurs after unplanned simplifications is more likely to be focused on repairing rather than enhancing quality of life. Under 'managing unpredictability', some guidelines for avoiding unplanned simplifications are suggested below (see page 227).

Although rarely recognised as such, liberal capitalist democracies have many simplifying mechanisms — social, political and economic — built into them. The pre-eminent example is the 'capital abandonment' in which economically unsuccessful enterprises are liquidated and replaced with new 'immature' enterprises which do not possess the dense networks of relationships accumulated by their predecessors. Politically, it is the periodic election of a new government, relatively free of 'baggage', which resets the complexity of a country's governance system. Socially, it is the replacement in positions of power of the ageing, set in their ways, by the young that allows a society's norms and values to evolve. Recognising when one of society's processes is also a simplifying process is a first step towards thinking through its effectiveness for that purpose.

One generic process for deliberately cycling between complexification and simplification in a hierarchical system is *centralisation–decentralisation*. Like the related processes of devolution and subsidiarity, decentralisation involves the transfer of decision-making and problem-solving responsibilities from a higher to a lower level of a sociopolitical hierarchy, for example, from a federal to a state government, from an agency to an individual. Communication, administration and negotiation costs are reduced by decentralisation but it is the benefits to be obtained from *coordinating* the activities of autonomous entities that eventually drives the system back towards integration and centralised control.

Modularisation or *compartmentalisation* (see page 186) is another simplifying process, leading a society away from criticality. It involves the organising of nodes (modules) which specialise in performing particular functions or tasks for society and which only interact with other parts of the system in a limited way. Modules are provided with the resources to maintain themselves as long as they provide their specialist services. The separation of governance into legislative, executive and judicial arms is an example. Modularisation implies simplification to the extent that solutions to problems arising within a module do not have to be coordinated with solutions to problems arising in many other functional areas. And while it has other benefits, such as its contribution to resilience and efficiency, modularisation has to be evaluated within a wider debate about balancing adaptation and adaptability (all adaptation involves closing off certain behavioural paths and hence a loss in adaptability, meaning the range of possible behaviours).

Downsizing Bigger societies tend to be more complex per se than smaller societies. Most obviously this is because as the number of nodes (people, organisations etc.) in a society increases arithmetically, the number of potential interactions between nodes increases geometrically (much faster). A second reason is that bigger societies tend to have more information processing levels, and hence opportunities for distortion in information flows ('Chinese whispers') and hence a need for further controls on information quality.

MANAGING UNPREDICTABILITY

The principle underlying rational choice between alternative actions is to pick the alternative with the 'best' consequences. What value is the rational choice model though if the consequences of possible actions cannot be foreseen with confidence?

Four types of knowledge about the future

Knowledge is a special sort of information, which, in turn, is an understanding of 'effective' differences — differences which have significant implications (Bateson 1979). Knowledge is information that the 'owner' is willing to assume to be true. Knowledge about the future can be of several types, including:

- Certain knowledge;
- Probabilistic knowledge;
- Uncertain knowledge;
- Possibilistic knowledge.

Certain knowledge

If we had the power to know the future it would mean that we could create mental images today of some focal subject at some future date which, come that date, would prove to have been accurate. We would have the gift of prophecy, the power to accurately predict the future, and we would know the future with certainty. In operational terms, knowing the future with certainty implies that one would be prepared to bet anything or everything on the predicted future eventuating.

We can distinguish *objectively certain* from *subjectively certain* future-knowledge. The difference between these is that most people would agree with a prediction of the future based on objectively certain knowledge (the sun will rise) but only the owner of subjectively certain knowledge has total confidence (high degree of belief) that the eventuating future will match hir imagined future.

Probabilistic knowledge

All knowledge which is not certain is *non-certain*. One well-studied form of non-certain (and hence deterministically unpredictable) knowledge about future states is probabilistic knowledge. If we are talking about the next occurrence of a future state which we know (believe unreservedly) from historical experience will be type 1 or type 2 … or type n, we may feel confident enough to assign an *objective probability* to that next occurrence. This objective probability will be the proportion of times that a future state of the type of interest has occurred in a set of past occurrences of that type of situation, for example, 'three years in ten it rains in March'. It is also assumed to be the proportion of times the future state will occur in future situations. Our knowledge of the future then, we feel certain, is as though it will be determined by spinning a roulette wheel where some of the ball-slots are marked 'future state occurs' and the rest are marked 'future state does not occur', for example, three slots on a ten-slot wheel are marked 'rain in March'.

Subjective probability is similar to objective probability in the sense that one's knowledge of the future is still that it will be as though determined by the spinning of a roulette wheel. The difference from objective probability is that the fraction of ball-slots marked 'future state occurs' is not based on historical observations of comparable past future states but on a personal (subjective) belief that is not readily analysable.

Uncertain knowledge

A future-gazer with *uncertain knowledge* of the future knows, believes with total confidence, or is willing to assume, that the eventuating future will closely match one of a limited number, N, of mental images of the matter of interest that s/he possesses. In a situation of strict uncertainty the future-gazer is unable to assign probabilities of occurrence to the N candidate states. Under the roulette wheel analogue, the uncertain future-gazer knows that each slot is marked 'Image 1 eventuates' or 'Image 2 eventuates' or … 'Image N eventuates' but s/he has no idea what positive fraction of all slots is assigned to what image.

Possibilistic knowledge

A future-gazer with *conjectural* or *possibilistic knowledge* of the future knows that the eventuating future could, imaginably, correspond with one or another of 1, 2, … N preview images of the future but s/he has no knowledge of whether there might be other images, N+1, N+2, … from which the eventuating future state could be drawn. In terms of the roulette wheel analogy, the identifier (1, 2, … N) of each preview image is marked on an unknown (non-zero) number of slots but the knower does not know the total number of slots on the wheel and hence can say nothing about the probability of outcomes 1, 2, … N.

Just as the words 'will' and 'likely' flag certain and probabilistic knowledge respectively, the words 'may', 'could' and 'might' all flag uncertain and possibilistic knowledge, for example, 'the winning number on this hidden roulette wheel could be (or might be), possibly (or uncertainly) three'. The term *scenario* was introduced in Chapter 1 to describe the possibilistic futures envisaged by diverse future-gazers. While it is not logical to talk about the probability of a scenario (because the number of slots on the 'futures wheel' is not known) it can be helpful, and is legitimate, to express the subjective judgment that it would be unsurprising (many slots), highly surprising (few slots) etc. if such-and-such a scenario eventuated (Shackle 1955).

With a few exceptions, possibilistic knowledge in the form of scenarios is the only knowledge we can have about the future, especially the deep future. Not only does this include knowledge of the consequences of proactive policies for achieving quality survival, it includes knowledge of the timing and scope of unplanned simplifications of the societal system and of changes in the global biophysical environment.

Guidelines for managing unpredictability

Having recognised that knowledge of the consequences of candidate policies is largely possibilistic, what does a policy-maker do about it? One response is to pick one unsurprising scenario describing the future of concern under each candidate policy and make the working assumption that it is certain to occur. Another is to hypothesise, for each candidate policy, a 'pseudo-probability' for each of a number of scenarios and proceed as though one's future-knowledge is probabilistic (risky) rather than possibilistic. Or, one can create a manageable number of scenarios for each candidate policy and proceed on the working assumption that the future will be uncertain, that is, assume that one of these will certainly occur. Any of these simplifying assumptions opens the way to using a range of decision-making aids that decision theorists have developed, for example, game theory, statistical decision theory (for example, Berger 1985). For example, game-theory thinking suggests that a decision-maker who is risk-averse should select the candidate policy which has a worst possible outcome which s/he prefers to the worst outcomes of other candidate policies. We have space only to note that these sorts of procedures exist, not to explore them.

The point is that simplifications such as these are used because existential decisions have to be made and, at least to date, there is really no intellectually satisfying way of incorporating possibilistic knowledge into policy design. That is, there is no obvious way of choosing, in terms of their relative consequences, between the candidate policies available for addressing some priority issue. Irrespective of the candidate policy chosen, any one of the envisaged or, indeed, an unenvisaged outcome could eventuate. Choice has unpredictable consequences. It is a difficulty which exists even before superimposing the further enormous difficulty of how to measure the degree to which any envisaged outcome would contribute to goal achievement, for example, to quality survival. This is why I can offer below only some fragmentary guidelines for better recognising non-certainty and unpredictability when developing future-making policies, plans and programs:

Divergent scenarios

Available resources will always limit the set of scenarios that can be created in any policy-design exercise aimed at improving the future. The challenge then is to make this limited set somehow representative of all possible futures. One way of interpreting this criterion is to say that one believes there is no plausible future that could eventuate from such-and-such policy that would be radically different from one (or a mix) of the scenarios envisaged. For example, when envisaging a policy's possible outcomes in terms of its quality survival implications, both an optimistic and a pessimistic scenario might be included.

Just-in-time decisions

It is a basic principle of decision making under non-certainty (meaning that one cannot be sure of the consequences of any decision taken and implemented) that you never make a decision before you have to. In that way you make every decision with the maximum possible amount of information, including information eventuating right up to the moment of decision.

Be sensitive to unintended consequences

All problems are embedded in the context of other problems and solving one problem tends to create or exacerbate other problems. The guideline here is simply to recognise that this is the case and make a particular effort to incorporate such unintended disbenefits into one's scenarios of a policy's consequences.

The so-called *precautionary principle* goes further, suggesting that policies with foreseeable harmful effects should not be implemented but redesigned. Are we doing things today that we will come to regret having done? Are we choosing to not do things today which we will regret not having done?

Beware of motes

Unplanned simplifications, whether internally or externally triggered, always have the potential to produce large rapid changes in society. They are difficult to foresee and hence stand to be underestimated in scenarios of policy consequences. The converse trap facing the scenariographer is that target changes are never easy to achieve, particularly in a mature society. This suggests the wisdom of erring on the side of anticipating under-achievement rather than over-achievement when foreseeing policy outcomes.

Monitoring and replanning

The best way of predicting the future is knowing what is happening today! That aphorism is pointing out that information about the state of things often flows so slowly in complex societies that speeding up such flows is equivalent to making a successful prediction. Monitoring the outcomes of previous decisions is the starting point for the continuous replanning that, ideally, is necessary in an unpredictable non-certain world. I say ideally for two reasons. One is that monitoring is expensive and therefore has to be selective, for example, monitor only major uncertainties or monitor the slow variables that managers tend to ignore. Two is that we do not know how to monitor many important aspects of an ever-changing world society, for example, fragility, senescence, global change, social justice etc.

Robust policies

One way of recognising that both better and worse outcomes are possible whatever policy is implemented is to try and construct policies which perform reasonably well no matter what outcome scenario eventuates. The usual cost of such *robust* or *resilient policies* is that while avoiding 'worst case' scenarios they forego any possibility of performing exceptionally well, that is, of being, apparently, highly *efficient*.

In the rare environment which is variable but not generating new forms of foreseeable variety, custom, tradition and routine may well offer sufficient robustness. Otherwise, one way of seeking robustness is to invest resources in constructing *contingency plans*, that is, specifying what will be done in the event of particular outcome scenarios eventuating. For example, what will we do if the reactor goes critical? It takes much effort to answer such a question. This approach may or may not involve 'warehousing' or reserving resources so that, if needed, they are quickly available to ameliorate unfavourable outcomes or capitalise on favourable outcomes. Thus firms need reserves of funds, inventory and labour to cope with non-certain markets. A more active way of holding resources in reserve is to invest them in experimental and research ventures which can be 'mothballed' and their resources released if necessary.

Building *redundancy* into programs is sometimes an option. Protection against foreseeable shocks which could destroy system components can be achieved by having 'backup' or redundant components available to take over the functions of lost components. Systems which are efficient in a stable environment become increasingly unstable as environmental risk increases. Redundancy confers stability.

Another proactive approach is to stabilise the external environment, making it less threatening if possible. Clearly there are contingencies which we are as yet unable to control, for example, strikes by large asteroids. However, there is a grey area where, through strenuous effort, perturbations in the environment can be dampened at an acceptable cost, for example, flood control, drought-proofing.

It can never be assumed that the benefits of making plans robust will outweigh the costs. For example, in a competitive market environment, firms which 'take out insurance' against a range of adverse scenarios eventuating (for example, by expending resources on a range of contingency plans) stand to be out-competed by any firms which successfully gamble on one particular scenario (business as usual?) eventuating and hence showing high apparent efficiency.

It may not be at all irrational for firms to gamble in this way and court bankruptcy. But for society as a whole, gambling on one scenario in the hope of, say, sharply lifting quality of life while courting social collapse, the stakes are much higher. For example, Joseph Needham (Ronan 1986) asks why China did not become the centre of world power, given that by 1500 CE it had gunpowder, the compass and printing, all before Europe. His tentative answer is that innovation and entrepreneurship threatened the emperors and were suppressed in the interests of political stability. The Soviet Union's 'jam tomorrow' policy of forced industrialisation is a more recent example.

But there are no algorithms for generating right answers. In principle, policy-robustness should be pursued until the costs of building in additional stability match the additional benefits.

Adapting to the unforeseen

Robust policies are a way of adapting to a variety of foreseeable futures but can something be done to anticipate unforeseen futures? For a start, can nature show the way?

Plant and animal species evolve, through a series of adaptations, to survive in a range of unpredictable habitats, that is, habitats where it is only feasible to have probabilistic, uncertain or possibilistic knowledge of the future. Each species' adaptations can be thought of as a suite of 'if … then' *response rules*, one for each eventuating state or group of states of the environment that the species is adapted to. Eventuation of a previously experienced state can trigger physiological responses, instinctual responses or learned responses. For example, mobility is an essential adaptation for animals dealing with local non-certainty in food supplies, safety etc. Other simple averaging behaviours cope with much variability, for example, gaining weight in good times and losing it in bad, seed dispersal and dormancy, spreading multiple births over a lifetime and a whole variety of schemes for gaining information about the environment and learning to utilise it.

On a somewhat longer time scale, evolution has produced mechanisms (gene mutation, recombination) which, under the influence of natural selection, maintain a species' level of genetic variability at a level appropriate to the variability of the environment. Part of the population, the part with the 'right' genes, will survive a particular sort of shock, for example, drought. Genetic variability is reduced in this process but then builds up again. Having different gene pools in a population, as a way of responding to imperfectly predictable events, is no different in principle from an individual having a variety of behaviours and physiological devices available for responding to higher frequency events. In ecosystems, having different groups of co-evolving species playing similar roles in the system's operations, but in slightly different ways — called functional redundancy — is a mechanism which protects critical functions in the face of imperfectly predictable events.

Extinction of the individual, the species or the ecosystem occurs when it has no pre-programmed response rule for an eventuating environment or cannot devise such a rule — cannot adapt — before being disrupted by the novel environment. Piaget (1971) regards adaptation as comprising assimilation and accommodation. *Assimilation* means encoding (recognising) the surprising information as a problem to be solved and *accommodation* means reorganising (self-organising) to create a behaviour that allows the surprising phenomenon to be dealt with, both immediately and if it should re-occur.

This brings us back again to the tricky concepts of adaptability and adaptable (see pages 216 and 221). *Adaptability* is the capacity to adapt to (live through) environmental fluctuations that have not been previously encountered. While it cannot be measured directly, there are some partial indicators available. For example, being adaptable necessarily means having a variety of behavioural options available but that may not suffice if this variety does not include an appropriate response to the particular novel environment. Similarly, having survived great change in the past may indicate luck rather than adaptability. There is in fact a *law of requisite variety* (Ashby 1960) which states that, to achieve appropriate regulation, the variety in the regulator (meaning the range of its behavioural options) must be equal to or greater than the variety of the system being regulated (environmental possibilities). Eventually, of course, all biological entities are overwhelmed by environmental fluctuations with which they cannot cope.

About the only guideline we can glean from nature is that species which have a history of generalised adaptation rather than specialised adaptation (see page 195) seem to have a greater variety of responses and hence to be more adaptable. Generalist species (for example, magpies) are those which have adapted in ways which extend their environmental niche rather than ways which improve their performance in their existing niche (for example, honeyeaters). For example, generalist species tend to be more mobile, more tolerant of environmental fluctuations (for example, warm-blooded) and/or more able to discriminate between different environments. Humans are particularly successful generalists, achieving the efficiencies of specialisation without the disadvantages, basically through the use of prostheses which, in turn, are a product of their great capacity to learn.

While having a variety of inherent responses would seem to be a necessary part of any strategy to survive (be pre-adapted to) unforeseeable future change, it must not come at too high a price in terms of adaptation to the existing environment. All adaptation involves closing off certain behavioural paths and hence a loss in adaptability. Finding a balance point between adaptation for surviving the present and adaptability for surviving the future is an endless challenge. Humanity's tendency of course is to err on the side of favouring the present.

In the case of human societies, *self-sufficiency* or *autarky* (including autarky at local, regional, national etc. scales) is a generalist strategy which has to be played off against free trade which is something of a specialist strategy. In the deep future, space settlement might be a generalist strategy.

Another important generalist strategy is *capital building*, meaning the accumulation of various types of flexible, uncommitted, unspecialised capital so that such will be readily available for coping with the unforeseen. For example, retaining land in an undeveloped state maximises the future uses to which it might be put. A population of broadly educated and co-operative people is another (see page 236). Developing generic rather than specialised technologies (see page 27) is another.

Beyond any elaboration which could be pursued here, guidelines on preparing for the unseen will continue to develop in line with the further application of systems thinking to the dynamics of societies (see page 248).

A SISYPHEAN TASK

The deep futures problem — managing the future so as to converge on quality survival — is a wicked or ever-changing problem which, I suggested in Chapter 5, can best be tackled in terms of responding, with the help of a portfolio of management guidelines, to an unrolling set of priority issues. For the purposes of this book, four such priorities were suggested. In this chapter, under the priority of guiding change, the search has been for guidance on coping with the surprising and the unforeseen, guidance on actively directing change, and guidance on recognising and typing change as it happens.

Thus, the first theme of the chapter is the inherent lack of stability, of equilibrium, in all phenomena — physical, biological, social, cosmological, personal. Given time, all things change. This seems obvious enough but it is only recently that seeing the world and its processes as equilibrium-seeking and inherently stable was the preferred conceptual model in many fields, with change, particularly large change, being seen as aberrant.

The chapter's second theme, and I give it the status of a working assumption, is that human agency, social or individual, can, to a limited extent, guide this ceaseless change in more rather than less preferred directions. I am thus rejecting the view that the complexities and non-certainties of societal change are too great to permit any meaningful attempt at their management; it is not pointless to struggle for the good society. Nonetheless, the task is Sisyphean, meaning one that requires continual effort while only ever paying off temporarily (Sisyphus was the mythical Greek who toiled to roll a giant boulder to the top of a hill every day, only to have it roll down again every night).

Methodologically, the task of nursing world society through endless change turns on being able to distinguish and differentially manage various recurring categories of change, including two which I present as particularly important: controlling fragility and senescence in over-mature societies; and making choices about what to do about an issue when the consequences of any such choices might be quite unforeseen or, at best, foreseen only as a family of scenarios, all plausible.

Deliberate simplification is a useful strategy for moving an over-mature society away from the twin dangers of gridlock and collapse which accompany complexification. Direct measures such as improving information flows can also help. As for the unpredictability problem, insurance against the eventuation of foreseeable adverse scenarios can be taken out in various ways including the adoption of robust policies based on contingency plans, built-in redundancy etc. Acquiring the adaptability to weather unforeseen outcomes and events for which, by definition, no specific preparations can be made, is a challenge for which few guidelines can be suggested. One guideline is to build up stocks of various types of flexible, uncommitted, unspecialised capital, ready to direct against emergent threats or to capitalise on emergent opportunities.

A third theme, probably warranting more attention than it has received, is the importance of comprehensively and continuously monitoring the dynamics of world society and its environment. Given that system behaviour can only be crudely predicted, and can range from quiescent to convulsive, there is a need for eternal vigilance, a need to know at once when system behaviour is beginning to change so that ameliorative or exploitative action can be initiated.

The overall conclusion which emerges from the chapter is that managing the dynamics of world society is indeed a Sisyphean task, one in which the collective will is forever cycling society between complexification and simplification, with one eye looking out for the unpredictable consequences of policies targeting priority issues and one looking out for the unforeseeable shocks which can cause great pain or, at worst, precipitate collapse.

Is there any alternative to this paradigm of clumsily steering a system, one never far from stalling or crashing, through a forest of scenarios? Given that it does not incur implementation costs, could society rely on self-organisation to move the world in preferred directions? The answer is no if your null hypothesis is that it would be just as surprising for a society left to its own devices to move towards as to move away from quality survival. Purposive effort can do just a little better than that I believe. What is important to remember is that, within the constraints set by society as a whole, self-organisation will periodically spawn new patterns of organisation and social interaction which will need to be detected, be evaluated and then encouraged or discouraged.

Social learning to the rescue?

This has been a methodological or even theoretical chapter insofar as it discusses generic guidelines and types of strategies for managing societal change in a variety of generic circumstances. But one crucial strategy has been left out and that is the acquisition of new knowledge through *social learning.*

This chapter discusses the management of societal change only in terms of what is already known about monitoring and diagnosing change and about creating and choosing between the families of possibilistic scenarios associated with policy alternatives. Looking beyond this, intelligent social learning promises new knowledge that will reshape our understanding of societal change, of what is currently unforeseeable and of the plausible consequences of policy choices. The world is not going to become predictable and we are not going to be able to shape the world as we wish, but intelligent and directed knowledge acquisition programs, particularly scientific research programs, will reveal new possibilities for actions and their consequences while discounting or rewriting currently foreseen possibilities.

It is because social learning is so fundamental to society's prospects for moving towards quality survival that it has been nominated as a priority issue and given its own chapter, rather than treating it too briefly in the present chapter. Chapter 7 explores some guidelines for making the social learning process as effective as possible and for ensuring that it is applied to priority issues.

7

GUIDELINES II: LEARNING FOREVER

HG Wells thought the future to be a two-horse race between knowledge and disaster. A century later, it is no clearer which is winning, just that the pace has increased. This chapter asks if the odds on knowledge can be systematically shortened.

A good part of this book so far is about identifying and making the best possible use of what societies already know as they pursue quality survival, for example, by turning it into decision-making guidelines. Clearly, what we know is not enough, at least within a framework where managing the future is interpreted as a matter of guiding world society towards quality survival via selective policy responses to a rolling set of priority issues. But, equally clearly, we can see that it might be more. It is to seize this opportunity that we now turn explicitly to some suggestions for making world society into more of a (social) *learning society* than it is now. A learning society is one in which high priority is given to the social learning task, that is, to the building up of a sufficient body of collective knowledge (useful information) to ensure quality survival.

Social learning was likened earlier (see page 192) to an evolutionary process in that innovative variations on existing production rules ('if ... then' rules) for maintaining society and its institutions are tried and adopted if judged to be improvements. One major advantage which social learning has over the genetic form is that society's candidate learning experiments can be simulated and compared in the mind's eye before deciding which is to be tried in reality. Natural selection, conventionally regarded as 'random search', lacks such foresight. Another major advantage is that social learning experiments can be tailored and re-tailored to society's priority goals of the moment, whereas natural selection's one-dimensional goal is reproductive advantage.

A potential limitation which social learning shares with natural selection is that it is unlikely to produce truly fundamental, transformational change in society. As in biology, macro-mutations tend to be non-viable. In Edgar Dunn's terms (page 192), social learning is appropriate for normal problem solving — improving the way the existing system works — but not for the extraordinary problem-solving called for when social learning experiments fail to achieve any goal convergence. Almost always, societies get fundamentally reorganised as part of a process of recovery from unplanned shocks and simplifications or, occasionally, from planned destruction as in a revolution. Still, to deliberately reorganise a society at all levels (see page 169) will always be massively risky, warranted only in the face of an extreme threat to survival or to quality of life. Nonetheless, there will be such occasions in the fullness of time and options for achieving controlled societal transformation need to be developed in advance.

FOUR PILLARS OF SOCIAL LEARNING

Accepting that world society needs a powerful social learning system to, we hope, get it comfortably through a boundless future, how might such a system need to be structured and organised? Our main focus in responding to this will be on the 'political' learning system and the generation of collective knowledge and less on the social or group learning that occurs within organisations and other voluntary associations. While *learning organisations* are valuable in themselves and as part of a learning culture (see below) their interests are short-term relative to our concern with managing the bigger problems and opportunities of nothing less than world society (Senge 1992).

If the core task of the social learning system is viewed as one of continuing to upgrade the steps involved in responding to an unrolling set of priority issues, the system will need, at least, the following subsystems:

1   An appreciation system (to use Geoffrey Vickers' [1968] term that identifies which tacit or explicit goals of the society are not coming any closer or, more urgently, are retreating. These can then become the focus for the learning process.

2   An options system for identifying existing policy suggestions, social technologies etc. for ameliorating priority problems or, finding nonesuch, for designing new candidate policies.

3   An implementation system for selecting and implementing one or more of the candidate policies.

4   A monitoring and evaluation system that checks progress and restarts the learning system over again when progress is unsatisfactory, for example, is the UN working?

The first important feature of a social learning system described in this way is its overt recognition that changes in social organisation are essentially empirical experiments on a dissipative complex system. Failure to understand this can and does massively distort the way society's resources are allocated. More broadly, if such a system is to function over a long period, it must be embedded in a supportive learning culture. And it must itself be a 'meta-learning' system, meaning that the learning system itself will have to evolve to meet the needs of an evolving world society as well as evolve in response to active attempts at learning how to better learn. Any worthwhile social learning system will be continuously experimenting to improve itself. We turn then to a brief discussion of ways of (a) nurturing and (b) boosting the core social learning system.

NURTURING SOCIAL LEARNING

What sorts of societies are likely to give high priority to the social learning task? History suggests that that they need not be democratic, egalitarian or peace-loving, although social learning to improve quality of life for ordinary people (as distinct from ruling elites) would seem more likely in such. Equally, it can be presumed that resources for supporting experimental social learning and science are less likely to be available in a chaotic society fighting for its daily survival.

Beyond these rather obvious preconditions, a learning society stands to be one which is culturally and structurally supportive of innovation (trying new ways to do things). By this I first mean that the population has a capacity for and positive attitude towards social learning and, second, that the society is organised to provide a wide range of opportunities to participate in social learning.

Education in a learning society

The basic resource of a learning society is a population of bright, educated, willing people.

Intelligence, being able to perceive relationships between things, plus having a store of relevant accessible knowledge, are primary determinants of a person's capacity for innovative problem-solving and hence for being able to contribute to social learning. Almost certainly, we can learn how to enhance or train intelligence more fully, including a role for active imagination (see page 110). And while it is education, formal and informal, which builds up relevant knowledge, we can continue to learn how to better store and access this knowledge in long-term and subconscious memory. We can also learn how to identify and train people who have specific intelligences, for example, mathematical intelligence.

A population which has been purposely educated for membership of a learning society seeking quality survival is likely to have a majority of people who have an integrated understanding of the world they live in. Some of the things this means are:

- Being scientifically and historically literate;

- Being aware of the great physical challenges that world society will presently face;

- Being aware of the possibilities and difficulties involved in building a successful life of one's own;

- Being aware of the psycho-social strengths and weaknesses which the human animal brings to the task of seeking quality survival;

- Being aware of how complexity, non-certainty and change constrain the degree to which the human lineage can shape its future.

A population which is willing, indeed enthusiastic, to participate in a learning society will have been imbued with learning-culture values and attitudes such as:

- Low dependence on authority, custom and tradition as a source of beliefs;

- Curiosity and a love of knowledge;

- Accepting of change and the need for ongoing change;

- Belief in the leveraged effectiveness and legitimacy of collective action;

- Awareness of the complementary roles of co-operation and competition as tools for producing social knowledge (see page 271);

- Respect for those contributing to social learning.

In addition to these population-wide characteristics, a portion of the population will have to be educated and regularly re-educated to master specialised knowledge. Indeed, if new technologies continue the current trend of drawing on several disciplines for their development (for example, photonics plus electronics), experts will need to understand vocabularies and fundamental concepts from related fields if they are to work effectively in multidisciplinary teams. As well as life-long learning, they will need long and demanding initial training, for example, multidisciplinary degrees.

Generating and maintaining diversity

Why might a diverse society promote social learning? Think biologically first. High biological diversity (variety) can be recognised at all levels in the hierarchical organisation of life on Earth. A species can be genetically diverse. A diverse ecosystem contains a wide variety of species interacting in numerous ways. Diverse land systems contain a wide variety of ecosystems. And so on. When its environment undergoes permanent change (for example, climate change), an ecosystem which is more rather than less diverse is correspondingly more likely to find, within itself, relationships that fit it to survive in the new environment; allow it to successfully reorganise. This can be either a process of adaptation — the environment changes and organisms change in ways that fit the new environment — or exaptation — past changes in a species fortuitously fit it for the new environment. Therein lies the importance of having different species with different responses to environmental change playing similar roles in the food chain (Chapin et al. 1997). Diversity provides natural selection with evolutionary fuel.

Analogously, a human society which is highly diverse has a wide variety of cultural groups (cf. species) playing a variety of interacting roles (for example, employees, participants, office holders) in the variety of organisations and institutions comprising that society's socioeconomic structure and infrastructure (cf. trophic structure). For example, the coexistence of a broad range of political and religious opinions (Rawls' 'reasonable pluralism' [1993: 134]) reflects diversity in a society's superstructure.

There is broad agreement that high diversity is preferable to low diversity if a society is to survive in a changing environment — simply because among its larger collection of behaviour patterns there is more likelihood of one being viable in the changed environment, for example, Jane Jacobs (1969: 98) argues that economically diverse cities are also resilient cities. However, it is a somewhat different question we are asking here. Is a highly diverse society more or less likely to be a learning society? Does the knowledge pool grow faster in a diverse society? In particular, is a diverse society more likely to direct its learning to the pursuit of social goals as well as more likely to survive environmental change?

With some qualifications, the answer is yes. One qualification is that diversity is normally correlated with complexity and there will be few possibilities for innovative experiments in social organisation if the society has diversified and complexified to the point of over-maturity or senescence. But, in a developing society, where the basic infrastructure, structure and superstructure have been established, a sufficient variety of social forms, functions, connections and tasks will create opportunities for experimental interactions and hence for new behaviours to emerge, for example, early agricultural villages were able to grow through a series of social inventions such as roles, records and the teaching of behaviour. Pattee (1969) reminds us of John Von Neumann's observation that unless you have a certain amount of complexity in a system you cannot get interesting interactions; but if you have too much you get gridlock.

A second qualification is that there is no particular reason, apart from being in the public interest, why the social learning that takes place in a diverse society because of the opportunities it offers for experimental inter-action should address that society's priority issues. Modern western society is a good example with its high levels of innovation in the private sphere, par-ticularly the economy, and its floundering government sphere. Similarly, a society of numerous loosely connected units may be diverse but lack the coherence to address society-wide issues. Diversity, with its promise of self-organising adaptability, is best regarded as a complement to goal-seeking problem-solving, with its promise of adaptation and control.

The starting point for a society seeking to encourage diversity relevant to quality survival is to provide operating resources to political, scientific, acad-emic, community etc. institutions where creative options for addressing pri-ority issues might emerge. Devolving political decision-making to as low a level as possible is one example. Social structures at a human scale give peo-ple power over their lives. In large social structures people feel insignificant, with the choice of conforming or being nothing (Fromm 1942). Subsidising experimental communities in deliberately contrived social and physical envi-ronments could be another way of diversifying. The importance ·of genetic diversity is easily overlooked (see page 239). Dissenters should be encouraged for they are the 'canaries' warning society that something is perhaps going wrong. Another clue is that history suggests that prosperity is the great pro-moter and protector of novel thought. More generally, diversity is best encouraged by using collective resources to create niches, but not to fill them.

BOOSTING SOCIAL LEARNING

We note two tasks under this heading. One is the need to learn how to improve the social learning process itself and the other is the need take an experimental approach to social learning.

Learning about learning

Here we are trying to identify research projects with the potential to increase the effectiveness of the social learning process per se.

First come the big scoping questions, questions which always need cur-rent working answers but which also need to be regularly revisited:

- Are there better phrases than this book's 'quality survival' as a shorthand goal, a landmark, for world society? Indeed, are there alternatives to 'goals' for driving narratives about the future of world society?

- Are there better ways of conceptualising world society's broad strategy for managing an expansive future than as a priority-issues strategy, that is, one of responding to an unrolling set of priority issues?

- Are there better ways of expressing the knowledge available for implementing this strategy than as 'guidelines'? Are there systematic procedures for constructing guidelines? How do they depend on context? How can they be considered simultaneously? Should a variety of guideline categories be elaborated, for example, indicative versus imperative guidelines?

Lasting mechanisms for researching and debating these panoramic questions will be needed. At the next level down come more specific questions about finding better methods within each of the learning system's four components of goal selection, options identification, policy selection and outcome evaluation. For example:

Selecting goals: What methods are available for systematically identifying priority issues? For updating the suite of priority issues? What is the relative importance of survival issues vis-à-vis quality of life issues? What sort of society do people need to live in to achieve self-actualisation? Should goals be expressed as states or as capabilities? What is an acceptable set of partial indicators of quality of life? How and when should that set be revised?

Assembling options: When does an issue demand the creation of novel policy instruments? How do we learn to purposively generate ideas for new social technologies which solve or pre-empt problems, exploit opportunities, reduce weaknesses and consolidate society's strengths (see Box 7.1)? Where does the development of material technologies fit in? Can the policy-design process be improved?

Evaluating outcomes: How do we test for goal convergence? Goal achievement? The need is for measurable indicators that, tracked over time, suggest whether world society is approaching or retreating from the societal goal of quality survival.

**BOX 7·1 SOME PRINCIPLES FOR DESIGNERS OF
NEW SOCIAL TECHNOLOGIES (AFTER COCKS 1992)**

It is not possible to anticipate the details of any future procedures which might be developed for routinely designing social
technologies, but the search and design principles behind those
procedures might well include, for example:

- The need to develop separate technologies for small parts of
  large problems (the 'adaptive muddling' principle);

- The importance of developing procedures which are accepted
  because they constitute 'instant carrot'. Things like the alphabet, the credit card, standard time, and penny postage were
  successful because it was in the immediate interests of people
  to adopt them (the 'instant feedback' principle);

- The importance of making maximum use of non-monetary
  values to motivate behaviour; conversely, the need to avoid
  solutions based on 'just throwing money at the problem' (the
  'leather medal' principle);

- The importance of harnessing self-interest to pursue public
  interest (the 'invisible hand' principle);

- The importance of viewing the problem from many perspectives (the 'alternative realities' principle);

- The need to redistribute resources among the stakeholders
  (the 'power sharing' principle);

- The need to recognise the existence of a public interest
  beyond immediate stakeholder interests (the 'beyond pluralism' principle);

- The need to engage the young and avoid generation drag
  (the 'dead wood' principle).

Experimental learning

Recognising that all goal-seeking responses to societal issues produce provi-
sional, 'flawed' solutions which are likely to spawn further wicked problems is
the beginning of enlightenment, as Prometheus might have observed from his
rock. One response is to despair and renounce purposive action as too problematic. Another is to embrace collective inaction in the neo-liberal belief that
solutions to society's problems will emerge from the self-interested interactions

of individuals and groups. If, however, the choice is made to continue proactively and collectively seeking quality survival, several improvements based on 'learning by doing' can be suggested:

Much can be learned from ecologists who study *adaptive ecosystem management*, the philosophy which contends that, because of inherent uncertainty and change, all policies are really hypotheses and that management actions are tests of those hypotheses. This represents a shift in focus from command-and-control presumptions of outcome-certainty, to seeing management as a flexible institutional process of continual assessment designed to increase understanding as well as achieve societal objectives (Gunderson et al. 1995).

Hazel Henderson (1998b: 227) recommends that all social innovations be introduced in 'pilot projects' — small, reversible, fail-safe experiments carefully monitored for unintended consequences. Sometimes it may be possible to institute a suite of pilot projects, all slightly different, and compare their outcomes, as if in a multi-factor but uncontrolled scientific experiment. When results are negative policy options can be redesigned; when positive the pilot can be expanded. Unfortunately, many real-world problems have to be tackled in a one-shot, all-or-nothing operation — one cannot build a freeway, or half a freeway, to see how it works.

The important role of *system failure*, whether unplanned or as a result of an experiment, is that it creates a window of opportunity for new policies. It also provides a test of one's understanding of the system (why did that happen?). Old, well-established social systems usually have to experience a visible failure before it is possible for them to adapt to a new environment (Thurow 1996). Milbrath (1989) says paradigm shifts in social organisation occur when the old paradigm is breaking down and society is becoming more turbulent.

Science reduces unpredictability

Several guidelines for improving collective decisions in an unpredictable world were given in Chapter 6. The question we ask here (despite Prometheus' nasty experience) which was not asked there is what types of new knowledge would be particularly helpful in refining an unpredictable future; as a reference point, useful new knowledge expresses itself through the adding and subtracting of possibilities from decision-makers' scenarios.

In general, the answer is new *scientific knowledge*, remembering that the sweep of science is from the molecular to the cosmic via the social and psychological. Historical knowledge of the past and factual descriptive knowledge of the present (what are the world's oil reserves?) should be included along with the process-understanding which science brings (how do things work?). Scientific progress involves recognising as impossible things we formerly thought possible and vice versa. Indeed, scientific progress is a cumulative and path-dependent speculation on the possibility or impossibility of things previously unimagined.

In more and more fields, science can suggest what might happen in the future and, provided that research efforts are resourced adequately, this should continue. Sometimes, possibilities can be reduced to uncertainties and uncertainties to probabilities. Successes currently come more readily in the natural than in the social sciences. As well as reducing the unpredictability of processes which society does not as yet attempt to manage, science produces the knowledge which underpins material and social technologies; these are the practical recipes on which so much of the repetitious day-to-day management of society is based. We step back then to take a broader view of the task of managing science and technology in a learning society.

MANAGING SCIENCE AND TECHNOLOGY

The role of technology, and more recently science-based technology, in shaping human history and the equally important role that most expect it to continue to play speckles this book (see pages 6, 27, 92 and 122). Most of the big hopes and fears of the modern world embody its influences. One view is that we are on a treadmill where every science-based solution to one of society's problems generates multiple problems in a Medusan nightmare. Conversely, there is no shortage of technological optimists who think technological progress will be able to solve all current and future social problems (Costanza 1989). The latter are focusing on winners and solutions while the sceptics are seeing the losers and their losses.

Here we are looking for clues on how to foster a research and development system which, in some way, has shifted to become more focused on the achievement of quality survival rather than on the commercial and military foci foreseen for 21st century science-technology in Chapter 1.

Such a shift could not happen in isolation of course, only as part of a wider reorientation of world society from today's market-driven globalisation to something more egalitarian and forward looking (see page 272). Each stage in this shift, if it happens, will create its own opportunities for a partial refocusing of the science system. Foreseeable movements in shift-enabling values include:

- A decline in consumerism and luxury consumption following community recognition that additional consumption contributes at a declining rate to quality of life past a certain point;

- Rising environmental and ethical concerns as new technologies lift the economy's capacity to manipulate the physical environment and its inhabitants — a concern backed up perhaps by an increasing share of purchasing power moving into the hands of non-government organisations, pension funds, government agencies etc., and by an increasing use of technology impact assessment.

In what follows, we are assuming an unequivocal community demand for science-based social learning to swing its focus towards the promotion of quality survival.

Reshaping the science and technology system

It is necessary to clarify several terms before turning to some guidelines that might prove useful in reshaping the science-based portion of the learning system. Science is conventionally divided into science for understanding, namely basic science, and science for manipulation, namely applied science. 'How does this work?' compared with 'What must I do to achieve that desired result?'. *Basic science* is what you do when you have no idea how to solve some priority problem; it asks what is causing the problem rather than asking, directly, the *applied science* question of how to solve that problem. The simple principle for organising scientific effort is to do basic research on those priority problems where there are no promising ideas to develop into technologies; do applied science on your other priority problems. Technologies are extensions by engineers of applied science's discoveries into 'recipes' for routinely manipulating the material world; they include generic and enabling technologies (see page 27) as well as task-specific technologies. To the extent that it aims to be ultimately useful, basic science is not quite the same as 'curiosity' science which seeks understanding as an end in itself.

Retaining the science culture

Asking what to keep is as important as what to change when contemplating the refocusing of the science–technology research system towards quality survival. Thus, in its current form there are several cultural features of that system which, it can be argued, contribute significantly to its high and accelerating rate of knowledge production — as well as being civilising.

One is the remarkable way in which science exploits and combines the virtues of both competition and co-operation as it adds to the world's knowledge stock. Individual scientists compete vigorously to produce 'breakthroughs' in understanding but most can switch easily into co-operative mode if this promises to leverage individual output. Similarly, teams of co-operators will compete until a higher level of co-operation promises synergy. We will return to the need to exploit the complementarity, the synergy, of competition and co-operation in all aspects of world-society's priority-issues strategy in Chapter 8. Science will be the exemplar.

Science works well because it is honest and open. While this may be changing with commercialisation, it is still predominantly the case that what is discovered is quickly available to all who are interested. Fraud is rare, simply because results can be verified.

Science works well because a majority of its practitioners have a high degree of intellectual freedom, a beneficence which facilitates the emergence of imaginative solutions to nature's puzzles. There must continue be a place for eccentric, obsessed scientists as well as for those who are less driven. It must be accepted too that most scientists will continue to be specialists because there are limits to the amount of knowledge that can be understood by an individual or group. Specialisation is needed to get to the depth of understanding from where problems with and improvements to reigning explanations can be perceived.

Moravec (1999: 200) says that the biggest impact of the post-Bacon scientific revolution has been to provide the world with a universal way of thinking, one which will not now be lost even if most of world civilisation is destroyed. While our understanding of that way of thinking grows with each Popper, Kuhn, Foucault etc., it remains, and must remain, based on the search, through observation, for the nature of the physical and social world.

Improved understanding of the sociology and the ratiocinative processes of the science and technology system can be used to manage it more sensitively. It needs to be understood that the accumulation of scientific understanding takes time and does not proceed smoothly. Apart from the Kuhnian paradigm shifts (Kuhn 1970) which rack science's disciplines periodically, understanding has to wait while data is slowly accumulated or until new tools are developed which allow new types of observations or, indeed, while the subconscious is sorting out the data it has. Overt diagnosis and encouragement of impending Kuhnian shifts and support for the development of new research tools (instruments, software etc.) are examples of management policies which might be considered.

Balancing technological, institutional and lifestyle change

We live in a world where an effective research and development system, one which is increasingly the creature of global capitalism, is producing new technological knowledge at what seems to most to be a very high rate — a positive feedback process where growth in knowledge in one field stimulates growth in knowledge in other fields. The commercialisation of new technologies into new products, particularly in the so-called knowledge-intensive industries which underlie the current Kondratieff cycle (see page 162), is driving accelerating change in the structure and size of both global and national economies. This in turn is driving 'catch-up' change in institutions as evidenced by ethical dilemmas, attempts to regulate new technologies, etc. Until prodded, institutions ignore the externality problems — the new patterns of benefits and costs — thrown up by technological change (Nelson and Soete 1988: 633). Bhopal, Three Mile Island and the development of DDT are good examples.

Thirdly, change is also imposing 'future shock' on individuals in the form of increasingly transient experiences of things, people, ideas, organisations and places (Toffler 1970). Transience erodes allegiances and hence the cohesion that creates a society out of individuals. The modern world is a 'runaway' world in which the pace and profundity of social change is starkly different from that of the pre-modern and Neolithic cultures to which people are adapted.

Many people try but fail to cope with such change. Many crave stability and do not want to cope with, for example, the constant learning that all this change demands. Worse, much of the change being imposed on people's lives is creating rather than addressing dissatisfaction, for example, unemployment, pollution. But it is not that simple. For those able to participate, the fruits of technological progress, delivered through the market, are seen as improvements to quality of life. Medical technologies are a good example.

What we have then is a question, one more applicable to this century perhaps than the many to come. Accepting the reality of a capitalist world wedded to the regular delivery of new technologies, is it feasible and desirable to slow the rate of technological change in order to slow the rate of change in people's lives and give society's institutions an opportunity to come to terms with new technologies?

The question is too narrowly framed. Scientific and technological progress may not be a sufficient condition for achieving quality survival, but it is certainly a necessary one. The challenge is so large that the innovation rate needs to be ramped up as soon as possible, not slowed down; ramped up though in 'public interest' areas that are of little interest to contemporary markets; historically, technological advance has served the economic rather than the ecological cause. The relevant question then is not the excessive rate of technical change but managing its direction and negative impacts.

If the community is genuinely demanding action to reduce the impact of technological change on quality of life and institutional capacity, and if the political will is there, much could be done without destroying the economy. Capping energy and material throughputs would reduce environmental impacts in a broad way (see page 290). More specifically, the social technology known as *technology impact assessment* has much to offer.

Technology impact assessment is the process of identifying the direct and indirect impacts, positive and negative, of the introduction of a new technology on the environment, the economy and various community groups of widespread use of a new technology.

The widespread diffusion of almost any new technology (for example, the mechanical loom) will usually have markedly different costs and benefits for different people in the community (for example, weavers and mill owners). While any decisions to regulate this diffusion process in the public interest are ultimately political, it is important that such decisions be supported by comprehensive identification of these costs and benefits. The significance of a new technology for both its direct beneficiaries and the broader community needs to be assessed at all stages from design proposal to post-obsolescence — not just prior to its release.

Some research priorities

Recall the master strategy which was suggested in Chapter 5 for shepherding the near-to-deep future towards quality survival. Reduced to a sentence, it is a strategy of responding collectively to an unrolling set of priority issues. The four priority issues suggested there for a first round of the strategy were: nursing the world through endless change; raising the quality of social learning (the subject of this chapter); anticipating deep-future challenges; and confronting near-future threats and opportunities.

If this 'priority issues' strategy is accepted, it follows that social learning in general and scientific-technological research in particular should focus, largely but not exclusively, on building the knowledge stock required to improve problem-solving in these areas. But our priority issues have been identified in such broad terms that choosing what to concentrate on in practice is still far from obvious. All that is being attempted in this section is to suggest a few candidate research themes in each priority area, enough to convey a flavour of the possibilities. And remember, the question of whether the projects suggested might or might not enjoy society's support is not being asked.

Science for social learning

The lack of methods for designing social technologies (see Box 7.1) as distinct from material technologies stands out here. Is it as John Platt (1966) suggests, that the solving of social problems lags behind technology because we have not organised the same sharp search for ideas to deal with them? Or is it that solutions to social problems are overtly political while new material technologies are apparently apolitical? If it is the latter, research into conflict resolution becomes a priority.

Next, research into improving the research process itself is necessary despite the putative success of the current research system in producing millions of research papers in thousands of journals. Can that output be maintained? Does each discovery get more and more expensive as we move further into the exploration of processes occurring at much larger and much smaller space–time scales than those of everyday life? Are there inherent limits to the rate at which information can be processed (Garriga et al. 1999)?

Here are some more researchable puzzles in science management: What sort of science leads to generic as distinct from task-specific technologies? How do you identify gaps in existing knowledge which are bottlenecks to suites of further discoveries? Can the speed at which different disciplines will advance be predicted? Can new research tools be developed more systematically? Can experimental science and simulation be combined more effectively? How can science be better organised to tackle more broadly defined problems using a wider range of expertise, for example, combining multi-disciplinary and trans-disciplinary science.

Perhaps basic science should be de-emphasised because there is a stockpile of it awaiting application and conversion to technologies? Or is the intellectual capital represented by basic science near exhaustion?

Researching society's dynamics

Much has been made so far of the idea that world society is a collection of dissipative or energy-degrading complex systems and that it will therefore behave in a variety of largely unpredictable but ultimately unsurprising ways. It is an idea that maps well into the chronicle of history with its eras of stasis, trend, forced and unforced change, turbulence, collapse and revival. Indeed history has to be the test bed for evaluating attempts to better model society's dynamics (infrastructural, structural and superstructural change) from a dissipative systems perspective. And it will be by comparing the historical behaviours of different societies that we will build a first catalogue of world-society's possible future behaviours.

Even though complexity research is still at an early stage, modest hopes can be held out for improvements in several directions. One should be our ability to diagnose what sort of era a societal system is in, something not always obvious. We might be able to produce early warnings of a change of era and a pruned list of the possible eras into which the societal system might move. And, best of all, we might learn to roughly predict how intervention could change the system's dynamics and in what general direction. Somewhere in the deep future the lineage may reach an understanding of the ultimate limits to prediction under complexity.

To avoid misunderstanding here, note that there are many processes within society which, because they are undertaken in a tightly controlled environment, are predictable in the sense that outcomes beyond a narrow band of possibilities would be surprising. For example, most technology recipes produce target outcomes reliably. Tractor factories produce tractors! Similarly, natural processes little affected by human intervention tend to complete their life cycles more regularly than societal processes fuelled by human agency. This is why natural resource managers can use scientific understanding to improve their plan-making. For example, conflagrations can be delayed by using regular control burning to keep a forest system simple. Here we are talking about research to help in managing fragility, senescence and non-certainty (see pages 219 and 225).

Science for the 21st century

Jumping ahead, Chapter 8 will divide the umbrella priority issue earlier called 'Confronting near-future threats and opportunities' into a handful of component issues and discusses how these might be addressed, not only in the 21st century, but also, because they will never wholly disappear, into the deeper future. In simplistic terms, they are the problems of war, poverty, injustice, environmental degradation and sociopathy; or, more positively, the goals of peace, material well-being, social justice, environmental protection and sociality.

Here we are simply making the point that scientific research in the standard linear-reductionist mode has much to contribute to the amelioration of these priority problems, towards meeting these challenges; and emphasising that research on priority issues is priority research. Purely as examples, here are five big research programs with the potential to change perspectives and strategies for responding to each of these five component issues:

1   War and peace: Methods of reducing and resolving conflict over natural resources (particularly water, oil and land) in the presence of strong population growth.

2   Poverty and material well-being: The psychology, sociology and politics of consumerism.

3   Injustice and social justice: Methods of preventing debilitating diseases found mainly in the third world, for example, malaria, schistosomiasis (to balance first world research on 'lifestyle' diseases).

4   Environmental degradation and protection: Ameliorating the quality of life consequences of capping energy use.

5   Sociopathy and sociality: What are the sufficient attributes of societies in which people feel secure, wanted, useful, empowered and able to grow? What is the psychology of self-actualisation?

What this list, an arbitrary one, suggests is that there are no readily imaginable magic bullets for solving world-society's priority problems and also that those problems are interrelated in the sense that making progress on one would seem to be a contribution to ameliorating the others. In its partiality the list also highlights the enormity of the task of comprehensively addressing world-society's near-future threats and opportunities.

Cosmic and planetary challenges

The longer the lineage survives, the more difficult the problems it will face; although it will face each new wave of challenges with greater capabilities (see page 128). At every stage the story could go either way — extinction or live on. One reason the late-universe problems we will face, and which we can perceive dimly now, are so threatening is because we cannot imagine the capabilities we will have to counter them. Many of the ultimate technologies that will be developed will use huge quantities of energy and carry an overhanging dread of unintended consequences prior to their initial trialling (just as the first atomic weapons did).

Because the stakes, the challenges and the lead-times are all enormous, and because the opportunity cost is high in terms of losing progress on contemporary problems, it would seem sensible to devote (as we do) a modest proportion of world society's scientific research efforts to the basic cosmology, basic physics and global science which might produce the knowledge we will need to survive — ants, not grasshoppers. As we become more skilled at managing world-society, resources for researching these distant challenges might become more available. In terms of managing the total research effort over centuries, one possibility is to step up basic research on distant problems when the rate of change of contemporary society needs to be slowed down.

Examples of 'long view' research themes which look promising and tractable at this time include:

*   Modelling the future of the Milky Way, including the bit part played by our solar system;

*   Modelling whole-of-globe environmental futures — geological, biological, biogeochemical, atmospheric;

*   Exploring the gravitational wave spectrum.

The last of these is particularly promising. Electromagnetic waves, discovered in the 19th century, have provided us with most of our knowledge of the universe. Exploring different regions of the electromagnetic spectrum has produced different sorts of knowledge. Optical astronomy gave us the expanding universe. Radio astronomy gave us cosmic background radiation. X-ray astronomy gave us neutron stars and black holes. Now gravitational radiation offers a completely new 'sense' for understanding the universe. A gravitational wave field moves (resonates) masses in the same way that an electromagnetic wave sets charged particles in motion. It can be detected by the 'tidal' forces it exerts on objects through which it passes (Blair 1999).

Finally, we should not be closed to researching 'science fiction' possibilities such as higher levels of consciousness and, should we see a way into them, forces currently unsuspected by contemporary science, for example, Sheldrake's (1988) morphic fields.

MANAGING STOCKS AND FLOWS OF KNOWLEDGE

The eschaton suggested above (see page 234) for world society's learning system was to build up a sufficient body of collective or social knowledge to ensure quality survival. As well as creating new knowledge in a focused and controlled way, the task includes the storage and dissemination of what will be and has been learned.

For 40 000 years, language was the only form of knowledge storage external to personal memory, for example, storytelling. Since then, the quantity of codified (meaning communicable as distinct from tacit or experientially learned) knowledge in society's *external storage system* has increased enormously with the successive invention of writing, printing and digital media. One estimate is that 90 per cent of all codified knowledge generated since Neolithic times has come in the last 30 years and that the doubling time for new knowledge is down to 15 years (Dodgshon 1998: 170). Only a few per cent of this is knowledge generated by formal research and development activities; most is a record of daily life no different from the clay wafers recording beer deliveries in ancient Mesopotamia.

In an ideal external storage system, all knowledge ever stored which would be useful for any societal or individual purpose would be immediately available on demand. This will be as true in a million years as it is today. But there are difficulties in achieving this ideal which society will have to try and overcome. And these exist despite the huge and growing storage and retrieval capacities of computerised information systems. We have space to mention some technical, institutional and delivery problems that arise in warehousing social knowledge.

Once new knowledge ceases to command day-to-day attention, it will be lost if it is not stored (for example, dying languages) but, given that all storage incurs costs, information which, it is judged, will never prove useful or prove minimally useful should not be stored. Conversely, it might be possible to identify exceptionally valuable knowledge, let us call it wisdom, for example, how to restore a collapsed society or make appropriate technology available to a post-holocaust society. Such judgments will consider, for example, whether knowledge is relevant to priority issues or foreseeable priority issues, whether it need not be stored because it could be re-created on demand and whether it is exoteric or esoteric. How difficult it is though to foresee what knowledge from today's knowledge pool the lineage might want to retrieve in, say, 100 000 CE; difficult but worth thinking about. A related question is the extent to which knowledge should be indexed, cross-linked and repackaged before storage or stored in conjunction with commentary on its context. Synthesising and generalising knowledge, both within and between disciplines, into broader and broader paradigms (for example, EO Wilson's [1998] 'consilience') makes it more transferable. But such improvements are costly and not necessarily available on demand.

At the other end of the pipeline, the primary challenge is to build a knowledge retrieval system that can filter and select from what is stored so as to provide maximally useful responses to queries, without overloading the inquirer. The possibilities, drawing on advances in areas such as artificial intelligence, are enormous. Among other criteria, such filtering systems would take account of the inquirer's existing knowledge and the context within which the knowledge was to be used. For example, because social, technological, and now natural environments are changing so rapidly, behaviour rules based on successful past experiences might become irrelevant or even misleading (De Greene 1993) — basing farming decisions on past rainfall records may already be an example. This trend stands to continue or even accelerate. A capacity to retrieve knowledge of the context in which past rules were successful might make their abandonment easier. Learning how to forget!

Once it is stored, how do you ensure that stored knowledge is never lost (cf. abandoned)? This is one of the hardest questions facing society's knowledge-keepers. Up to a point, just making a memory collective makes it less vulnerable to destruction. Well-made books survive for a long time under 'benign neglect' but digital media degrade or become unusable very quickly; there are viewing problems, scrambling problems, linkage problems and physical degradation problems. At present, digital information has to be re-stored every few years. Nor is the Internet-to-come likely to be the answer; it has been described as 'one giant global computer that … doesn't really work; it can't be fixed; no one understands it; no one is in charge of it; it can't be lived without; and it gets worse every year' (see www.longnow.org accessed 29 April 2002).

And whatever the physical form of the external storage system, it will have to be managed by institutions which last for millennia, a problem discussed by Tonn (2001) in relation to the management of nuclear waste. Such institutions will have to be able to weather political and economic change and to remain focused on the allotted task. Also, as in Asimov's *Foundation* trilogy (1995–1996), they will have to be designed to withstand long periods of neglect. Tonn considers alternative stewardship arrangements including community, private, religious or government responsibility and suggests a secular non-profit organisation as the best option.

There could be another useful long-term role for well-credentialed guardians of the external storage system, what we might call 'stirring the knowledge pool'. Memes and ideas in good currency are used in decision making because they are in the community's short-term memory, the upper levels of the knowledge pool so to speak. Just as today's media largely determine what ideas will command public attention, it should be possible to enrich decision processes by 'deep remembering', systematically upwelling long-forgotten knowledge back into public awareness. Most debate is ignorant of how similar issues have been viewed or have evolved in the past.

RECAPITULATION

This chapter is built on two presumptions. One is that world society is committed to the quality-survival goal, that is, high quality of life for most people into the indefinite future. The other is that one necessary condition for achieving this goal is to make world society into a learning society where high priority is given to the social learning task, that is, to the building up of a sufficient body of collective knowledge to ensure quality survival. The chapter is concerned only in passing with learning in pursuit of short-term personal or sectional interests.

Clearly there is much that will have to be learned if world society is to survive various cosmic and planetary challenges ahead. Not quite so clearly, because it can also be seen as a lack of political will, world society seems to lack the knowledge to meet the basic quality-of-life needs of a significant fraction of the world's population and the higher needs of a large majority.

Hackneyed as it may seem, the big impediments to achieving basic quality of life for most have been and will continue to be war, poverty, injustice and environmental degradation.

From here the chapter moves to explore two questions. What sort of society stands to be a learning society and how should social learning be organised in terms of institutions and their tasks?

The chapter identifies a diverse society with members who are (a) educated to have an integrated understanding of the world and (b) socialised to support and participate in social learning as one predisposed to be a learning society. A society which is diverse in terms of its cultural groups, individuals' roles and range of problem-solving organisations can bring a wider variety of knowledge-bases and 'thinking styles' to bear on its social learning problems and hence improve its chances of finding innovative solutions to them.

On the second question, should world society adopt a strategy of 'responding collectively to an unrolling set of priority issues' for managing the future, then it follows that the preferred output from the social learning system will be knowledge which reduces uncertainties encountered when designing policy responses to those priority issues. In line with the tentative set of four priority issues suggested in Chapter 5, the search would be for knowledge which improves the social learning process itself; knowledge which improves society's capacity for guiding its own dynamics; knowledge for better addressing perennial substantive issues such as war and poverty; and knowledge for responding to distant cosmic and planetary challenges.

The chapter emphasises that all social learning must be seen as experimental and iterative. Starting with a perception of important goals which are receding or being poorly achieved, a set of candidate policy responses is designed and, following the choice and implementation of one of these candidates, outcomes are monitored to see if goal achievement has improved. Failure means that further mental models of policy options and their consequences will have to be designed.

Institutionally, there is no obvious alternative to a science–technology research and development system. Nothing else has the potential to successfully produce a flow of knowledge rich enough to reduce unpredictability for policy makers and problem solvers across the immediate and future spectrum of priority issues. Some examples are given. The existing science system has many desirable features which would seem to be worth retaining, for example, its openness, its intellectual freedom. The idea that technological progress should be slowed when institutions fail to cope with its consequences and people cannot adjust is rejected. Rather, the challenge is to find resources to further grow the science system — given the size of the knowledge pool that is and will be required to support the quest for quality survival. Notwithstanding, institutions will have to be established which disinterestedly assess proposed and emerging technologies in terms of their environmental, social and economic impacts and reject those found lacking. Conversely, institutions to identify unfilled technology niches are equally needed.

More broadly, the research and development system itself will need to be continuously revised via a political process of questioning its goals, ethics, strategies and the forms in which it delivers knowledge.

Finally, the chapter looks for guidelines on how accumulating knowledge might best be stored and retrieved over millennia and longer. The difficulties loom larger than the solutions. The overall message though is that it is worth attempting to create a collective learning system which continuously grows and refocuses as it produces knowledge for solving contemporary and foreseeable priority problems.

8

GUIDELINES III: WORKING ON PERENNIAL ISSUES

This is the last of three chapters identifying and discussing ideas for policy guidelines for a world society committed to pursuing the goal of quality survival via a strategy of responding collectively to an unrolling set of priority issues. Chapter 6 addressed the possibility of guiding the behaviour of an endlessly and unpredictably changing world. Chapter 7 asked what has to be done if world society is to become a learning society in which high priority is given to creating the knowledge considered necessary for quality survival.

Here, under the umbrella of the priority issue 'Confronting near-future threats and opportunities', the focus is on finding guidelines for selectively addressing four clusters of 'sub-issues' or component issues which are absolutely and enduringly and interactively related to the achievement of high quality of life for most people, certainly in this century and probably for as long as the lineage is recognisably human. Expressed in 'threat and opportunity' form, as in Chapter 7, they are:

- Social relations (sociopathy and sociality; participation and alienation);
- Global governance (injustice and social justice; war and peace);
- Production and distribution (poverty and material well-being);
- Environmental degradation and protection.

Once again, notwithstanding its generality, there is no suggestion that this list is exhaustive. Nor is there any suggestion that following any single set of guidelines can move world society from its present state where all these threats and opportunities commingle to one where these matters are no longer of concern. The chapter is best regarded as a small contribution to improving the improvable, to exploring how these enormous issues might be steadily progressed by a world society which has become committed to a quality survival goal. While such commitment would be surprising, remember that world society is in a period of 'destructuring and simplification' (see page 6) from which new paradigms might well emerge.

Given the wealth of literature on solving the world's problems, can a book on surviving well over the very long term offer anything approaching a new perspective on what might be tried? In a very modest way, the answer is yes — but not in the form of specific policies or new organisational principles or new ideology. How then?

First, the quality survival perspective offers a comprehensive criterion for critiquing policy suggestions across all policy areas. If we are committed to quality survival, it is incumbent on us to ask of any problem-solving proposal how it offers to better meet the needs of the world's people and their descendants? What does this policy mean for everybody's grandchildren? Does it rise above parochial self-interested short-termism? Does it have a global rather than a national perspective? Is it acceptable in terms of both inter- and intra-generational equity? Conversely, those who reject the quality survival goal for world society can reasonably be asked what ends their policy suggestions are directed towards.

More generally, the deep-and-wide view demands knowledgeable critiques of the almost invisible conventional wisdoms that underlie most policy, for example, the virtues of capitalism, liberal democracy, economic growth etc. All things pass and it is important to think about what might emerge or be encouraged in their place. In similar vein, the deep-and-wide view highlights the need for policies compatible with processes that are 'invisible' through a small space–time window — Kondratieff cycles, global change, creeping Fascism, modernisation and other residues of history. Even though it cannot address specific issues from the distant future, the deep-and-wide perspective challenges the here-and-now perspective, the short-termism and parochialism, that most policy displays.

MANAGING SOCIAL RELATIONS

Under this heading, I am looking for guidelines for managing two aspects of social relations, each with significant quality-of-life implications. One, named as *Sociality and sociopathy*, is about managing the background against which all interpersonal relations in complex societies take place. The other, under the heading of *Participation and alienation*, is about managing the attitudes which determine individuals' willingness to contribute to maintaining and reproducing their societies. That last sounds manipulative, and it is to an extent, but it is equally about the need for societies to create environments in which people will want to contribute.

Managing sociality and sociopathy

My starting assertion here is that societies in which sociality is high and sociopathy low are conducive to high quality of life for their members. *Sociality* means there is a prevailing attitude in which members of a society tend to regard others, even strangers, as their metaphorical brothers and sisters. A society where sociality is high is *fraternal* or *sisterly*.

Sociality implies social relationships marked by the expression of such behaviours as nurturing, fellowship, goodwill, empathy, altruism, love, affection, concern, trust, agape, civility, collaboration, togetherness, belongingness, inclusiveness, mutualism, cohesion, loyalty and solidarity. Sociality is a large part of any society's *social capital*, defined earlier (see page 47) as widespread amicable relations between people. Similarly, *social health* is Wolfe's (circa 1989) term for indicating widespread satisfying relations and interactions between individuals and groups, especially joint endeavours. *Sociopathy* on the other hand is a set of attitudes under which most people tend to regard others as enemies to be mistrusted and exploited. Tribalism, territoriality and hostility- indifference to others characterise sociopathy.

Sociality is important for two reasons. In a society where sociality is the norm, many of the individual's higher needs which have to be met if a quality life is to be achieved (see page 136) will, to some extent, be automatically satisfied, including the needs for safety, security, belongingness and affection, esteem, respect and self-respect. More than that, policies intended to promote sociality and avoid sociopathy can themselves further satisfy human needs. The second importance of sociality is that it is indicative of a co-operative society, meaning one in which people easily and readily come together to exploit the synergies of collective action (see page 138). It is also one starting point for approaching other major goals which will appear later in this chapter — moderate consumption, world peace, social justice and a quality environment; a society of 'team players' stands to be a more just and environmentally superior society.

Both sociality and sociopathy have their roots in the behaviour of our hunter–gatherer forebears who evolved instinctive and useful appetencies for co-operation within the group and for hostility towards outsiders (see page 116). It needs to be recognised that both appetencies still exist even though, apart from a limited role in stimulating social criticism and as an indicator of unmet needs, sociopathy has no apparent function in a complex society. The question then is whether sociopathy should be left to die out (unlikely), be actively eliminated if possible or encouraged on the basis of the diversity it brings with it.

Almost certainly sociopathy is too dangerous to encourage, as can be easily done. Human behaviour is very malleable and children can be brought up to hate or to be fraternal–sisterly and co-operative. For example, children in lightly supervised playgroups teach each other co-operation. Such socialisation is easy in a society which is already fraternal–sisterly simply because most behaviour is imitative. People treat each other much as they themselves are treated. However, under conditions of stress, insecurity, crisis and declining expectations, sociality tends to be replaced by sociopathy. Along with treating those causes, as part of restoring quality-of-life prospects, sociality has to be actively nurtured by teaching and example.

Deceit, including self-deceit, plays a major and complex role in interpersonal relations (Giannetti 1997). A good example is Homer's Odyssey which is about little else. Given the importance to sociality of being able to trust that one is not being deceived, educating people to understand and detect deceit would seem to be a guideline for building or rebuilding sociality. Finally, if it is correct that the real functions of symbolic 'grooming' and gossip are to keep social groups together (Blackmore 1999: 96) then another simple guideline for nurturing sociality is to encourage these activities.

Managing participation and alienation

Despite the fact that societies exist to benefit individuals, many humans have a profound ambivalence towards their social role (Campbell 1972), particularly in societies where a right to pursue one's own interests vigorously is recognised and approved. *Alienation* is an unwillingness to play one's perceived social role.

From the time of the first agricultural civilisations until the end of the Middle Ages religious authority and physical duress (for example, slavery, serfdom) were the main instruments of social control, that is, for ensuring people's *participation* in the work of running the society. Most of the time people were socialised into accepting the legitimacy of the society's demands on them, revolting only when quality of life, by the standards of the day, became intolerable. Tradition is a glue that holds society together while stress is building up to some breaking point (Buchanan 2000: 189).

While religious authority and duress remain important (there are still 27 million slaves in the world), social control of people's behaviour has loosened in many societies since then, following the rise of individualism and

Enlightenment values (including the classic liberal principles of government by consent and the right to be represented in decisions that affect one's interests). Also, a high rate of evolution in production systems since the industrial revolution has made it difficult for people's value systems to evolve rapidly enough to provide them with a rationalisation for what they have to do to survive (see page 110). In fact, the productivity of many modern societies is such that tight social control is no longer as necessary for survival, for example, a few per cent of the population can produce food for all (as long as the cheap energy lasts!).

The loosening of total social control over people's behaviour for these several reasons, has probably facilitated the emergence of both sociopathy and alienation, even as it has given people discretionary time and freedom for innovative problem-solving and various social movements, as well as for self-actualisation. Ramphele (2000) suggests that balancing the tension between individual freedom and being a social being, balancing individual autonomy against social control according to circumstances has become the most important trade-off facing all societies, present and future.

Encouraging sufficient participation

Dubious methods

Unwilling participation and participation achieved by manipulation, deception and indoctrination are incompatible with high quality of life. In principle, most people support the right of a legitimate state to monopolise the use of coercive physical power to deter certain sociopathic behaviours; but not to enforce a society's demand that an individual make some designated contribution. History suggests that societies where participation is based on compulsion are susceptible to regression or disintegration when the power balance eventually changes. In fact, terror is not needed (Huxley 1959: 116). A modern state can keep behaviour within bounds by making it exhausting and difficult to live a non-conforming life, for example, by erecting bureaucratic obstacles. Surveillance that eliminates privacy may be all that is needed.

But it may not be just the state imposing conformity for its own reasons (see below). Heilbroner (1993: 113) points out that in times of social crisis the people often turn towards authoritarianism in the belief that it is better able to cope than democratic structures. People will not tolerate a society where they are subject to periodic upheavals. A good example is Fascism. It brought stability to fluctuating economies by reducing freedom at a time when there was a stalemate between democracy and what is nowadays called neo-liberalism (Polanyi 1944; 2001). Stability of expectations is clearly an important part of quality of life. Even in quieter times, many are willing, with help from the state, to sacrifice freedom and democracy for security.

If social control has to be imposed, is the carrot preferable to the stick? Reinforcing desired behaviour may be more effective than punishing undesirable behaviour. Skinner (1971) for one believes that human freedom is a myth and that society's best hope for survival is to condition people to want to do what is socially necessary, not by propaganda or concealed manipulation but by 'training' them with rewards.

Achieving social control by manipulating people's emotional responses has always been (temporarily) effective, whether orchestrated by leaders, proselytisers or advertisers. Appeals to territoriality, xenophobia, blood, guilt, shame, lust, greed, status (the list goes on) commonly produce responses which conflict with a reasoned analysis of people's best interests (but see page 111 f.). Emotional responses are enriching, provided they do not get out of control. They are best treated as first suggestions. From a quality-of-life perspective, a society is needed where people are mature enough to recognise when they are being manipulated and to manage their responses. This is quite achievable if it is actively sought through education. Society itself needs to recognise that emotional manipulation of large numbers of people stands to blow back and destabilise social organisation in diverse ways; its role must be small.

Combining emotional manipulation with deceit — lying, propaganda, misinformation, disinformation etc. — is additionally dangerous in terms of possible repercussions for societal stability and quality of life. People particularly resent being deceived by a government. The circumstances will be few in which deceit can be argued to be a legitimate instrument of social control.

In general then, coercion, manipulation, conditioning and deceit have, at best, limited legitimacy as instruments of social control. Where then do we turn? The two possibilities presented below emphasise the importance of leadership and the importance of the social contract in managing participation.

Constraining the powerful

A useful start to finding guidelines which might encourage willing participation (what can I do for my society?) is to ask why people, particularly non-elite people, do so often feel ambivalent about their social roles. One recurring answer is that many people sense they have very little choice but to accept a flawed social contract which has been imposed on them by sociopathic and self-interested elites.

One of history's recurrent themes is the 'treason of the elites'. A society of any complexity requires that some of its members coordinate and direct the activities of the majority (see page 201). With few exceptions, these elite minorities have used their power to advance and protect their own interests at the expense of majorities. Reforms and concessions which have improved quality of life for the majority have most commonly come only in response to the threat of civil unrest from the 'dangerous classes' (Wallerstein 1995). During quieter times the elites seek to reclaim such concessions. The prime example of modern times is the creation of welfare states after the Second World War as a response to Fascism and Communism; and their winding back with the demise of Communism.

For a world society with a social goal which includes high quality of life for most, the implication of this reality is, first, to limit the power of elites to what is functionally necessary and, second, to protect rights and freedoms which have been already won, and then extend them. Here are some possible guidelines:

- Honour genuine service to society, that is, other than the by-product of self-interest;
- Educate elites to recognise the existence of a public interest beyond immediate stakeholder interests;
- Promote an understanding of the will to power (see page 167);
- Find ways of aligning the interests of rulers with ruled;
- Foster 'power sharing' procedures and participatory democracy in all institutions;
- Look for ways of 'flattening' hierarchies and devolving power;
- Distribute and interlock power widely across institutions, for example, church, state, military, business, academia, justice system;
- Dilute power by recognising many forms of successful participation, for example, sport, art, science, teaching, community service;
- Clarify the ways in which institutional procedures structure the distribution of power and influence;
- Proscribe the inheritance of wealth and position;
- Reshuffle power in each generation;
- Discourage dynasties; encourage cross-class breeding (!);
- Identify society's elite positions and a maximum tenure for which each can be occupied;
- Institute procedures for redistributing resources away from elites, for example, progressive tax regimes;
- Create procedures for disclosing the material interests of elites;

- Treat corruption harshly;

- Create independent procedures for publicly identifying winners and losers from political decisions;

- Work to extend individual rights and freedoms and then institute procedures which obstruct their withdrawal (see below);

- Create structures that specifically protect human rights when they come under sudden pressure;

- Make the social contract as explicit as possible (see below).

It needs to be accepted that, irrespective of society's structure, many people will continue to seek power into the foreseeable future and that many of these will try to use power to enhance their own status and self-interest. Policies such as those just listed make sociopathic behaviour more difficult but also carry costs, for example, losing wisdom and experience when competent and public-spirited office holders are forced to step down at the end of their tenure. Nonetheless, while it may not always be so, at this stage in society's development, the need is to redress an entrenched bias towards the interests of elites. And, like the undermining of feudalism by the emergence of rich and powerful non-aristocrats, including merchants and landed gentry, that might take centuries — and be no more successful.

People with highly specialised knowledge pose a particular problem in complex societies. They are asked to make judgments about choices which others cannot understand (for example, reproductive technologies) or check for bias. There is no neat answer but society has to be prepared to make greater efforts to understand complex issues and to delay decisions until understanding between specialists and non-specialists is satisfactory (Kucher 2001). Perhaps greater use might be made of 'anti-experts' whose role is to argue against complex proposals.

It is one thing to try and rein in 'bad' leaders, but can anything be done to pre-select or encourage the emergence of 'good' leaders? Progress towards quality survival depends heavily on the principled conduct and goodwill of its elites; unlike what happened in other European countries, Bulgaria's Jews survived the Holocaust because its leaders spoke out. Is there some reliable way of weeding out cowards, parasites, knaves and fools? I fear not. How do you avoid people who will hastily over-react in a crisis (a common political failing)? One small comfort is that if good leaders do emerge they will be imitated by their successors. It probably helps for aspiring leaders to have gained the perspective that comes from having lived in several cultures, for example, Gandhi, Marx.

Importance of the social contract

It was suggested earlier (see page 51) that people in modern societies live under a tacit social contract wherein society has a responsibility to attempt to provide some sort of rising standard of living in return for the individual citizen fulfilling certain obligations and accepting certain responsibilities to the society. It is a very imperfect arrangement but one way of edging history beyond social organisation based on compliance with religious or ideological authority or strong social taboos (Jantsch 1975: 282). And it leads to the notion of *citizenship* — societies exist to benefit individual members called citizens.

Here I am suggesting a strong and explicit social contract as society's primary instrument for both meeting the individual's needs (the basis of quality of life), and ensuring the individual's willing participation in the work of maintaining and reproducing society and, perhaps, in social learning (the basis of survival). The social contract's basic idea is one of a fair system of co-operation between and within generations (Rawls 1993). On one side of this contract, society has a responsibility to protect and promote a negotiated, evolving set of individual rights. On the other side, each citizen has a duty to contribute to the smooth functioning of society.

The late John Rawls was a leading proponent of rights-based social-contract thinking, defending it from various criticisms, including the utilitarian criticism that we ought to seek to maximise the aggregate well-being of a society's members regardless of how that aggregate is distributed between people (Rawls 1993). Utilitarians are committed to the position that when a conflict occurs between individual rights and general well-being, the latter takes precedence. Egalitarians believe in focusing on the organisation of society to achieve equality of opportunity or equality of outcome (equal quality of life for all?). The guideline being suggested here, loosely based on Rawls, is that satisfying people's rights under the social contract is overwhelmingly more important than anything else and, beyond that achievement, improvements in quality of life should come from further extending the rights recognised in the social contract. It is a model which focuses on steadily raising minimum quality of life rather than average or 'total' quality of life. It denies the periodic claim that all social-contract models assume self-interested contractors and therefore have no room for compassion or altruism or sociality.

Space permits a few comments, presented as assertions worth debating, on the possible content of an evolving social contract. It will be helpful if I use the language of 'freedoms, aspirations and duties' as well as that of 'rights and responsibilities'.

It is important for the individual to have the right to challenge the social contract without being excluded from it. No contract can cover all contingencies and all have large tacit components (Hodgson 1999a). Knowing where society is heading allows the individual to assent to (or question) that contract in a more informed way. More strongly, every society has a responsibility to its members to explain its collective purpose; every citizen has a right to be informed of that purpose. Further, it is processes of challenge and debate which will drive improvement in the social contract. Nor should the possibility of different groups negotiating somewhat different social contracts within one society be rejected.

A good starting point is John Locke's belief that a civil society is one in which the individual gives up the right to judge and punish others. That can be juxtaposed against the classical four freedoms of religion, speech, press, assembly — to which Franklin Delano Roosevelt added freedom from fear and hunger (Stiglitz's foreword to Polanyi [1944; 2001]).

Under current socioeconomic structures, society relies on employment as the individual's main way to ensure freedom from hunger. In this situation, people surely have a right to meaningful work and a living wage, along with a presumptive responsibility to contribute to the wealth of society by seeking and earning a living through employment or self-employment. Society has a corresponding right to ensure that children are socialised to want to become fully contributing members of society, notwithstanding the dangers here of a drift towards an unacceptable level of social engineering. Open debate on the education process is the safeguard there. While it will normally be in society's interests to provide people with a good education (see page 236), such must also be recognised as part of a right to be employable.

Other individual responsibilities for the smooth running of society include a duty to play an informed role in the political process (at least to vote) and a presumptive duty to obey the law; perhaps also to serve in peacekeeping forces.

While civil (for example, the right to own property, the right to sue) and political (for example, the right to vote) rights are passably well recognised and protected in the western democracies (five out of ten?), social, economic and environmental rights are scarcely recognised, even by governments striving to provide *opportunities* to enjoy these dimensions of life. The reason for this, as much as anything, is that governments just do not know how to guarantee social, economic and environmental rights. Nevertheless it is rights in these areas which will be extended as the social contract evolves. Examples include:

- A right to be treated without a priori discrimination, for example, children, women, minority groups;

- A right to be healthy. The community has a responsibility to ensure that everyone has access to adequate healthcare and the individual has a responsibility to care for hir own health;

- A right to an effective standard of communications and to a standard of transport that allows one to participate fully in the life of the community;

- A right to clean air and water and a responsibility to keep the community's air and water clean;

- A right to enjoy the natural world and a responsibility to protect it;

- A right to play a useful role in society;

- A right of access to effective legal representation (something more than the legal right of equality before the law);

- A right in old age to an adequate income and access to humane residential and community care;

- A right to pain relief and a right to die when you have stopped growing or helping others to grow;

- A right to have children provided that this is balanced by taking responsibility for their physical and mental health at birth and beyond.

It has to be acknowledged that there are difficulties surrounding the adoption of a rights-based social contract as an institutional foundation for achieving high quality of life and willing citizenship. If the social contract is legally enforceable, for example, through a bill of rights, what happens when rights conflict (that is, cannot be satisfied simultaneously) or their achievement is clearly infeasible? What happens to irresponsible individuals? How will rights be protected from erosion? Where do new rights come from? How updated? These are matters to be worked on over time. One small idea is that new rights might be consolidated in steps, moving from a charter of *good intentions* to the status of *legitimate aspirations* before being codified as *rights*.

Notwithstanding, is world society ready for a social-contract approach to fostering participation? While most of us retain at least some need for external authority in our lives, people's capacities to be consciously inner-directed rather than externally directed have been increasing more rapidly for several thousand years. Already the concept of citizenship in western societies is evolving to include more rights and responsibilities for individuals. I am suggesting that people are mature enough and responsible enough (more than just law-abiding) for this to continue and be seen as the primary way forward. An alternative and less reassuring view might be that no choice exists between inner-directed and externally-directed social control, not so much because self-discipline has flourished but simply because external authority, particularly religious authority, has declined in our times.

I turn then to the future role of religion, not just as an instrument of social control, but also as an expression of people's need to understand the world and as a way of experiencing the world.

What is to become of religion?

Having a religion means believing in and taking actions to please a divine or supernatural power. Pleasing actions include participating in customs and rituals and behaving in accordance with a prescribed moral code. Religious belief-systems commonly extend to stories about the creation and early days of the world. Religion has been absolutely central to the organisation of human societies for thousands of years, evolving with the economic system of the times to direct individuals in the performance of their socioeconomic roles. Shared behaviour in accord with a shared religion has also been a means of bonding people within groups and differentiating them from other groups, thus enhancing co-operation within the group and hostility towards other groups (see page 108).

The switch from magic-based and propitiatory religions to today's great religions, with their emphasis on personal morality and self-actualisation in a difficult world, began in the first millennium BCE as the old religions lost their effectiveness as social-control instruments (see page 153). As Toynbee (1971: 48) puts it, all the great historic philosophies and religions — Buddhism, Christianity, Islam and Judaism — have been concerned with overcoming egocentricity. All see the same problem and offer the same solution — egocentricity can be conquered by love. Similarly, the ethics of different religions are not all that different because their common aim is to inculcate the compliance and sociality which makes community life possible. And, to achieve this, all suggest some form of the guideline that one should live in a way that allows others to live in the same way, for example, the golden rule, Kant's categorical imperative that no behaviour can be regarded as morally unimpeachable unless it can be recommended in principle to everybody.

The dimension of religion which has eroded most in recent centuries has been its beliefs about world history. Science's first blow to religion's myths was the discovery that the Earth travels around the Sun. Discoveries about the age and size of the universe and the origin of species have cast doubt on histories guided by divinities and hence on the reality of the divinities themselves, for example, Nietzsche's 'death of God'. History has contributed its darts too with accounts of corruption within religion.

Looking to the future, should religion be encouraged or discouraged? In general, religious beliefs continue to be a constraint on social learning and an ongoing source of enmity between groups (having found the truth, it is unsettling to find that others have too). But they are important in providing an intellectual framework and social environment in which people can build identity and organise personality, particularly in times of change. They can be doorways to reverence, mystical experience and deep self-knowledge — Jesus, Mohammed, Socrates and Buddha were all trying to make people more conscious of themselves and awaken them to their full potential (Armstrong 2001). Most importantly, they preach, and often exemplify, the brotherly and sisterly love on which sociality is based. Both Kant and JS Mill thought there was a place for organised religion in society to act as a carrier of such moral values.

Are there non-religious belief systems that encourage sociality without encouraging inter-group and inter-faith enmity and which are not opposed to new ideas? There are systems based on belief in a supernatural but non-divine power such as astrology, pantheism or deep ecology. There are secular systems based on a belief in naturalism and rationalism and these include post-Enlightenment humanisms and political ideologies (including nationalism). With the decline of traditional religion, alternatives have also emerged in the form of all-encompassing beliefs in lifestyles based on a practice, for example, psychoanalysis, vegetarianism.

All of these, with the possible exception of humanism, are 'closed' systems of beliefs and intolerant to a greater or lesser degree. Most are neutral with respect to sociality. Humanism is a philosophy which puts human progress at its centre — HG Wells' version in *The Conquest of Time* (1942) reads like a socialist tract. I came close to labelling myself a scientific humanist in the Introduction to this book and probably succeeded when arguing in Chapter 3 for quality survival as a sensible goal for world society. Most forms of humanism want and encourage people to make the most of themselves as they are. *Transhumanism* though is a philosophy that humanity should strive towards, and can succeed in reaching, higher levels of physical, mental and social development. But while humanism might encourage sociality, it is only religion which brings the authority of the divine, with its awesome promise of justice delivered from another realm, to that task. Few people will be able to make a satisfactory 'religion' out of the worship of humanity.

Recognising the positive and negative impacts of religions and other belief-systems on social relations, what is to be done? Perhaps nothing. Millions already live ethical lives without religion or other belief systems and, in time, the bulk of humanity might learn to live ethically without religion. Meanwhile, accepting people's existential need to find something to live by, society should encourage the proliferation of creeds and belief systems, even as it provides people with an education that allows them to discriminate between such systems and to understand their psychological function. Being religious should be a matter of well-informed personal choice. Also, as is evidenced by the growth of new religious movements, freeing up the rate at which belief systems can evolve does allow people to better match their inner lives to the realities of social organisation.

Finally, encouraging a variety of belief systems brings a diversity of perspectives to society and weakens the possibility of one group imposing universal values on all. But, to combat the antipathy that develops between revelatory religions, different faiths should be encouraged to understand and respect each other and recognise that while divinity has become known in different forms in different cultures, all preach the redemptive power of love.

Making good use of co-operation and competition

In co-operative behaviour, two or more parties agree on how resources will be used to achieve an agreed objective. In competitive or adversarial behaviour, two or more parties strive at the same time for an objective which can only be achieved by one of those parties. Both co-operative and competitive behaviour can be distinguished from coerced behaviour in which one party is placed by another party in a situation where they have almost no choice of behaviours.

The processes of co-operation and competition have been recurring motifs in this book, starting with their complementary roles in biological evolution — all biological hierarchies are forms of co-operative behaviour and competitive selection drives phylogenesis. They appear as social instincts in early primate societies and as partly learned, partly instinctual, behaviours in hunter–gatherer times (see page 116). Successful hunter–gatherer groups achieved a balance between two tendencies: amity within the group and enmity to other groups. In today's world society they are found together in a variety of social, political and economic processes (see page 197). Thus, market capitalism is a competitive process operating in a framework of behavioural rules created by co-operation, the use of money and legal contracts being the obvious examples. Indeed, all competitive processes (unlike conflictual ones) take place in an environment of constraining rules delineated by prior co-operation and, unless they have been coerced, all competitors are co-operating with each other to the extent that all have agreed, perhaps tacitly, to take part in a codified competitive process.

Here we are looking for guidance on the respective roles of competition and co-operation as *tools* for progressing a quality-survival strategy of selective policy responses to a rolling set of priority issues.

Mutualism and individualism

While all societies use both co-operative and competitive processes, those that tend to favour co-operative processes are thought of as mutualistic and those that tend to favour competitive processes are individualistic (see page 120). Should world society be actively pushed in one direction or the other, now or in the future?

As Kropotkin (1904; 1915) notes, the tribe, village and medieval city were all organised around the idea of mutual aid and support. Then came three centuries in which mutual aid organisations were actively discouraged and, beginning in the middle of 18th century, a flowering of the idea that the only secure basis for the maintenance and progress of society was individualism.

Many are the virtues claimed for the individualistic, competitive society — from economically and politically efficient to socially innovative and liberating. The mutualistic, co-operative society is not so widely championed but is also claimed to be economically efficient in its own ways; socially, it can be presumed to nurture sociality and participation rather than sociopathy and alienation.

Efficiency, output achieved per unit of input, is a difficult concept, even under a narrow interpretation of the term 'output', that is, immediate and one-dimensional. It becomes almost meaningless when it is recognised that taking any action precludes other actions and sets off cascades of consequences — all forms of 'output' which should be taken into account when calculating efficiency.

In the economic sphere, competition can save resources and free them for other uses, but, if competition is too fierce, businesses fail and their resources are wasted. Co-operation can save resources too, by reducing uncertainty about the behaviour of others and by permitting specialisation. And co-operation wastes resources when securing agreement on action takes much time and effort. So, both processes can both waste and save resources (see page 186).

Similarly, both processes can create and destroy economic diversity. When competition leads, as it tends to, to a single monopolistic 'winner' then other modes of production are lost. However, if the 'losers' create new markets or related niches in the existing market and occupy them, diversity is regained.

Firms tend to search for new routines and increased profits only when profits fall below some acceptable 'satisficing' level (Nelson and Winter 1982). Cooperation too reduces the variety of 'solutions' that are subjected to practical testing but it also produces novel solutions because of synergistic interactions between the collaborators.

In political and cultural life also, too much competition is destructive. Survival rather than functionality becomes the goal. Too little competition (for example, a one-party state) means that the search for better solutions to problems is stultified. People try hardest in moderately competitive situations. Both competitive individualism and co-operative mutualism appeal to self-interest, the former quite directly and the latter when people understand indirect reciprocity (see page 116). Both processes have altruistic elements.

The point being made is that both co-operative and competitive processes have their strengths and weaknesses and there is no reason to have a dogmatic belief in either as tools for progressing quality of life. The guideline which suggests itself is that society should continually ask where and when a strengthening or weakening of co-operative or competitive processes would be most valuable. And how this should be approached.

What sorts of co-operation and competition?

In general, co-operation and mutualism involve creating semi-autonomous, non-adversarial, collaborative, voluntary etc. institutional arrangements for addressing priority issues. In the 21st century, two sorts of initiatives are likely to be particularly valuable — those which foster co-operation at intercultural, international and global levels and those which aim to reduce major uncertainties such as threats of political, economic or environmental instability. Situations where a weakening of co-operation might be warranted include collusive partnerships intended to damage others in direct and major ways, for example, cartels.

Managing competition and individualism is more problematic than managing mutualism. Most competitive, adversarial processes take a short-term view and have a tendency to reinforce inequality, alienation and sociopathy, all inimical to quality survival. For this reason, when competition does not lead to even apparent efficiencies or innovations, it should be modified. For example, competition among consumers for positional goods (for example, harbour views) and opportunities (for example, quality education) is normally based on wealth and purchasing power. Less divisive alternatives (for example, sharing, ballot) at least need to be considered. Overall though, it is difficult to think of situations where competition should be proscribed automatically.

All proposals for new competitive processes should be formally assessed for their potential benefits and disbenefits among diverse stakeholders (especially those with the lowest quality of life). People need to be informed of the consequences of willingly participating in such processes and the rules need to be patent. People need to be taught how to handle failure under competition. Competitive processes where the penalty for failure is very high need to be restructured into several low-penalty stages.

Another useful guideline is that every attempt should be made to create societal processes which synergistically interweave co-operation and competition. The scientific research community was quoted earlier (see page 244) as a good example of this. Trade associations for collectively managing marketing and public relations are another example. Co-operation itself will work better if it is competitive in the sense that lots of alternatives are debated before an agreed plan is selected. Alexander (1979: 224) likewise makes the point that we co-operate best during inter-group competition.

Conflict, the recognition of incompatible objectives, can make little or no contribution to quality survival and, wherever possible, should be converted into competitive or co-operative processes. A large part of the process of formal conflict resolution is the attempt it makes to uncover common purpose among the antagonists (Borgeryd 1998). Just how diachronic competition, that is, between generations, should be conceptualised and managed is an open and difficult question (but see page 142).

MANAGING GLOBAL GOVERNANCE

In Chapter 1 several geopolitical scenarios for the 21st century were offered, centering on a declining US hegemony, changing alliances among major powers and a succession of wars (see page 9). This may be the politics of reality but it is also a continuation of the system of interactions between states which, over hundreds of years, has failed to manage global conflict and oppression. But Chapter 1 also notes a growing recognition that a globalising world needs global governance and a high level of inter-nation co-operation if most people are to have access to a reasonable spectrum of life opportunities (see page 52). And from times as turbulent as ours, the emergence of an effective system of global governance would not be totally surprising. Here we are looking for guidelines that might help in the establishment of a global governance system and for addressing two basic quality-of-life issues that any such system will have a responsibility to confront, namely conflict and oppression.

Can world society be governed?

There can be no permanent answer to the question of how world society should be organised politically. Inevitably, as times change, so do political solutions. The guideline being suggested here is that the 21st century is an appropriate time for moving towards a world federation in which nations can both co-operate and develop individually (Polanyi 1944; 2001). Federation is a well-tried form of political union. The version being suggested here, like the Australian federation, leaves all responsibilities not specifically covered in the articles of association, to the individual state.

Should a world federation be built from the ground up or by reforming and extending the UN? It is difficult to envisage any scenario where a world federation arises outside the platform of the UN. Despite being undemocratically controlled by Security Council members and their vassals in their own short-term interests, such a transformation is not inconceivable. It would have to start with another charter-making conference — San Francisco Two. Resistance would be strongest from the United States and China, the current and aspirant hegemonic powers. Since 1989 the United States has increasingly believed that it can run the world as its empire in everything but name and this is the perception that would have to change; not only that it cannot do this, but also that it does not want to do so (Rubenstein 2001). The latter may be hard for a country which seems locked into an economic and political need for external enemies (Kwitny 1984). Progress may also have to wait on prior federations in Europe, Africa and Latin America. Many setbacks can be expected.

Membership of the world federation would be open to any state accepting the UN's Universal Declaration of Human Rights, a remarkable document. Secession from the federation would require a people's referendum to protect against self-serving leaders. Indeed, as flagged earlier (see page 85), the people might need to be represented directly, as well as through their states, in a legitimate world federation. Procedures for suspending states breaking the federation's laws would have to be established, as would procedures for disadvantaging free riders. The massive funding required to run a world federation would probably come in part from taxes on all international transactions including trade, capital and communications and in part from taxes on resource use (for example, fossil energy, land clearing) and pollution (for example, carbon emissions). International companies might be taxed on some mix of their profits, assets and dividends.

No state is going to act against its perceived national interest, so what would be the benefits of federation membership? Given that the federation's goal would be to seek quality survival, there would be obvious immediate material benefits for disadvantaged third world countries pursuing modernisation. More broadly, the world's capacity to solve its problems would benefit from an enhanced sociality, stability and predictability in international relations. Within nations, the federation's standards might provide benchmarks and arguments for those working to strengthen the social contract. Having universal standards would also mean that no state was disadvantaged commercially by engaging in socially and environmentally responsible trade and production.

We turn more specifically now to some guidelines for a world federation willing to move strongly against two toxic destroyers of quality of life for hundreds of millions — war and oppression.

Reducing war and conflict

Let me start with a bright idea. Hazel Henderson (1998b: 229) includes a United Nations Security Insurance Agency in a list of desirable new global institutions. Nations could buy insurance against potential aggression with premiums being used to fund peacekeeping and conflict-resolution contingents. Perhaps, to further boost the fund, those major powers that are heavily involved in arms sales and nuclear proliferation should be taxed on these activities. Other ideas with further potential to ameliorate the horrors of war include the new International Criminal Court, disarmament negotiations and weapons conventions (for example, banning anti-personnel mines). Community and international peace organisations should be given every encouragement. The prevention of war is a responsibility the world has to keep nibbling at on diverse fronts. Given a goal of quality survival, the costs of war outweigh any possible gains.

The overarching guideline for preventing war and conflict is that the world, whether federated or not, should be run as a participatory and pluralist democracy, as explained below for the nation state (see page 277). But what happens when conflict does appear? Traditional international relations models (for example, Morgenthau and Thompson 1985) assume conflict (having incompatible goals) inevitably turns to war unless constrained by deterrence, that is, the threat of deadly retaliation. Given the prevalence of war, it has to be assumed that deterrence is not applied sufficiently or that the theory is wrong and deterrence does not deter, for example, Korea, Vietnam. The non-traditional view, my preference, is that inter-group conflicts can frequently be resolved without (further) deadly violence if the underlying frustrated needs of the conflicting parties (see page 167) can be teased out, through a well-understood process, and if the parties then jointly search for political solutions satisfying both sets of needs. Having said that, resource-based conflicts being driven by population growth do seem depressingly intractable.

The conflict-resolution approach has some successes to its credit but, once spear-rattling, demonisation, historical revisionism and counter-accusations have commenced, conflicting parties find it difficult to come together in this way. A period of violence seems, almost, to be first necessary. It may be that conflict-resolution methods will have to prove themselves, as is happening, at the domestic and community level before being accepted for use in international and 'tribal' conflicts. Nonetheless, conflict-resolution conferencing, conducted in secret, should be offered to all parties in actual or potential war situations (Burton 1996). The importance to a people of just having their group identity recognised by others cannot be over-emphasised.

Reducing oppression and discrimination

Oppression is the imposition of unjust or unfair burdens on one part of a population by another more powerful part of the population (Following Rawls [1971], I am treating justice and fairness as synonymous). Discrimination is weak oppression.

In a general way, powerful elites have always fought the expansion of ordinary people's rights (see page 261) and, to the extent that it has conflicted with their own interests, restricted ordinary people's access to opportunities such as health and education services (opportunities that, in time, will come to be regarded as social and economic rights). Here, beyond that starting point, we are talking about the uneven way in which basic rights and opportunities are further distributed among different segments of the global population. Around the world, to different extents in different countries, there are categories of people who get a particularly bad deal from their societies. To paraphrase Orwell's dictatorial pig, 'All folk are unequal, but some are more unequal than others'. The guideline being suggested here is that world society, and all its nations and communities, have a responsibility to reduce this oppression and, in doing so, make an enormous contribution to the goal of high quality of life for most. Indeed, it can be argued that reducing oppression is the most effective and single most important task in the ongoing struggle for the good society.

Who are these oppressed, low-power groups and what are some of the ways in which their rights and opportunities are denied? The list, depending on circumstances, includes women, children, the aged, the very poor, immigrants, indigenous peoples, ethnic and religious minorities, prisoners, homosexuals, rural people, the disabled, slaves, indentured labourers, dissidents, colonial and ex-colonial peoples and coming generations.

As individuals, the oppressed suffer both institutional bias and interpersonal prejudice. Members of all of the listed groups have differences which allow them to be categorised, consciously or subconsciously, as outside the 'tribe' or not fully human and hence not to be treated in a fraternal–sisterly way. Being hated, feared and despised is an enormous impediment to being treated fairly.

Most justice systems, not excluding those in first world countries, are biased against disadvantaged groups. Even the law as written may recognise them as different and may not recognise some forms of oppression as illegal. Judicial and police bias and corruption are common. Complaints get ignored. Rights get ignored. Justice is delayed and not transparent. Proper legal representation is unavailable. Those reaching prisons, places where torture and cruelty are not uncommon, are further discriminated against. The justice system is the prime example but other bureaucracies and institutions, in their own way, can be just as oppressive and discriminatory.

As peoples, the two notable ways in which the oppressed are treated unfairly by the international community are through denial of political self-determination and through economic exploitation, meaning the failure of reciprocity, for example, irresponsible foreign investment, unfair product prices. Denial of a meaningful voice in world affairs is a third example.

What is to be done?

A goal of quality survival for world society admits no alternative to supporting the marginalised, dispossessed, disadvantaged, weak and oppressed; but just how that is to be done is not so clear. I will suggest several guidelines at each of the international, national and personal levels.

Internationally, the UN Universal Declaration of Human Rights, the Convention on the Elimination of All Forms of Discrimination Against Women and the 1989 UN Declaration on the Rights of the Child are good places to start. These documents must be explained to people everywhere. All national governments should be asked to reaffirm them. Groups monitoring breaches of human rights should be strongly supported, along with groups lobbying for practices to change. Abusers of human rights should be tried in the International Criminal Court. There is nothing new here, just a recognition of the need for more vigour. More will become possible if the world federates. Also, given the important role of national justice systems in the reduction of oppression, special support should be offered to nations trying to achieve required reform.

Because it is difficult to generalise on when independence movements should be supported, a first guideline here might be that the international community pay particular attention to monitoring the protection of human rights in such situations. The problem of economic exploitation as a form of oppression will be commented on below (see page 283).

At a personal level we are all heirs to prejudice against 'outsiders'. Recognising this is a first step towards reducing prejudice. In time, as peoples interbreed and as our emotions and instincts come under tighter forebrain control, prejudice might decline naturally. We will learn to detect our own 'moral partiality' operating, that is, our remarkable capacity to see our own actions as morally justified. In the shorter term, prejudice is best fought by arranging shared experience, particularly situations where opportunities for slowly building trust are present. Sporting teams for people from mixed backgrounds provide a simple example. More broadly, it is the participation of all groups, including low-power groups, in legitimate political processes which has the potential to subdue prejudice. This is what has to be facilitated. Notwithstanding, the threat of prejudice being inflamed by unscrupulous leaders will remain until, as a species, we become more mature. We turn then to the lead role of democratic government in reducing oppression and discrimination.

Participatory and pluralist democracy

My first guideline here is that at a national political level, the institution which can do most to counter oppression and discrimination is a participatory and pluralist democracy focused on constructing a strong rights-based social contract — just as it is the institution promising to deliver quality-of-life gains to non-elite but non-oppressed majorities. Recall that a participatory process is one which genuinely considers the views of all affected people. While democracy, at a first approximation, is majority rule, pluralist democracy is majority rule restrained by a range of values including the power of countervailing institutions (for example, bureaucracy, unions) and the rights of minorities and oppressed groups (see page 13).

Part of the spirit of pluralist democracy is a willing acceptance of a broad range of world views (Rawls' [1993: 134] 'reasonable pluralism'). That range cannot be too broad though if it is believed that a measure of cultural and social homogeneity is essential to representative (cf. direct) democracy as a decision procedure, especially in a centralised sovereign state, that is, voters will only entrust legislative power to candidates somewhat like themselves.

Devolution has previously been mentioned as an instrument for encouraging diversity (see page 237) and for confronting complexity (see page 184), but it is also a very direct way for the less powerful to participate in decisions that affect them. It means actively transferring national-government powers, not only to regional and local governments, but also to not-for-profit participatory organisations in the community sector such as citizen action groups, self-help movements and social movements. More generally, the challenge is to create what Pateman (1970) calls a *participatory society* rather than just a participatory political system. A participatory society seeks to democratise as many institutions as possible and to devolve power from larger to smaller institutions wherever possible. It might be argued that a high level of participation could threaten a society's stability and so encourage authoritarianism but, on balance, participation protects against oppression and discrimination while meeting people's socio-biological needs for status and identity.

As a reference point, participation can be contrasted with corporatism and adversarialism. Corporatism means a few big players (unions, business) bargaining directly with government over policy. In adversarial processes conflicts and disputes are 'resolved' by destroying the legitimacy of the opposition and using power to impose solutions coercively.

So, how is participation to be achieved? There is a voluminous literature on empowerment and social development through participation which we do not have space to review (but see Cocks [1999] Ch 6). Pateman (1970: 8) warns that generating genuine participation is demanding of resources and slow to produce results.

MANAGING PRODUCTION AND DISTRIBUTION

Chapter 1 reported a variety of scenarios for the world economy in the 21st century, mostly bounded by the perception that what that system produces and distributes for consumption will continue to be guided by some form of market capitalism, distorted and regulated to a greater or lesser degree. And the not-uncommon view that market capitalism will be replaced in time as the world economy's guidance system was also introduced — along with noting the shortage of plausible ideas about what might replace it.

One thing we can do here is to look for guidelines for managing the world economy over the next few centuries under the assumption that a strong world federation will be in place. There is a more immediate task though and that is to clarify what is expected of the world economy under a social goal of quality survival. Then we can ask whether meeting that expectation is physically feasible. It is only if what is being asked of the physical economy is reachable in principle that it becomes relevant to ask what system of incentives, constraints and opportunities might achieve it in practice.

Without pondering over why it is so, it is clear that at no time over the last 6000 years has economic activity provided the bulk of the species with a reliable, modest level of material well-being, even by the standards of the times. That conclusion is true today and it would be unsurprising if it remained true for the rest of the century.

What is expected of the economy, call it the *target economy*, can be extracted from the social contract (see page 264), starting with food, clothing and shelter for all, including future generations. Beyond these basics, the economy should be able to offer the opportunity to access reasonable education, health, transport and communication/information services. And the economy should operate so as to ensure the continued availability of clean air, clean water and natural areas to enjoy. Workloads and the working environment should not be destructive of people's health.

Because the present global economy does not produce anything like this basket of goods and services, the question of whether it could physically do so can only be answered by modelling, and the necessary modelling has not been done. Such modelling, a form of quantitative design exercise, would project a staged transition, a developmental pathway, from the present pattern of production of consumption goods and services and of investment in physical capital to those of the target economy — industry by industry and country by country. It would take time to replace the capital mix producing today's goods and services with a mix that, using plausible technologies, could produce the target mix of consumption goods.

Factors that would have to be recognised when attempting to design such a transition scenario for the world's physical economy include:

- Growth projections for the world population and workforce;

- Preferred rate of investment in a new suite of capital goods appropriate to the needs of the target economy (remembering that all investment reduces current consumption);

- Preferred rate of investment in improving sociopolitical institutions, social relations and social learning (including research and development);

- The probable need to divert 'luxury' consumption in the existing economy into basic consumption in the target economy;

- Preferred rate of investment in 'insurance' against unpredictable contingencies, for example, redundant capital, backup systems;

- Increasing amounts of energy that will be needed to extract each tonne of fossil energy and each tonne of minerals from declining reserves;

- Technologies and instruments assumed to be available for counter-ing air and water pollution;

- Changes in the availability of renewable resources such as water and forests;

- Time and resources needed to train a workforce with a different skills mix, for example, more teachers and health workers.

Attempts to design a transition path to a new physical economy might show that there are many ways or, conversely, no apparent ways of doing so. If there are multiple transition possibilities, which is preferred? For example, the fastest transition might reduce consumption in the immediate future to unacceptable levels.

My own intuition, based only on some experience in modelling the Australian physical economy, is that it would be physically possible to trans-form the present world economy into the target economy over 5 or 6 decades but that once achieved it would become increasingly difficult to sustain that performance for subsequent generations, even accepting projections of a decline in world population after 2070 or so. Factors militating against longer-term sustainability in this sense might include the need to adapt to resource depletion, climate change, land degradation and to disruptions from war and other contingencies. Even a transition lasting several generations, no matter how well managed, would impose the high rates of change which so often bring great social pain.

Ideology is not the answer

Assuming for discussion purposes that a transition to the target economy is physically possible, the emotive question arises as to the institutional arrangements — resource allocating mechanisms — which might bring that transition about. Traditional ideology is not the answer. Theory and practice suggest that neither market liberalism nor a centralised command economy of the socialist–communist variety could deliver a target economy, especial-ly one with the mixture of resilience and adaptability required to respond to environmental change and consumer-preference changes. In anything remotely approaching a pure form, history shows that both systems encounter popular resistance. The cumulative processes of divergence which accompany competitive self-interest offend the sense of fairness that many have. Conversely, there is no place for the driving force of self-interested innovation in a command economy. Market failures abound in one and gov-ernment failures in the other. And while mixtures of these polar ideologies (for example, embedding markets in a socialist society, worker co-operatives in market society) have also been devised (see Polanyi 1944; 2001; Cockshott and Cottrell 1993, Hodgson 1999a: 40), they too appear inadequate as over-arching institutions capable of transforming the present world economy to a target economy.

It seems we have little choice but to 'muddle through', starting with the existing world economy and where possible, improving those institutional arrangements most unfavourable to quality survival. Somewhat sadly, there is no case for attempting to impose anything more revolutionary. Even here, the problem immediately arises that there are no international mechanisms for regulating the global economy in the interests of quality survival. Bodies like the World Trade Organisation and the International Monetary Fund are more interested in strengthening and protecting the global economy than in the wellbeing of ordinary people. To come up with any guidelines that might make a difference in quality survival terms, I will have to first assume some form of federation of world states has already emerged. Redirecting the world economy will be more a matter of ongoing politics than of putting the 'right' economic system in place.

Guidelines for two priority issues

On that basis, what might be priority issues for a world federation seeking to create a global economy which offers most people a chance to live in modest comfort? Let me suggest two candidates, both structural and both covering a number of constituent issues: reforming the operating environment for cor-porations in the global economy and influencing global investment patterns.

Reforming the corporate operating environment

Despite libertarian efforts to minimise the role of the state, it is inescapable that the creation and maintenance of property rights and functioning market institutions requires the sustained intervention of the state (Hodgson 1999a: 82). Even a simple contract like writing a cheque relies for its efficacy on both a level of trust and a whole system of collective arrangements. But, while business needs the state, the state, as agent of the people, equally needs busi-ness to deliver goods and services that satisfy human needs and, through employment, to distribute purchasing power.

The importance of this mutual dependency is that it provides a basis on which world business and a world federation of states might begin negotiat-ing an explicit social contract based on rights and responsibilities in the man-ner of the social contract between the state and the individual (see page 264). In recognition of the complexities of such a *state-business contract*, negotiations might start with aspirations perhaps rather than formal rights.

Apart from the state's responsibility to enforce the legal system on which business relies, what might corporations most want from the state in such a contract? Low taxes certainly, but also healthy social relations characterised by sociality and willing participation (see page 257) by a healthy, educated workforce. The state is being asked to provide business with its human resources and with a low-cost, stable and predictable social and regulatory environment in which to operate, for example, trust and honesty reduce transaction costs for business, just as trust is undermined by overuse of contractual negotiation and the cost calculus. But equally, given the importance of wages and employment conditions in setting individual attitudes to social relations, the state will be asking business to provide working environments that meet employees' needs.

More generally, the state's basic demand on business would be that it should be socially and environmentally responsible. For example, as suggested by Peter Senge (1999), the duty statements of company directors might be modified to recognise that their legal duty to make money should not be at the expense of 'the environment, human rights, public safety, the community or the dignity of employees'.

Umbrella organisations for mega-corporations and the like could be expected to drive a hard bargain when negotiating a worldwide state-business social contract. The state's strong position in such negotiations is under-recognised, although the state's negotiators may not always have the interests of ordinary people at heart (see page 261). Still, if a world federation were to emerge, the completion of a state-business-social contract as one of its products would not be too surprising.

A social contract between employee unions and the state or a state-business-unions social contract are other possible avenues to reforming the world economy's operating environment. Note though that negotiation between a few large players over a social contract is not corporatism insofar as it is the broad social framework which is being negotiated, not deals on particular issues.

A three-way social contract between unions, business and the state might even be able to address the challenge of separating sustenance from work. Modern states live with the contradiction of demanding that all work to get their share, even when there is not work for all. Worse, much effort goes into growing the economy to create jobs, even though much of that growth is relatively 'jobless', destructive of the environment and productive of consumer goods that add little to the quality of people's lives. Sharing work and leisure may be part of the answer, but the key is to find ways of rewarding those whose undoubted contributions fall outside the requirements of the economy. Perhaps a widespread acceptance of everyone's right to a minimum income is all that is needed.

Influencing global investment patterns

From a quality survival perspective, the 21st century global economy is failing in several very obvious ways which, it can be assumed, a world federation would seek to address using the full range of policy instruments at its disposal:

*   Under-investment in health and education;

*   Economic stagnation and exploitation in peripheral regions of the world economy;

*   Under-investment in renewable-energy generation;

*   Largely uncontrolled atmospheric, freshwater and marine pollution.

The sorts of programs which a world federation might seek to negotiate with member states include the use of the federation's tax revenues to:

*   Establish quality health and education systems in disadvantaged countries and in disadvantaged regions of other countries;

*   Establish quality legal systems where requested, including systems of business law;

*   Establish banking systems which specialise in micro credit and credit for import replacement ventures in disadvantaged countries;

*   Establish effective transport and communications systems in disadvantaged countries.

In terms of regulatory and legislative programs, a graded tax on fossil energy use would be a high priority, that is, graded to be lower in disadvantaged countries. Such a tax would encourage the global transition to renewable energy as well as lowering relative business costs in disadvantaged countries. In the richer countries it would hasten the dematerialisation of the economy, that is, the transition to a services economy, and reduce the rate at which renewable and non-renewable resources both entered the economy and left it as unprocessed residues (pollutants). Tradeable permits to use energy (joules per capita) might be another way to boost national income in disadvantaged countries, at least in the earlier stages of their economic development. Nothing happens without energy!

Another high priority would be a world trade agreement which eliminated discrimination against disadvantaged countries, even discriminated in their favour perhaps.

The above suggestions are largely concerned with redressing the economic disadvantages of countries where quality of life is glaringly low. Why? It does not require much of a sense of fairness to see that this is how the social goal of reasonable quality of life for all can be most rapidly approached. It is a judgment which is reinforced by understanding that economic growth declines in its capacity to contribute to quality of life as it saturates demands for material goods.

Many more guidelines could be suggested for the task of managing the 21st century global economy but it is time to turn to a fourth massive challenge for any emerging world federation to consider — managing the Earth system, not just in the 21st century but into the deep future.

MANAGING THE GLOBAL ECOSYSTEM

The Earth's physical systems (crust, oceans, atmosphere) plus its biota or life forms can be usefully viewed as a single worldwide ecosystem. As described earlier (see page 125), this global ecosystem, through a complex web of feedback processes, has maintained, for 1500 million years, the ambient levels of carbon, oxygen, temperature and water vapour and the accessible levels of essential cell nutrients within the limits compatible with life's survival.

While there have been long periods of little change or slow change in these state (of the system) variables, there have also been abrupt changes. Life forms themselves have evolved, fluctuated in numbers and, usually, disappeared. Life forms and physical systems have co–evolved, forcing change on each other and change in the range of values of state variables under which life can survive, for example, the oxidation by aerobic bacteria of, first, the Earth's crust and then the oxygenation of the atmosphere. As well as being changed by life itself, physical conditions in the global ecosystem have also been changed by outside forces indifferent to anything that happens in the biosphere, for example, deep vulcanism, fluctuations in the Sun's luminosity.

Not that this has all happened uniformly. In different parts of the world, the global ecosystem's subsystems, its biomes, are climatically, geologically and biologically different and the environmental limits within which each can survive are also different, for example, rainforests cannot survive under polar conditions.

Each of the major glacial–interglacial cycles of the last two million years resulted in vast sweeps of various biomes advancing and retreating across the world's continents. Those pushed back have generally survived in small patches, waiting to 'surge' (it could take centuries) across the landscape when conditions change; just as will happen in the next glacial if the necessary remnant patches survive the land use changes imposed by humans since the interglacial began (see page 88). It goes back much further of course. The history of global plant cover over the last 65 million years, particularly forests, is characterised by flux, not stability, and that flux is likely to continue (Tallis 1991: 368). None of the biomes and large ecosystems we see today are permanent.

Where are we now?

What is interesting about the global ecosystem during the current interglacial is that one species (us) has increased its numbers enormously, partly at the expense of other species which have declined or become extinct as humans have captured the energy sources on which those species relied. For example, humans commonly replace mature ecosystems supporting many species with immature but more productive ecosystems such as crops. Equally important-ly, humans have learned how to capture the Earth's store of fossil-fuel energy and, for the first and last time, are using it, at very high rates, to support an increasingly complex form of social organisation and to support an increasing population. Also, it is mostly fossil energy which powers the prostheses (for example, bulldozers) that allow humans to divert other species' energy sources to human use.

All this human activity has produced clearly identifiable changes, beyond the experience of the last 500 000 years in many cases, in the Earth's land surface, oceans, coasts, atmosphere, water cycle and biogeochemical cycles (see page 60). This is in addition to the losses of species and ecosystems. While nobody knows, these global changes have the potential to abruptly switch the global ecosystem (a dissipative complex system after all) into an alternative mode of operation (see page 57) which is much less hospitable to humans and other life 'as we know it'.

The second great trauma lurking in the global ecosystem is that the human population, like most populations that grow explosively, may decline as rapidly as it grew; perhaps when the fossil energy runs out, perhaps when society gets too complex to keep functioning.

This then is the background against which we have to think about managing the global ecosystem into the deep future.

Strategic guidelines

What does world society realistically want from the global ecosystem? In a thousand years perhaps nothing but a place to stand, depending on psychic change and technological progress. Today though, and into the foreseeable future, we want the global ecosystem to supply us with, at least:

- A breathable atmosphere;

- Fertile farmland and land for settlements;

- A climate which remains within the variability range of post-glacial temperature and rainfall regimes;

- Non-renewable resources for the economy, primarily minerals and fossil fuels;

- A non-declining harvest of natural products (fish, timber etc.);

- A global ecosystem which is biologically diverse.

And, to the extent that change is inevitable, we want it to be at a rate that gives us time to adjust the infrastructure and structure of world society to the new conditions. It is because we want to maintain these *ecosystem services* (see page 60) and because they are all under some degree of threat that management of the global ecosystem is a priority issue.

At the global scale, there are two paramount (and linked) causes of the existing and foreseeable decline in the delivery of these ecosystem services. One is population growth and the other is the amount of energy used by the global economy. Not only does every extra person spark a new demand for energy to be used in meeting that person's material needs, there is a patchy global trend towards using more energy to provide more goods and services per head.

It can be suggested then that just as the regulation of global energy use was seen above (see page 283) as central to the management of the global economy, it is central to the management of the global ecosystem. Thus a world federation, acting through a world energy authority perhaps, might cap world energy use and set up a market for trading energy-use rights. This could be combined with a permit system in which different forms of land transformation and land use intensification (see page 60) required different numbers of energy-use credits. As with the global economy, compensation arrangements for disadvantaged countries would be needed.

Before turning from energy capping to the equally important issue of guiding world population, and to the question of depleting non-renewable resources, we discuss the question of managing the world's biodiversity at the regional (cf. global) level.

Managing biodiversity

To maintain some ecosystem services, the requirement is for biomass (that is, any sort of life) rather than biodiversity (that is, a wide variety of species and habitats in all parts of the world). In the short term, crops can replenish the atmosphere and yield surface water, just as forests do. Over decades, perennial vegetation which is not diverse may still suffice to recycle water to the atmosphere and maintain regional or continental rainfall and temperature patterns. Nonetheless, the question remains, does loss of biodiversity, either of species or habitats, threaten a violation of the conditions under which life can persist? While the answer is that it probably does not, a reversion, at least on a large scale, to much simpler ecosystems stands to be highly disruptive of human societies. For example:

- Every human still depends to some extent on the natural products of relatively undisturbed ecosystems, for example, wild fish, timber from forests;

- Whether or not it is because they evolved as hunter–gatherers in mature ecosystems, humans obtain joy and aesthetic pleasure from encountering a variety of species and habitats, that is, biodiversity has amenity value;

- As we come to slowly believe, post-Darwin, that other animal species have a right to exist and not be cruelly treated, we are led to seeing the conservation of biodiversity as ethically correct.

Loss of biodiversity is a direct by-product of land clearing and of each subsequent step down the path to ever-more intensive land use which ends in paved cities or mining operations. Indirectly, land-use intensification leads to pollution and other off-site effects which further destroy biodiversity. The message then is that biodiversity loss is important in itself, important as a precursor to climatic and land use change and important as an indicator of the ever-increasing economic activity which meets people's material needs.

The challenge is twofold. First to minimise the biodiversity loss associated with any economic activity. Second, to forego economic activity when the costs in terms of biodiversity loss and other environmental costs such as pollution and climate change are unacceptably high. Easier said than done! All I can offer here are a few examples of guidelines which communities might refer to when deciding whether to accept or reject development proposals that involve land-use intensification:

- As far as possible do not develop areas where biological diversity is particularly high, for example, coral reefs, rainforests;

- Protect ecosystems found in the sorts of environments predicted to expand under climatic change;

- Manage the harvesting of goods and services from natural areas very carefully, that is, sustainably. This includes water as well as plant and animal products;

- Divert proposals for intensive land uses to areas already cleared and developed (most biodiversity is lost in the initial clearing);

- Reject development proposals that fragment or dissect intact ecosystems;

- Protect natural areas which are large enough and undisturbed enough to be self-managing. Systems which retain most of their naturally evolved species survive disruption better than systems from which many species have been lost;

- Give particular protection to rare and endangered species. Over longer periods, conditions always change and today's rare species, if they have been allowed to survive, might become the 'keystone' species of new ecosystems where their particular attributes give them a competitive advantage. High diversity is the key to smooth evolution;

- Recognise that every local population of a species is worth protecting. The loss of any local populations of a species reduces its genetic diversity. When a species loses genetic diversity it is more susceptible to population crashes under environmental change;

- Recognise that it is particularly difficult to protect biodiversity in the hinterlands of large cities where economic values from competing land uses are always high;

- When making plans that will guide future land use, it is important to consider as large an area as is politically possible because this maximises the likelihood that both economic and environmental values can be accommodated;

- Think of the biosphere as Posterity's Earthgarden (see page 207).

Managing the gene pool and people numbers

For most of its existence the human population has been growing at a rate proportional to the square of population size and it is only in the last few hundred years that this ever-accelerating rate of growth has begun to fall. Just as global energy use might decline of its own accord as fossil fuels are used up, global population might follow demographic projections and begin falling later this century, after 2070 say (see page 40). Or it could be sooner (and sharper) if threshold population densities are reached at which hormonal controls switch in and drive fertility down even faster than indicated by the present demographic transition — an evolutionary adaptation with obvious survival value in terms of conserving food supplies (see page 74). For example, women in concentration camps stop menstruating.

Is it possible to suggest a long-term target for the world's population, apart from wanting to avoid a roller coaster of disruptive ups and downs? Catton (1980) says that the only solution is that we must learn to live within the world's intrinsic 'carrying capacity', not trying to artificially enlarge it by digging up energy supplements left over from past eras. Unfortunately, 'carrying capacity' is a slippery concept, dependent on what standard of living is assumed and difficult to quantify even when the data are available (Cocks 1996: 98).

Still, as a first guideline it can be suggested that world society think in terms of reaching a more-or-less stable population within the next 200 years such that, in principle if not in practice, most people can live in modest comfort without relying on fossil energy or an excessive share of the energy flowing through the biosphere to meet their needs. What that figure is depends, among other things, on the availability of renewable energy supplies and the proportion of primary energy flow through the biosphere which is diverted into directly supporting humans as distinct from other species. We can be sure though, even without doing the sums, that it will be less than the present six billion.

Almost certainly, the present world population is not in balance with its environment; natural resources are shrinking even as the population which needs them is growing. Given the threats to ecosystem services posed by current energy use and population levels, there may be a place for a further precautionary guideline, namely to stabilise population at a level which requires a considerably smaller fraction than the current 40 per cent of the biosphere's primary energy flow to be diverted to human use — perhaps 30 per cent or 20 per cent. The figure is arbitrary but intended to suggest a major reduction.

There seem to be few arguments against this suggested loose strategy of stabilising world population over the next 200 years at a level considerably below 6 billion. But perhaps there are ways in which a population well above the present level could improve quality survival prospects? The trend towards living in big cities would obviously continue and cities do produce innovative ideas. Or, more generally, more people means more clever people to tackle the challenges of quality survival. Perhaps population growth would hasten the advent of a global brain (see page 113)? These are thin ideas and no basis for a long-term population strategy.

There remains the possibility of a genetic argument in favour of a larger population, but again there is none. While the population remains in the billions there is no prospect of the species losing the genetic diversity which may allow it to adapt physically and psychologically to persistent new environments, particularly those of large cities. Nor is there any place, at this stage in the evolution of the lineage, for attempting to manage breeding behaviour to produce people with an enhanced capacity to achieve high quality of life. The quality survival challenge is a matter of social and not genetic learning.

Indeed, it could be argued that if an attempt is to be made to breed humans suited to a particular sort of environment, it should be the sort of environment that might exist after the collapse of the current civilisation. That would require establishing and isolating populations in 'experimental' environments and imply a quite unacceptable level of social engineering. Perhaps the more general point to be made here is that the current diversity of environments within which humans live and breed together should be maintained insofar as this will give the species a basic stock of relatively uniform genetic types on which to draw. In practice this simply means that humans, particularly indigenes, should continue to occupy all parts of the world.

But equally, from a genetic perspective, there must be a free flow of genes within and between populations of genetic types. Inbred populations tend to have weak immune systems, meaning they are susceptible to diseases. The incest taboo has a very sound biological basis. The genetic requirement for species survival is a neither more nor less than a single, diverse human gene pool.

This means that barriers to interbreeding between classes within societies and between societies should be kept low. Darlington (1969: 674) suggests that even moderate inbreeding has frequently endangered a governing class, not through producing defectives but merely by stabilising a type which has lost its functional value. Between societies, migration is an important way of stirring the gene pool, once antipathies due to differences of creed, social standing etc. have died away.

Just as inbreeding can have advantages and disadvantages, a high degree of outbreeding can increase abortion and peri-natal mortality rates and the proportion of extreme individuals, that is, creatives and mental, social or sexual defectives (Darlington 1969: 674). If managing the human gene pool is seen to be the task, the challenge is to balance inbreeding and outbreeding. But, to my knowledge, there are no clear-cut rules or institutions for doing so in modern societies (except of course to always avoid the sort of genetic isolation of populations that might eventually see the lineage split into more than one species and threaten conflict).

Managing depletion of non-renewable resources

The central question in managing non-renewable resources such as fossil fuels, fossil water, minerals and (many) agricultural soils is whether the rate at which they are being currently used up should be slowed in order to delay the time when they are effectively exhausted. The purpose recognised in such proposals is normally presented as one of taking action to treat future generations fairly. Under this book's suggested social goal of quality survival, slowing depletion might also be viewed as an insurance against extinction, should we encounter difficult times ahead when having some non-renewables left would be particularly useful. One point we will ignore in the present discussion is the fact that, over geological time, non-renewables may eventually regenerate naturally.

In principle, the depletion question is answered by identifying and valuing the changes in benefits and disbenefits that would accrue to different groups, present and future, if depletion were to be slowed by mechanisms such as tradeable depletion quotas, taxes on the use of virgin materials or mandatory recycling (see Cocks 1999, chapter 4). In practice, such assessments are plagued by massive non-certainties and unavoidable subjective judgments.

All I can offer here are some brief arguments for and against strict control of depletion rates. And I will focus on metallic minerals rather than fossil-fuel use which I have already suggested to be in need of long-term regulation.

Opponents of depletion control point out that the global economy is already dematerialising steadily, implying a declining demand for minerals. Recycling discarded products is also increasing and becoming more efficient and that implies a reducing need for virgin minerals to be brought into the economy. Non-metallic substitutes for many metals (for example, fibre optic cable) are being steadily invented and this trend will increase as extraction costs for metallic ores rise (see page 66). Extraction costs could actually decrease if we develop technologies in the future that allow us to retrieve metals from low-grade ores, for example, by using nanotechnology or genetically modified bacteria which consume and concentrate metals. To constrain the global economy at this time by rationing renewables may put growth at risk and, with it, the research which produces substitutes for metals.

Opponents conclude that reserves of metallic minerals are unlikely to be exhausted in the foreseeable future and that use rates will be most conveniently and efficiently determined by market forces. They delight in pointing out that predicted exhaustion dates for various metals in the famous 'Limits to growth' study (Meadows et al. 1972) have already proved wrong.

Responding to these arguments, proponents of depletion control point out that any movement towards savings through dematerialisation is being swamped by the growth of the global economy. And that while the ratio of recycled secondary metals to primary metals has increased somewhat, a recovery rate of even 70 per cent implies that existing stocks in circulation would virtually disappear within five years.

They also point out that energy input and pollution residues per tonne of metal produced are increasing as the richest ores are successively used. One tonne of copper in the United States at the beginning of the 20th century produced 50 tonnes of tailings waste. Today the figure is 250 tonnes of tailings waste. The problem is that much of the cost of land and water pollution coming out of mining operations is not paid for by the producer which immediately suggests to an economist (Daly 1982) that unmanaged rates of depletion are likely to be higher than the rate at which marginal social benefits equal marginal social costs, that is, there is a sound economic case for some constraint on depletion rates.

One possible (arbitrary) basis for a depletion control program is the 'hundred year rule' which states that world society should not extract more than 1 per cent of remaining proven reserves of any non-renewable resource in any given year. This means that there will always be a 100-year supply for future generations, but the annual quantity actually supplied will vary as proven reserves vary.

On the assumption that this cap on production is worldwide and being managed by a world federation or similar, revenue from auctioning the annual quota would help fund the federation's operations. An alternative way, more helpful to disadvantaged countries, would be to allocate each country a share of the quota in proportion to population and allow countries to use their share or auction it for use elsewhere. The view lurking here is that mineral reserves are a resource belonging in some sense to all of humanity, and to future generations.

Capping the annual production of non-renewables which are in strong demand stands to hasten the development of substitution technologies, extraction technologies, recycling technologies and, in general, the trend to dematerialisation. These are benefits to be balanced against price rises flowing from increased production costs.

Depletion quotas which regulate the production of non-renewables could be combined with measures to encourage recycling and reuse of products containing non-renewables. Any tax on 'virgin' materials entering the production process for the first time could be combined with a legal requirement for some products to contain more than a certain percentage of recycled materials. Industry is already learning to design products with recycling in mind.

Overall, the use of taxes, quotas etc. has the potential to not only delay the exhaustion of non-renewables but to stimulate our learning to economise on their use and replace them with renewable substitutes early enough to avoid shocks like the jumping oil prices of the 1970s. Having said that, the case for regulating the depletion of non-renewable metallic minerals does not seem nearly as strong as the case for regulating global energy production and use. Regulation would be expensive and difficult and it is not clear just how much market failure there is in its absence.

CHAPTER OVERVIEW

This chapter is a recognition that world society has to cope successfully with the near future if it is to have any prospect of surviving well throughout the deep future. As Keynes might have said, unless you look after the short run, there is no long run. The chapter looks for a succinct perspective on each of four families of priority issues (social relations, governance, economy, environment) which confront world society in the 21st century and which, in some form will continue to confront it for many centuries.

Reflecting on the particular guidelines suggested for addressing these issues, several meta-guidelines emerge:

It is a globalising world and these issues are global issues which beg to be addressed at a global scale (as well as, but not instead of, at regional and local scales). That is why I have found it useful at a number of places in the chapter to assume that the world's nation states have federated to form a world government of some sort. Without the possibility of co-operative joint action by the peoples of the world, there does not seem to be a lot that can be done about a number of these matters.

Unless you can make an assumption about what world society is trying to achieve (I assume it to be quality survival) there is no basis for evaluating and comparing suggested guidelines for managing world-scale threats and opportunities (if you don't know where you are going, it does not matter which bus you catch).

Many, if not most, of the guidelines suggested as having the potential to make the largest contributions to the quality survival task, involve curbing the self-interest of the powerful and/or boosting the opportunities of the weak and disadvantaged. The search is for fairness in a world which is failing to meet human needs.

9

STORIES TO LIVE BY

Once and once only for
each thing — then no more.
For us as well. Once.
Then no more ... ever.
But to have been as one,
though but the once,
with this world,
never can be undone.
(RM RILKE, from the 'Ninth Duino Elegy')

BACKTRACKING

Let me start this final chapter by recapitulating what this book has done. Chapters 1 and 2 reviewed a multitude of scenarios and opinions on what the world and human through to post-human society might be like politically, socially, psychologically, technologically, economically and environmentally — over the 21st century and, more panoramically, for the rest of time. Chapter 3 argued that it is legitimate and useful for societies to have collective goals and suggested quality survival (high quality of life for most people into the indefinite future) as an appropriate goal for an emerging world society.

As a preliminary to asking if and how world society can be moved by purposive collective action towards quality survival, Chapter 4 reviewed thinking from various disciplines on how societies change over time. The most useful conclusion was that the societal tendencies (dynamics) which history detects strongly parallel behaviours observed and inferred in energy-degrading complex systems elsewhere in nature, for example, the tendency to pass through a life cycle.

Chapter 5 looks for a quality-survival strategy which is compatible with this 'historical complex system' view of world society. The suggested best-available answer is a strategy of responding collectively and selectively to a rolling (ever-changing) set of priority issues, meaning those judged at the time to have a particular bearing on whether the lineage can achieve quality survival.

Chapters 6, 7 and 8 move a small way towards demonstrating how such a strategy might be implemented. All three chapters are concerned with suggesting guidelines that the policy machinery of world society could consider if it were formulating responses to some priority issues (author's choice in this case), viz how to manage an ever-changing historical complex system (Chapter 6), how to boost the rate at which society acquires the knowledge it is going to need to survive well (Chapter 7) and how to tackle the social, political, economic and environmental issues that demand attention now and into the foreseeable future (Chapter 8).

What I have constructed is an argument where each chapter proceeds on the assumption that the reader has accepted the working conclusions (because that is all they are) of previous chapters. That is, while each chapter lengthens the chain of conditional argument, the reader is free to slip away at any time if it all gets too preposterous.

But when the argument is done, it turns out that I have also constructed what amounts to the bones of a normative scenario, meaning a description of how I would like world society to develop during this century and beyond, including happenings such as:

- Adopting a big generous goal such as quality survival;

- Working towards a world federation as a basis for organising collective action on issues of global concern;

- Identifying a first set of such priority issues akin to those I suggest here as important and then identifying some guidelines on how those issues might be addressed.

My preference is not tightly prescriptive though. There are several ways I would be happy to see world society developing as long as the core of my scenario was retained, that is, a world society which takes its future into its own hands and comprehensively considers its options for moving itself into the near and then the deep future. It is a scenario which, looking back one day, may turn out to have also been descriptive. That is, even though it would be surprising, there is no reason in principle why it should not happen this way.

But, if world society does move to take charge of its own future, it will also mean that a critical mass of people have come to believe, with some passion (that is, enthusiasm), that such a shift can and should happen — *carpe diem,* in the destructive element immerse. Just wanting to survive well will be a major determinant of whether the lineage does survive well. So also will be having a passion for knowledge, a thirst to understand the world and ourselves. Nonetheless, while there are few things sadder than people asking 'Is this all there is?', I cannot argue that people be passionate, only hope.

STYLE, ATTITUDE AND ROLE

Beyond passion, the habitual attitudes and feelings which humans have towards their lineage and to the long cosmic play they have been cast in will be as important as their capacity for rational strategy development, if quality survival is to be anywhere near approached. This chapter's primary message is just that — successful management of the deep future will need to draw on both heart and head (see page 110).

The reason is simple. Just as a contract can never cover all the understandings in a business relationship (see page 171), thinking about how to manage the future can never anticipate all the situations that will have to be dealt with. The lineage, I am proposing, needs metaphorical role models to guide its behaviour through the gaps that thought has had to leave unanalysed. While attitudes and feelings are intangibles which are difficult to discuss as determinants of quality survival, they are nevertheless real and important and I want to suggest something of what might be needed. The most direct way of doing this is to present several of these putatively helpful attitudes and feelings as my own; and risk the perception of egotism.

I identify strongly with the lineage personified earlier as Posterity. The cosmic-scale historical play in which Posterity has a role is only half over. It has been a story of growing complexity which, once it is familiar, is enchanting and mind-stretching — from energy to matter to stars to planets to life to mind to self-awareness to world society. Fancy that!

When it comes to Act Two of the cosmic play, Posterity can help to write the script. That includes the option of writing herself out by falling victim to rogue technology. It may include struggles with other scriptwriters, planetary and cosmic forces say, who are indifferent to who stays in the play. Posterity is determined to stay but if the time to depart does come, then, whether we are squeezed out or snuffed out, let it be a graceful exit; I want to belong to a lineage that dies like Socrates. It is a bonus that the very attitudes and style that foster quality survival are autolectic, rewarding in themselves.

Nietzsche, quoted by Rollo May (1953: 67), says a person is known by his or her 'style', that is, by the unique 'pattern' which gives underlying unity and distinctiveness to his or her activities. Applying this to the lineage, Posterity's style is very much about the ways in which she plays her multi-faceted role. Already in this book she has been cast as a dragon slayer (see page 128), an Earth gardener (see page 207), a Sisyphus (see page 231) and a Prometheus (see page 242). Such metaphors or allegories are powerful, readily understood models of how to behave in particular situations and of what could be the results. Most importantly, the attitudes and behavioural or ethical styles they spark in people are readily shared as stories, as myths in the making, as common understandings of the task at hand. For example, just as the lineage will have to be, Posterity the dragon slayer is self-reliant, not dependent on authority figures to tell her what to do. She revels in her growing powers.

Posterity the Earth gardener too is autonomous, forever making deci-sions which parallel choices to be made in guiding world society into the deep future. She is constantly beset by mild optimism and mild pessimism. The first prompts her to see and confidently seize opportunity. The second reminds her that nothing is easy. In their extreme forms, optimism distorts judgment and pessimism kills the will to act (see page 145). We must suc-cumb to neither a complacent nor a doomsday view of reality. Posterity mostly plays the Earth-gardener role as a cautious nurturing optimist, calm-ly accepting the task she has been given. Or sometimes as an optimistic meliorist, convinced that the lineage can make a significant contribution to achieving quality survival, even though this is a belief that cannot be 'proved'. No existential anxiety for her!

The fable of the grasshopper and the ant provides Posterity with two more metaphorical roles. The industrious, even Promethean ant (Prometheus means 'forethought'), who can see into the wintry future and stores provisions now is a model for a lineage which can see great challenges in the deep future and starts to make provisions for them now, for example, building a learning and co-operating society. But it is no less important to be a grasshopper at times, a bon vivant with a sense of humour. Quality survival is too important a matter to be taken totally seriously, even in a world where so many are hurt-ing. That way lies a loss of perspective. I suggest something of the philosophy of Omar the Tentmaker:

> How long, how long, in Infinite Pursuit
> Of This and That endeavour and dispute?
> Better be merry with the fruitful Grape
> Than sadden after none, or bitter, Fruit.
> ....

> Ah, fill the Cup:-what boots it to repeat
> How Time is slipping underneath our Feet.
> Unborn Tomorrow and dead Yesterday,
> Why fret about them if Today be sweet!

Sometimes Posterity sees life and the cosmic play as a joke, none funnier than Douglas Adams' (1980) portrayal of Earth as an insignificant planet obstructing an intergalactic freeway in an unfashionable part of the galaxy. Humans too are enormously funny if you see them through James Thurber's eyes.

Of the other roles which it will at times be valuable for Posterity to play (mystic, gambler, lover, artist, steward, voyager etc.), one is particularly important, albeit a little difficult to explain. Call it the 'successful human' role for want of a better name. My suggestion here is that human life is a metaphor for the life of the lineage, that the lineage can learn much about how to play out its evolutionary role by observing how psychologically and socially successful humans construct their once-only life-long stories (and vice versa perhaps, that is, how the unsuccessful fail). Posterity's challenge to achieve quality survival is strongly comparable to the challenge everyone faces of making his or her own life a success.

As individuals, we struggle through childhood and adolescence to form a stable and integrated personality which will allow us to cope with life's travails, find a means of sustenance, form family and social relationships, develop skills and take on big defining projects, quests and tasks (Parker 1973). The successful are not locked into the legacies of genes and culture, but pick what is useful from both. Most importantly, the successful learn in adolescence that the essence of managing one's life is self-discipline, the foregoing of short-term gratification (or accepting short-term pain) in return for long-term gain. Failure to give this sort of unifying, persisting form to one's life leads first to neurosis as a second-best source of structuration and then to psychosis with its associated loss of contact with reality. Hostility is commonly an expression of anxiety about this threat of disintegration. When they are accepted as useful guides to reality, emotions, including the dark ones, can be consciously managed. Loving and participating draw the individual into society while self-actualisation comes with the development and ongoing exercise of one's individual talents.

The lineage too needs to see itself as being on a life's journey in a world and universe which are also traversing their (somewhat longer) life cycles. Indications are that Posterity is now an adolescent. Her physical and mental powers have increased sharply in the last 3000 years but her emotional development is slower. Not having yet learned to empathise with others, she can be thoughtlessly cruel and a bully. Like other adolescents, she is fascinated by technology and unconcerned about death, or even about planning her life a few generations into the future.

She has yet to choose a vocation that will shape her adult life in concert with steadily mastering the skills that vocation demands. She wants to be free but has not quite learned to tolerate the insecurity that goes with freedom. Indeed, she sometimes still likes to be told where her boundaries are. She enjoys competition and direct co-operation but is still ambivalent about indirect co-operation. Her need to belong attracts her to a gang life where competition with gangs of 'others' becomes an end in itself. Enough. I blush for these easy generalisations about adolescence but the point remains, human life is a powerful metaphor for the life of the lineage. And, within that metaphor, the central lesson is that just as you and I respond to the existential challenge — the challenge of finding ourselves here — by imposing meaning on our lives, so must the lineage.

Whether it is quality survival that becomes the inspirational image of the future that draws world society forward is less important than that there be one. As in Periclean Greece or the Renaissance, shared convictions bring creative forces together and give society a core of meaning. What I am emphasising, romantically perhaps, is the importance of some such vision emerging from this present period of transition and doubt. And, to go with it, the best rolling game plan that informed, clear thinking can devise.

Thank you for your attention.

APPENDIX:
BASIC PROPERTIES OF DISSIPATIVE
(ENERGY-DEGRADING) SYSTEMS

The fundamental property of dissipative systems (Glansdorff and Prigogine 1971) is that they continuously take in energy, physical materials and information (a patterned form of energy with special properties) from their environment and continuously excrete (dissipate) materials, information and degraded energy — energy of a lowered quality in terms of its capacity to do work — back into the environment, for example, waste heat. Within its boundaries, a dissipative system's intake of energy, materials and information is used to build and maintain persistent processes called structures. If it stops taking in energy, it ceases to exist. Systems which are continuously exchanging energy, physical materials and information with the surrounding environment are called open systems, meaning open to the environment. Such systems can be contrasted with impermeable closed systems which, eventually, irreversibly 'run down' to a static equilibrium state from which the system, because it has run out of usable energy, cannot change further.

Dissipative systems are also inherently *hierarchical, complex* and *self-organising*. A hierarchical (nested) system can be largely decomposed into successive sets of increasingly constrained subsystems, for example, nation, region, community. Its observed behaviour differs according to the space–time scale at which it is observed. For example, if it is observed through a coarse space–time window then the dynamic behaviour of the higher level (more inclusive) components of the system will be apparent, and vice versa. Properties which only become apparent when the system is observed through a coarser window are called *emergent properties*, for example, the properties of a forest are not apparent from the properties of its individual trees.

A *complex system* is one in which many of the interactions — cause–effect links — between its various component subsystems are organised into positive and negative feedback loops. A feedback loop is a chain of cause–effect links (transfers) between the components of a system such that the chain starts and ends on the same component (circular or mutual causation). A negative (positive) feedback loop is a feedback loop such that a causal change in any component tends to dampen (amplify) activity in that loop.

The way in which a complex system behaves over time depends on the mix of positive and negative feedback loops operating within it. Four commonly observed behaviour patterns are exponential growth (in systems dominated by a positive feedback or *autocatalytic* loop), exponential decay (in systems dominated by a negative feedback loop), sigmoid or S-shaped growth (indicating the presence of a positive loop linked to a negative loop that is due to some limiting factor) and oscillation towards a limit (which usually indicates the presence of a negative feedback loop with a time delay built into it).

Other dynamic possibilities for complex systems include steady-state behaviour, cyclical behaviour, chaotic behaviour, sigmoid growth with oscillations and overshoot followed by collapse. A system showing *steady-state behaviour* remains in just one state over the period during which it is being observed. Such systems, like all *orderly* (non-chaotic) systems, tend to be sparsely connected via short feedback loops. Or, putting this another way, 'orderly' systems have limited numbers of states they can occupy out of all possible states. A system showing *cyclical behaviour* passes through a repeating sequence of states (sets of structures).

A system which is behaving *chaotically* appears to be behaving randomly (without any pattern to the sequence of states it assumes) but is actually behaving in a way which is the resultant of several to many of its components independently following their own fixed behaviour rules. Many apparently random chaotic systems are actually obeying power laws, meaning that they generate output events in such a way that when the size of the event being considered is doubled, the event becomes X times as rare (X being the 'power' referred to). For example, double the size of an extinction event, measured as families lost, and it becomes four times as rare in the evolutionary record. Chaotic systems tend to have a dense network of causal connections between their components (Kauffman 1995). They are inherently unpredictable — chaotic systems which differ only minutely at time zero rapidly diverge. As the density of a chaotic system's connections falls, it passes a critical value called 'the edge of chaos' beyond which it behaves in an orderly rather than chaotic manner. It seems, empirically, that being at the edge of chaos is commonplace for many types of complex systems.

When the environment of a complex system or a subsystem of a complex system changes (fluctuates) in terms of the delivery of energy, materials or information, the system is said to be disturbed or perturbed, meaning that it gets 'pushed' into a sequence of states different from the sequence (cycling, oscillating etc.) that it would have followed in the absence of a perturbation. Depending on how *resilient* the system is, it will return to the behavioural pattern it was following prior to being perturbed. This is called *homeostatic stability*. The complete set of states, the region of state-space, into which a system can be pushed and from which it can still return to its former behavioural pattern is called a *basin of attraction* or *domain*. Thus, a highly resilient system is one with a large basin of attraction, a system which will resume its previous behaviour even after a large perturbation. The particular behaviour pattern to which a perturbed system will return, from wherever it has been pushed within a basin of attraction, is called an *attractor*, for example, a point attractor, a cyclical attractor, a chaotic attractor.

If, however, a perturbation is so large that it pushes the system outside its current basin of attraction, the system will either collapse or enter another basin of attraction. When a complex system collapses, the number of links in the network of cause–effect links among its subsystems is significantly reduced and the former system's collection of subsystems no longer behaves as a coherent whole. *Catastrophe theory* suggests that system collapse proceeds rapidly at first and then more slowly because rate of change is proportional to complexity.

A *self-organising system* is one which can move to alternative basins of attraction when appropriately disturbed. An appropriate disturbance will necessarily be either exogenous or endogenous. An *exogenous disturbance* is a fluctuation in the system's external environment. An *endogenous disturbance* in a self-organising system is a fluctuation in the external environment of a component subsystem (that is, a fluctuation which is external to the subsystem but internal to the system) which is itself self-organising (self-reorganising might be a more understandable term than self-organising).

Moving to a new basin of attraction is called a *structural change* or *phase shift* or *phase transition* (Clayton and Radcliffe 1996) and the changed behaviour of the system once it enters a new basin of attraction is called *emergent behaviour*.

A self-organising system which moves through a sequence of basins of attraction is said to follow a *trajectory*. If a self-organising system's trajectory takes it through a large number of small basins of attraction, its behaviour is said to be *unstable* (and vice versa). Kauffman (1995) asserts that an orderly system near the edge of chaos (near some critical level of connectivity between components) is likely to be unstable and readily moved to a new basin of attraction.

A large part of understanding self-organising systems in particular disciplines is concerned with understanding the conditions under which different classes of such systems pass through particular sorts of trajectories. For example:

- Organisms tend to pass through a developmental trajectory with phases called birth, immaturity, maturity, senescence, and death;

- Species tend to move through a line of descent called a lineage in which population grows, declines and ends in extinction;

- Ecosystems and societies tend to pass through a succession of stages from birth to death also.

In fact, while it can be interrupted at any time, and perhaps diverted, all self-organising systems which have any living components (cf. physico-chemical components only) have a tendency to follow a basic immaturity-maturity-senescence trajectory. This basic developmental or 'life cycle' trajectory, at least up to maturity, is characterised by an increasing rate of energy intake, increased storage of usable energy in system structures, increased connectivity between system components and, near maturity, increasing susceptibility to collapse.

Self-organising systems which, within certain environmental limits, tend to renew (maintain) themselves and reproduce themselves (that is, are self-renewing and self-reproducing) are *autopoietic systems*. Living organisms are examples. They contain information (genes) which, in an appropriate environment, acts as a recipe for the self-replication process, the core of which involves building up a new organism from a detached part of the old organism. Self-reproduction or self-replication is an evolutionary strategy for overcoming the entropy imperative, the tendency for self-organising systems to complexify and become susceptible to collapse.

Structural change in a system can be evoked by a large change in some driving variable — called a shock — or a small 'trigger' change, sufficient to edge some driving variable (a variable determining the delivery of system inputs) system past some critical threshold value (for example, a resource runs out). An example of the latter is a particular type of structural change called a *bifurcation*. Here, the system changes smoothly until some driving variable approaches a critical value but, once this value has been minimally exceeded, the system will behave in one of several markedly different ways, depending on imperceptibly small differences in values of other variables during the previous history of the system (Capra 1996). The behaviour of self-organising systems reaching a bifurcation point is unpredictable. A *flip* is a common type of structural change, one involving a rapid step-wise change or discontinuity in some aspect of the system's behaviour.

REFERENCES

Adams D (1980) *A Hitchhiker's Guide to the Galaxy*, Harmony Books, New York.

Alexander RD (1979) *Darwinism and Human Affairs*, University of Washington Press, Washington.

—— (1987) *The Biology of Moral Systems*, Aldine De Gruyter, New York.

Allen TFH & Starr TB (1982) *Hierarchy: Perspectives for Ecological Complexity*, Chicago University Press, Chicago.

Argy F (1992) *A Long Term Economic Strategy for Australia: An Interim Report for the Committee for the Economic Development of Australia*, Longman Cheshire, Melbourne.

Argyris C (1976) *Increasing Leadership Effectiveness*, Wiley, New York.

Armstrong K (2001) *Buddha*, Penguin, New York.

Arquilla J & Ronfeldt D (eds) (1997) *In Athena's Camp: Preparing for Conflict in the Information Age*, Rand, California.

Ashby WR (1960) *Design for a Brain: The Origin of Adaptive Behaviour*, Chapman & Hall, 2nd edn, London.

Asimov I (1995, 1996) *The Foundation Saga (Foundation, Foundation and Empire, Second Foundation)*, Paperback Editions, Harper & Collins, London.

Australian Science & Technology Council (1995) *Management of Neurodegenerative Disorders in Older People 2010: Science and Technology Requirements*, Australian Government Publishing Service, Canberra.

Ausubel JH (1998) Resources and environment in the 21st century: Seeing past the phantoms, *Journal of the World Energy Council*, July, pp. 8–16.

Ausubel JH & Marchetti C (1996) Elektron: Electrical systems in retrospect and prospect, *Daedalus*, 125(3): 139–69.

Bak P (1996) *How Nature Works: The Science of Self-Organised Criticality*, Copernicus, New York.

Bandura A (1971) *Social Learning Theory*, General Learning Press, New York.

Barraclough G (1991) *Main Trends in History*, Holmes & Meier, New York.

Bateson G (1979) *Mind and Nature: A Necessary Unity*, Wildwood House, London.

Beck U (1992), *Risk Society: Towards a New Modernity*, (first published 1986), Sage, London.

Bell D (1973) *The Coming of Post-industrial Society: A Venture in Social Forecasting*, Basic Books, New York.

Berger JO (1985) *Statistical Decision Theory and Bayesian Analysis*, Springer-Verlag, New York.

Berlin I (1999) *Concepts and Categories, Philosophical Essays*, Pimlico, London.

Berry BJL (2000) A pacemaker for the long wave, *Technological Forecasting and Social Change*, 63: 1–23.

Bion WR (1961) *Experience in Groups: And Other Papers*, Tavistock, London.

Birch C (1975) *Confronting the Future: Australia and the World: The Next Hundred Years*, Penguin, Melbourne

Blackmore S (1999) *The Meme Machine*, Oxford University Press, New York.

Blair D (1999) The future of astronomy: Exploration of the gravitational wave spectrum, in Burdyuzha U & Khozin G (eds) *The Future of the Universe and the Future of our Civilization*, World Scientific, Singapore, pp. 59–68.

Blau PM (1955) *The Dynamics of Bureaucracy*, University of Chicago Press, Chicago.

Blumenfeld Y (ed) (1999) *Scanning the Future: 20 Eminent Thinkers on the World of Tomorrow*, Thames & Hudson, London.

Bongaarts J (1998) Global population growth: Demographic consequences of declining fertility, *Science*, 282(5388): 419–20.

Borgeryd A (1998) *Managing Intercollective Conflict: Prevailing Structures and Global Challenges*, Department of Political science, Umea University, Umea, Sweden.

Bossel H (1998) *Earth at a Crossroads: Paths to a Sustainable Future*, Cambridge University Press, Cambridge.

Boulding E (1978) Futuristics and the imaging capacity of the West, in Maruyama M & Harkins AM (eds), *Cultures of the Future*, Moulton, The Hague.

Boyd R & Richerson PJ (1985) *Culture and the Evolutionary Process*, University of Chicago Press, Chicago.

Broad CD (1925) *The Mind and its Place in Nature*, Routledge & Kegan Paul, London.

Bronner ME (1996) The road to Q-infinity, *Population and Environment*, 17(5): 373–90.

Bronowski J (1973) *The Ascent of Man*, British Broadcasting Corporation, London.

—— (1977) *A Sense of the Future: Essays in Natural Philosophy*, MIT Press, Cambridge, Massachusetts.

Brown H (1986) *The Wisdom of Science: Its Relevance to Culture and Religion*, Cambridge University Press, Cambridge.

Buchanan M (2000) *Ubiquity: The Science of History*, Weidenfeld & Nicolson, London.

Burdyuzha U & Khozin G (eds) (1999) *The Future of the Universe and the Future of our Civilization*, World Scientific, Singapore.

Burnet M (1970) *Dominant Mammal*, Heinemann, Melbourne.

Burton JW (1972) *World Society*, Cambridge University Press, Cambridge.

—— (1996) *Conflict Resolution: Its Language and Processes*, Scarecrow, London.

—— (1997) *Violence Explained: The Sources of Conflict, Violence and Crime and their Prevention*, Manchester University Press, Manchester.

Caldwell J (1994) *The Course and Causes of Fertility Decline*, IUSSP Distinguished Lecture Series on Population and Development, International Conference on Population and Development, Cairo.

Calvin WH (1997) *How Brains Think: Evolving Intelligence, Then and Now*, Basic Books, New York.

Camilleri J & Falk J (1992) *The End of Sovereignty? The Politics of a Shrinking and Fragmenting World*, Edward Elgar, Aldershot.

Campbell DT (1972) On the genetics of altruism and the counter-hedonic components in human culture, *Journal of Social Issues*, 28(3): 21–37.

Camus A (1946) *The Stranger*, Alfred Knopf, New York.

Capra F (1996) *The Web of Life*, Doubleday, New York.

Carey J (1999) *The Faber Book of Utopias*, Faber & Faber, London.

Carroll J (1997) The middle-class quake, *The Australian Review of Books*, 2(1): 18–19.

Castles I (2000) *Reporting on Human Development: Lies, Damned Lies and Statistics*, Academy of the Social Sciences in Australia, Occasional Papers Series 1/2000, pp. 55–82.

Catton W (1980) *Overshoot: The Ecological Basis of Revolutionary Change*, University of Illinois Press, Urbana.

Cerny PG (1995) Globalisation and the changing logic of collective action, *International Organisation*, 49(4): 595–625.

Chapin FS, Walker BH, Hobbs RJ, Hooper DU, Lawton JH, Sala OE & Tilman D (1997) Biotic control over functioning ecosystems, *Science*, 227: 500–504.

Chapman PF & Roberts F (1983) *Metal Resources and Energy*, Butterworth, London.

Childe G (1942) *What Happened in History*, Penguin, London.

Clapperton CM (1990) Quaternary glaciations in the southern hemisphere: An overview, *Quaternary Science Reviews*, 9: 299–304.

Clayton AMH & Radcliffe NJ (1996) *Sustainability: A Systems Approach*, Earthscan Publications, London.

Coase RH (1937) The nature of the firm, *Economica*, 4: 386–405.

Coates J (1994) *The Highly Probable Future: 83 Assumptions About the Year 2025*, World Futures Society, Bethesda, Maryland.

Coates J, Mahaffie JB & Hines A (1996) *2025 — Scenarios of US and Global Society Reshaped by Science and Technology*, Oak Hill Press, Greenboro, North Carolina.

Cobb A (1998) *Thinking About the Unthinkable: Australian Vulnerabilities to High-Tech Risks*, Parliamentary Library, Parliament of Australia, Research Paper 18, 1997–98.

Cocks D (1992) *Use With Care: Managing Australia's Natural Resources in the 21st Century*, University of New South Wales Press, Sydney.

—— (1996) *People Policy: Australia's Population Choices*, University of New South Wales Press, Sydney.

—— (1999) *Future Makers, Future Takers: Life in Australia 2050*, University of New South Wales Press, Sydney.

Cockshott WP & Cottrell AF (1993) *Towards a New Socialism*, Spokesman, Nottingham.

Costanza R (1989) What is ecological economics?, *Ecological Economics*, 1: 1–17.

Cottrell F (1955) *Energy and Society: The Relation Between Energy, Social Change and Economic Development*, McGraw-Hill, New York.

Courchene T (1993) Glocalisation, institutional evolution and the Australian federation, in Galligan B (ed), *Federalism and the Economy: International, National and State Issues*, Federalism Research Centre, Australian National University, Canberra.

Cravalho EG (1994) Biomedical technologies, in Sheffield C, Alonso M & Kaplan MA (eds), *The World of 2044: Technological Development and the Future of Society*, Paragon, Minnesota.

Croce B (1941) *History as the Story of Liberty*, Allen & Unwin, London.

Csikszentmihalyi M (1993) *The Evolving Self: A Psychology for the Third Millennium*, Harper Collins, New York.

Dahl RA (1999) *On Democracy*, Yale University Press, New Haven, Connecticut.

Dahrendorf R (1959) *Class and Class Conflict in Industrial Society*, Stanford University Press, San Francisco.

Daly H (1982) The steady-state economy: What, why and how?, in Birrell R, Hill D & Stanley J (eds) *Quarry Australia? Social and Environmental Perspectives on Managing the Nation's Resources*, Oxford University Press, Melbourne.

Daly MT & Logan MI (1989) *The Brittle Rim: Finance, Business and the Pacific Region*, Penguin, Melbourne.

Dark KR (1998) *The Waves of Time: Long-Term Change in International Relations*, Pinter, London.

Darlington CD (1969) *The Evolution of Man and Society*, Allen & Unwin, London.

Darwin C (1859) *The Origin of Species by Means of Natural Selection Or the Preservation of Favoured Races in the Struggle For Life*, Random House (The Modern Library), New York.

Darwin CG (1952) *The Next Million Years*, Rupert Hart-Davis, London.

DAS (Department of Administrative Services) (1996) *DAS — Claiming the Next Twenty Years*, Report of the Preferred Futures Project, Department of Administrative Services, Canberra.

Davies P (1983) *God and the New Physics*, Dent, London.

Dawkins R (1982) Universal Darwinism, in Bendall DS (ed), *Evolution from Molecules to Men*, Cambridge University Press, Cambridge, pp. 403–25.

De Greene KB (1993) The growth of exhaustion, *European Journal of Operational Research*, 69(1): 14–25.

—— (1994) The rocky path to complex-systems indicators, *Technological Forecasting and Social Change*, 47: 171–88.

Debray R (1967) *Revolution in the Revolution? Armed Struggle and Political Struggle in Latin America*, Penguin, London.

Dennett D (1995) *Darwin's Dangerous Idea: Evolution and the Meanings of Life*, Simon & Schuster, New York.

Depew D & Weber B (1995) *Darwinism Evolving: Systems Dynamics and the Genealogy of Natural Selection*, MIT Press, Cambridge, Massachusetts.

Diamond JM (1992) *The Third Chimpanzee: The Evolution and Future of the Human Animal*, Harper Collins, New York.

—— (1997) *Guns, Germs and Steel: The Fates of Human Societies*, Jonathan Cape, London.

Dibb S (1995) Swimming in a sea of oestrogens: Chemical hormone disrupters, *The Ecologist*, 25(1): 27–31.

Disney J (1994) Imaginative and pragmatic partnerships, in Economic Planning Advisory Commission, *Ambitions for our Future*, Report 3 of *Shaping our Future:*

National Strategies Conference, Australian Government Publishing Service, Canberra.

Dodgshon RA (1998) *Space: A Geographical Perspective on Change*, Cambridge University Press, Cambridge.

Dollar D & Kraay A (2000) *Growth Is Good for the Poor*, World Bank, Economic Growth Research Papers, www.worldbank.org/research/growth/, accessed 16 September 2000.

Donald M (1991) *Origins of the Modern Mind: Three Stages in the Evolution of Culture and Cognition*, Harvard University Press, Cambridge, Massachusetts.

Dörner D (1997) *The Logic of Failure*, Addison-Wesley, Massachusetts.

Douglas R (1996) Human survival: The importance of demographic, epidemiological and health transitions, in Furnass B, Whyte J, Harris J & Baker A (eds), *Survival, Health and Wellbeing into the Twenty First Century*, Nature and Society Forum, Canberra.

Doyal L & Gough I (1991) *A Theory of Human Need*, Macmillan, London.

Drexler KE (1986) *Engines of Creation: The Coming Era of Nanotechnology*, Anchor Books, New York.

Drucker P (1997) The global economy and the nation-state, *Foreign Affairs*, 76(5): 159–71.

—— (2001) The next society, *The Economist*, 3 November, Survey, pp. 3–20.

Dunn ES (1971) *Economic and Social Development: A Process of Social Learning*, Johns Hopkins, Baltimore.

Dupont A (1999) Scarce seafood could spark wars, *Australian Financial Review*, 7 July, p. 14.

Durkheim E (1893; 1964) *The Division of Labour in Society*, (trans. G Simpson), Free Press, New York.

Dyson E (1998) *Release 2.1: A Design for Living in the Digital Age*, Penguin, London.

Dyson F (1979) Time without end: Physics and biology in an open universe, *Reviews of Modern Physics*, 51(3): 447–60.

Dyson F (2000) There's gold in them there trees, *Good Weekend Magazine*, 1 January, pp. 35–37.

Eckersley R (1995) Values and visions: Youth and the failure of modern Western culture, *Youth Studies Australia*, 14(1): 13–21.

Eco U (1995) Ur-Fascism, *New York Review of Books*, 22 June.

Economic Planning Advisory Commission (1995), *Investment and Economic Growth*, Commission Paper No. 9, Australian Government Publishing Service, Canberra.

Eisler R (1998) Conscious evolution: Cultural transformation and human agency, in Loye D (ed), *The Evolutionary Outrider: The Impact of the Human Agent on Evolution*, Praeger, New York, pp. 191–207.

Elkins DJ (1995) *Beyond Sovereignty: Territory and Political Economy in the Twenty-First Century*, University of Toronto Press, Toronto.

Ellyard P (1998) *Birth of Planetism*, Melbourne University Press, Melbourne.

Elwell FW (1991) *The Evolution of the Future*, Praeger, New York.

Emery F, Emery M, Caldwell G & Crombie A (1975) *Futures We're In*, Centre for Continuing Education, Australian National University, Canberra.

Emy HV (1993) *Remaking Australia: The State, the Market and Australia's Future,* Allen & Unwin, Sydney.

Encel S (1979) The future of work, education and leisure, in *Prospect 2000: A Conference on the Future,* Australian and New Zealand Association for the Advancement of Science, Perth.

ESCAP (Economic and Social Commission for Asia and the Pacific) (1996) *Forum on Environmental and Urban Geology for Sustainable Development of Fast-Growing Cities,* Economic and Social Commission for Asia and the Pacific, Bangkok.

Etzioni-Halevy E (1981) *Social Change: The Advent and Maturation of Modern Society,* Routledge, London.

Evans G & Grant B (1995) *Australia's Foreign Relations in the World of the 1990s,* Melbourne University Press, Melbourne.

Fagan B (1996) *World Prehistory: A Brief Introduction,* Harper Collins, New York.

Fagan RH and Webber M (1994), *Global Restructuring: The Australian Experience,* Oxford University Press, Melbourne.

Falkenmark M (1998) Dilemma when entering 21st century — Rapid change but lack of sense of urgency, *Water Policy,* 1(4): 421–36.

FAO (Food and Agriculture Organisation) (1994) Review of the state of world marine fishery resources, *FAO Fisheries Technical Paper,* 335.

Flannery T (1994) *The Future Eaters: An Ecological History of the Australasian Lands and People,* Reed Books, Sydney.

Forrester JS (1961) *Industrial Dynamics,* MIT Press, Cambridge, Massachusetts.

Frankel B (1987) *The Post-Industrial Utopians,* Polity Press, Cambridge.

Freud S (1963) *Civilization and its Discontents,* The Hogarth Press, London.

Friedman G & Lebard M (1991) *The Coming War With Japan,* St. Martin's Press, New York.

Friend J (1992) Genes help rattle the food chain, in Gastin D & Mitchell C (eds), *Creating the Future,* published by *The Australian,* Sydney.

Fromm E (1942) *The Fear of Freedom,* Routledge, London.

Fukuyama F (1992) *The End of History and the Last Man,* Free Press, New York.

Fuller RB (1969) *Utopia or Oblivion: The Prospects for Humanity,* Penguin, Harmondsworth, England.

GACGC (German Advisory Council on Global Change) (1993) *World in Transition: Basic Structure of Global People-Environment Interactions,* Economica Verlag, Bonn.

Galligan B (1995) *A Federal Republic: Australia's Constitutional System of Government,* Cambridge University Press, Cambridge.

Galtung J & Inayatullah S (eds) (1997) *Macrohistory and Macrohistorians: Perspectives on Individual, Social, and Civilizational Change,* Praeger, London.

Garriga J, Mukhanov V, Olum K & Vilenkin A (1999) Eternal inflation, black holes and the future of civilizations, in Burdyuzha U and Khozin G (eds), pp. 42–52.

Giannetti E (1997) *Lies we Live By: The Art of Self-Deception,* Bloomsbury, London.

Gibbon A (1993) Where are 'new' diseases born? *Science,* 261: 680–1.

Giddens A (1979) *Central Problems in Social Theory: Action, Structure and Contradiction in Social Analysis,* Macmillan, London.

—— (1998) *The Third Way: The Renewal of Social Democracy,* Polity Press, London.

Gilland B (1995) World population, economic growth, and energy demand, 1990–2100: A review of projections, *Population and Development Review*, 21(3): 507–39.

Glansdorff P & Prigogine I (1971) *Thermodynamic Theory of Structure: Stability and Fluctuations*, Wiley, London.

Goldstone J (1998) The problem of the 'early modern' world, *Journal of the Economic and Social History of the Orient*, 41: 249–84.

Goleman D and Gurin J (eds) (1995) *Mind Body Medicine: How To Use Your Mind for Better Health*, Choice Books, Australian Consumers Association, Sydney.

Goodman DSG & Segal G (1995) *China Without Deng*, Thompson, Sydney and New York.

Gorer G (1966) *The Danger of Equality and Other Essays*, Cresset Press, London.

Graham-Smith F (ed) (1994) *Population: The Complex Reality*, issued by the Royal Society, published by North American Press, Colorado.

Greider W (1997) *One World, Ready or Not: The Manic Logic of Global Capitalism*, Simon & Schuster, New York.

Griffiths PE & Gray RD (2001) Darwinism and developmental systems, in Oyama S, Griffiths PE & Gray RD (eds), *Cycles of Contingency: Developmental Systems and Evolution*, MIT Press, Cambridge, Massachusetts, pp. 195–218.

Grubler A & Nakicenovic N (1991) Long waves, technology diffusion and substitution, *International Institute for Applied Systems Analysis Review*, XIV(2): 313–42.

Grubler A, Jefferson M, McDonald A, Messner S, Nakicenovic N, Rogner HH & Schrattenholzer L (1995) *Global Energy Perspectives to 2050 and Beyond*, World Energy Council, London.

Gunderson LH, Holling CS & Light SS (eds) (1995) *Barriers and Bridges to the Renewal of Ecosystems and Institutions*, Columbia University Press, New York.

Halal H (1993), World 2000: An international planning dialogue to help shape the new global system, *Futures*, 25(1), 5–21.

Haldane JBS (1932; 1937) *The Inequality of Man*, Penguin, Harmondsworth, England.

Hall CAS, Cleveland CJ & Kaufmann R (1992) *Energy and Resource Quality: The Ecology of the Economic Process*, University Press of Colorado, Niwot, Colorado.

Hall PA (1993) Policy paradigms, social learning and the state: The case of economic policy making in Britain, *Comparative Politics*, 25(3): 275–96.

Hall S, Held D & McGrew T (eds) (1992) *Modernity and its Futures*, Polity Press in association with the Open University, Cambridge.

Hammond A (1998) *Which World? Scenarios for the 21st Century*, Shearwater, Washington.

Handy C (1994) *The Empty Raincoat: Making Sense of the Future*, Hutchinson, London.

Hardin G (1993) *Living Within Limits: Ecology, Economics and Population Taboos*, Oxford University Press, Oxford.

Harnad S (1982) Consciousness: An afterthought, *Cognition and Brain Theory*, 5: 29–41.

Harris M (1977) *Cannibals and Kings: The Origins of Cultures*, Vintage Books, New York.

—— (1979) *Cultural Materialism: The Struggle for a Social Science of Culture*, Vintage Books, New York.

Hartcher P (1996) First World War highlights Asia risk, *Australian Financial Review*, 25 October, p. 16.

Harth E (1999) Perspectives, in Blumenfeld Y (ed), *Scanning the Future: 20 Eminent Thinkers on the World of Tomorrow*, Thames & Hudson, London, pp. 97–106.

Harvard Working Group on New and Resurgent Diseases (1995) New and resurgent diseases: The failure of attempted eradication, *The Ecologist*, 25(1): 21–26.

Hawking SW (1988) *A Brief History of Time: From the Big Bang to Black Holes*, Bantam Books, Toronto.

Hegel GWF (1807; 1971) *Phenomenology of Mind*, (trans. JB Baillie), Allen & Unwin, London.

—— (1837; 1944) *Philosophy of History*, (trans. J Sibree), Wiley, New York.

Heidmann J (1989) *Cosmic Odyssey*, Cambridge University Press, Cambridge.

Heilbroner R (1993) *21st Century Capitalism*, Norton, New York.

—— (1995) *Visions of the Future: The Distant Past, Yesterday, Today, and Tomorrow*, Oxford University Press, New York.

Henderson H (1998a) Breaking points, *Australian Financial Review*, 4 December, pp. 1–2, 8.

—— (1998b) Economics and evolution: An ethos for an action researcher, in Loye D (ed) *The Evolutionary Outrider: The Impact of the Human Agent on Evolution*, Praeger, New York, pp. 215–32.

Hirschman AO (1991) *The Rhetoric of Reaction: Perversity, Futility, Jeopardy*, Belknap, Cambridge, Massachusetts.

Hirst P (1997) *From Statism to Pluralism: Democracy, Civil Society and Global Politics*, UCL Press, London.

Hobsbawm E (1994) *Age of Extremes: The Short Twentieth Century, 1914–1991*, Michael Joseph, London.

Hodgson GM (1999a) *Economics and Utopia: Why the Learning Economy is not the End of History*, Routledge, London.

—— (1999b) *Evolution and Institutions: On Evolutionary Economics and the Evolution of Economics*, Edward Elgar, Cheltenham.

—— (2002) Darwinism in economics: From analogy to ontogeny, *Journal of Evolutionary Economics*, 12: 259–81.

Holland JH (1995) *Hidden Order: How Adaptation Builds Complexity*, Addison-Wesley, New York.

Holling CS (1973) Resilience and stability of ecological systems, *Annual Review of Ecology and Systematics*, 4: 1–23.

—— (1987) Simplifying the complex: The paradigms of ecological structure and function, *European Journal of Operations Research*, 30: 139–46.

Homer-Dixon TF (1991) On the threshold: environmental changes as causes of acute conflict, *International Security*, 16(2): 76–116.

Hulbe CL (1997) Recent changes to Antarctic Peninsula ice shelves: What lessons have been learned?, web journal, *Natural Science*, vol. 1, article 6, http://naturalscience.com/ns/articles/01-06/ns_clh.html, accessed 23 July 2002).

Huntington SP (1994) The clash of civilizations, in Clesse A, Cooper R & Sakamoto Y (eds), *The International System After the Collapse of the East-West Order*, Dordrecht, The Netherlands.

Hutton W (1996) *The State We're In*, rev. ed., Vintage, London.

Huxley A (1938) *Ends and Means*, Chatto & Windus, London.

—— (1959) *Brave New World Revisited*, Bantam, New York.

Huxley J (1953; 1963) *Evolution in Action*, Harper & Row, New York.

Jacobs J (1969) *The Economy of Cities*, Pelican, London.

Jantsch E (1975) *Design for Evolution*, Braziller, New York.

—— (1980) *The Self-Organising Universe: Scientific and Human Implications of the Emerging Paradigm of Evolution*, Pergamon, Oxford.

Jaspers K (1953) *The Origin and Goal of History*, Routledge & Kegan Paul, London.

Jaynes J (1976) *The Origin of Consciousness in the Breakdown of the Bicameral Mind*, Houghton Mifflin, Boston.

Jones S (1993) *The Language of the Genes: Biology, History and the Evolutionary Future*, Harper Collins, London.

Joslyn C, Turchin F & Heylighen F (1997) *Cybernetic Immortality*, http://pespmc1.vub.ac.be/CYBIMM.html, accessed 8 August 2002.

Jouvenel B de (1964) Surmising forum, *The Spectator*, 12 June, p. 787.

Kahn H & Bruce-Briggs R (1972) *Things to Come*, Macmillan, New York.

Kahn H & Weiner AJ (1967) *The Year 2000*, Macmillan, New York.

Kahn H, Brown W & Martel L (1976) *The Next 200 Years*, Morrow, New York.

Kasting J (2000) The evolution of earth's climate, Paper to *Science in an Uncertain Millennium,* American Association for Advancement of Science, Washington DC.

Kauffman S (1995) *At Home in the Universe: The Search for Laws of Complexity*, Penguin, London.

Kavka GS (1982) The paradox of future individuals, *Philosophy and Public Affairs*, 11: 105–09.

Kennedy P (1989) *The Rise and Fall of the Great Powers: Economic Change and Military Conflict from 1500 to 2000*, Vintage Books, New York.

Kennon PE (1995) *The Twilight of Democracy*, Doubleday, New York.

Keys D (1999) *Catastrophe: An Investigation into the Origins of the Modern World*, Arrow, London.

Knight A (1987) The self-indulgent article, *Economist*, 7 February.

Koestler A (1967) *The Ghost in the Machine*, Arkana, London.

Kondratieff ND (1926) Die Langen Wellen der Konjunktur, *Archiv für Sozialwissenschaft und Sozialpolitik*, (German translation of Russian original), *Band*, 56: 573–609.

Krasner SD (1988) Sovereignty: An institutional perspective, *Comparative Political Studies*, 21: 66–94.

Kropotkin P (1904; 1915) *Mutual Aid: A Factor of Evolution*, Heinemann, London.

Kucher P (2001) *Science, Truth and Democracy*, Oxford University Press, Oxford.

Kuhn TS (1970) *The Structure of Scientific Revolutions*, University of Chicago Press, Chicago.

Kwitny J (1984) *Endless Enemies: The Making of an Unfriendly World*, Congdon & Weed, New York.

Langford D (1979) *War in 2080: The Future of Military Technology*, Cassell, Sydney.

Larson ED, Ross MH & Williams RH (1986) Beyond the era of materials, *Scientific American*, 254(6): 34–41.

Lasch C (1995) *The Revolt of the Elites and the Betrayal of Democracy*, Norton, New York.

le Bon G (1947) *The Crowd: A Study of the Popular Mind*, Benn, London.

Leach L (ed) (1995) *The Alliance Alternative in Australia: Beyond Labor and Liberal*, Catalyst Press, Sydney.

Leslie J (1996) *The End of the World: The Science and Ethics of Human Extinction*, Routledge, London.

Lévi-Strauss C (1958; 1963) *Structural Anthropology*, Basic Books, New York.

Lindblom CE (1959) The science of muddling through, *Public Administration Review*, 19: 79–99.

—— (1965) *The Intelligence of Democracy: Decision Making Through Mutual Adjustment*, Free Press, New York.

—— (1977) *Markets and Politics*, Basic Books, New York.

Linstone HA (1994) New era-new challenge, *Technological Forecasting and Social Change*, 47: 1–20.

Lorenz K (1963; 1966) *On Aggression*, 1st edn 1963, (trans. M Kerr Wilson 1966), Harcourt Brace, New York.

Lovelock JE (1989) *The Ages of Gaia: A Biography of our Living Earth*, Oxford University Press, Oxford.

Loye D (ed) (1998a), *The Evolutionary Outrider: The Impact of the Human Agent on Evolution*, Praeger, New York.

—— (1998b) Evolutionary action theory: A brief outline, in Loye D (ed), *The Evolutionary Outrider: The Impact of the Human Agent on Evolution*, Praeger, New York, pp. 168–89.

Lutz W (ed), 1994, *The Future Population of the World: What Can we Assume Today?*, Earthscan Publications, London.

Lutz W, Sanderson W & Scherbov S (2001) The end of world population growth, *Nature*, 412: 543–5.

Maddox J (1998) *What Remains to be Discovered*, Macmillan, London.

—— (1999) The unexpected science to come, *Scientific American*, 31 December, pp. 5–11.

Mannion AM (1995) Biodiversity, biotechnology, and business *Environmental Conservation*, 22(3): 201–09.

Marchetti C (1987) Infrastructures for Movement, *Technological Forecasting and Social Change*, 32: 373–93.

—— (1991) *On Mobility*, First progress report to OMV-IIASA (International Institute for Applied Systems Analysis), Laxenburg.

Martin P & Lefebvre M (1995), Malaria and climate: Sensitivity of malaria potential transmission to climate, *Ambio*, 24: 200–07.

Maslow AH (1954) *Motivation and Personality*, Harper, New York.

—— (1968) *Toward a Psychology of Being*, Van Nostrand, New York.

May R (1953) *Man's Search for Himself*, Delta Books, New York.

May RM, Lawton JH & Stork NE (1995) Assessing extinction rates, in Lawton JH & May RM (eds), *Extinction Rates*, Oxford University Press, Oxford, pp. 1–24.

Mayr E (1994) The new evolutionary pluralism, in Campbell JH & Schopf JW (eds), *Creative Evolution?*, Jones & Bartlett, Boston.

McMichael AJ (2001) *Human Frontiers, Environments and Disease: Past Patterns, Uncertain Futures*, Cambridge University Press, Cambridge.

McNeill WH (1979) *Plagues and People*, Penguin, London.

McRae H (1994) *The World in 2020: Power, Culture and Prosperity: A Vision of the Future*, Harper Collins, London.

Meacher M (1982) *Socialism with a Human Face: The Political Economy of Britain in the 1980s*, George Allen & Unwin, London.

Meadows DH, Meadows DL, Randers J & Behrens WW (1972) *The Limits to Growth*, Universe Books, New York.

Merton RK (1957) *Social Theory and Social Structure*, rev. ed., Free Press, New York.

Milbrath LW (1989) *Envisioning a Sustainable Society: Learning Our Way Out*, State University of New York Press, Albany.

Mills CW (1959) *The Power Elite*, Oxford University Press, New York.

Milne G (1997) Howard sees global change in Clinton's embrace of IT, *The Australian*, 30 June.

Modelski G & Perry G (2002) 'Democratization in the long perspective' revisited, *Technological Forecasting and Social Change*, 69: 359–76.

Modis T (2002) Forecasting the growth of complexity and change, *Technological Forecasting and Social Change*, 69: 377–404.

Moravec H (1999) *Robot: Mere Machine to Transcendent Mind,* Oxford University Press, Oxford.

Morgenthau H & Thompson KW (1985) *Politics Among Nations: The Struggle for Power and Peace*, 6th edn, McGraw Hill, New York.

Morrison R (1999) *The Spirit in the Gene*, Cornell University Press, Ithaca.

Müller HJ (1967) What genetic course will Man steer?, *Proceedings of 3rd World International Congress on Human Genetics*, pp. 521–43.

Myrdal G (1944) *An American Dilemma*, Harper, New York.

Naisbitt J (1994) *Global Paradox: The Bigger the World Economy, the More Powerful its Smallest Players*, Morrow, New York.

Negroponte N (1995) *Being Digital*, Hodder and Stoughton, Sydney.

Nelson RR & Soete LLG (1988) Policy conclusions, in Dosi G, Freeman C, Nelson R, Silverberg G & Luc S (eds), *Technical Change and Economic Theory*, Pinter, London, pp. 631–35.

Nelson RR & Winter SG (1982) *An Evolutionary Theory of Economic Change*, Belknap Press, Cambridge, Massachusetts.

Netherlands Scientific Council for Government Policy (1995) *Sustained Risks: A Lasting Phenomenon*, Report to the Government No. 44, The Hague, The Netherlands.

Nicolis G & Prigogine I (1977) *Self-Organisation in Non-Equilibrium Systems: From Dissipative Structures to Order Through Fluctuations*, Wiley, New York.

North DC (1993) *Economic Performance Through Time*, The Nobel Foundation and the Royal Swedish Academy of Sciences.

North RD (1995) *Life on a Modern Planet: A Manifesto for Progress*, Manchester University Press, Manchester.

Odum HT (1983) *Systems Ecology: An Introduction*, Wiley, New York.

Oliphant M (1992) The Sun as Earth's saviour, in Gastin D and Mitchell C (eds), *Creating the Future*, published by *The Australian*, Sydney.

Olson M (1982) *The Rise and Decline of Nations: Economic Growth, Stagflation and Social Rigidities*, Yale University Press, New Haven, Connecticut.

Ornstein R & Ehrlich P (1989) *New World / New Mind*, Doubleday, New York.

OSCA (Office of Strategic Crime Assessments) (1996) *The Strategic Setting: A Discussion Paper*, Canberra.

OTA (Office of Technology Assessment) (1988) *Technology and the American Transition*, Congress of the United States, Washington DC.

Pardon EA & Clark WC (1995) Sustainable development as social learning: Theoretical perspectives and practical challenges for the design of a research program, in Gunderson et al. (eds) *Barriers and Bridges to the Renewal of Ecosystems and Institutions*, Columbia University Press, New York, pp. 428–60.

Parker CM (1973) Regression and Psychotherapy, unpublished MA thesis, Australian National University, Canberra.

Parsons T (1949) *The Structure of Social Action*, 2nd edn, Free Press, Chicago.

Pateman C (1970) *Participation and Democratic Theory*, Cambridge University Press, Cambridge.

Pattee HH (1969) Physical conditions for primitive functional hierarchies, in Whyte LL, Wilson AG & Wilson D (eds), *Hierarchical Structures*, American Elsevier, New York, pp. 161–71.

Patten BC, Jorgensen SE & Auerbach SI (eds) (1996) *Complex Ecology: The Part-Whole Relation in Ecosystems*, Prentice Hall, New Jersey.

Peters R (1995) The culture of future conflict, *Parameters*, 25(4): 18–27.

Piaget J (1971) *Biology and Knowledge*, University of Chicago Press, Chicago.

Pinker S (1997) *How the Mind Works*, Norton, New York.

Pinstrup-Andersen P (1994) *World Food Trends and Future Food Security*, International Food Policy Research Institute, Washington.

Platt J (1966) *The Step to Man*, New York, Wiley.

Plotkin HC (1994) *Darwin Machines and the Nature of Knowledge: Concerning Adaptation, Instinct and the Evolution of Intelligence*, Penguin, Harmondsworth, England.

Polanyi K (1944; 2001) *The Great Transformation: The Political and Economic Origins of our Time*, Beacon Press, Boston.

Poleman TT (1996) Global hunger: The methodologies underlying the official estimates, *Population and Environment*, 17(6): 545–68.

Popper KR (1972) *Objective Knowledge: An Evolutionary Approach*, Oxford University Press, Oxford.

Potter VR (1990) Getting to the year 3000: Can global bioethics overcome evolution's fatal flaw?, *Perspectives in Biology and Medicine*, 34(1): 89–98.

Prehoda RW (1967) *Designing the Future: The Role of Technological Forecasting*, Chilton, New York.

Putnam RD (1993) *Making Democracy Work: Civic Traditions in Modern Italy*, Princeton University Press, Princeton, New Jersey.

Ramphele M (2000) Unleashing humanity's full capacity, *Australian Financial Review*, *Friday Review*, 10 November (edited version of Hawke lecture), pp. 4–5.

Rawls J (1971) *A Theory of Justice*, Harvard University Press, Cambridge, Massachusetts.

—— (1993) *Political Liberalism*, Columbia University Press, New York.

Regis E (1990) *Great Mambo Chicken and the Transhuman Condition: Science Slightly Over the Edge*, Penguin, London.

Reich RB (1991) *The Work of Nations: Preparing Ourselves for 21st Century Capitalism*, Simon & Schuster, London.

Reich W (1946) *The Mass Psychology of Fascism*, Orgone Institute, New York.

Rescher N (1980) *Unpopular Essays on Technological Progress*, University of Pittsburgh Press, Pittsburgh.

Richardson WN & Stubbs TH (1976) *Evolution, Human Ecology, and Society*, Macmillan, New York.

Ridley M (1995) *The Red Queen: Sex and the Evolution of Human Nature*, Penguin, New York.

Rittel H & Webber M (1973) Dilemmas in a general theory of planning, *Policy Sciences*, 4: 155–69.

Romer P (1994) The origins of endogenous growth, *Journal of Economic Perspectives*, 8: 3–22.

Ronan C (1986) *The Shorter Science and Civilization in China: An Abridgement of Joseph Needham's Original Text*, vol. 3, Cambridge University Press, Cambridge.

Rooney D & Mandeville T (1998) The knowing nation: A framework for public policy in a post-industrial knowledge economy, *Prometheus*, 16(4): 453–67.

Rostow WW (1953) *The Process of Economic Growth*, Oxford University Press, London.

Rousseau JJ (1762; 1968) *The Social Contract*, Penguin, London.

Roy O (1994) *The Failure of Political Islam*, Harvard University Press, Cambridge, Massachusetts.

Rubenstein RE (2001) Basic human needs: The next steps in theory development, *International Journal of Peace Studies*, 6(1): 51–8.

Russell P (1982) *The Awakening Earth: The Global Brain*, Ark, London.

Salthe SN (1993) *Development and Evolution: Complexity and Change in Biology*, MIT Press, Cambridge, Massachusetts.

Sandel MJ (1996) America's search for a new public philosophy, *The Atlantic Monthly*, 277(3): 57–74.

Sartre JP (1975) *Existentialism and Humanism*, Methuen, London (reprint of 1948 edn).

Saunders C (1994), Constitution, democracy and the future, in Economic Planning Advisory Commission, *Ambitions for our Future*, Report 3 of *Shaping our Future: National Strategies Conference*, Australian Government Publishing Service, Canberra.

Sceats M (1992) Global village spanned by a web of optical fibre, in Gastin D and Mitchell C (eds), *Creating the Future*, published by *The Australian*, Sydney.

Schaer R, Claeys G & Sargent LT (2000) *Utopia: The Search for the Ideal Society in the Western World*, Oxford University Press, Oxford.

Schon DA (1971) *Beyond the Stable State: Public and Private Learning in a Changing Society*, Penguin, Victoria.

Schumpeter JA (1934) *The Theory of Economic Development*, Harvard University Press, Cambridge, Massachusetts.

—— (1942) *Capitalism, Socialism and Democracy*, Harper, New York.

Schwartz JH (1999) *Sudden Origins: Fossils, Genes and the Emergence of Species*, Wiley, New York.

Schwartz P (1991) *The Art of the Long View*, Doubleday, New York.

Self P (1993) *Government by the Market: The Politics of Public Choice*, Macmillan, London.

Selye H (1978) *The Stress of Life*, McGraw-Hill, New York.

Senge PM (1992) *The Fifth Discipline: The Art and Practice of the Learning Organisation*, Century Business, London.

Senge PM (1999) Though the eye of the needle, in Gibson R (ed), *Rethinking the Future*, Nicholas Brealey, London, pp. 122–46.

Shackle GLS (1955) *Uncertainty in Economics and Other Reflections*, Cambridge University Press, Cambridge.

Sheffield C, Alonso M & Kaplan MA (eds) (1994) *The World of 2044: Technological Development and the Future of Society*, Paragon, Minnesota.

Sheldrake R (1988) *The Presence of the Past: Morphic Resonance and the Habits of Nature*, Collins, London.

Shuman JN (1978) Cultural heterogeneity in social systems, in Maruyama M & Harkins AM (eds), *Cultures of the Future*, Moulton, The Hague.

Simon HA (1973) The organisation of complex systems, in Pattee HH (ed), *Hierarchy Theory: The Challenge of Complex Systems*, Braziller, New York, pp. 1–27.

Simon HA (1982) *Models of Bounded Rationality*, MIT Press, Cambridge, Massachusetts.

Simpson D (1992) Age of stimulation for retirees, in Gastin D & Mitchell C (eds), *Creating the Future*, published by *The Australian*, Sydney.

Singer M & Wildavsky A (1993) *The Real World Order: Zones of Peace/Zones of Turmoil*, Chatham Publishers, New Jersey.

Singer P (1992) It's all a question of ethics, in Gastin D and Mitchell C (eds), *Creating the Future*, published by *The Australian*, Sydney, p. 11.

Singer SF (1994) Transport and communications, in Sheffield C, Alonso M & Kaplan MA (eds), *The World of 2044: Technological Development and the Future of Society*, Paragon, Minnesota.

Sinnott EW (1950; 1962) *Cell and Psyche: The Biology of Purpose*, University of North Carolina Press, (Harper Torch edn 1962).

Skinner BF (1971) *Beyond Freedom and Dignity*, Knopf, New York.

Slaughter R (ed) (1993) The knowledge base of futures studies, Special edition of *Futures*, 25(3): 227–374.

Smith AC (1969) Systematics and appreciation of reality, *Taxon*, 18: 5–19.

Snooks G (1996) *The Dynamic Society: Exploring the Sources of Global Change*, Routledge, London and New York.

Snyder A (1999) The genius within, *The Australian*, 12 November, p. 12.

Somervell DC (1946) *Abridgement of AJ Toynbee's A Study of History Vols I–VI*, Oxford University Press, London.

Spengler O (1932; 1961) *The Decline of the West*, abridged edn, Allen & Unwin, London.

Stapledon O (1930; 1966) *Last and First Men: A Story of the Near and Far Future*, Penguin, London.

Starr C (1996) Sustaining the human environment: The next two hundred years, *Daedalus*, 125(3): 235–53.

Sterelny K (2001) *The Evolution of Agency and Other Essays*, Cambridge University Press, Cambridge.

Stove DC (1995) *Darwinian Fairytales*, Avebury, Aldershot.

Strain MB (1997) *The Earth's Shifting Axis: Clues to Nature's Most Perplexing Mysteries*, ATL Press, Shrewsbury.

Tainter JA (2000) Problem solving, complexity, history, sustainability, *Population and Environment*, 22(1): 3–41.

Tallis JH (1991) *Plant Community History: Long Term Changes in Plant Distribution and History*, Chapman & Hall, London.

Tawney RH (1920) *The Acquisitive Society*, Harcourt Brace, New York.

Taylor G (1996) *Cultural Selection*, Basic Books, New York.

Taylor SR (1998) *Destiny or Chance: Our Solar System and its Place in the Cosmos*, Cambridge University Press, Cambridge.

Teilhard de Chardin P (1959; 1964) *The Future of Man*, (trans N Denny), Fontana, London.

Tenner E (1996) *Why Things Bite Back: New Technology and the Revenge Effect*, Fourth Estate, London.

Thurow L (1996) *The Future of Capitalism: How Today's Economic Forces Will Shape Tomorrow's World*, Allen & Unwin, New York.

—— (1999) The third industrial revolution, *Australian Financial Review, Friday Review*, 2 July, pp. 1–2, 8–9.

Toffler A (1970) *Future Shock*, Bodley Head, London.

Tonn BE (2001) Institutional design for long-term stewardship of nuclear and hazardous waste sites, *Technological Forecasting and Social Change*, 68: 255–73.

Toulmin S (1972) *Human Understanding*, Princeton UP, New Jersey.

Toynbee A (1934–1961) *A Study of History*, 12 vols, Oxford University Press, London.

—— (1971) *Surviving the Future*, Oxford University Press, London.

Turchin VF (1977) *The Phenomenon of Science*, Columbia University Press, New York.

UNDP (United Nations Development Program) (1996) *Human Development Report 1996*, Oxford University Press, Oxford.

van Asselt M, Beusen A & Hilderink H (1996) Uncertainty in integrated assessment: A social scientific perspective, *Environmental Modeling and Assessment*, 1(1–2): 71–90.

Van Creveld ML (1991) *On Future War*, 1st UK edn, Brassey's, London.

Varis O (2002) Belief networks: Generating the feared dislocations, in Beck MB (ed), *Environmental Foresight and Models: A Manifesto*, Elsevier, Amsterdam, pp. 169–205.

Vickers G (1968) *Value Systems and Social Process,* Penguin, Harmondsworth, England.

Victor DG (1990) *Liquid Hydrogen Aircraft and the Greenhouse Effect,* Working Paper 90–02, International Institute for Applied Systems Analysis, Laxenburg.

Visser J & Hemerijck A (1997) *'A Dutch Miracle': Job Growth, Welfare Reform and Corporatism in The Netherlands,* Amsterdam University Press, Amsterdam.

Vitousek PM, Mooney HA, Lubchenco J & Melillo JM (1997) Human domination of the earth's ecosystems, *Science,* 227: 494–9.

Wagar WW (1989) *A Short History of the Future,* Chicago University Press, Chicago.

Waldrop MM (1992) *Complexity: The Emerging Science at the Edge of Order and Chaos,* Penguin, London.

Wallerstein I (1974) *The Modern World System: Capitalist Agriculture and the Origins of the European World Economy in the Sixteenth Century,* Academic Press, New York.

—— (1983) The three instances of hegemony in the history of the capitalist world-economy, *International Journal of Comparative Sociology,* XXIV, 1–2: 100–08.

—— (1995) *After Liberalism,* The New Press, New York.

Watt KF (1992) *Taming the Future: A Revolutionary Breakthrough in Scientific Forecasting,* Contextured Web Press, Davis, California.

WCED (World Commission on Environment and Development) (1987) *Our Common Future,* Oxford University Press, Oxford.

Weber M (1905; 1958) *The Protestant Ethic and the Spirit of Capitalism,* (trans T Parsons), Charles Scribner's Sons, New York.

Weir A (1999) Flight into danger, *New Scientist,* 7 August, no. 2198: 42–43.

Wells HG (1942) *The Conquest of Time,* Watt, London.

Westley F (1995) Governing design: The management of social systems and ecosystem management, in Gunderson et al. *Barriers and Bridges to the Renewal of Ecosystems and Institutions,* Columbia University Press, New York, pp. 391–427.

Wheeler JA (1977) *Foundational Problems in the Special Sciences,* Reidel, Dordrecht.

Wicken JS (1987) *Evolution, Thermodynamics, and Information,* Oxford University Press, Oxford.

Wilkin DC (1996) Accounting for sustainability: Challenges to landscape professionals in an increasingly unsustainable world, *Landscape and Urban Planning,* 36: 217–27.

Wills C (1998) *Children of Prometheus: The Accelerating Pace of Human Evolution,* Perseus, Reading.

Wilson C (1972) *New Pathways in Psychology: Maslow and the Post-Freudian Revolution,* Gollancz, London.

—— (1980) *Frankenstein's Castle,* Ashgrove, Sevenoaks.

—— (1984) *CG Jung: Lord of the Underworld,* Aquarian Press, Northamptonshire.

Wilson EO (1975) *Sociobiology: The New Synthesis,* Harvard University Press, Cambridge, Massachusetts.

—— (1998) *Consilience: The Unity of Knowledge,* Vintage Books, New York.

—— (2000) Wringing literature from science, *Australian Financial Review, Friday Review,* 30 July 30, p. 6.

Wilson P (1996) Australia climbs the defence dollars table, *The Australian,* 5 July.

Wolf ER (1982) *Europe and the People Without History*, University of California Press, Berkeley.

Wolfe A (c1989) *Whose Keeper?: Social Science and Moral Obligation*, University of California Press, Berkeley.

Wolfe JA (1985) Distribution of major vegetation types during the Tertiary, in Sundquist ET & Broecker WS (eds), *The Carbon Cycle and Atmospheric CO_2: Natural Variations Archaean to Present*, Geophysical Monographs 32, American Geophysical Union, Washington DC, pp. 357–75.

World Resources Institute (1996) *World Resources 1996–97*, World Resources Institute, Washington DC.

INDEX